STRENGTH
FOR THE DAY

Karen Pearson
EDITOR

Pacific Press®
Publishing Association
Nampa, Idaho | www.pacificpress.com

Cover design: Daniel Añez
Cover design resources: vecteezy.com, generated by AI Photo Pro
Interior design: Aaron Troia

Copyright © 2024 by General Conference Corporation of Seventh-day Adventists®
Printed in the United States of America
All rights reserved

The authors assume full responsibility for the accuracy of all facts and quotations as cited in this book.

Scripture quotations marked ESV are from The Holy Bible, English Standard Version® (ESV®), copyright © 2001 by Crossway, a publishing ministry of Good News Publishers. Used by permission. All rights reserved.
    Scripture quotations marked KJV are from the King James Version of the Bible.
    Scripture quotations marked *The Message* are from *The Message*, copyright © 1993, 2002, 2018 by Eugene H. Peterson. Used by permission of NavPress Publishing Group. Represented by Tyndale House Publishers, Inc.
    Scripture quotations marked NASB are from the New American Standard Bible®, copyright © 1960, 1971, 1977, 1995, 2020 by the Lockman Foundation. All rights reserved.
    Scripture quotations marked NET are from the New English Translation (NET Bible®), copyright ©1996–2017 by Biblical Studies Press, LLC. All rights reserved. Used by permission.
    Scripture quotations marked NIV are from THE HOLY BIBLE, NEW INTERNATIONAL VERSION®. Copyright © 1973, 1978, 1984, 2011 by Biblica, Inc.® Used by permission. All rights reserved worldwide.
    Scripture quotations marked NKJV are from the New King James Version®. Copyright © 1982 by Thomas Nelson. Used by permission. All rights reserved.
    Scripture quotations marked NLT are from the Holy Bible, New Living Translation, copyright © 1996, 2004, 2007, 2013, 2015 by Tyndale House Foundation. Used by permission of Tyndale House Publishers, Inc., Carol Stream, Illinois 60188. All rights reserved.
    Scripture quotations marked NLV are from the *New Life Version*, copyright © 1969 and 2003. Used by permission of Barbour Publishing, Inc., Uhrichsville, Ohio 44683. All rights reserved.

To order additional copies of this book, call toll-free 1-800-765-6955, or visit AdventistBookCenter.com.

Library of Congress Cataloging-in-Publication Data

Names: Pearson, Karen, editor.
Title: Strength for the day / Karen Pearson, editor.
Description: Nampa, Idaho : Pacific Press Publishing Association, [2024] | Summary: "A collection of
   365 devotional thoughts for women to encourage and strengthen faith"— Provided by publisher.
Identifiers: LCCN 2023058756 | ISBN 9780816370085 | ISBN 9780816370092 (ebook)
Subjects: LCSH: Women—Prayers and devotions.
Classification: LCC BV4527 .S7436 2024 | DDC 242/.643—dc23/eng/20240222
LC record available at https://lccn.loc.gov/2023058756

May 2024

About the Editor

Karen Pearson loves nothing more than to share stories of Jesus and His love—and the difference He longs to make in our lives. She has served in women's ministries, pastoral ministry, and prayer ministries and has an active speaking and writing ministry. She loves to hear stories from women around the world and believes everyone has a remarkable Jesus story to share.

Dear Reader,

The North American Division (NAD) Women's Ministries team welcomes you to the 2025 edition of the women's devotional book. We are pleased and grateful that all proceeds from the sale of the book in the NAD will be used exclusively for scholarships in our territory. We are praying that you will be blessed this year as you read devotionals from women like you—real women with real stories of God's love and providence in their lives. We look forward to hearing from you, and we hope that you will be inspired to submit your own stories to share with others.

DeeAnn Bragaw is the director of NAD Women's Ministries. She joined the Women's Ministries Department in July 2021. Bragaw previously served as the Women's Ministries director and Prayer Ministries coordinator for the Rocky Mountain Conference. She is passionate about showing the world the love of Jesus as beautifully expressed through His women!

Erica Jones, the assistant director of NAD Women's Ministries, joined the department in 2014. Her background in youth ministry has given her a heart for teens and their struggles. Combined with her media experience, this background made it easy for her to find her ministry niche in the department—teen girls and social media. Erica lives with her four-legged children: Boots, the cat, and Maisy, the miniature shepherd mix.

Heather-Dawn Small

If there were a twentieth-century Hall of Faith such as Hebrews 11, Heather-Dawn's name would be included. She was a woman of faith and prayer and was known as an avid Bible student and journaler. She doted on her children and dearly loved her husband. Creativity helped her relax from her many responsibilities and travels, and many enjoyed receiving her original cards. During her travels to meet and minister to women, she listened to them, mentored them, and loved them. And the women she encountered loved her in return.

One of her focuses was this devotional book series, constantly encouraging women to write entries and to share the compilation—in part because the proceeds help young women further their education. She loved the idea of empowering women, discipling them so they could be their best and in turn share the good news of Jesus Christ.

Heather-Dawn's favorite word was *joy*. She often stated and wrote, "Don't let anyone steal your joy." To the very end, she practiced the motto, "I choose joy"—joy in her Savior, joy in salvation, and joy in the marvelous women around the world who are making a difference.

—Ardis Dick Stenbakken

Women Helping Women

There is an aspect of this book that is unique

None of the contributors have been paid—each has shared freely so that all profits may go to scholarships for women. Recipients of the Women's Ministries scholarships are talented women who are committed to serving the mission of the Seventh-day Adventist Church.

General Conference Women's Ministries scholarship fund in the North American Division

All profits from sales of the Women's Ministries devotional book in the North American Division support women's higher education in Seventh-day Adventist colleges and universities in the United States and Canada.

Purpose of the women's devotional book

Among Friends, published in 1992, was the first annual women's devotional book. Since then, the proceeds from these devotional books have funded scholarships for Adventist women seeking to obtain higher education. But as tuition costs have soared in North America and more women have applied for assistance, funding has not kept pace with the need. Many worthy women who apply must be turned down.

Recognizing the importance of educating women—to build stronger families, stronger communities, and a stronger church—each of us can help. Together we can change lives!

There are many ways to support our sisters

- Pray for women worldwide who are struggling to get an education.
- Tell others about the Women's Ministries scholarship program.
- Write for the women's devotional book (guidelines are available).
- Support women's education with a financial gift or a pledge.

To make a gift or receive materials, send us the following information:

Name _____

Street _____

City _____ State/Province _____

Postal Code_____ Country_____

Email_____

To contact us:

Women's Ministries Department Phone: 443-391-7265
9705 Patuxent Woods Drive Email: ericajones@nadadventist.org
Columbia, MD 21046 Website: https://www.nadwm.org/

The scholarship application and devotional book writers' guidelines are available on our website.

January 1

The Palm Tree as a Symbol

The righteous will flourish like a palm tree.
—Psalm 92:12, NIV

Entering a new year, we all wonder what kind of a year it will be: What joys or challenges will it bring? Will we be strong and graceful? Will we gain a new experience of God's abundant presence in our lives?

Once, during my childhood, I heard a sermon on Psalm 92:12. Growing up in places deprived of palm trees, I was impressed with the list of characteristics they possess that resemble a godly life. Later, I forgot most of them, but the impression was so memorable I started to research the subject. I found out that palm trees are evergreen—a symbol of everlasting life, immortality, and eternity.

Palm trees are visually distinctive. They are easily identifiable in any landscape due to their unique shape and form. If a band is placed around a palm tree's trunk, as the tree grows, it will break the band. The bands become deeply embedded in the trunks of other kinds of trees. Palm trees are also strong and durable and do not easily break in a storm.

Palm trees can flourish in a desert. Their strong roots grow down deep into the soil, where they find the water needed to survive. Palm trees are surprisingly fruitful, producing different fruits, nuts, and oils. They are valuable and the older the tree, the sweeter its fruit. Palm trees' leaves and bark can be used in multiple ways.

Palm trees provide shade and shelter for travelers, birds, and animals. They also protect other varieties of trees. Citrus trees often grow under palms, where they are protected from excessive heat and sunshine.

The promise in Psalm 92:12 has become profoundly encouraging to me. As I consider the beauty of the palm tree, I am reminded that as disciples of Jesus, we should be unique and distinctive, strong and durable, rooted in God and well nourished by His Word. Christians should flourish and bear fruit even in a desert, serve people in multiple ways, and help them grow. As we grow older, we should become sweeter and more like Jesus—evergreen in faith, hope, and love.

Galina Stele

January 2

Finding the Rest in *Restore*

And he said, "My presence will go with you, and I will give you rest."
—Exodus 33:14, ESV

A new year has begun! *What is my theme word for this year?* I asked myself. The word would need to be relevant; one that would make a difference in my life. *Joy? Hope? Trust?* Then the word *restore* popped into my mind. Our family has restored houses, cars, and gardens. *Restore* has always been a good word for this do-it-yourself kind of woman. I like to get the job done. *Restore* sounds energetic. Yes, it is exactly my kind of word.

With my typical get-it-done attitude, I enthusiastically began learning more about my word. Eventually, in lights brighter than sunshine on snow, four letters stood out: *r-e-s-t*. Seriously? "There is no time to rest, God," I mumbled. But those four letters continued to invite me. So how does *restore*, an action word, fit with *rest*, a quieting word? And what does it look like in this busy, type A life of mine? I was unsure, but I knew I had to find out.

Slowly, I began to see that the challenges of the previous year had worn me down. My joy quotient measured close to zero. My mind would ruminate without purpose, and while I could still hustle with the best of them when needed, I would crash when done. Could God be suggesting a pause in all my efforts? Was He hinting at something more to life than getting through my endless to-do lists? Did He want to be first and last on my list in every situation?

I love my quiet time. When I pray and pause in His Word, the Scriptures encourage and energize my heart and mind. But I noticed that as my day progressed, I would lose that sense of His peace, joy, and connection. When life demanded more than I could give, I would jump right in to find a solution. The results were not always positive. I began to sense a need for His presence to stretch throughout my day.

So, what would happen if the first thing I did in any situation—joyous or junky—was to pause for a moment and rest in His presence? And in the pause, recognize He is with me—within me. With that realization, I could release to Him whatever is going on.

A weight has rolled off my shoulders. Yes, God is changing me. I am learning that to restore, I must first rest. It is quite a new adventure with Him. And somehow, my to-do lists are still getting done.

Lynn Ortel

January 3

New Every Morning

They [the LORD's compassions] are new every morning;
great is your faithfulness.
I say to myself, "The LORD is my portion;
therefore I will wait for him."
—Lamentations 3:23, 24, NIV

Yesterday, I received a parcel in the mail containing next year's devotional book for women. I have received an author's copy of these books for the last thirty years. This beautiful book, *New Every Morning*, was written by women from around the world, sharing what God means to them and inviting others to start their day with thoughts of Him. Some stories tell of pain, others of joy, but all invite us to turn to Jesus, our best Friend, in every situation. He knows and understands what life is like for us because He lived on Earth and had close contact with many women. Through His loving and respectful attitude toward women, Jesus showed the society of His time that its treatment of women was not what God had intended when He created *Ish* and *Isha*—man and woman—in His image. As Jesus saw their problems and had compassion, so He sees women today. He sees what we struggle with and invites us to let Him carry our burdens each day.

As I look at the long row of women's devotional books in my bookcase, I realize that life has changed a lot in the last thirty years. Events have come and gone, my children have grown, and situations are different. Some of the things I wrote about in the earliest books do not even exist anymore. But one thing has not changed: God is still there, taking care of us. Jesus is still our Friend in whom we can trust. He has not changed. And every morning He is there, waiting for us to start our day with Him, offering us encouragement and counsel for all our problems, though sometimes He asks us to wait until we understand what He is saying to us.

During His time on Earth, He recognized the pain that sin had caused the women He encountered, and He knows that we need His loving support as God's daughters today. He still sees in us the image of God in which He created us. He wants to help us reflect this image so others can see it as well.

The Lord is our portion; therefore, let us wait for Him. And as we ask and wait, He will transform our lives.

Hannele Ottschofski

January 4

Your Story

Your eyes saw my unformed body;
all the days ordained for me were written in your book
before one of them came to be.
—Psalm 139:16, NIV

Don't you love being in control? Knowing exactly what is going to happen next? And even if you do not, having the certainty that if you do not like what is happening, you can just click the backspace key and start over? Wait. Did I say backspace key? Yep. I did. I am talking about writing. It is addictive. When I write, I am in control. Even when I get mad at my characters, I can still tell them what to do. I can push and stretch and cut the plot to fit the mold I have created in my mind.

But real life is not like that. I get lost easily in real life. The plot gets tangled, and I do not always live up to the character I am supposed to be. Sometimes I get dressed, look in the mirror, and think, *Something could go wrong. I may make a big mistake today, and my whole life could be ruined.* Though we are in control of our decisions, we are not always in control of our circumstances. But do not worry! This story you are living—though I have not read it, I know one thing—if you have the right Author writing it, it is going to have a happy ending. I promise.

God does not need a backspace key. He is so great at this that He will just pick up where you are in that complicated plot and, slowly but surely, pull all the tangled strings free. Every. Last. One. That conversation you are nervous about having with someone? He will write it. That plot twist you cannot even see? He will take care of it.

So now, when I look in the mirror, I can say, "Wow! I cannot wait to see how He is going to keep this story going. I wonder if He will sprinkle a little humor into this chapter today." (Believe it or not, some authors do like to see their characters happy.)

My story is still being written, and every day He adds a new page. Each day I know I draw closer to my happy ending.

What about you? Who is writing your story? The Master Author promises, "I know the plans I have for you," . . . "plans to prosper you and not to harm you, plans to give you a hope and a future" (Jeremiah 29:11, NIV).

Sasha De Dios

January 5

Ralph-if and His Neighborhood

*"Fear not, for I have redeemed you;
I have called you by your name;
You are Mine."*
—Isaiah 43:1, NKJV

I can still picture it: my first "book," written in blue magic marker on orange construction paper; the pages stapled together with way too many staples. I remember my dad proudly showing off my first written masterpiece to neighbors and family. It was a "masterpiece" with a huge mistake. I did not know how to spell *Ralph*—the name of the hero in the story—correctly. Somehow, I spelled it with an *if* in it. *Ralif*? *Ralfif*? I do not remember how I spelled it, but I do recall that when I learned about my mistake, I just included it in the story. Ralph had an "if" for everything. The entire story focused on all of the young boy's "ifs" for everything that happened around him in his neighborhood. My mistake was redeemed and became the central theme of his story. This redemption of a mistake is much like what God does in our lives.

God takes our mistakes, the things we get wrong, and the hard things thrown at us, and He redeems them. He speaks into the devastating moments with grace, loving-kindness, and unending mercy—and redeems. And like with "Ralph-if," He often wants to use these parts of our stories to impact others. The very parts of our stories we wish we could hide are often the stories where we see God most powerfully in our own lives, and they brings courage and hope to others.

One of my mistakes was a suicide attempt at eighteen. It was a source of shame and something my parents said we would never speak of again. And yet I knew God wanted me to tell that story when another family faced a similar crisis. With fear and trembling, I shared how God had led me in that moment and turned my life around. My story brought them courage and hope. Similarly, a friend thought of her divorce only as a source of pain and shame. God transformed her story with healing and blessing and turned it into a powerful message of courage for others. Another friend is a survivor of domestic violence—something she hid from her family for years. Now she walks alongside others, bringing hope and teaching churches and people how to best minister to hurting people.

Our God not only redeems but also brings beauty and hope from our pain and wounds.

Tamyra Horst

January 6

What a Friend

*Now this is the confidence that we have in Him,
that if we ask anything according to His will, He hears us.*
—1 John 5:14, NKJV

One evening Jesus and His disciples were on the Sea of Galilee when a sudden storm threatened to capsize their boat. The terrified disciples asked Jesus for help after their own efforts had failed. With one simple command, "Peace, be still!" Jesus lulled the raging sea back into tranquility (Mark 4:35–41, NKJV). Like the disciples, my prayers were mostly for big things. I did not think it was necessary to "bother" God with mundane problems. But as I grow older, my life experiences have taught me otherwise. Now I pray without ceasing, even for simple things.

Practicing a healthy lifestyle has reduced but not removed my hypertension, which I am genetically susceptible to. One December my blood pressure had been unusually high for several days, so I went to see my cardiologist. At her office, parking is usually limited. On that visit, I spent more than two hours in the doctor's office, and my husband could not find a place to park in that time.

A week later, as I drove back for the results, my repeated prayer was, "Dear God, please help me to find a parking space." My hopes were dashed when I saw a line of cars circling like ants searching for food. "Please, Jesus, please, I don't want to be late." Just then, I saw a car backing out. I quickly swung into the space as another car circled around. "Thank You, God! Thank You, Jesus," I repeated, grateful to make it in time for my appointment.

Praise God, the results were negative. I decided to buy a gift for the office staff, which meant giving up my precious parking space. How could I expect God to provide another one? My plan was to turn on the car's hazard lights and pull up to the front for a few minutes. But to my surprise, a car backed out as I approached. I pulled in and cried, "Lord, You are too good to me. I don't deserve this." The staff were grateful for the gift, and I was doubly blessed.

Regarding prayer, Joseph M. Scriven penned these words:

> O what peace we often forfeit,
> O what needless pain we bear,
> All because we do not carry
> Everything to God in prayer.*

Oh, what a Friend!

Maureen Nembhard

---
* Joseph M. Scriven, "What a Friend We Have in Jesus," 1855, public domain.

January 7

I Am With You Always

*Yea, though I walk through the valley of the shadow of death,
I will fear no evil: for thou art with me;
thy rod and thy staff they comfort me.*
—Psalm 23:4, KJV

It was a beautiful evening, and I had just finished an overdue visit to my hairdresser and returned to my car. It was really dark as I put the key in the ignition and turned on the engine. Then I saw it: low beam headlight failure! *No problem*, I thought. *I can just use the high beams as needed.* To say I was overconfident as I drove off would be an understatement, but I knew I would be on well-lit roads in twenty minutes. Or so I thought.

I realized this was not the best solution when I saw blue-and-red lights flashing at the scene of an accident at the first major intersection. My heart sank. Now I would have to take a detour on an unfamiliar road. My overconfidence disappeared, and I prayed, "Lord, have mercy."

If I had been able to turn left, that would have been great. I knew the alternate way through the mall parking access roads, but because of the accident, there was only one way. I had to go right. That night right seemed wrong for me. However, as I turned right, there was one thing I could thank God for: the police were too busy with the accident to take time to notice my low-beam dilemma.

As I turned onto the unknown one-lane road, there were no streetlights. I felt helpless on a dark road with my one low-beam light. I could not see my way. But God heard my cry and gave me peace. I know God heard because there was every reason to panic.

The GPS was not helpful, and I could not see a safe place to stop and call my husband. Thank God, my GSS (Good Shepherd System) was working; I could depend on Psalm 23:4. "Thou art with me," I prayed as I followed a few cars headed in the same direction as home.

Finally, I saw a familiar road, but I was in the wrong lane. I needed to get over to the left-turn lane. I put on my left indicator, and a road angel graciously allowed me to slip into the correct lane. "Thank You, Jesus," I exclaimed. That back road had never looked so good! It was well lit, and I was more familiar with it. I soon made it safely home. The Good Shepherd had fulfilled His promise yet again. "I am with you always" (Matthew 28:20, KJV). Another tested and proven promise from the Lord! Thank You, Lord!

Claudette Garbutt-Harding

January 8

God's Provisions Are Beyond Amazing

*And my God shall supply all your need
according to His riches in glory by Christ Jesus.*
—Philippians 4:19, NKJV

On a hot afternoon late one summer, I decided to go to my bedroom and rest. While resting, I pondered the recent turn of events in our lives. My contract with GIZ Zambia (German Agency for International Cooperation) had ended several months before, and my husband had been out of work for more than two years. We had used up our savings finalizing our retirement home and paying school fees for our five children. My thoughts turned to the girls' schoolbags. They needed to be replaced, and school was set to open in a week. As my thoughts lingered on how we would replace their bags, I somehow drifted to sleep.

A few minutes into my nap, I was awakened by a phone call. Looking at the number, I recognized it was from my sister who resides abroad. Eagerly, I answered her call, and after exchanging pleasantries, she quickly got to the point of why she was calling.

She wanted to alert me that she had forwarded some boxes containing an assortment of goodies for the family back home. She wanted my husband to facilitate the picking up of the boxes. Her next words literally had me crying tears of thanksgiving. She said she had included two schoolbags for the girls among the other goodies she was sending. She did not understand why I was sobbing. After composing myself, I told her that a few minutes before drifting to sleep, I had been thinking about the girls' bags, which needed changing, but I could not quite figure out how I was going to do it with the financial challenges we were facing. But here was God making provision in a way I had not anticipated—through her. The promise in Isaiah came alive in my mind: "It shall come to pass that before they call, I will answer; and while they are still speaking, I will hear" (Isaiah 65:24, NKJV).

As I thought of how I had been fretting and worrying only a few minutes earlier, I felt rather ashamed of myself that I had failed to trust God and His amazing provision. He makes provision even before we become aware of our needs. He supplies what we need according to His riches in glory. Before we call, He answers, and while we are yet speaking, He hears. What an awesome God we serve!

Charity Hanene Nchimunya

January 9

More Than Corn

Your eyes saw my substance, being yet unformed.
And in Your book they all were written,
The days fashioned for me,
When as yet there were none of them.
—Psalm 139:16, NKJV

I went home to Louisiana, United States of America, for a visit, and while there, I stayed with a friend. We spent Sabbath afternoon on her back porch talking and enjoying nature. From the porch, we could see hummingbirds feeding from the feeder. A beautiful white bird sunbathed at the edge of the pond, and tall, majestic oaks lined the perimeter of her property. As beautiful as her backyard was, it had not always looked that way. As we sat and talked, she shared with me this story.

One day her husband asked her to go with him to look at some property he wanted to buy. When they arrived at the property, she could not believe her eyes. It was a huge cornfield. She did not understand why her husband wanted to buy a cornfield. He explained that he wanted to raise their children in the country. My friend was not in favor of the plan. Her husband responded, "You have to see the vision." She truly tried, but when she looked, all she could see was corn. After many discussions, they decided to buy the property.

Her husband graded the land and made it suitable for their mobile home. Later, he and his son dug a pond and filled it with fish. Then he sectioned off small plots for gardening and built a gazebo next to the pond. Finally, he built my friend her dream home. She shared with me how she had thanked her husband for seeing a vision for their land even when she could not. Now, after thirty years, there is nowhere else she would prefer to live.

Often in life, we look at others or even ourselves and see only corn, unable to see past the rough exterior and apparent mess. However, when God looks at us, He sees our future. With that future in mind, He begins to work, molding and shaping us into the vision He has had for us all along. Even before we were born, God was working on that vision. It does not matter how we stray or stay in the cornfield—God never forgets the future He has planned for us.

I cannot wait for the day when I stand on the sea of glass, cast my crown at His feet, and thank Him for seeing more than corn in me.

Carmalita Green

January 10

Beautiful

He has made everything beautiful in its time.
—Ecclesiastes 3:11, NKJV

She walked into my office and sat down on the couch. I listened as she made statements I had heard many times over the years. She felt ugly and unlovable. She felt she was not good enough. Others have come into my office with a lack of confidence, motivation, hope, or sense of purpose. They are unsure they can manage all the difficulties they are facing.

Along the pathway of life, this woman, like so many others I have worked with, was led to believe she was unworthy and a mistake. Too often, society, social media, friends, or family make statements and act in ways that reinforce the belief that we must change something about ourselves to be good enough. If left unchecked, these thoughts can fuel depression, anxiety, and hatred toward self and others. While I saw a beautiful woman walk into my office that day, she did not see herself the same way. We began a journey that would help her learn that she was worthy, beautiful, and lovable. Her life did have purpose.

The journey to healing begins with the recognition that God created people "in the image of God . . . ; male and female He created them" (Genesis 1:27, NKJV). A few verses further, it states He saw everything He made, and it was very good (verse 31). In Jeremiah 1:5, God says, "Before I formed you in the womb I knew you; before you were born I sanctified you" (NKJV).

We have all been beautifully and purposefully created. We are loved beyond imagination. "God so loved the world that He gave His only begotten Son, that whoever believes in Him should not perish but have everlasting life" (John 3:16, NKJV). God not only put His Son's life on the line for us but also wants us to partake in strength, confidence, and fullness of purpose that is divine in nature. That is an incredible statement to make, but 2 Peter 1:4 says we are given "exceedingly great and precious promises, that through these [we] . . . may be partakers of the divine nature" (NKJV). These verses take my breath away.

God made each of us in His image. We have been made "very good," and we have access to a divine power that can take us through all trials. Let us encourage each other to turn away from the things offered by humans and accept God's offer to be partakers of His divine nature.

Beatrice Tauber Prior

January 11

Danger in the Shadows

He stores up sound wisdom for the upright;
He is a shield to those who walk uprightly;
He guards the paths of justice,
And preserves the way of His saints.
—Proverbs 2:7, 8, NKJV

I enjoy spending time in nature, hearing the birds sing and the bees buzz as they travel from flower to flower, and watching the gentle sway of the trees in the breeze. I love feeling the sun shining down on me. Nature is a testament to God's creative power and is a soothing balm to my troubled soul.

I live in a neighborhood with a lake surrounded by trees and shrubs. Walking trails curve behind a retirement village to a golf club and lead under an overpass bridge. The foundation of the bridge is formed with large rocks skillfully stacked on top of each other. One Sunday morning I decided to follow the footpath toward the golf course rather than circle the lake. As I walked by the foundation of the overpass, I heard a noise and, in my peripheral vision, saw something drop to the ground. I glanced down and was so startled that I jumped back and ran down the path as quickly as I could. A thin gray snake had fallen from the rocks onto the path in front of me and began to slither on the footpath near my feet. Yikes!

As I recovered from the unexpected incident, I began to think: *How many times have I passed under that bridge and failed to see the snake hiding between the rocks? If I had not run away, would it have tried to attack me?* In reflecting on my own life, how many times do I see something but not recognize the danger lurking behind the action, intent, or behavior? How many times does God try to catch my attention before I listen and obey?

In 1 Peter 5:8, the Bible refers to Satan as a roaring lion who is actively trying to lead us away from God. But remember, there is Someone more powerful than Satan, and His name is Jesus. When we have Jesus, we have light and direction for our footsteps (Psalm 119:105), wisdom to discern right from wrong (Proverbs 2:6), and trust in God for all things (Proverbs 3:5). We also have access to the armor of God, which is a hedge of protection against the deceptions of Satan (Ephesians 6:10–20). This includes the belt of truth; the breastplate of righteousness; the shield of faith; the helmet of salvation; and the sword of the Spirit, which is the Word of God. My dear sisters, Jesus is our protection against the evil one who lurks in the shadows!

Jenny Rivera

January 12

Nothing Is Wasted for Jesus

Mary took a pound of very costly oil of spikenard, anointed the feet of Jesus, and wiped His feet with her hair. And the house was filled with the fragrance of the oil.
—John 12:3, NKJV

There are so many things I would love to do, things I would love to learn, books I would love to read, hobbies and interests I would love to pursue, mountain trails I would still love to hike, and more places I would love to see. But there is just *never* enough time!

There is never enough time to do all I long to do for Jesus either. I used to think I would never grow up and get old, and I would always have endless energy. But now, at forty-seven, I am realizing my years on this earth may already be half gone. I sometimes ask myself, *Was it a waste that I never did this or that while I still could? Was it a waste that I never got married or got to be a mom? Was it a waste that I did not hike more mountains or go on more sightseeing adventures? Was it a waste that I did not hide myself away and write more books instead of helping others with their needs? Should I have been more protective of my life and time?*

Then Jesus reminds me of Mary. Those watching Mary pour the costly spikenard on Jesus' feet thought she was being wasteful. She spent her whole life savings on that spikenard. The money could have been put to much better use, they said. But with Jesus, nothing spent for the kingdom and nothing spent to help others by honoring the King of kings is ever wasted. So, tears pour down my cheeks as Jesus softly whispers to my heart once again, "Melody, in love and joy, you have also poured out your spikenard, the best years of your life and youth, at My feet! Your gift has not been wasted! You could have had anyone, had any life—you could have spent all your years protecting yourself or doing whatever you wanted, but instead, you have chosen Me! Your life in ministry has not been wasted."

Friends, it is not wrong to stop and take time to smell the roses and take time for those we love. It is not wrong to get married and raise a family—especially if we are doing so for Jesus! I wish I had gotten to experience this joy. The point is, this life is not meant to be all about us. It is about pouring our broken flask of spikenard at His feet however He calls and commissions us. We each have only one life to spend. Let it be spent for Jesus. Let us make this life count for eternity!

Melody Mason

January 13

Anchored by Faith

What, then, shall we say in response to these things?
If God is for us, who can be against us?
—Romans 8:31, NIV

In the midst of a world paralyzed by a global pandemic and economic uncertainty, I found myself nearing the end of my contract. The thought of facing unemployment weighed heavy on my heart. But amid the chaos, a glimmer of hope emerged. Against all odds, I secured a remarkable job opportunity—a senior global role that allowed me to work remotely.

The process was not without its challenges. After enduring four rigorous interviews, I was elated to be offered the position. However, my joy was quickly dampened by a sudden realization. My passport, essential for onboarding and compliance purposes, had expired. Due to the pandemic, the passport renewal process was plagued with long waiting times and uncertainty. Fear crept in as doubts swirled in my mind. How could I navigate this roadblock?

In moments like these, unwavering faith becomes my anchor. I turned to prayer—my default response in times of trouble. I fervently prayed, reminding myself that God had granted me this opportunity and would not abandon me now. I cried out, "You have brought me this far, and I know You will make a way."

As the days ticked by, my worries grew. The Friday before my scheduled start date, just when my desperation peaked, an email arrived. It was from the company, informing me that they had the technology to verify my status and gather the required information remotely. A wave of relief washed over me, and tears of gratitude streamed down my face. At that moment, I could not help but marvel at the wonders of God's provision. Time and time again, He had shown His unwavering love and faithfulness. He not only blessed me with an incredible job opportunity during uncertain times but also orchestrated a solution to my passport dilemma.

I was reminded of the promise, "If God is for us, who can be against us?" (Romans 8:31, NIV). Truly, nothing can stand against His plans for our lives. In the face of adversity and seemingly insurmountable obstacles, He will make a way where there seems to be no way. There is no challenge too great and no hurdle too high. His love and guidance will carry us through! We can trust Him!

Sharon Hudson Iyayi

January 14

Generosity

"Blessed are the merciful, for they shall obtain mercy."
—Matthew 5:7, NKJV

Like so many others, Celia lost her job during the pandemic. As she watched the bills pile up and her family in need, she decided to go out and ask for help. She went from house to house, and people were kind and gave her some food to take to her family. Before returning home, she decided to stop at one more house that seemed to belong to someone rich. Celia rang the doorbell, and after sharing her needs, she was met with harsh, rude words.

"I just lost my job," the man said. "I have a lot of problems, and yours do not interest me. My family is struggling too. So, I do not, I cannot, and I will not help you. Go away, and leave me alone with my battles!" As soon as he finished speaking, he slammed the door violently.

After a few minutes passed, Celia courageously rang the doorbell again. When the man saw her the second time, he became even more irritated. "I have already told you I have nothing for you. Go away and do not bother me anymore!" Then Celia kindly reached into her basket and handed him some food she had just been given. "I did not come to ask for anything; I came to share what I have received so your family can also eat tonight." Under the man's disbelieving gaze, she turned and walked away, happy to have been able to help and thinking to herself, *Nobody is so poor that they cannot give nor so rich that they do not need to receive.*

What motivates someone so needy to share what little she has? Generosity. This is the characteristic of one who has compassion, nobility of character, and excellence of purpose. To be able to stop thinking about our own needs is a gift given by God to those who trust in Him and surrender to His plans.

The world touts the belief that personal success is individually earned and deserved. What matters are my needs, my success, and my ideas. Everything is egocentric. But Jesus taught the opposite of that. He said, "Blessed are the merciful, for they shall obtain mercy" (Matthew 5:7, NKJV).

The postpandemic world needs people who feel the pain of others and who care about them, even if they do not receive anything in return. Just as Jesus cares about our every need, we are to care for others.

Sueli da Silva Pereira

January 15

What Does It Take?

*Be not forgetful to entertain strangers:
for thereby some have entertained angels unawares.*
—Hebrews 13:2, KJV

I decided to run some errands after work and drop by the mall. I wanted to get done and get back home before it grew too dark. In a city like Toronto, Canada, it is difficult to ignore the homeless crisis, and on my way to the local Shoppers Drug Mart, a man sitting on the ground asked for spare change. "I'm sorry," I replied as I walked past him, barely making eye contact.

While ringing up my items at the checkout counter, another man came up behind me with a few items and wanted to know if I would buy them for him. He had gone to every aisle asking for help. "No, I'm sorry," I said again as I paid for my lip products, even though I could have helped him. He walked away, unable to get what he needed, and I went my way.

I continued on to Yorkdale Shopping Centre, one of the most luxurious malls in the city. While making my way through the subway tunnel, I saw a man sitting in the middle of the walkway, holding a red Tim Hortons coffee cup and begging for change. Like everyone else, I walked past him, but only a few steps inside the mall, I was convicted. I turned and walked back hurriedly, but he was nowhere to be seen. On the subway railing sat the empty Tim Hortons cup.

I have played various scenarios in my mind over the years. Maybe someone gave him what he needed, and he left. Or maybe he was frustrated with being invisible and left hungry. Whatever it was, I have always felt the man at the Yorkdale subway station was an angel, sent to put me to the test to see whether I would help someone in need. In the span of three hours in one day, I missed three opportunities to make someone's day a little easier, all because of my fear and prejudices—my preconceived ideas as to what each person would do with the money. None of my thoughts were about the person's well-being.

What does it take to be a true follower of Christ? It is more than going to church, returning tithes, and fellowshiping with other believers. It is about growing into the character of Christ and putting the needs of others before our own. It is about loving as He loves, making a difference in the lives of others in His name. Oh Lord, forgive us! May we have Your heart and share Your love with those in need, especially the poor.

Jonsaba C. Jabbi

January 16

Kindness Always Returns

Cast your bread upon the waters,
For you will find it after many days.
—Ecclesiastes 11:1, NKJV

Many years ago my aunt shared this true story with me. Glendora Martin was small in stature, but she had the kindest heart. Everyone in the village affectionately called her "Sister Glen." For years, she worked as a shop attendant in a small superette in St. John's, Antigua.

One day, when a local workman forgot his lunch at home and did not have time or money to find something to eat, he was told to go and ask for Sister Glen. In desperation, the young man explained his situation, and Sister Glen opened her purse and gave her last $5.00 to the stranger. He purchased a cheese sandwich and a bottled soda. Everything came to $4.95.

Years later, Sister Glen decided to open her own shop. When the workmen came to start building, she asked how much they would charge for labor. One man said he charged $150.00 per day.

"What about you, sir?" Glendora asked the next workman.

"I will tell you when we finish the job," he replied.

"But I don't operate like that," the little lady retorted. "You have to tell me up front so I can budget properly."

"It's OK; it won't be anything you cannot afford," he said.

When the building was finished, Sister Glen asked, "Well now, Mr. Thomas, how much do I owe you?"

"Five dollars," was the reply.

Sister Glen was startled. "Five dollars? You have worked for weeks, and now you say I owe you only five dollars? I do not understand!"

It turns out that when Mr. Thomas was a teenager, he forgot his lunch at home one day, and someone sent him to Sister Glen. Now, many years later, he was able to repay her kindness. Sister Glen invited him to church the following Sabbath, and after he received Bible studies, she had the joy of seeing him baptized.

I am reminded of Jesus' words: "Inasmuch as ye have done it unto one of the least of these my brethren, ye have done it unto me" (Matthew 25:40, KJV).

Hyacinth V. Caleb

January 17

Being Christian

Be kind and compassionate to one another.
—Ephesians 4:32, NIV

I love to travel. You never know what adventures await. Once I was returning from Kanyakumari, India, to Delhi, where I was to board a bus to Jaipur. I reached Delhi and, the following morning, got onto the bus bound for Jaipur. The weather had been warm, and the bus was not as comfortable as I had hoped.

Seated opposite me were a mother and her young son. The mother was busy on her mobile phone, and the son was left to entertain himself. He tried to get his mother's attention, but sadly, it seemed the mobile phone was more tempting than the company of her ten-year-old son.

The bus was moving at a tremendous speed, and I must say, the bus driver was driving somewhat recklessly. Many times I felt my heart skip a beat. The sudden jerks caused by his slamming the brakes were enough to make anyone dizzy. It proved to be too much for the boy, and he threw up. Oh mercy! You can imagine the smell. The other passengers made faces, changed seats, and so on. To my surprise, the mother, too, started to scold the poor child. I knew she felt embarrassed. I saw the dilemma she was in. I wondered how to be of help to this mother and her child.

Fortunately, I had lots of newspapers with me that I had used to wrap some breakable items. Unwrapping them meant risking them being broken. But I felt clearing the mess was more important. I spread the newspaper on the mess, and it did help. The people came back to their seats. Some offered paper wrappings if they had any. One old lady blessed me and placed her hand on my head.

The bus finally reached its destination, and I disembarked. The woman whom I had helped was waiting for me outside the bus, and she asked me, "Are you a Christian?" I was not entirely sure why she wanted to know, but it taught me an important lesson: Christians ought to be different. People should be able to tell we are Christians by the way we love and treat others. Since then, I have always tried to be kind and helpful.

Dear Father, help me to always be kind and compassionate to my fellow beings.

Rita Gill

January 18

Lord, Do I Need a Fence?

*As the deer longs for streams of water,
so I long for you, O God.*
—Psalm 42:1, NLT

The early morning light welcomes me as I sit down at my dining-room table for devotions. Looking out my patio door, I smile at the faces staring back at me. Several deer, frozen in place by my movement, have stopped grazing and are waiting to determine whether they are safe. I love to watch them walk across the yard or nibble the leaves off the bushes; their velvet ears and brown eyes wary of any possible danger. But honestly, I am generally not too fond of the deer in my neighborhood. They eat everything in sight—bushes, gardens, flowers, and other things I wish they would leave alone!

Many of the flowers I love to enjoy throughout the summer are like candy to the deer, so those blossoms are no longer in my yard. I once set a pot of flowers down by the garage instead of placing it up on the deck, and a couple of days later, when I got home from work, a pot full of empty stems greeted me. People tell us if we really want a garden around here, it must be enclosed in at least a six-foot-tall fence!

And deer are constantly crossing the streets, darting out unexpectedly, sometimes causing serious accidents. In fact, our son hit a deer on his motorcycle, causing the deer's early demise, wrecking the motorcycle, and sending our son to the hospital for several days.

So, this morning, as the deer and I lock eyes, Psalm 42:1 rises up in my mind: "As the deer longs for streams of water, so I long for you, O God" (NLT). I sense Jesus inviting me to consider whether I am as determined to guard my time with Him as I am to guard my flowers from the deer. Are there treasures in His Word I am not experiencing because I have been letting other things "eat" into the time He would love to spend with me? Time He could use to cause His character to bloom in my life? Have I "put a fence" around that time?

Oh, Jesus, I do thirst after You! My soul longs for You! Today I choose to surrender my priorities to You. Please let Your Living Word create the beauty of holiness and the fragrance of God in my life!

DeeAnn Bragaw

January 19

Have a Gray Day

Rejoice in the Lord always. I will say it again: Rejoice!
—Philippians 4:4, NIV

I am just going to come right out and say it: autocorrect has it in for me! It is true! I type, and it changes my correctly spelled words to something else. Something that does not make sense. Something outright *wrong*! Recently, autocorrect has been playing a new game with me. Every time I type the word *great*, it changes it to *gray*. Today my autocorrect adventure left me with this sentence typed to my daughter who is away at college for the first time: "Have a gray day!" Autocorrect strikes again! *Lord, help me!*

Of course, there is a spiritual parallel or two to examine here. When we do our best to create something *great* in our day, relationships, and workplace, Satan steps in and changes our (often correct) actions into something gray.

What is a girl to do with all this gray? Philippians 4 is my go-to gray-day chapter. Verse 4 begins, "Rejoice in the Lord always." And to add emphasis, it repeats, "Rejoice!" How can we rejoice, be happy, or be at peace when our great has been painted gray? Read on, sister. "Let your gentleness be evident to all. The Lord is near" (verse 5, NIV). How much gray would be lifted by simply remembering that the Lord is nearby? Right here with us? In us?

"Do not be *anxious* about anything, but in every situation, by *prayer and petition*, with *thanksgiving*, present your requests to God. And *the peace of God*, which transcends all understanding, will guard your hearts and your minds in Christ Jesus" (verses 6, 7, NIV; emphasis added).

In the gray moments, when our situation has been altered or when we have been wronged, let us not lose heart. Fix Satan's autocorrect by remembering Philippians 4. Rejoice! Remember that God is present. Be gentle. Pray. Rejoice. Claim God's gift of peace, and turn the gray back to great in the power of the Lord. I pray He will paint His greatness over your grayness today. Rejoice, my sister. Rejoice! (Read all of Philippians 4 for more instruction on how to keep your spirits up in challenging situations. The entire chapter is gold.)

Mary K. Haslam

January 20

I Have a Dream

I can do all things through Christ who strengthens me.
—Philippians 4:13, NKJV

The 1960s were a time of many challenges. Between the Vietnam War and the tragedy of several assassinations, including that of the president of the United States of America, we were all left needing hope. In 1963, during this tumultuous time, civil rights leader Dr. Martin Luther King Jr. gave his "I Have a Dream" speech. It was inspiring and powerful, filled with eloquent words about his dream for a day when there would be no more prejudice toward people of color. All people should be judged by the content of their character.

When Jesus was answering the question about the greatest commandment, He said, "Love your neighbor as yourself" (Matthew 22:39, NKJV). This sums up how we should treat everyone. Jesus came to Earth to show us how to achieve this. He sacrificed His life so we can have life—a changed life in which we think of others first and, ultimately, an eternal life after He returns to take us home.

So, this is my dream: that each day I will wake up having grown closer to Jesus and be more like Him in character.

I have a dream that the Holy Spirit will guide me in everything I say and do so I can reflect the love of God.

I have a dream that I will always treat others the way I want to be treated—with love, compassion, and respect.

I have a dream that when I make a mistake, I will own up to it, ask God's forgiveness, and move on.

I have a dream that all people will recognize who Jesus really is one day and accept His gift of salvation.

And last but not least, I have a dream of being a blessing to others, and even though I have made a multitude of mistakes, those others will see I have been forgiven—and that they can find the same path to forgiveness. I am thankful my walk with God grows each day. I am still a work in progress, but with Christ at my side, all things are possible. What is your dream today?

Jean Dozier Davey

January 21

Red Bus Ride Home

You drew near on the day I called on You,
And said, "Do not fear!"
—Lamentations 3:57, NKJV

My college years were very hectic for me. I was studying for my registered general nursing qualification in Port of Spain, Trinidad. During that period, I was also pursuing a course of study in psychology in Saint Augustine, Trinidad. During that time, I met the director of nursing for the Port of Spain General Hospital, who was also studying for the same qualification. We became buddies and would travel together from evening classes using the public transport service.

There were two public transport services for the island. One of the services ran buses that were painted blue and white, and the other used buses that were painted red and white. The blue-and-white buses were less expensive, and they ran until 8:00 P.M. each evening. The red-and-white buses ran until 9:00 P.M. Our classes ended at 7:30 P.M., which allowed us just enough time to catch a blue-and-white bus.

One evening we attended a tutorial that had been scheduled ahead of an upcoming exam. It was lengthy and ended up finishing much later than the regular lecture time. As we left the class, we knew that the bus had already left because it was usually on time. At the bus stop, we contemplated what to do, as our tickets were only for the earlier, cheaper service. We tried hitching a ride from vehicles passing by, to no avail. We must have been there for more than half an hour with no change in our predicament. It was getting late, with fewer and fewer vehicles on the road, and we were no closer to getting home.

With our anxiety levels getting the better of us, we remembered to pray. The prayer was short and to the point. No sooner had we finished praying when the headlights of a bus appeared in the distance. And it appeared to be the headlights of the blue-and-white bus. But when it got closer to where we were standing, it was a red-and-white bus. We clambered aboard hurriedly. The driver did not ask for tickets. Nor did he stop for the many passengers waiting along the bus route. Our next stop was the Port of Spain bus terminal. We knew that God was waiting on our call. He is waiting on your call, too, but you must "seek first the kingdom of God and His righteousness, and all these things shall be added to you" (Matthew 6:33, NKJV).

Cheryl-Ann Hudson-Victory

January 22

Eager Expectation

*"Therefore I say to you, do not worry about your life, what you will eat
or what you will drink; nor about your body, what you will put on.
Is not life more than food and the body more than clothing?
Look at the birds of the air, for they neither sow nor reap nor gather into barns;
yet your heavenly Father feeds them. Are you not of more value than they?"*
—Matthew 6:25, 26, NKJV

It was springtime, and a mother robin had decided to build her nest between the upper downspout and the gutter of our house. Every morning, as I sat at my breakfast table, I saw this faithful mother bird bringing her tiny offspring their breakfast. As she approached the nest, it was such a beautiful sight to see the baby birds lift their heads with eager expectation and open their mouths to receive their food. These babies had no choice in their menu and did not know what their mother had brought. The helpless chicks depended on her for survival. Gladly, they received their food, believing she would not bring them anything harmful. Mother robin knew just what her babies needed and brought only that which would satisfy their nutritional needs. She was doing her duty faithfully because that was her nature. God is like this and more. His nature is love.

As farmers prepare for planting, they eagerly expect the seed to germinate and produce a bountiful harvest. They have come to expect year after year that the sun will rise every day and the rain will fall in its season. Both are necessary for the growth, development, and maturity of their crops.

With eager expectation, we wait and trust our daily needs will be met by God. Just like the mother robin, He knows what is good for us. Just as the baby robins opened their mouths to receive from their mother, we are encouraged to open our hearts and minds for God to pour out His blessings and fill us with His Holy Spirit, His love, and His goodness.

He forbids us to worry because He knows our needs even before we ask. What we will receive will far exceed our expectations because He has promised to do for us "exceedingly abundantly above all that we ask or think" (Ephesians 3:20, NKJV).

Therefore, let us surrender all our cares and anxieties to God and wait with eager expectation on our faithful heavenly Father.

Lydia D. Andrews

January 23

Who Is in Charge?

In all your ways acknowledge Him,
And He shall direct your paths.
—Proverbs 3:6, NKJV

Welcome to the club! The nail-biting, hair-pulling, skin-scratching society of those who are weak in the faith. We know how it feels to be too stressed to be blessed. We have experienced the look from others that silently demands, *What is your problem, Christian?*

I have come to the conclusion that one of the chief weapons in Satan's arsenal is stress generated by fear. It is difficult to trust God when I am stressed and filled with fear. Summarizing various dictionary definitions of *stress* teaches us that *stress* is a force that strains or deforms; a mental or physical tension caused by a sense of dire urgency. I shudder when I recall the times I have been stressed to the max. Some examples include learning of a family member's accident or illness, expecting an important item in the mail that did not arrive, more people turning up for dinner than I had been prepared for, or failing to meet a financial obligation on time.

I finally learned over the years that being stressed does not hasten the item's arrival or cause my family to get in touch. It does not bring peace and calm, and it never reduces anger or fear. So why have I worried instead of trusting God?

In God's Word, Christ instructs us not to worry about what we shall eat, drink, or wear (Matthew 6:25–34). And He tells us to "seek first the kingdom of God and His righteousness, and all these things shall be added to you" (verse 33, NKJV). In other words, God is in charge. We can trust Him. In Luke 10:41, Jesus reminds Martha that she is "worried and troubled [stressed] about many things" (NKJV). In other words, she should, rather, relax and spend more time with Jesus like her sister, Mary.

Stress and worry will never change a situation. Only waiting on the Lord and trusting Him with all our hearts can do that. So, stop the nail biting! Choose not to worry or be anxious about anything! Cast all your cares on Him (see 1 Peter 5:7)!

Lord God, fill us with Your holy presence. For it is only as You direct us that we can ever learn to trust more and stress less. Thank You for being in charge. Amen.

Helen O. Byoune

January 24

He Cares for You

*Fear not, for I am with you;
be not dismayed, for I am your God;
I will strengthen you, I will help you,
I will uphold you with my righteous right hand.*
—Isaiah 41:10, ESV

Have you ever faced circumstances in your life that left you wondering, *Why me?* I remember an incident that occurred a few years ago. One sunny Tuesday morning I drove to a nearby store to purchase a gift for a friend. Unfortunately, while returning to my car, I fell and broke the little finger on my left hand. Unable to use my left hand, even though I am right-handed, I was not able to do as much around the house or in the garden. More importantly, it became difficult to care for my ninety-six-year-old mother, who was now my responsibility.

As a result, one of my sons, who was out of work at the time, came to assist me. Shortly after he arrived, my daughter-in-law, who had also lost her job, decided to join him. No sooner had she arrived than my orthopedist informed me that I would need surgery to correct my broken finger. The surgery was performed soon after, and on the following Thursday, my mom fell and broke her hip. I thank God every day that my son and daughter-in-law were around to assist me and especially to help with my mom when so many things happened all at once.

Because of her broken hip, my mom had to be moved into a nursing home for therapy. A month after entering the nursing home, she fell again and had another break in her hip. Ultimately, she succumbed to her injuries and passed away soon after.

In each unfortunate circumstance, God was visible. He sent the help I needed just when I needed it most. Miracles—too many to mention here—were performed one after the other as the Lord found ways to provide for both families throughout these difficult times.

The Bible reminds us,

> Trust in the LORD with all your heart,
>   and do not lean on your own understanding.
> In all your ways acknowledge him,
>   and he will make straight your paths (Proverbs 3:5, 6, ESV).

God takes care of His own, and we should never doubt His power to make provision for our needs because He is an on-time God. We can safely trust in Him, believe in Him, love Him, and have faith in Him. He will always see His children through.

Maureen H. Moncrieffe

January 25

Angels, Scooters, and SUVs

For he shall give his angels charge over thee.
—Psalm 91:11, KJV

There are numerous stories of angel encounters, but how blessed I was to encounter not one but two angels! One Thursday afternoon, with my dinner still warm on the stovetop, I knew I had about twenty minutes before my husband would come in to eat. The Weedwacker wheezed tiredly as he cut the tall grass near the wire fence. Should I disturb him to tell him I was going for a stroll? No. I would be back before he came inside. Or so I thought.

The downhill walk in my quiet neighborhood was uneventful. I admired the puffy bright clouds and the mango trees still laden with late-season fruit. With the brilliant sun shining warm in the October sky, it was soon time to return home. Did I have time for a few extra steps? I could get in about twenty if I turned right instead of left. I turned right. The next thing I knew, I was face down on the uneven asphalt, broken glasses in my hand, dentures bent, teeth broken, and lips swelling. This was bad. I tried getting up without success. This was really bad!

That is when I heard what I would later realize were angelic voices. "Lady, are you all right?" The young rider had rested his scooter on the grass before rushing to my side.

Another young man in a black Jeep stopped and asked, "Do you need help?"

Without waiting for an answer, the two young men scooped me up, lifted me into the Jeep, and asked, "Where do you live?"

I looked into their youthful faces, "You know that you are angels, right?"

No comment from either one. Just a smile I will never forget.

In about three minutes, I was home, where my husband, still thinking I was safe inside, was shocked to see me bruised and in distress. The young driver explained as much as he could while I went inside to tend to my wounds.

I have rewound the mental video of that accident hundreds of times since it happened. And each time I realize I could have died or been more seriously injured. I could have broken a bone or two, a vehicle could have run over me, and on and on. But instead, my Savior sent two angels and gave me this testimony. The promise is for you too. Are you in any sort of distress? Claim God's promise: "He shall give His angels charge"—maybe even on a scooter!

Annette Walwyn Michael

January 26

Guardian Angel on Guard

For the angel of the LORD is a guard;
he surrounds and defends all who fear him.
—Psalm 34:7, NLT

My first posting after completing my internship in pastoral ministry was in a remote place on the islands of Fiji. Whenever I went out, I had to walk through an area where drug addicts lived. It was dangerous for a single female. Sometimes I had to walk through their village several times a day and sometimes at night too. One night a group of them came toward my house, but they were in for a surprise. They did not expect to meet up with my little guardian angel. I named him Canine.

Shortly after I arrived to take that assignment, I found a little puppy in a ditch close to my house. I took him in, bathed him, warmed him up, fed him, and basically saved him from death. He quickly grew. Every night he would sleep on my front porch, with his paws crossed and his head nestled over them. Every so often, he would lift his head and scan the horizon. Inside, I slept peacefully, knowing he was there.

On that night, as he scanned the horizon, he saw several intruders approaching the house. Their intent was not friendly. Canine barked his lungs out and charged at the group. He frightened them, and they quickly abandoned their mission. My faithful friend then went about circling the house the whole night, barking fiercely, making sure nobody came near my house from any direction. He continued that tour of duty for a few nights. Afterward, he settled back on the front porch with his paws again crossed and his head nestled over them. Every so often, he would scan the horizon.

When some kids would come over during the day, wanting to pick mangoes from the tree in my backyard, they could not get past Canine. I thanked God for sending that guardian angel to look after me, a single female pastor, as I lived and worked in a dangerous place. Truly, "the angel of the LORD is a guard; he surrounds and defends all who fear him" (Psalm 34:7, NLT).

Do you have a story about your guardian angel? We all have a guardian angel. At that time, mine was my faithful dog. Have you ever had someone in your life who looked after you in such a way that it could only have been an angel? Then you have a story to share!

Romina Lata Masih

January 27

A Fiery End

*For he will order his angels
to protect you wherever you go.*
—Psalm 91:11, NLT

"I don't even like to think about that bike. It almost killed me!" My son and I were reflecting on some of his adventures as a teenager.

First, it was the skateboard. He was always good at improvising. We lived in the country, so he had no access to skateboard parks and found his own way to practice his skills. Our four-bedroom house has a full basement, so he got his thrills by sailing up a sheet of plywood he had propped against the high basement wall. Across the floor and up to the ceiling he would go, circle back down, then do it over and over again. To my knowledge, he never had a spill.

Then came the trail bike. How he loved the freedom of riding in the woods, over the trails and through the fields, until one day the unthinkable happened. The bike hit a rock and threw him headlong into an oak tree. When he regained consciousness and could walk, he staggered through the woods, not knowing where he was going. He was found by an acquaintance, who drove him home. His eyes were swollen shut, and his nose and right cheekbone were broken and cut. It took a long time for him to heal and be ready to ride again. His friend retrieved the bike and the helmet, which was destroyed beyond use. My son had started out that day without his helmet but had second thoughts and had come back for it; otherwise, this story would have had a tragic and entirely different ending.

Another day he came rushing in, panic on his face and in his voice. The bike had caught fire in our field, and the flames were heading toward the house. There was no 911 emergency number in those days, so, hands shaking, I found the volunteer fire department's phone number and called for help. To our relief, they arrived in time to put out the fire before the house was endangered. So ended the trail bike adventures, and not a moment too soon.

My son is now a grandfather and has survived even more adventures and misadventures. The Lord has been faithful to see him safely through them all. How thankful we can be for such mercy and grace—and for guardian angels!

Lila Farrell Morgan

January 28

Are You Thirsty?

*"But whoever drinks the water I give them will never thirst. Indeed, the water
I give them will become in them a spring of water welling up to eternal life."*
—John 4:14, NIV

It was a summer Sabbath, and I was at the historic Seventh-day Adventist church in Washington, New Hampshire, United States of America. We had the morning service and potluck lunch, and I led the afternoon cemetery tour for our group of visitors who had come from all over. After the tour, some left while others were walking on the Sabbath Trail.

I noticed a young backpacking couple reading the marker about the history of the site. The old dirt road in front of the church is part of the fifty-mile Monadnock-Sunapee Greenway Trail that goes between two mountains. It was common for backpackers to pass by. I approached them, welcomed them, and let them know that although there was no electricity on the site, we did have solar-powered modern bathrooms, and they were welcome to use them. The man replied, "You have modern bathrooms? Does that mean you have a water source?"

"Yes, there is water in the bathrooms," I replied, "and it is safe for washing. But we don't recommend that you drink it. If you want drinking water, we have that in the foyer of the church and in the pavilion."

The couple exchanged glances and smiled as he replied, "We would love some water to drink!"

We went to the foyer of the church, and they both drank deeply. Then he took out an empty canteen and filled it up. That is when I realized they had been out of water. No wonder they looked so tired. I wondered how long they had been hiking without anything to drink. I directed them to the pavilion, where I knew my husband was, and I went about tidying up the church. When it was time to go home, my husband asked me to check the trailhead donation box. He had emptied it earlier but had seen the backpacking couple put something in. Sure enough, there was a single large bill in the box. *They had certainly placed a high value on a little bit of water*, I mused to myself.

As water provides life to our bodies, so Jesus provides everlasting life to all who believe and claim His gift. Just like water to the thirsty, Jesus satisfies our innermost needs.

Marsha Hammond-Brummel

January 29

Give Me Water!

He said to me: "It is done. I am the Alpha and the Omega,
the Beginning and the End.
To the thirsty I will give water without cost from the spring of the water of life."
—Revelation 21:6, NIV

As I read today's text, Revelation 21:6, during my morning devotional time, I vividly remembered a time when I was willing to pay almost anything for even a little water.

I had been flying from Germany to Tanzania when my colon started bleeding—more like gushing, it seemed to me. I aborted my flight in Johannesburg, South Africa, and was examined by a doctor in the airport. He suggested I see my own doctor as soon as possible. I tried desperately to get a flight back to Germany, but the airlines would not cooperate. Finally, I was able to get a business-class ticket home to Maryland on Air France, transiting through Paris. I called Frankfurt, and my husband insisted he would meet me at the airport in Paris. As I waited for my flight, I drank orange juice and water, which were available in the business lounge.

By the time I arrived in Paris, I was still bleeding, and I was starting to pass out at the slightest exertion. It was a long walk from where my plane had landed to the gate to meet Dick and my flight home. I was getting desperate for water—a sign of shock, I am told. Suddenly, along the side of the concourse, there was a kiosk selling water. "How much for a bottle?" I asked. Five euros. It seemed exorbitant to me, but I did not hesitate to pay for it.

As I sipped my expensive water, I remembered a story recorded by John. He tells us that Jesus had to walk through Samaria—not because it was the only way but because He wanted to meet a Samaritan woman who was open to His word. They met at Jacob's well. I have been there, and the well is deep, and the water is cold. It was a lot of work for this woman to draw water. In their conversation, Jesus said, "If you knew the gift of God and who it is that asks you for a drink, you would have asked him and he would have given you living water" (John 4:10, NIV). When the woman questioned this, He added, "Everyone who drinks this water will be thirsty again, but whoever drinks the water I give them will never thirst. Indeed, the water I give them will become in them a spring of water welling up to eternal life" (verses 13, 14, NIV).

Are you thirsty like I am? We, too, are promised that now, today, and on the new earth we can have that "water without cost from the spring of the water of life" (Revelation 21:6).

Ardis Dick Stenbakken

January 30

Heaping Coals of Fire

Do not let sin have power over you. Let good have power over sin!
—Romans 12:21, NLV

I am a very competitive person, and I like to win! Winners get a prize, a reward, or a trophy. Paul writes, "Dearly beloved, avenge not yourselves, but rather give place unto wrath: for it is written, Vengeance is mine; I will repay, saith the Lord. Therefore if thine enemy hunger, feed him; if he thirst, give him drink: for in so doing thou shalt heap coals of fire on his head" (Romans 12:19, 20, KJV).

I read this text and decided I would do just that. A coworker had been very mean and said some unkind things to and about me. I went on vacation and returned with a gift for her—a souvenir from my travels. She was so caught off guard, she started to sweat, turned red, and had absolutely nothing to say! I would say she was feeling those coals of fire on her head.

Soon after that experience, I read, "If thine enemy be hungry, give him bread to eat; and if he be thirsty, give him water to drink: for thou shalt heap coals of fire upon his head, and the Lord shall reward thee" (Proverbs 25:21, 22, KJV). I thought, *All right! Why was this promise mentioned twice in the Bible? When I do this, the Lord Himself will reward me! I will get a prize!*

The competitive side of me got excited. *Now I need to find another enemy, heap on coals of fire, and collect my reward! Why can't I find an enemy? Where is an enemy when you need one?* The words of Jesus rang loudly: "But I say unto you, Love your enemies, bless them that curse you, do good to them that hate you, and pray for them which despitefully use you, and persecute you" (Matthew 5:44, KJV). While I concluded that heaping coals of fire brings a reward, perhaps I should rather be seeking the ultimate reward.

Sometimes we get caught up in this life, chasing things out of our reach. We need to take a breath and refocus. The writer of Hebrews points us to Abraham, who "was looking forward to the city with foundations, whose architect and builder is God" (Hebrews 11:10, NIV). If we want to win the most important reward of all, we should remember this promise: "Look, I am coming soon, bringing my reward with me to repay all people according to their deeds" (Revelation 22:12, NLT). In Christ, we are all winners. Amen!

Sylvia A. Franklin

January 31

All I Need

"Therefore do not worry about tomorrow, for tomorrow will worry about its own things. Sufficient for the day is its own trouble."
—Matthew 6:34, NKJV

Once I had a patient who was nervously facing a risky surgery. As they shared with me their struggle to come to grips with what was happening, they mentioned prayer and God. I told them that I had lived long enough to know life was not always fair and that we do not always know why something happens. I added that God promises strength only for today—not for tomorrow. The strength to face the surgery would come when the time came. Not before. What they needed to work on was today because that is when God had provided the needed strength. I shared that there had been times in my life when I had wondered how I would survive, but I found I was always given the strength. Even though, looking back, I was not always sure how I survived it, and I wondered whether I could survive it again, I know that the God who gave me strength then can do so again, and that is all I really need to know.

During my college career, I had to deal with both scholastic and personal challenges. What I told my patient, and what I tell others, is that even though God did not prevent the school, work, financial, and other challenges, He was with me through them.

Though I did not provide care for this patient after our conversation, when I was back in the room helping the primary nurse, they thanked me for what I had said.

As I write this, our world is in chaos. Many times I have found myself drawing strength from the challenges I have faced in the past as a means of strength for today. Today's challenges can help provide strength for tomorrow. I think this old song had it right: "He's still working on me to make me what I ought to be."* God reminds us in His Word, "As your days, so shall your strength be" (Deuteronomy 33:25, NKJV). Jesus' words to the disciples are still valid today: "Do not worry about tomorrow" (Matthew 6:34, NKJV). "Do not worry about how or what you should speak. For it will be given you in that hour what you should speak" (Matthew 10:19, NKJV). He is all we need, and that is enough for today.

Melinda Ferguson

---

* Joel Hemphill, "He's Still Working on Me," 1980, Hemphill Music and Family and Friends Music.

February 1

And Yet . . .

"Though he slay me, yet will I hope in him."
—Job 13:15, NIV

After my fifth cancer scare in three years, to say I was feeling a little like Job was an understatement. Four different types of cancer and precancerous lumps turned up in rapid succession. One of the cancers, melanoma, visited twice—and yet will I hope in Him.

Charles Ellicott's Bible commentary calls the sentiments in Job 13:15 an "expression of living trust."* I think that is why this verse resonates so much with me. To me, living trust, living hope, signifies perpetual motion. An "expression of living trust" in our good God is not something I say once and forget. It is something I express again and again, daily, sometimes hourly, as each new wave of fear and uncertainty threatens to engulf me.

Chemotherapy and surgery, and yet will I hope in Him.

Radiation treatment and immunotherapy, and yet will I hope in Him.

Anticancer tablets and their side effects for the next decade, and yet will I hope in Him.

So how did Job get to a place of "and yet"? How can I? Like Job, I learned to be careful whom I surrounded myself with during cancer treatment. I tried not to spend time with people who judged my choices or scolded me for taking—or not taking—this or that treatment.

When my mind's natural tendency was toward catastrophic thinking, I memorized Bible verses or listened to quieting music. A friend encouraged me to read a psalm a day, and often, the psalm perfectly captured my mood—foul or fair. It was as if the psalmist were in my head!

I tried to take care of myself—body, mind, and spirit. I would rise early and walk for an hour. I avoided doomscrolling on my devices and switched off the twenty-four-hour news cycle. I fed my mind with good books and filled my spare time with uplifting activities and journaling.

Like Job, the more I reflected on God's character, the more I learned to trust that He had a deeper purpose in my difficulties. While I wait to see that unfold, I trust Him to keep me in His grace. "Indeed, this will turn out for my deliverance" (verse 16, NIV). "I will wait for my renewal to come" (Job 14:14, NIV). Yes, this is hard, and yet will I hope in Him.

Denise Murray-Goods

---

* Stanley Leathes, "Job," in *A Bible Commentary for English Readers*, ed. Charles John Ellicott (London: Cassell, 1897), s.v. "Job 13:15."

February 2

No More Tears

*"And God will wipe away every tear from their eyes;
there shall be no more death, nor sorrow, nor crying.
There shall be no more pain, for the former things have passed away."*
—Revelation 21:4, NKJV

One day when a friend asked me to take her to the farmers market, I experienced uncontrollable weeping. Just hearing those two words, *farmers market*, brought back a flood of memories. It was the last thing my mother and I did together before she died. I had gone to visit her in South Carolina, United States of America, while I recuperated from a fractured ankle.

Each morning I would get her coffee from McDonald's, and we ended our day with a Southern home-cooked meal prepared by my mother. Seven years later, it is still not easy recalling these events. It was late February when my mother asked me to ride with her to the farmers market. I said yes, and off we went, stopping along the way at the roadside where farmers would come to sell their fruit, peas, and veggies. However, the farmers market was in another city close to where Mama would go to get her beautiful collard greens.

We spent the whole day going to the places she loved, visiting with longtime friends and family in rural South Carolina. I had no idea it would be the last day I would see my mother alive! The following day I headed back to Alabama, and just two short weeks later, my mother died from lung cancer. What a brave warrior! She was strong and powerful in her illness. There were no visible signs she was sick and that I would never see her alive again. My reaction to the mere mention of the farmers market allowed me to see how tender my emotions were now that I had become part of that group whose mothers had left them through death.

I now understand more deeply our Father's love when He says, "And God shall wipe away all tears from their eyes; and there shall be no more death, neither sorrow, nor crying, neither shall there be any more pain: for the former things are passed away" (Revelation 21:4, KJV). And Isaiah 25:8 says, "He will swallow up death in victory; and the Lord God will wipe away tears from off all faces" (KJV).

What a glorious day that will be! What a loving Father to give us such comfort and hope. How *I love Him*! If you love Him, too, say Amen!

Lenora Dorf

February 3

Light as a Feather

"Come to me, all you who are weary and burdened, and I will give you rest. Take my yoke upon you and learn from me, for I am gentle and humble in heart, and you will find rest for your souls. For my yoke is easy and my burden is light."
—Matthew 11:28–30, NIV

Cancer. Diabetes. Divorce. Money struggles. Family relationships. Gas prices. Recently, there have been many opportunities for disappointment, distraction, confusion, and hopelessness.

Some years ago my friend Toni shared something inspiring about feathers. She told us that despite the burdens we go through, the Lord does not want us carrying even a featherweight of concern or worry. She asked, "Do you know how much a feather weighs?"

Of course, we said, "Nothing! Feathers do not weigh anything!"

She responded, "That's right! Nothing!"

This story has stayed with me for years, and I have had quite a few opportunities to share it with others. When I do, there have often been tears shed, then a sense of relief, and finally, an abiding peace. Some have shared stories of coming across a feather while working in their garden or in some unusual place. Another lady told me that after her sister passed away, she had chosen to keep a metal feather she had found among her belongings as a special memento. She was not sure why at the time, but she said it felt like it was something meaningful. Many others have shared their stories of feathers with me.

Wow, Lord! This story has traveled from heart to heart, just like a feather floating on the breeze, moving beyond the original story I shared!

If you are going through challenges of any kind today, here is an idea for you. Use any web browser to search for images of an outline of a feather or a coloring page of one. Print it out on card stock, if possible. Print a few. Grab some crayons, coloring pencils, or watercolor paint, and decorate it. You can do this individually, with your family, or with a group.

Put it in a place where you will see it often, and when you are having one of those moments, this symbolism will remind you how much weight the Lord wants you to carry. His shoulders are strong and broad enough to bear any burdens or cares you have to give Him.

May your journey be light as a feather and filled with peace.

Kim Denyse Brown

February 4

His Peace

And let the peace of God rule in your hearts,
to which also you were called in one body; and be thankful.
—Colossians 3:15, NKJV

Thou wilt keep him in perfect peace,
whose mind is stayed on thee: because he trusteth in thee.
—Isaiah 26:3, KJV

One Sabbath evening I listened to a Christian television station as the gospel group Bibletones sang a song with the words "God is so good, He's so good to me; He took away my burdens, set my spirit free."* I reflected on how God had led me during the past week, and I had to agree with the musicians: God is good to me. As I acknowledged His peace, I praised God for His goodness.

So many things are happening all around us wherever we are. We have experienced a pandemic that has not fully left us, and other plagues have arisen and are moving around in our atmosphere. During the time of the pandemic, a war began between Russia and Ukraine, which has resulted in further economic strains worldwide. Adding to that, wild shooting sprees by unscrupulous individuals occur across our land, killing and disrupting the lives of innocent people. During these trying times, domestic abuse and other forms of violence continue to plague us. To address and correct the ills of domestic violence, our Women's Ministries' End It Now initiative serves as a sterling program.

In our human frailty, we sometimes do not understand why troubles come upon our world and affect our lives. We wonder when these things will end and peace will come to our global village. Even though much of the world's troubles may be far removed from where we live, we still experience the ripple effects in one form or another. We sorrow and mourn with those who are suffering and likewise in our own sufferings.

In this sin-sick world, our hope is Jesus Christ, who alone can deliver, heal, restore, and save us. He can give us His peace and enable us to dwell where we are until He returns to take us home. Jesus encouraged His disciples, "In Me you may have peace. In the world you will have tribulation; but be of good cheer, I have overcome the world" (John 16:33, NKJV).

Elizabeth Ida Cain

---

* Jamie May, "God Is so Good," Bibletones, *Subject to Change*, 2021.

February 5

Do Not Worry

"Fear not, for I am with you;
Be not dismayed, for I am your God.
I will strengthen you,
Yes, I will help you,
I will uphold you with My righteous right hand."
—Isaiah 41:10, NKJV

I listened to the words sung by the children with their crystal-clear voices, and the message penetrated deep into my heart: be faithful until the Lord comes.

I watched the fifty or so kids from the camp sing their hearts out. As I listened, they sang with youthful exuberance. Deeply moved, I choked back my tears and sang along with them. My thoughts went up to God in heartfelt prayer: *Lord, fulfill these words in their lives. Help them to be faithful to the end.*

Life often charts a course different from the one we expect. Nothing is stable anymore. Our world is going through turmoil and is changing very quickly. The whirlwind of trouble and change makes us dizzy. But we are not lost. All of these things show us that the second coming of our Lord Jesus Christ is now ever closer.

Even though we may be experiencing trials, confusion, and restrictive legislation, by faith, we can look confidently ahead. We can live boldly because we know that one day we will see the fulfillment of Jesus' promised return. We will live in a place where

> pain cannot exist. . . . There will be no more tears, no funeral trains, no badges of mourning. . . . "For the former things are passed away.". . .
> . . . From Him who created all, flow life and light and gladness.*

If the burdens of life are weighing you down today, if the trials seem too great, look to Jesus and trust His promises. As the writer to the Hebrews so clearly reminds us, "Be content with what you have, because God has said, 'Never will I leave you; never will I forsake you' " (Hebrews 13:5, NIV).

So, do not worry. Be patient, "for yet a little while, and He who is coming will come and will not tarry" (Hebrews 10:37, NKJV).

Liliana Radu

---

* Ellen G. White, *The Great Controversy* (Nampa, ID: Pacific Press®, 2005), 676, 678.

February 6

And the Award Goes To . . .

Blessed are they that do his commandments, that they may have right to the tree of life, and may enter in through the gates into the city.
—Revelation 22:14, KJV

The presentation of the Grammy Awards is one of the most star-studded events that takes place in the United States of America. This award ceremony is presented by the Recording Academy to recognize outstanding achievements in the music industry, and a great deal of preparation goes into an event like this. If you have ever watched this event, you may have noticed how the nominees—the stars—are dressed. Their hair, outfits, and makeup are just right. Everything is perfect. Their speeches are well prepared, and for many, I imagine the after-party celebrations are the highlight of the evening.

I have often wondered about the second coming of Jesus. How much preparation are we making for this event? Are we diligently sharing the good news of Jesus, the Bright and Morning Star? What about our lifestyle? The way we choose to live life each day? Is there a marked difference between the way we speak and dress compared to the people of the world?

When Jesus comes, He will be coming with awards. Instead of the highly prized gramophone trophy given to the winners at the Grammy Awards, He will give each of His faithful ones a crown filled with stars. So, as God's children, let us be in the world but not of the world. May we not allow the world and its practices to draw us away from preparing for this glorious event, which is soon to take place.

The winners at the Grammy Awards give acceptance speeches. What will my acceptance speech be? I think I will be speechless! There will be no red carpet in heaven; instead, we will walk on streets of gold. And we can only begin to imagine what Jesus has in store for us. The Bible says, "But as it is written, eye hath not seen, nor ear heard, neither have entered into the heart of man, the things which God hath prepared for them that love him" (1 Corinthians 2:9, KJV).

My dear sisters, let us be faithful. Let us ask Jesus every day to prepare us for the greatest event of all ages. Even so, come Lord Jesus!

Joan M. Leslie

February 7

Lessons on Aging

What is your life? You are a mist that appears for a little while and then vanishes.
—James 4:14, NIV

I always longed to have my mother's beautiful white hair, but I gave little thought to the aging process that brought it about. As I have aged, I have learned lessons along the way, and here are four of them: First, treat your body right. I have made a healthy diet my medicine. I exercise regularly and spend quality time with God. At the age of sixty, I did not feel or look old, and my medical history, though not perfect, was better than many my age and younger.

Second, if you can laugh at yourself, it does not matter who else does. Somehow, threescore and ten snuck up on me. I have learned the hard way to prevent falls by walking slowly, reducing climbing, and not turning around suddenly. I now calculate how I will get up before bending down to retrieve anything. Aches come and go in places I did not know existed. Squeaks follow me, not from my shoes but from my knees. I am now aging! Thank God all of these are manageable and often cause me to laugh at myself.

Third, commune with God continuously. My prayer and praise life has skyrocketed. As I open my eyes each morning, I thank God I am alive, I can see, my mind is sound, and I can hear myself thanking Him. As I get out of bed, I thank Him that I can stand and walk by myself. Devotion in my garden reaches greater heights and continues throughout the day. If I mislay something in the house, which happens more often now, I ask Him to find it for me, and often, as I open my eyes, I am led to it. I pray more for protection as I leave the safety of my home and give thanks as I return. I thank Him more for food and shelter, as I see many on the streets without either. I take nothing for granted.

Fourth, befriend young people. Over the years, God has blessed my life with the friendship of many young people whom I encourage and pray for. I thank Him for them. They have kept me young at heart, and now they are becoming invaluable as death takes my peers away. Aging can be as good as you make it or as bad as you allow it to be.

I now yearn for the Second Coming, and while I strive to live a better life each day, I look forward to living eternally on the earth made new.

Cecelia Grant

February 8

I Still Matter

"He will renew your life and sustain you in your old age."
—Ruth 4:15, NIV

Growing up on the beautiful island of Barbados, I never envisioned myself getting old, much less reaching eighty-two. I thought I would always be young and energetic, so I did not plan for old age. Now, here I am. Unexpectedly, old age knocked on my door, and before I could respond, it walked in, took up permanent residence, and refused to leave. It has caused me to slow down and left me unable to do the things I once enjoyed. However, I try not to let it ruin my life. I have learned that the more involved I am in helping others, the less time I have to think about myself.

This past Easter God gave me the idea to call some of my retired friends and former colleagues to let them know I was thinking of them and to tell them that even in their senior years, they still mattered. Some had downsized and moved away to be nearer to families. They, too, are experiencing a decline in being able to do the things they once enjoyed.

The day following Easter I made six calls, including one to my ninety-eight-year-old former handbell choir director. She was delighted! We laughed and reminisced about the good old days, and before we parted, she said, "Thank you for thinking of me and calling. It made me feel special." Another call was to a former boss whom I worked with forty-three years ago. He was happy and thanked me for my contribution to his department's success during my tenure of service. He commented that he was following in my footsteps and was writing a book. I encouraged him to keep writing.

A later call was to a dear friend—the pianist at my wedding more than fifty-three years ago. She returned my call on her way home from work. We chatted for several minutes. At the end of our conversation, she remarked, "Every night after I come home from work, I cry. Tonight I did not cry. Thank you for calling me." Her beloved husband had succumbed to pancreatic cancer some months before.

Old age is a blessing from the Lord, but sometimes, we may not see it that way. I am thankful that God continues to give me special moments to brighten the lives of fellow travelers on the road of life. No one is ever too old to inspire or encourage others.

Shirley C. Iheanacho

February 9

Old Age

They shall still bring forth fruit in old age; they shall be fat and flourishing.
—Psalm 92:14, KJV

If I live to see my next birthday, I will have reached fourscore years on this earth. A tad more than the age recorded by Moses: "The days of our years are threescore years and ten; and if by reason of strength they be fourscore years, yet is their strength labour and sorrow; for it is soon cut off, and we fly away" (Psalm 90:10, KJV).

I was thinking about how Sarah got her wish for a baby, though she was 90. God called Moses at the age of 80 to confront Pharaoh. And Abram was led at 75 to leave his homeland and become the father of a new nation. The oldest living man was Methuselah at 969 years (Genesis 5:27). Older or infirm people are not always judged fairly, being seen as slow, out of step, or out of date. But, while the length of their days may not be a goal, everybody wants to feel that their life's purpose is fulfilled.

A friend of ours was struggling with amyotrophic lateral sclerosis (Lou Gehrig's disease), which has rendered her hands and feet useless. She confided that a colleague encouraged her with the suggestion, "Even in a wheelchair, you can still counsel people. Make videos and a vlog!" Hope came flooding back.

Like David, I do not want to be cast aside in my old age (see Psalm 71:9). God has given me a mind and His Holy Spirit. God can still use us. I recently read two promises that have rebooted me. In the first, Isaiah shares God's pledge with us:

> "I will be your God throughout your lifetime—
> until your hair is white with age.
> I made you, and I will care for you.
> I will carry you along and save you" (Isaiah 46:4, NLT).

The second promise is found in Psalm 92:12–14. *Matthew Henry's Commentary* on Psalm 92:14 reads, "The last days of the saints are sometimes their best days, and their last work is their best work. . . . Perseverance is the surest evidence of sincerity."[*]

My prayer each day is, "*Use me, Lord.*"

Elinor Harvin Burks

---

[*] Matthew Henry, "Psalm 92, Verses 7–15," in *Matthew Henry's Commentary*, accessed December 5, 2023, https://www.biblegateway.com/resources/matthew-henry/Ps.92.7-Ps.92.15.

February 10

Do You Love Jesus?

We love Him because He first loved us.
—1 John 4:19, NKJV

When the question is asked, "Whose side are you standing on?" I wish to reply, "I am standing on the Lord's side!" Some people may not know that they have taken sides, but there are only two marshaled forces: those of good and those of evil. In this controversy between Christ and Satan, no human being can remain an onlooker. We are all active participants in a battle that rages every day.

If you choose good and godly principles and obedience to God's law, this shows your loyalty to God. Act like a rogue, and Satan welcomes you with open arms because you are on his side. We serve whom we love. Because God calls us to witness of Him, I like to ask people if they love the Lord. It can serve as a springboard into deeper spiritual conversations.

I once asked a church sister, "Do you love the Lord?"

She responded, "What stupid question are you asking me?"

I replied, "I just want to know if you love the Lord."

She seemed upset. "Well, you asked me a very silly question, and a silly question deserves a silly answer." That ended the conversation.

Then I met a businessman I knew and posed my question to him: "Sir, do you love the Lord?"

His eyes lit up. "Do I love the Lord? I most certainly love the Lord!" He was delighted.

I joyfully confessed, "I love Him too!" And from that conversation, we began to speak about the signs of Christ's second coming.

Aunt Glen, my ninety-year-old aunt who is the matriarch of our family, asked me, "How are things with you?"

I responded positively. As the phone conversation continued, I wanted to ask whether she still loved the Lord. So I posed my question to her: "Aunt Glen, do you love the Lord?"

Without any hesitation, she responded, "There is no one else to love but Him."

Different answers to the same question. Some responses took the conversation deeper, and some answers ended the conversation.

My friend, I ask you, "Do you love the Lord?" I pray your response will be, "Yes! I love Him because He first loved me."

Hyacinth V. Caleb

February 11

Anyway

For I am convinced that neither death, nor life, nor angels, . . . nor things that are present, nor things to come . . . will . . . separate us from the love of God.
—Romans 8:38, 39, NET

"Do you have anything in your pocket?" There in the center of the store aisle, I looked down into the face of a little girl. Her face bore the telltale signs of Down syndrome. I was trying to do some long-overdue grocery shopping while a caregiver stayed with my failing husband. But sleep deprivation had me struggling to make sense of where I should head next. Away from answering questions from hospice workers, laundering soiled bed linens, and preparing specialized meals, I felt lost. My knees wanted to buckle, and tears threatened to flow. But I must stay on schedule.

"Do you have anything in your pocket?" the child repeated. Before I could answer, a small, grimy hand dug into the front pocket of my snow-white tunic. "Nope, it's empty," she pronounced. "I couldn't find anything in there. Do you know my grandma?" A middle-aged woman chatting nearby glanced at the child and then winked at me before resuming her conversation. "My grandma's talking to that lady over there. So, do you know Grandma?" When I shook my head no, the little girl said, "That's OK for now if you don't. I love you anyway." With that, she tenderly laid her smudgy face against my white-tunicked tummy. And for a long, unexpected instant, short, chubby arms did their best to encircle my waist. I literally felt the love while salty tears nearly breached my eyelids before returning to lower tide levels.

Have you ever reached out to a stranger, only to realize they did not know Someone who was special to you? I have. And maybe, as with me, their appearance, apparel, aroma, or lifestyle put you off, and your subliminal response toward them revealed it. I wish instead I had intentionally conveyed in word or gesture a clear "That's OK for now. I love you anyway." If I had let them know I loved them anyway, maybe they would have better understood that God does too. That neither death, nor life, nor things present or to come, nor depression or divorce, nor abuse, nor impending widowhood or a changing life landscape could ever separate them from God's love. Going forward, I will try to be more like that little girl who, on a painful, tearful day in a big-box store, offered assurance that she—and God—loved me anyway.

Carolyn Rathbun Sutton

February 12

The Tender Voice of the Lord

"Today if you hear His voice, do not harden your hearts."
—Hebrews 4:7, NASB

Hearing the voice of God in the midst of the turmoil of the world is, above all, a privilege for us. In a world where screams and moans transcend the imagination and shake the intellect, the Master's soft voice is a relief in the wilderness of existence.

It is necessary to relearn to hear God's voice—in the whisper of the breeze, in the song of the bird, in the joke of a child, or in the serenity of prayer. The voice of Jesus brings comfort and courage in the face of fear and struggle. His voice reaches us wherever we find ourselves and gives us peace. He can turn impatience into calm, ingratitude into gratitude, anxiety into serenity, and disappointment into victory. His love redeems us and brings us from darkness to light.

It is when we sit by His side and let Him speak to our hearts that we realize the healing power of His presence. Jesus patiently waits for an opportunity to be with us. He does not invade our privacy. He respects the freedom of choice given to every human being, but oh, how He craves time with us! He longs to bless each moment with us. Where the Master dwells, there is peace, joy, and love, even in times of anguish and suffering. The power that emanates from Christ is able to supply all our needs.

He speaks to us through His Word, which has the power to heal our deepest wounds. His promises bring hope and rest to weary souls. Those who invite and delight in the Savior's presence experience how great our Lord is.

If you hear the voice of God today, do not harden your heart with doubt or unbelief. Allow yourself to experience something extraordinary—give yourself a moment alone with the One who moves the entire universe to be by your side. Then you will be able to understand that there is no greater love than the love of God! A life away from the Lord is a life without purpose, but a moment at His side is enough to give meaning to our existence. It is in the love of the Father that true happiness is given to us. It is in the arms of the infinite Lord that we find peace.

What does God want to share with you today? Be still, and listen for His voice. "Come close to God and He will come close to you" (James 4:8, NASB).

Sueli da Silva Pereira

February 13

Trust Him in All Things

But if we hope for that we see not, then do we with patience wait for it.
—Romans 8:25, KJV

As I sat down to write, my thoughts were focused on the impossibility of the situation before me. My heart ached, my mind raced, and my emotions felt as though they were having the time of their lives at a trampoline event. To be honest, I had already decided to give up.

As I read the love letter he had written so many years ago, I was jolted into the reality that I was depending on my own strength to make it through. The more I read, the more I saw my need for God. I needed to unite with Him and work through those stubborn feelings of hurt, disappointment, and anger, which would take time and therapy. I bowed my head in prayer, and in an agonized whisper, I cried out, "Lord, help me!"

It was then that God reminded me in His great love letter, the Holy Bible, that He is all-powerful (Matthew 28:18, KJV). He "will perfect that which concerns me" (Psalm 138:8, NKJV). He wants me to wait on Him (Micah 7:7) and asks me to trust Him in all things (Proverbs 3:5). And finally, He will ensure that the trials of this life produce testimonies that draw others to him (1 Peter 4:12, 13).

A ray of Sonshine peeked through the clouds of discouragement, and I saw a glimmer of hope. God's love letter, in unity with the Holy Spirit, had done it again. It had lifted up Jesus and drawn me to Him.

I thank God that He pursued me. He reminded me so eloquently that He loves me, died to save my soul, and continues to advocate and provide for me. After spending time in His Word, I felt loved, treasured, and protected. I was persuaded that although I could not see how this particular situation would work out, I had to place it in God's hands.

Are you facing any situations that seem impossible, with no solution in sight? Please join me in prayer, and lay each impossible thing before the Lord. Though we may not see the way forward, God does. We can pour out our hearts to Him and allow Him to teach us how to wait on Him. "Be still, and know that I am God" (Psalm 46:10, KJV).

Let us call out to our heavenly Father, "Lord, I believe; help thou mine unbelief" (Mark 9:24, KJV).

Linda McClellan

February 14

The One My Heart Loves

I found the one my heart loves.
—Song of Solomon 3:4, NIV

My husband and I recently sat behind two aged couples in church. (I realize, of course, that *aged* is a relative term. We ourselves are considered aged by many, if not most!) They were a study in consideration and care, and they served as a great blessing to me that Sabbath.

One couple appeared to be in their nineties and were about the same size—tiny. Her entire outfit was skillfully crocheted at a level way beyond my abilities. Her hair was beautifully coiffed, and the gentleman was just as dapper as could be.

The lesson began when they got up for the opening hymn. The struggle ended with them both on their feet, though I was not sure if they were helping each other up or holding each other up. But up they got, arms around one another, and both sang energetically.

The struggle to get back down and, a little later, onto their knees for prayer and back up again played out similarly. But smiling sweetly at one another all the while, they managed quite nicely. They were a joy to watch, and I only hope Rick and I are as much a pleasure to behold twenty years from now.

The other pair was also a delight. They were, I believe, a little younger, and they both wore hearing devices supplied by the church. A moment of levity occurred when he snatched the aid she was wearing off her head and put it on his own, evidently preferring it. She wrestled it back. But they, too, held hands, smiled, helped each other up and down, and generally appeared to be in love.

I do not know for sure that these two couples were in long-lived marriages, but I like to think so. I imagine them being married as youngsters and holding on till now. That takes some doing.

I came away encouraged by what I saw and thinking, too, of our marriage relationship with Jesus. It is doable also. He does all the heavy lifting, to be sure, but we agree to be in the relationship and to stay in it. We get helped up, held up, and just held.

So, let us smile and hang on! No matter our age!

Carolyn K. Karlstrom

February 15

Emotions in the Psalms

*But I trust in your unfailing love;
my heart rejoices in your salvation.
I will sing the LORD's praise,
for he has been good to me.*
—Psalm 13:5, 6, NIV

Reading Psalms often shocks me, especially when we see the author vent in all sincerity to God, without holding back. Why, then, when we go to pray, do we start with "Our heavenly Father, thank You for Your blessings," when what we really want to do is explode and vent about how stressed, tired, and in need of help we are? God can handle it, I am sure!

Because we are guarded around everyone else, we often act the same way around God. We may be guarded because we feel we are strong and do not need to express ourselves. It could also be that we fear rejection or judgment from people around us. The sad truth is that all of us need a safe space to vent every once in a while. When we read the following sentences, we understand that even Bible characters dealt with great frustrations from daily life: "May the LORD cut off all flattering lips, and the tongue that speaks proud things" (Psalm 12:3, NKJV). "O LORD, heal me, for my bones are troubled. My soul also is greatly troubled" (Psalm 6:2, 3, NKJV). These Bible characters knew that the best place to take those frustrations was to Jesus.

I know I did not quote the most intense verses that sometimes pop up in the Psalms—the ones that leave us embarrassed or shocked that someone actually said such things out loud. However, I think those grenade verses are there to teach us we can truly, completely, safely vent to God. Our prayers do not need to be scripted by religious formality that results in their becoming a kind of mantra we play on repeat. We can be real with God. He is there to listen. He loves us, and He longs to help us grow and heal from whatever situation we are in.

Some days, or most days, it is hard to deal with our "neighbor," or the "brethren," as we like to say. That is totally normal. Some days we get angry because we see "the wicked prosper" (Jeremiah 12:1, NKJV). Some days we are frustrated because the enemy seems to have the upper hand. But God is there on the good days and the bad days. He is always there. So take it all to Jesus; He knows who you really are, and He loves you. God sees our flaws, but He also sees what we can be if we trust our lives, including our emotions, to Him.

Yvita Antonette Villalona Bacchus

February 16

Only God Can Satisfy My Soul

O God, listen to my cry! Hear my prayer!
—Psalm 61:1, NLT

There are moments when we feel dejected, with everything in disarray. We feel isolated, discouraged, and depressed. It seems we are separated from God and blocked in by difficulties, and we cannot cope. We have the overwhelming impression that nobody understands us.

If your heart is heavy or downcast today, hold on! Do not give up because God has a plan for your life. He will fulfill the promises He has made to you. Psalm 61 reminds us that in times of distress, sorrow, pain, or discouragement when we come into the presence of God, our hearts become quiet. We know that He is very close to us, and His presence reassures and comforts us. This psalm reminds us of something very important, something we sometimes forget: God is the only One who can satisfy our souls and grant us the peace, joy, and comfort that we so desperately need.

He is listening as no other can. Sometimes our husbands, parents, and friends may not have time to listen because they are too busy to hear what our hearts want to share. Like us, they are human and may not be in the mood to be with us when we need them. But God will always be there. He listens to our cries. He feels our despair, pain, and sadness. Our Savior is with us—not sometimes—but all the time. And He can satisfy our souls if we believe in Him.

In the presence of God, we can say with the psalmist:

> I waited patiently for the Lord to help me,
>   and he turned to me and heard my cry.
> He lifted me out of the pit of despair,
>   out of the mud and the mire.
> He set my feet on solid ground
>   and steadied me as I walked along.
> He has given me a new song to sing,
>   a hymn of praise to our God.
> Many will see what he has done and be amazed.
> They will put their trust in the Lord (Psalm 40:1–3, NLT).

When we seek God with all our hearts, whatever we may be facing in life, we will find peace on every level. As Isaiah reminds us, "The Lord's arm is not too weak to save you, nor is his ear too deaf to hear you call" (Isaiah 59:1, NLT). Surely, God will hear us, save us, and satisfy our souls.

Fabienne Maslet

February 17

For Your Entertainment

Turn my eyes away from worthless things;
preserve my life according to your word.
—Psalm 119:37, NIV

Our pastoral team chose to preach a sermon series on various human emotions. When the lead pastor preached about desires, he mentioned the Motion Picture Production Code.* This set of guidelines was developed and used in the movie industry to ensure good taste prevailed, no profanity would be used, and no suggestive nudity or ridiculing of the clergy would appear on the screen. The Production Code was strictly followed through most of the 1950s but slowly eroded over time due to the impact of television and the influence of foreign films, which were not bound by the Production Code.

I remember watching television programs with good moral messages. Some even included stories that showed the blessing being said over family meals. How times have changed! The entertainment industry no longer follows the Production Code in its pursuit of increased viewers and generating higher box-office revenues and ratings. Movies regularly encourage revenge and vigilante justice. Religion and religious persons are routinely mocked, with a few notable exceptions. There are also movies and television programs that humanize evil and evil agencies. Fortunately, there are still informational and educational documentaries and biographical movies that delight and inspire us.

Just like the Production Code, God's instructions are often ignored. Paul instructed, "Finally, brethren, whatsoever things are true, whatsoever things are honest, whatsoever things are just, whatsoever things are pure, whatsoever things are lovely, whatsoever things are of good report; if there be any virtue, and if there be any praise, think on these things" (Philippians 4:8, KJV).

We must be careful what we behold because it is "by beholding we become changed."† Carelessness can erode our love for God and alter the choices we make. God's Word reminds us, "But we all, with unveiled face, beholding as in a mirror the glory of the Lord, are being transformed into the same image from glory to glory, just as by the Spirit of the Lord" (2 Corinthians 3:18, NKJV). Let us fix our eyes and our minds on the Lord.

Barbara Burris Neequaye

---

* *Encyclopaedia Britannica Online*, s.v. "Hays Office," accessed November 16, 2023, https://www.britannica.com/topic/Hays-Office.
† Ellen G. White, *Christ's Object Lessons* (Battle Creek, MI: Review and Herald®, 1900), 355.

February 18

Beautiful News

*How beautiful on the mountains
are the feet of those who bring good news,
who proclaim peace,
who bring good tidings,
who proclaim salvation,
who say to Zion,
"Your God reigns!"*
—Isaiah 52:7, NIV

Running into the house one day after school, one of our children excitedly announced that their class was going on a field trip to the zoo in a few days. Children love the excitement of having something to look forward to.

What about us? Are we excited about the good news, and do we look forward to sharing it? The good news we believe in remains unique and relevant in the world today. To some, a postmodern and post-Christian world is a difficult field in which to labor. It is a time when many people feel their personal journey, their individual experience, and their relative truth are more valuable than an old organized and institutionalized religion that they consider outdated.

However, what I believe and the values I hold on to, my understanding of prophecies and doctrines, and my unique religious experiences should not be hidden because I think people do not want to hear them. Through my study of the Scriptures, my participation in a community of faith, and an open heart toward others, I grow. When I see how the good news affects my life, my choices, my thoughts, and my habits, I discover its value and meaning—and I become excited!

Yet the peace and hope in Christ that come from my knowledge of His Word should not make me feel superior to anyone. We are responsible and accountable to God for what we know and are learning. Jesus invites us to be His disciples and to make disciples. So how do we share the good news with others today? Are we keeping our light "under a bushel" (Matthew 5:15, KJV), trying to fit in rather than sharing what makes us different?

The good news should be shared with a discerning attitude. We must build bridges rather than walls of division. The message is beautiful not only to the one who shares it but also to the one who hears it. God's good news will break down barriers and open prison doors.

As you study Jesus' life, notice His meek, loving, and compassionate attitude. Note how He shared good tidings, proclaimed salvation, and declared, "My God reigns!" May God reign in our lives as we grow and share the good news.

Nilde Itin

February 19

Do We Hear His Voice?

After the fire there was the sound of a gentle whisper.
—1 Kings 19:12, NLT

When I studied communication, I realized that listening is an important part of communication that has largely been neglected. Why? Because people typically do not listen. We hear, but do we really listen? If humans listened, many of the world's problems would be reduced. When the law is neglected because humans hear but do not listen, crime rises to ever higher levels.

Complete communication is when a message is sent through a good channel and received through good listening and understanding, and feedback is returned. But because most receivers do not listen, senders never get any feedback, so a lot of incomplete messages are left hanging. Communication can be spoken loudly or softly, through body language or written words. Often, it is spoken communication that suffers the most.

The Bible describes the prophet Elijah waiting to hear from God, and God sending different modes of communication to the prophet. Was he listening? Did he hear? Was he expecting God to speak through the strong wind that tore the rocks loose, the earthquake, or the fire (1 Kings 19:11, 12, NLT)? Instead, God chose to speak in a gentle whisper. What can we learn from this? We must listen carefully to hear God's voice talking to us all the time.

I had tried several times to hear God's voice but could not say for sure that I had heard Him. But one day I sat very quietly after my devotion, and it dawned on me that I heard a voice telling me to get an umbrella and put it in my bag. It was ninety degrees outside, and there were no rain clouds in the sky. I obeyed—and just five minutes after leaving home for a doctor's appointment, it started to rain heavily. All I said was, "Thank You, God." That day I understood how to listen and hear the still, small voice of the Holy Spirit.

If you are wondering whether God honestly has the time to tell someone about an umbrella, all I can say is that He did it for me. And it helped me a lot. All we must do is listen for His voice. Whether it is regarding a major or minor problem, it will always help. So, do you listen? Do you want to listen? Let us not push the Holy Spirit away. He wants to communicate with us. We just need to be still—and listen.

Mabel Kwei

February 20

Drip-Drop Miracle

"Before they call I will answer;
while they are still speaking I will hear."
—Isaiah 65:24, NIV

The faint scratching of a pencil on paper signified the completion of one more item on the morning's to-do list. I closed my eyes for a moment, and visions of unfinished items jockeying for pole position appeared like the eighth notes of a Rachmaninoff concerto—at times discordant but always dramatically racing along.

Next, I headed to the garage to wait for my mother to go shopping. As I approached the passenger side of the car, I felt an unexpected sensation. It was raining in my garage! It took a minute for my brain to process, especially since sunshine and blue sky peeked in from the windows. I looked up, and a fat drop of water fell on my face. Yes, it was indeed raining in my garage. Possibilities flitted across my mind. I could ignore it, or I could face reality. There was a leaking pipe in the house. As a newly single mom who had recently moved to an unfamiliar area, my options were limited. Though I was an expert with the screwdriver and the hammer, I knew nothing about plumbing, and I did not know a plumber.

I trudged back inside and frenetically started to make a series of phone calls, all with negative outcomes. The house plumbing was no longer under warranty. The twenty-four-hour emergency plumbing service was only taking messages. Calls to other plumbers went straight to voicemail.

Suddenly, I remembered I had randomly called a handyman to help with some yard work a few weeks before. Would he know a plumber? I called, and providentially, he was just finishing up a job and could come to investigate the issue. After he arrived, I stood staring at the hole in the garage ceiling as he removed wet insulation. He explained that a myriad of issues could cause the leak. It just so happened that the first pipe he checked was the one leaking. He just happened to have the right tools in his truck to fix the issue.

In that moment, I imagined God saying, "See, even though everything seems chaotic and broken, I still see you; I still provide." Even before I felt that first drop of water on my head, God had appointed an available helper with all the right tools. My drip-drop miracle serves as a reminder that even though I walk through valleys of uncertainty, God is always with me.

Charmaine Houston

February 21

Nothing Is Hopeless With God

*"But they do not know the thoughts of the Lord,
And they do not understand His plan;
For He has gathered them like sheaves to the threshing floor."*
—Micah 4:12, NASB

I read this verse one morning in my devotional, and it stuck out to me. I have read Micah before and honestly have struggled at times to understand the minor prophets. After I had read the verse a couple of times, it hit me. I do not know God's thoughts or His plans, but He does. I cannot see what is coming, but He can.

The nations had surrounded Israel, and from where they were positioned, they felt confident of a sure victory. If you were in Israel at this time, things were looking very bleak and hopeless. You may have even found yourself saying, "This is hopeless!" But then God stepped in. His plan overruled everything Babylon had declared. They did not know the Lord's thoughts or understand His plan. What looked hopeless at one point in time was turned into hope and deliverance when God directed it that way. The situation changed from bondage to freedom. And that is the difference between what we can see or imagine and what God can see and makes possible in His power.

While I may see only the mile in front of me, God sees the whole route I am traveling. He sees it with all its possibilities and problems. Micah reminds me that though I do not know the Lord's thoughts or understand His plans, that is OK. I do not need to know them because He does, and that is all I need to remember. We can rest assured that His plans are always right and lead to what is best for us—even when we do not understand them at the time.

So, the next time you find yourself thinking that things are not going to happen or that a situation is hopeless when it did not go the way you thought it would, remember that we do not know God's plans. He has set things in motion that He has planned for our ultimate good. When we trust His plans and not our own, everything will work out the way it should.

If today, dear sister, you find yourself in a place of uncertainty or disappointment, you are in a good place, for it is here where God can work. Trust in God's thoughts and plans for you. They will always work out in the right way and at the right time.

Debra Snyder

February 22

Together at Last!

*And we know that all things work together for good . . .
to them who are the called according to his purpose.*
—Romans 8:28, KJV

For I know the thoughts that I think toward you . . . to give you an expected end.
—Jeremiah 29:11, KJV

Finally, my four siblings and I were going to be reunited! We had not had a reunion in more than thirty years. I was excited, ecstatic, and overjoyed. A few weeks before the reunion, my husband and I flew into Sangster International Airport in our beautiful hometown of Montego Bay, Jamaica. So far, everything was going according to my well-laid plan.

Then came the first disappointment. It landed with a thud! Due to unforeseen circumstances, my sister had to cancel her travel plans. Then, as if this were not enough heartbreak, the second disappointment landed like a ton of bricks on the very day of the reunion! One of my two brothers fell ill and had to be taken to the hospital. After a very long wait in the emergency room waiting area, he was admitted and transported to the ward. My other siblings alternated with me in supporting our ailing brother. We were devastated. There would be no reunion. What would have been more poignant than a reunion of siblings who had not been together for more than thirty years? Though we did not know it, God had interrupted our plans for a very good reason.

After much reflection, I turned my thoughts to Romans 8:28. We had wanted this reunion, but God knew that my brother was quite ill and needed medical attention. "God moves in a mysterious way His wonders to perform"!*

Life does not always give us beautiful, sweet-smelling roses. We must sometimes walk through the thorns and get pricked. But even when we face disappointments and feel crushed, we can remember that God's way is always the best for us. God knows the end from the beginning. Though our joyful reunion did not take place, the good news is that my dear brother's life was saved, and we are, indeed, grateful.

I look forward to that glorious heavenly family reunion when, by God's grace, we will be together at last. To God be the glory!

Winsome Joy Grant

---

* William Cowper, "God Moves in a Mysterious Way," 1773, public domain.

February 23

God's Goodness Knows No Limits

O taste and see that the LORD is good: blessed is the man that trusteth in him.
—Psalm 34:8, KJV

My family and I were fulfilling our missionary stint in London, England. Previously, we had traveled to the United States of America, where my husband, Horace, had pursued further theological studies. Now we were farther away from Jamaica, our island home, than ever before. Since we were stationed in London, my sister Yvonne, who was teaching mathematics back home in one of the high schools, seized the opportunity to submit her application for the teacher-exchange program to teach in London for a year. London covers a vast area of square miles and is further divided into sections designated by the four cardinal points.

My sister and my family eagerly awaited the response to her application. Late one afternoon the telephone rang, and I answered it. It was a long-distance call from my sister in Jamaica. We listened with bated breath as she told us that she had received a reply from the teacher-exchange program. "You would never believe it, but listen to this," she exclaimed as she began to read her response letter to us. "Your application is accepted, and you are assigned to teach at Willesden High School in London." Shrieks of rapturous delight emanated from our lips. Why the outburst? Willesden High School was only a stone's throw away from the Willesden Seventh-day Adventist Church, which was one of the churches that came under the precincts of my husband's pastorate.

We were tireless in our praises as we recounted how God had orchestrated everything in His great wisdom. Within a few weeks, Yvonne arrived in London and lived with us during her stay there. She had a wonderful experience with the staff and students at Willesden High School and enjoyed the fellowship of the people in our churches. And to top it all, she was able to visit a few European countries. Yvonne was indeed blessed by her London teaching experience, and we also were truly blessed.

What a great and marvelous God we serve! He is interested in every detail of our lives and works for our benefit so that we can give Him all the praise and the glory He rightly deserves.

Bridget S. Taffe

February 24

I Have Seen God's Guidance

And Jesus answered and said to them, "Truly I say to you, if you have faith and do not doubt, you will not only do what was done to the fig tree, but even if you say to this mountain, 'Be taken up and cast into the sea,' it will happen. And whatever you ask in prayer, believing, you will receive it all."
—Matthew 21:21, 22, NASB

When I was growing up, my mother took my siblings and me to the Catholic Church. One day my grandmother, who was a Seventh-day Adventist, asked my mom if I could accompany her to church. I honestly believe the Spirit of the Lord told my mom to consent. I soon attended church every Sabbath, and I really enjoyed it! I joined Pathfinders and, later, Adventist Youth.

Eventually, my grandmother asked my mom if I could be baptized, and she agreed. I was baptized at the age of seven and have been a part of the church ever since. However, my journey was not always smooth. You see, I struggled to understand the doctrines. I vividly remember praying silently to the Lord and telling Him about my doubts about the Sabbath, diet, and some of the other beliefs of Adventism.

My heavenly Father, who knows all things, orchestrated sermon after sermon over the years specifically for me. I felt like He was saying, "My child, I know you do not understand, but be encouraged; this message is prepared specifically for you." And so it was; every doubt that I had was answered through messages from the pulpit. Throughout the years, as I have seen God's guidance in my life, I have also developed a habit of communicating with my heavenly Father. Through this channel, He has guided me, and yes, I have seen His mighty hand at work in my life, especially in helping me to remain in good faith.

I look forward to the beautiful home He has prepared for me. I long to see Him, and I look forward to saying the words of the apostle Paul: "I have fought the good fight, I have finished the course, I have kept the faith" (2 Timothy 4:7, NASB).

What about you? Do you have any doubts today? What are your struggles? Is there something keeping you from saying yes to Jesus? I pray you will choose to give up all your doubts and say, "Yes, my Lord, enter into my heart."

Marleni Brant-Pomare

February 25

Just Happenstance?

"Before I formed you in the womb I knew you,
before you were born I set you apart." . . .
"Alas, Sovereign LORD," I said, "I do not know how to speak; I am too young."
—Jeremiah 1:5, 6, NIV

I grew up in the village of Kanye in Botswana. As a little girl, I was hindered from discovering my talents because of shyness. Though I was a good student at school, I was too quiet to be recognized as anyone of note by my peers. It was only in my last two years of middle school that I realized I was a good athlete. In high school, I excelled in track and field competitions. Bit by bit, I discovered myself and grew from strength to strength as I served God and the people around me.

When I moved from Kanye to take up residence in the small mining town of Jwaneng, I thought I was only doing so to join my husband, who lived and worked there. I just happened to bring my niece, who was a Seventh-day Adventist, to come and stay with us in Jwaneng. A visiting pastor, Dr. Riley, came and preached in Jwaneng, and my niece invited me to go with her to listen to the sermons. Consequently, I ended up being baptized into the Seventh-day Adventist Church. Were those all just happenstances? What do you think?

Now, instead of working simply to impress people, I am using my talents to serve God. We sometimes tend to tell our Creator all about ourselves and nothing else. But remember, He created us. He was the One who formed us. He knows all about us and what He can do through us. So when He says, "My daughter, I want you to go there and do this for Me," it would be impudent for us to tell God what we believe we should do instead.

We cannot tell Him anything He does not already know. Neither can we teach Him how to do His work. He reminds us that He knew us before we were formed in our mother's womb. We would do well to inquire of Him for wisdom rather than try to tell Him what to do.

So, my sister, you, too, have been gifted and blessed with unique talents. Whatever it is that you have been skeptical of doing, just try it and see what God will do for you. We each have a specific work to perform. We can do it in His strength and for His glory. Do not ever doubt it!

Bogadi Koosaletse Ndzinge

February 26

God's Perfect Timing

For he will command his angels concerning you
to guard you in all your ways.
—Psalm 91:11, NIV

This story took place more than fifty years ago, but I remember it as if it happened today. I was only eighteen, a young, inexperienced woman, and had just moved from Rio Grande do Sul to São Paulo, Brazil. One of my sisters lived near there at that time, and I moved in with her. I did not have many financial resources because I was a student, and my brother-in-law used to pick me up on his bicycle after school each night.

As soon as I got a part-time job, I saved enough money to study dactylography, which is the scientific study of fingerprinting. I was also able to pay the bus fare to and from school.

One night I left school at about ten-thirty and walked to the bus stop. It was very cold and dark. I looked at both sides of the street and saw absolutely nobody. The street was deserted, and I began to feel afraid. I quietly prayed and asked God to take care of me and keep me safe until I reached home. It was very cold, and I tried to cover my face against the winter wind with my coat collar.

Suddenly, a tall young man approached me and said he would like to talk with me. I felt something was off, and I told him I did not want to talk. He insisted and got closer. At this time, I felt his intentions were not good, and my heart was beating really fast. There was nobody there to help me, and even if I screamed, no one would hear.

But then, from nowhere, two police officers showed up and came toward me. They asked me if the man was bothering me. I said, "Yes!" But he sarcastically told the officers, "Do you think I do not know how to talk to a lady?"

The officers asked him to show his ID, and he began to look for it, searching in all his pockets. He could not seem to find it. In the middle of this confusion, the bus arrived, and I jumped inside as fast as I could. My heart was still beating hard, but I felt so relieved and grateful. God had sent not one but two angels to save me that night. His timing was perfect!

Whenever you are afraid, remember that God is only a prayer away.

Eva Cleonice Kopitar

February 27

Do I Have a Guardian Angel, Lord?

*Because you have made the L*ORD *your dwelling place—*
the Most High, who is my refuge—
no evil shall be allowed to befall you. . . .

For he will command his angels concerning you
to guard you in all your ways.
—Psalm 91:9–11, ESV

It was about two o'clock in the morning, and I was on my way to Houston, Texas, in the United States of America, to spend Thanksgiving with my family. I knew I was getting low on fuel, yet I passed by a filling station off Interstate 35, telling myself, *I'll stop at the next one.* Approximately three miles later, I came over a hill to find a traffic jam that stretched out as far as I could see.

My heart sank. Why had I not stopped for fuel when I had the chance? As the traffic inched along, my anxiety began to increase. Then, up ahead, I saw a car stopped beside the road. An older gentleman stood helplessly beside it. As I reached his car, it appeared there was a woman in the car with him, so I said a prayer and pulled over. It felt like we both needed help!

They said they had been broken down since nine o'clock that night, and no one had stopped to help. This was in the days before the convenience of cell phones, but I had a bag phone in my trunk that I could make an emergency call from. As I opened my trunk, a voice behind me said, "Are you the one who called for help?" Surprised, I turned around to see a tow truck. The driver of the truck said he would help the older gentleman and that I needed to take the next exit. At that point, it was no more than a hundred yards ahead. He said I would be able to turn around and go back to the station for fuel.

If I had ever doubted the existence of guardian angels before, I never did after that night! After that experience, I know there are angels among us. We had not called for help, and I am still not sure that exit existed prior to God's intervention. But God was watching, and He sent an angel to help me and the older couple who had been broken down beside the road for hours.

The gas station attendant told me to take the county road that ran along the interstate so that I would not have to get back into that traffic jam. And just like that, my gas tank was full, and the traffic problem was solved!

Thank You, Jesus, for sending an angel in our time of need.

Jo Shuck

February 28

Teach Me Silence

A fool's mouth is his destruction, and his lips are the snare of his soul. . . .
Death and life are in the power of the tongue.
—Proverbs 18:7, 21, KJV

Perhaps, for many, the sound of silence drives the mouth to speak. How many times do we wish we could hit rewind and take back the words spoken in haste before thinking through a situation? How often have resentment, pain, and distrust caused us to speak in retaliation? It only makes things worse. Most of us, if we are truthful, have made that mistake more than once. Or perhaps we have said something about someone else, true or not, that we wish we could take back. How we would love a do-over. Sad to say, do-overs are not always possible and are not guaranteed. However, we do not have to beat ourselves up because our blessing is found in the fact that we serve a God of second chances.

Each day God's blessings are refreshed and renewed. This does not mean we do not need to confess our sins to the Lord and apologize to the ones we have wounded. But God is so merciful, so full of grace, and so loving and kind. He bids us draw near to Him and whispers in our ear, "My dear daughter, 'This is the way, walk ye in it' [Isaiah 30:21, KJV]." He bids us come into His presence and seek His face. His grace is extended with nail-scarred hands to each of us. All we need to do is accept His gift of love.

Today, when you hear His voice, surrender all to Him and follow His will. He will direct your path. We can ask Him to teach us how to listen and how to think before we speak. He will take away the harsh tones and angry affects that mar our countenance. He will take our heart of stone, give us a heart of flesh, and re-create in us His likeness and loveliness.

I know He can do this for you because He is transforming my life. I am learning to listen more, speak less, and weigh my responses before I speak. If you feel discouraged, remember this counsel and be encouraged: if you fail "and are betrayed into sin, do not feel then you cannot pray . . . but seek the Lord more earnestly."* May the God of second chances refresh your life today!

Edna Andrews-Rose

---

* Ellen G. White, *Our High Calling* (Washington, DC: Review and Herald®, 1961), 49.

March 1

Easy?

Live at peace with everyone.
—Romans 12:18, NIV

There is a curious text buried in Matthew 10. Jesus is speaking to His disciples: "Think not that I am come to send peace on earth: I came not to send peace, but a sword. For I am come to set a man at variance against his father, and the daughter against her mother, and the daughter in law against her mother in law. And a man's foes shall be they of his own household" (Matthew 10:34–36, KJV). These are the words of the Prince of Peace!

In a perfect world, we would be at peace with everyone because we would all be living in love. But we do not live in a perfect world. Our words and actions are not always loving. Neither are the words and actions of anyone else, including our families. When it comes to family issues, we tend to hide the details in a bubble of normalcy. That is not necessarily a bad thing, but it can make us forget that others may have similar struggles. We clash, and feelings get hurt. Thankfully, I am responsible only for my actions. "If it is possible, as far as it depends on you, live at peace with everyone" (Romans 12:18, NIV). "Everyone" includes the rude cashier, the aggressive driver, the customer service rep, and our families. Remember, we will not be called to account for their behavior. We will only answer for our own.

So how would Jesus want us to behave toward others? Luke records Jesus' words:

> "If you love only those who love you, why should you get credit for that? Even sinners love those who love them! And if you do good only to those who do good to you, why should you get credit? Even sinners do that much! And if you lend money only to those who can repay you, why should you get credit? Even sinners will lend to other sinners for a full return.
>
> "Love your enemies! Do good to them. Lend to them without expecting to be repaid. Then your reward from heaven will be very great, and you will truly be acting as children of the Most High, for he is kind to those who are unthankful and wicked. You must be compassionate, just as your Father is compassionate" (Luke 6:32–36, NLT).

This is not easy, but we are not called to do what is easy. We are called to be like Jesus. In His strength, we can be kind and compassionate, both inside and outside of our homes.

Ann Trout

March 2

From Out of the Heart

"A good man brings good things out of the good stored up in his heart, and an evil man brings evil things out of the evil stored up in his heart. For the mouth speaks what the heart is full of."
—Luke 6:45, NIV

When she walked into the room, all eyes drifted in her direction. She looked amazing. Her outfit was beautifully coordinated. Her hair was perfectly coiffed. She had a lovely figure, and she knew how to present herself very well. Yes, her outward appearance was impressive.

But shortly after the meeting began, someone stepped on her proverbial toes. When she opened her mouth and responded to the apparent injustice, the expressions of admiration suddenly turned to shock. As I listened to the exchange, I was filled with great disappointment. The verbal exchange soon stopped, but a sense of sadness lingered as we left the meeting. I allowed some time to pass before addressing the situation with both parties and made some suggestions as to how the situation could have been handled differently. They both eventually agreed, but the well-dressed lady did so with some reluctance. She felt she had been wronged and felt justified in having defended herself.

As I remembered the verbal exchange several days later, it reminded me of the beautiful red-and-yellow apple sitting on my fruit tray. It looked perfect, as if it had just been picked from the tree. I was hungry, so with great anticipation, I washed it and split it down the middle with a knife. To my horror, it was black inside except for a thin layer of white flesh closer to the skin. I was so disappointed. I had been fooled by its external beauty.

Jesus' words of admonition came to mind: "The mouth speaks what the heart is full of" (Luke 6:45, NIV). It is not an easy thing to control our tongues. We tend to respond instinctively with harsh words when we feel attacked. Then comes the regret. Even though we apologize, scars are left on our hearts and on the hearts of others.

To guard my words, I have made David's words my mantra: "I said, 'I will guard my ways, lest I sin with my tongue; I will restrain my mouth with a muzzle' " (Psalm 39:1, NKJV). "Create in me a clean heart, O God, and renew a steadfast spirit within me" (Psalm 51:10, NKJV). If my heart is clean, my words will be good and kind.

Sonia Kennedy-Brown

March 3

More Than Enough Food in My Pantry

"Give, and you will receive. Your gift will return to you in full—pressed down, shaken together to make room for more, running over, and poured into your lap. The amount you give will determine the amount you get back."
—Luke 6:38, NLT

There were precious, hungry mouths to be filled and two very concerned, confused parents who had no idea where their next meal would come from. My husband and I quietly discussed the situation before us. The immediate need was to provide food. We could assist the family in solving other issues later that day or at some other time. For now, we would share from our own pantry to help this family.

After we reached home, my husband went in search of a large enough box as I headed to the pantry. I prayerfully surveyed the items in front of me. *Lord, please show me what I need to put in this box.* As I picked out a variety of cans, packets, and boxes of food, I thought about how each item could contribute to a meal.

We did not have ready cash to give this family, but there certainly was enough food for both our families. In fact, we had much more than we needed. My husband brought a second box, and we filled that too. On our way back to the family, we thought about them. If we had not visited their home, we would have had no idea of their dire need. Later that evening, after dropping off the boxes of food, I went back to our pantry. We still had enough food. Even after sharing with the other family, there was still enough to share again.

Whenever we give, God has a way of supplying all that we need. The more we give, the more we are given in return. Perhaps today is a good time to assess the pantries in our lives. How about our faith pantry? Our trust pantry? How about our gratitude pantry? Our help pantry? What about our love pantry? Let us check our pantries. We will find more than enough to share something with someone today. Let us practice giving love, kindness, and a helping hand. God has given us so much—and we have more than enough!

God has promised to supply in abundance when we give to others. We can trust Him with our pantries.

Gloria Barnes-Gregory

March 4

Hospitality

Offer hospitality to one another without grumbling.
—1 Peter 4:9, NIV

The ringing telephone matched the nighttime howling Midwestern wind. My pastor husband, just home from a board meeting, went to answer it.

"I'm sorry we can't give you money for food, but we'd be glad to see that you receive something to eat. Tell me about your family and where you are located."

After several minutes, I heard my husband say, "Let me give you directions to our house. We will feed you and put you up for the night. In the morning, we will see how we can help you."

The father expressed his gratitude. The family would be right over.

I checked the clock; it read 10:15 p.m. I groaned slightly and slid out of bed. The text "And let us not be weary in well doing" (Galatians 6:9, KJV) followed me all the way to the kitchen.

While my husband switched on the porch light and checked the extra bedroom for stray toys, I prayed silently for guidance in fixing a meal the family would like. *Everyone likes potatoes*, I thought, so I quickly put some on the stove and found some applesauce for the baby.

By 10:50 p.m., the table was set, and a warm meal was waiting on the stove. At 11:00, we surmised that the family had made a wrong turn but should arrive any minute, but 11:30 came and went. Fifteen minutes later, my husband turned off the porch light and announced bedtime. Anger, frustration, and exhaustion knotted my stomach. I was hurt. A see-whether-I-care attitude occasionally tempts me, but the Lord is good and gently reminds me, "We must gather warmth from the coldness of others."* Our gift had been rejected, but that must not stop us from continuing to give.

"The Bible lays much stress upon the practice of hospitality. Not only does it enjoin hospitality as a duty, but it presents many beautiful pictures of the exercise of this grace and the blessing which it brings."† Hospitality is a tool to encourage people and point them heavenward.

Marybeth Gessele

---

* Ellen G. White, *Testimonies for the Church*, vol. 5 (Mountain View, CA: Pacific Press®, 1948), 136.
† Ellen G. White, *Testimonies for the Church*, vol. 6 (Mountain View, CA: Pacific Press®, 1948), 341.

March 5

Little Things

So then, be careful how you walk, not as unwise people but as wise, making the most of your time, because the days are evil.
—Ephesians 5:15, 16, NASB

As I sat down to begin my morning devotions, I realized I was thirsty, so I went to the kitchen to get something to drink. I walked through the kitchen door and saw the dishes I had washed the previous night still in the drainboard. I packed them away.

When I finished, I noticed the laundry basket in front of the dryer. It reminded me there was still a load of clothes in the dryer and one in the washer. I placed the dry clothes into the basket and moved the ones in the washer to the dryer. Then I wondered why I had originally come into the kitchen.

When I remembered, I looked at the clock and realized I had used a big chunk of my devotional time doing little things. I shook my head as I retrieved a bottle of water from the fridge and headed back to my devotional area. I felt annoyed at how easily distracted I had been by what I call "little things"—things that are not urgent and can be taken care of at a later time.

The dishes had been in the drainboard all night. They could have stayed there until I had finished my devotions—or even later. The same could be said for the clothes in the dryer and the washer.

I was thankful I did not have to go to work that day so I could complete all my devotional activities. However, if it had been a workday, I would have had to decide what to leave undone: the devotional thought, Bible reading, Sabbath School lesson? What about my prayer time before and after my devotions? Would I skip my reflection time? All of these are vital in my personal devotion time.

As I sat down to begin my devotions that morning, I asked God to forgive me for being distracted. I thanked Him for reminding me how easy it is to get caught up by the "little things" and asked Him to help me not be distracted from my time with Him by them.

The moments we spend with God are precious. They equip us for our day, give us strength for our Christian journey, and prepare us for the kingdom. Watch out for those "little things"!

Barbara J. Walker

March 6

More Light

Now we see things imperfectly, like puzzling reflections in a mirror, but then we will see everything with perfect clarity.
—1 Corinthians 13:12, NLT

"Now, keep your eye on the spot in the center. Do not let it follow the flashing lights," instructed the surgeon. *Focus, concentrate, find a spot, and hold it there,* I told myself. A few seconds later, I heard him say, "Excellent, all done!" For anyone who has had cataract surgery, this may sound familiar.

I listened closely to the doctor's specific instructions: "Be sure to wear your eye patch while sleeping or taking a nap for the next few days. Follow the printed schedule for eye drops," and several more details. I left the office wearing dark sunglasses, determined to follow all the instructions. Those cataracts had certainly dimmed my vision, but now the second eye had been successfully finished.

As I prepared for bed that evening, my eyes fell upon the information sheet attached to all my prescriptions. You know the one, with all the tiny print? I glanced at it and could not believe my eyes—I could read it with ease! I was so excited, I almost felt like crying. The story of the blind man's joy after Jesus had healed him flashed through my mind. And then a verse in 1 Corinthians kept repeating itself:

> "No eye has seen, no ear has heard,
>   and no mind has imagined
> what God has prepared
>   for those who love him" (1 Corinthians 2:9, NLT).

My improved eyesight is nothing compared to what God wants for all of us. As I thought about the specific instructions from my doctor, I could see a spiritual comparison that was good for all of us. "Concentrate! Don't follow the flashing lights! Keep focused!" There is much in life to distract us from keeping our eyes on Jesus. Flashing lights come in all shapes, sizes, and colors, but God has given us a map, the Bible, to help us navigate this often crazy world. Each day we get a clean slate to begin again with Jesus. Our eyes cannot imagine what has been so wonderfully planned for us. Even with my much-improved eyesight, I want more light—I want the spiritual light that draws me closer to knowing God's plan and desires for me. Won't you join me on this daily journey?

Rita Kay Stevens

March 7

The Blessing of Sight

*"I will lead the blind by ways they have not known,
along unfamiliar paths I will guide them;
I will turn the darkness into light before them
and make the rough places smooth.
These are the things I will do;
I will not forsake them."*
—Isaiah 42:16, NIV

*Blessed are those whose help is the God of Jacob,
whose hope is in the Lord their God.*
—Psalm 146:5, NIV

He stood there on the median, with his white cane raised, indicating his desire to cross the busy motorway. We could not stop without causing an accident, so I prayed that God would cause another vehicle to see him in time to stop and allow him to cross. Or perhaps a passerby would come along and guide him to the other side of the busy street. Thoughts of the inability to see lingered with me, and I tried to imagine the difficulties sightless people experience daily. I could only conclude that they must cope with the help of God to navigate each day successfully.

The ways of the omniscient, omnipresent, and omnipotent God are past finding out. He takes care of all His children in each of their different circumstances. I thank God for enhancing the other senses of the physically blind, making a way to help them function effectively and live productively. I feel blessed to be able to see, and I give thanks and praise to God.

As I do, however, I also think of how desperate it would be to have physical sight but be spiritually blind. To have spiritual sight is to be in Christ Jesus, the One who knew us from our mother's womb. He is the One who guides and watches over us always. We lack nothing when we are in Christ because He makes us whole and supplies all our needs.

I am therefore encouraged today, knowing that I have spiritual eyesight because I am in Christ Jesus. He is the One who "gives sight to the blind, the Lord lifts up those who are bowed down, the Lord loves the righteous" (Psalm 146:8, NIV).

I praise God for lifting up those who are bowed down. I am grateful that out of the gloom and darkness, the eyes of the blind will one day be opened to behold Christ Jesus. On that day, we will all rejoice—all those "whose hope is in the Lord their God" (verse 5, NIV).

Elizabeth Ida Cain

March 8

Finding the Light

Do not gloat over me, my enemy!
Though I have fallen, I will rise.
Though I sit in darkness,
the Lord *will be my light.*
—Micah 7:8, NIV

Whenever I think about the Israelites and their exodus from Egypt, the guiding pillar of cloud by day and fire by night always sticks out to me the most. It was always there and shone through the darkest night, guiding and showing them the way to go. I have always wanted that experience for myself. How I wish there was a literal cloud I could see. Living in the light is not always easy. Sometimes, when we look at others, it may seem that the light just follows them—God's presence, success, and blessing. But God's light is always available to everyone, ready to guide us, even when we feel the farthest away.

I remember one summer I felt exactly like that—far away from God and a failure in my own life. I just knew something had to change. I remember standing on a balcony and wishing I did not have to face life anymore. I did not have the courage to die, but neither did I have the courage to live in the right way.

Later that day, I walked slowly outside when some friends of the family I had not seen in a while walked up. They began enthusiastically telling me what a blessing I was to others and how valuable I was to God. I hoped they had not noticed that the light had died out of my eyes and that I felt far from being a blessing to anyone. I felt convicted. Once again I knew I had to choose to step back into the light and share it with others. I had a purpose and a reason to live.

Though I did not realize it that night, I have seen how, over and over again, I am reminded that the deepest, dark holes we fall into are never too deep for that light to reach us. God's mercy is unchanging, and His light always shines deeper into our hearts, souls, and lives than we can imagine. God is only waiting for us to accept His grace and peace in our lives. In those circumstances, when we feel that everyone is against us and life is not worth living, God is ready to give us a reason to live. He is ready to give us the power to help us choose the light each new day and through each trial we face.

In a world growing increasingly darker, let us join hands and choose to live in the light.

Anne Crosby

March 9

Will We Be Ready?

For the Lord himself shall descend from heaven with a shout, with the voice of the archangel, and with the trump of God: and the dead in Christ shall rise first.
—1 Thessalonians 4:16, KJV

This morning, while watering my garden, I noticed the dew on the roses. The beautiful pink blooms glistened and sparkled in the early morning sunlight. They reminded me of the lyrics, "I come to the garden alone, while the dew is still on the roses."*

Then I remembered this song was my great-grandmother's favorite song. She had a rose garden, a vegetable garden, a berry patch, carob trees, a pomegranate tree, a fig tree, and rows and rows of aloe vera. My great-grandmother loved to be in her garden early in the morning, tending her plants. A woman of faith, she loved God and had a special place in her house where she would kneel three times a day and pray for her children, grandchildren, the church, and her neighbors. My great-grandmother was involved with a group at her church called Willing Workers. These women worked hard and provided scholarships and gifts to young people headed to college. They also helped young mothers who needed things for their children.

I was with her in her home when she died. She had gotten up as usual and opened all the curtains to let the sunshine in. My great-grandmother had her devotions, lay on her bed, and went to sleep in Jesus. She was faithful in this life, and I know she will hear the words, "Well done, thou good and faithful servant: thou hast been faithful over a few things, I will make thee ruler over many things: enter thou into the joy of thy lord" (Matthew 25:21, KJV).

I would like to be like her and share love and not hate with those in the world around me. Our world is full of hate and violence. People are angry and want to hurt others. We see it on the news every day—hate crimes, ignorant behaviors, and violence toward women and children. We know we are living in the last days of Earth's history. Will we strive not only to make a difference but also to be a difference in the world? Will we show God's love to our families and those in our sphere of influence? Jesus is coming soon. Let us be God's hands and reach out to a hurting world.

Eva M. Starner

---

* C. Austin Miles, "In the Garden," 1912, public domain.

March 10

The Least of These

"He will reply, 'Truly I tell you, whatever you did not do for one of the least of these, you did not do for me.' "
—Matthew 25:45, NIV

We often think we need to wait for momentous circumstances before doing the good we are asked to do. Perhaps driving a van load of specialists to help in refugee camps or coordinating training for the hard-to-reach peoples of Mount Kinabalu, Malaysia. Maybe organizing a clothes-collection drive for the needy or sending survival items to those living in medical isolation.

But what about the smaller things around us that we tend to neglect? The blank faces that pass us on our daily commute? The searching eyes we are afraid to look into? The outstretched hands we are afraid to touch?

The old man who sweeps the roads around the block I live on often raises his hand in a high-five gesture. Mostly, I respond with a bright "Hello," or I raise my own high five that breezes past his upheld hand—close but never quite touching. Today was different. Something made me connect my high five to his. The connection remains etched in my mind.

As our two hands touched, it took a moment for it to sink in that my hand had actually touched his. Then his toothless grin broke into mirth, and his cackle was so loud I was caught by surprise, as were the passersby who witnessed this exchange. At first, the look of censure on one face escalated into outright disdain at me for touching dirty, unwashed hands. On the other side of the road, surprised, bemused looks greeted me. Perhaps some who are reading this right now might wonder about my seemingly rash act of touching dirt-infested hands that may have touched goodness knows what!

But the chain reaction was priceless. I treasure it still. As the old man danced a little jig, a cheer from another road sweeper filled the air, and broad smiles spread across the faces of onlookers. The austere looks melted into smiles and unspoken thoughts of *What did I just witness?* For a little while, everyone present was bathed in the joy of this one shared moment.

Whatever we do not do for the least of these, we do not do for Jesus! What does God's Word challenge us to do? How is the Disciple Maker inviting us to show His love to the least of these?

Jessy Quilindo

March 11

Look Here—*Now!*

"Before they call I will answer."
—Isaiah 65:24, NIV

Three words. Each letter stood about ten feet tall on a highway billboard as we sped along on our way to church. And in the split second I happened to look up and see the words, I knew they were meant precisely for me. It was no accident that I looked up at that moment. God had been listening to my internal ruminations about a nagging problem. A problem I had been picking the scab off whenever one began to form and bring healing to my attitude. And now it was festering. So God, who knew where the billboard was and how soon we would be passing it, directed my eyes just in time to see those punch-to-the-gut words flash by: *Let it go.*

Whoa! Someone was speaking to me. Those words were definitely being used by Someone to counsel a needy passenger in the car speeding down the road. The whooshed-by message put a screeching halt to my inner grumblings and poor-me mental gymnastics. Since that day, that one short command has served as a frequent reminder of when God gave me the gift of letting go of what was slowly but surely poisoning me from within. And God has popped those words into my mind at other times, easing me over the wailing wall of *woe is me.*

God uses whatever works to get our attention. Whether it is a still, small Voice or a huge highway sign, He tailors His attention-getting methods to our specific needs. Sometimes it is immediate, and sometimes it happens over a period of years. Our loving Father is constantly reaching out to each one of us on this planet.

In one of my favorite Bible verses, we are told that Jesus, who is the true Light, is He who "lighteth every man that cometh into the world" (John 1:9, KJV). Did you catch that astounding revelation? What a magnificent truth to absorb: every person who has ever been born on this planet, in some way that we do not exactly comprehend, has been and continues to be reached, or lit, literally by Jesus Christ, the Son of God.

So, if you feel alone or forgotten, depressed or unworthy, lift up your eyes and remember that the God who is love (1 John 4:8, KJV) is the same God who has your name graven on the palms of His hands (Isaiah 49:16, KJV). Whatever is holding you back, *let it go!*

Christine B. Nelson

March 12

Solitude

*And, behold, the L*ORD *passed by, and a great and strong wind rent the mountains, . . .
but the L*ORD *was not in the wind: and after the wind an earthquake;
but the L*ORD *was not in the earthquake: and after the earthquake a fire;
but the L*ORD *was not in the fire: and after the fire a still small voice. And it was so,
when Elijah heard it, that he wrapped his face in his mantle, and went out,
and stood in the entering in of the cave. And, behold, there came a voice unto him.*
—1 Kings 19:11–13, KJV

I can truly appreciate how Elijah felt on that fateful day when he had to run for his life from an angry woman. He must have felt elated after he had accomplished such a feat for the cause of God. He had all the prophets of Baal slain but now his life was threatened. All alone, he felt forsaken by God and wanted to die. God saw him as he lay asleep under the juniper tree and later manifested His presence to him in a still, small Voice.

God comes to us in the silence of our thoughts. In the midst of our pain, He shows up—sometimes unexpectedly—but He is always there.

It is in solitude where I find peace. It is in silence that I can steal away to Jesus and hold sweet communion with Him. When we are alone, just the two of us, I experience true peace. I am comfortable enough to unveil myself, remove my pretenses, and be who I am. I confess my faults—those hidden, darling sins known only to Him and me. I feel free to be myself, and so I tell Him about my loneliness, my isolation, and my want to just be by myself in my little world. I let Him come in, and I open up to Him. He is such a wonderful Friend. I know I can trust Him. He will never disappoint me. No matter what I do that is contrary to His will, when I confess my sins, He will always say, "I forgive." He will never stop loving me.

In solitude, we hear the voice of God more distinctly, just as Elijah did in 1 Kings 19. When we feel discouraged and depressed to the point of wanting to die, when we feel all alone, God will send His angel to encourage and strengthen us, and He did with Elijah. Oh, how He renews us, picks us up, and sets us firmly on our feet!

May the Lord help us, dear sisters, to stop, wait, and listen for His voice as He comes to rescue and restore us.

Kollis Salmon-Fairweather

March 13

Move Now!

*For everything there is a season,
a time for every activity under heaven.*
—Ecclesiastes 3:1, NLT

"Move now!" I woke up to these words one Sunday morning a few years ago. Certain I must have misunderstood, I closed my eyes and tried to block out the two-word command. You see, we had just packed up my parents' home after their death, and the last thing I wanted to do was pack up another house—our house.

There it came again, "Move now!" This time I was certain it was the Holy Spirit speaking to my heart, instructing my husband and me. I knew we needed to take action. Two years prior, my husband, Vondell, had been diagnosed with multiple sclerosis, and at some point, living in our two-story home would pose a problem. Besides, we needed to downsize. The children were gone, and it was just us. We had agreed a one-level home in a senior community would be ideal.

After reading my devotions and having a long talk with the Father, I shared with Vondell what had been revealed to me. Immediately, we searched my tablet for homes in our target community and discovered a lovely house listed for sale. This was unusual, as residents rarely left that coveted neighborhood. The following day our real estate agent arranged for us to view the home. "Perfect," we agreed. The real estate agent submitted a bid, and we waited. A week went by without a word. We prayed, sure that this was the house God had chosen. The next week we received word our bid was not accepted.

Disappointed, I prayed, "Father, I thought You said, 'Move now!'" The response came back, "I did, but that is not the house I have in mind for you." So we searched other listings and viewed several senior communities with houses we assumed would fit our needs. Again, we came up empty. The price was beyond our budget, the house needed more work than we were prepared to do, or the community was too distant from family.

Again, the Holy Spirit nudged me back to our target community. Another house had become available! Unlike the first house, this house was in pristine condition, with new hardwood floors, an updated kitchen, fresh paint, and a large patio. We prayed, and this time He said, "Yes!" For everything there is a season. Allowing God to lead is the sure way forward.

Yvonne Curry Smallwood

March 14

No Better Time

Always be prepared to give an answer to everyone who asks you to give the reason for the hope that you have.
—1 Peter 3:15, NIV

I was recently looking for a job after relocating to a new country. After submitting many applications, one company responded positively. An interview was arranged for the next day at 8:00 A.M., but I would need to travel at least an hour to get to the interview on time. I made sure to set the alarm to wake me up by 6:00 A.M. The alarm rang at the set time, but my body did not respond. As the alarm kept switching to snooze, I thought I still had time to sleep a little more. When I finally roused, it was 7:30 A.M., far too late to make it in time for the interview. In short, I lost the opportunity I had longed for so badly. I learned a vital lesson that morning: the best time to wake up to an alarm is just after it has sounded. A minute later may be too late.

Acts 16 tells of the ordeal Paul and Silas went through on their missionary journey to Macedonia. Paul wished to go to Asia, but the Holy Spirit forbade them. In a night vision, Paul saw a man from Macedonia fervently requesting they come over to Macedonia. Paul could not miss God's voice directing them to where they were needed most. He immediately set sail with Silas, stopping first in Philippi, where they baptized Lydia and her household. They faced many trials and were ultimately stripped, beaten, and put in stocks in the most secure part of the prison.

Why did the Holy Spirit lead Paul and Silas into a situation where He knew they would face such an ordeal? God knew He could trust them. In their anguish, they "prayed, and sang praises unto God" (Acts 16:25, KJV). What faith! God responded with an earthquake that shook the foundation of the prison, flinging open all the doors. Before the night was over, the jailer and his household became believers.

Paul and Silas knew there was no better time to pray and sing praise to Him who has saved us than when all the alarm bells of a broken world are tolling loudest. Jesus is coming soon—there is no better time for us to share our faith. Jesus encourages us, "Now when these things begin to happen, look up and lift up your heads, because your redemption draws near" (Luke 21:28, NKJV). Can you hear the alarm bells ringing?

Mary Opoku-Gyamfi

March 15

Wrinkles Away

*And to present her to himself as a radiant church, without stain
or wrinkle or any other blemish, but holy and blameless.*
—Ephesians 5:27, NIV

Ironing on a hot summer's day? Yes! There I was, with a load of clean shirts before me, waiting to be ironed. My husband and sons would need their shirts to be ready to wear to church early the next morning. So I tackled the task. One by one, I ironed the shirts, using steam as necessary to smooth away even the tiniest wrinkle. Once they had been ironed, I hung them neatly on a rack. While I ironed, working with the heat and steam, I knew my family was worth it!

As I reached for each shirt, arranging it carefully on the ironing board, I thought about our spiritual garments. They were washed in the blood of the Lamb when we invited Jesus into our hearts and accepted His sacrifice in atonement for our transgressions. But that is only the beginning. To be ready for His second coming, our garments must be ironed—our characters transformed. With the iron of the Holy Spirit, through the heat and steam of trials, God smooths away every wrinkle in our character. He is diligently, tenderly preparing us for His kingdom. Every time heat is applied, a wrinkle is smoothed away. Each trial and heartache we endure reveals how important we are to our heavenly Father.

He calls us to "be perfect, therefore, as your heavenly Father is perfect" (Matthew 5:48, NIV). Jesus holds the iron in His hand. He feels the heat, too, so you and I can be ready, pure and faultless, without a wrinkle or any other imperfection!

Paul invites us to "give thanks in all circumstances; for this is God's will for you in Christ Jesus" (1 Thessalonians 5:18, NIV). When we feel the heat of trials and tribulation, instead of complaining, why not praise God? Do we trust Him? If we do, we will cry out, "Yes, Lord! Thank You! Please smooth away all my wrinkles." One day soon we will thank Him face-to-face for the time He invested in preparing our heavenly garments.

Lord, thank You for Your Holy Spirit, who prepares my character for Your kingdom. Help me to endure the heat while You gently smooth all my wrinkles away! In Jesus' name, amen.

Rhodi Alers de López

March 16

God's Plans Bring Success

"He responded, 'The Lord, in whose presence I have lived, will send his angel with you and will make your mission successful.'"
—Genesis 24:40, NLT

It had been a grueling three months of study, assignments, quizzes, and exams leading to the final certification exam, for which a 70 percent grade was required to pass. I had lost two days of study due to an office emergency and another day driving to a family funeral. I also missed one of the two-day in-person reviews while attending the funeral. It did not look good for my grades. Despite all of this, the Lord delivered a stunning 86 percent grade on the exam! God answered our prayers.

Now I was headed home. *Nothing can go wrong*, I thought as I praised God for the victorious certification achievement. I arrived early at the airport and returned the rental car, but in my rush, I boarded the wrong shuttle. *No problem*, I thought. *I will remain on the shuttle until we reach the American Airlines terminal, get my preordered wheelchair, and proceed to my gate.* However, I discovered everyone had to exit the shuttle at the Delta terminal. There I stood, with three pieces of luggage and a carry-on bag, needing a wheelchair due to my upcoming knee surgery. I struggled to get inside the terminal and asked God to help. A gentleman in an airport uniform offered to assist me. He secured a wheelchair and kindly said, "I can help you with that."

He loaded my luggage onto the wheelchair, and we headed toward the American Airlines terminal. As we chatted away, I forgot to check my luggage in. Arriving at the gate, my "angel" unloaded my luggage. Then another "angel" informed me my flight was at another gate; the gate I was at was for an earlier flight. When I requested permission to board this earlier flight, I was asked, "Do you have any luggage checked in?" Praise God! The mistake of not checking in my luggage earlier turned into a blessing. I was now eligible for the earlier flight.

Circumstances, mistakes, and oversights often appear to obliterate our plans, but they may place us directly within God's plan. His direction brings great peace and joy! Even when we experience severe turbulence, as occurred on the flight, we can rest in perfect peace, secure in His hands, because He knows His plans for us. Isn't He amazing?

Miriam Battles

March 17

Enjoy the Flight

*Some trust in chariots and some in horses,
but we trust in the name of the L*ORD *our God.*
—Psalm 20:7, NIV

I was again on an airplane, ready for a flight. As we taxied to the end of the runway, the pilot announced we were about ready to take off. "Make sure everything is put away and tighten your seat belts." I started to think, *I have no idea who this man is. I have never seen him, I do not know his name, I do not know where he came from, his training, or anything about him. Yet I am trusting my life to him. He may fly me over oceans, mountains, and deserts, and I am trusting him.* As the flight began to take off, he made a few more announcements and then said, "So just sit back, relax, and enjoy the flight." It turned out to be quite a bumpy ride. I had to trust not only the pilot but the structure of the plane itself, but obviously, I arrived at my destination.

One time on a transpacific flight, a young woman sat next to me. I found out that she was not a Christian. We hit a patch of seriously turbulent air, and after we hit a particularly hard jolt, she exclaimed, "Oh God!" I turned to her and said, "Yes, that is who you should be talking to. That is who I trust." In Psalm 56:3, we read, "When I am afraid, I put my trust in you" (NIV).

Every day we place our trust in so many people and things: elevators, medical personnel and the medications they prescribe, church leaders, family, fire alarms—the list goes on and on!

Who and what do I trust? I wonder, *Can I apply that to my Christian experience?*

The hard part comes when we have to decide between one or more options. When I get on an airplane, I cannot choose the pilot. But when I decide what to buy or study, which career or spouse to choose, the decision-making gets harder. That is when we have to pray, seek God's Word, and ask for advice from those we trust and who follow the Lord. Then we can "trust in the LORD" with all our hearts, and "not depend" on our "own understanding. Seek his will in all" we do, "and he will show" us "which path to take" (Proverbs 3:5, 6, NLT).

Otherwise, we are likely to get in trouble. As Job said, some things we trust in are as fragile as a spider's web (Job 8:14, NIV).

Put your trust in the only One who can always be trusted, then sit back and enjoy the ride.

Ardis Dick Stenbakken

March 18

The Blessing of Missed Connections

*If you make the L*ORD *your refuge,
if you make the Most High your shelter,
no evil will conquer you;
no plague will come near your home.*
—Psalm 91:9, 10, NLT

Anthony, my youngest son, was in the army and was stationed at Mainz, Germany. After he shipped out, he celebrated his twentieth and twenty-first birthdays by himself. I was adamant that he would not spend another birthday without seeing me. I did not have money for the trip, and I had never been to Europe, but I found work caring for a woman in my neighborhood and put two hundred dollars each month into savings. I donated plasma through plasmapheresis twice a week and added fifteen dollars each time to my savings. I skipped paying my mortgage for one month and added five hundred dollars into my account. I prepaid the travel agent and was on my way!

My son had taken leave and met me at the airport in Frankfurt, Germany, and we began our trip. Together, we toured twelve countries, including Belgium, Liechtenstein, Luxembourg, Austria, Italy, France, Switzerland, and England. What a wonderful experience we shared!

We said goodbye at the Frankfurt Airport as I waited in line to board my plane home. The plane remained on the tarmac for four hours. No one could get off the plane. The flight attendant told us the airline would hold our connecting flight in London. Finally, we learned someone had checked in luggage but had not boarded the plane. We watched workers remove our bags and place them on the tarmac. Each one was checked against the passenger list and then returned to the hold.

When we arrived at Heathrow Airport in London, England, our connections had departed. Every one of us had to be rerouted. We were given vouchers for food to compensate us for the long wait. I was sent to New York, United States of America, and finally to Detroit, Michigan, where I had started my trip a month before. As I drove to my home in Columbus, Ohio, it was cold and dark.

What a day! Only later did I hear of the horrific deaths on Pan Am Flight 103 over Lockerbie, Scotland. I was stunned. My flight was Pan Am 103, whose flight plan was from Frankfurt, over Lockerbie to Heathrow, and on to Detroit.

My prayer session that night was longer than usual. My prayers were full of gratitude and deep introspection as I pondered the mission God intended for me.

Patricia Hook Rhyndress Bodi

March 19

Follow the Solid Word

*"The Lord your God in your midst,
The Mighty One, will save;
He will rejoice over you with gladness,
He will quiet you with His love,
He will rejoice over you with singing."*
—Zephaniah 3:17, NKJV

My dad loves to drive. When I was younger, he drove a taxi during the week, and on Saturdays, he would drive us kids to see family and friends in the evening. We looked forward to those trips and to the treats he would buy for us. Even as an adult, I counted on my dad to drive me to places that were too far to drive on my own.

Once I had to attend a job function six hours away. I called Dad, and he gladly agreed to drive me. We had a wonderful time. After we started toward home, rain began to pour. I sat next to my dad, completely confident that we would get home safely. Dad was very careful, and he had a history of being a safe and successful driver.

As Dad drove through the night and the rain pelted the car, I wondered aloud if he could still see clearly enough to drive. He responded kindly, "Don't worry, Rose. If you just watch the white line on the right as you drive, your car will keep straight. Just follow the solid white line!"

It has been a long while since Dad gave me this advice. Though I had been driving for many years, I had not paid attention to the significance of following the solid white line until that night. Now, when I drive in the dark and the way seems hard, I think of my dad, and I follow my father's counsel.

I have a Father in heaven who left me very specific guidelines as I go through life's journey. When I am afraid and unsure, He tells me not to fear because He is with me. When life is hard, He assures me that He will never leave me. My Father has a history of telling the truth and a record of keeping His promises. He is very near in good and tough times.

Our heavenly Father is Dad to us all. He loves us and reassures us that He is our God, and He is in the midst of our lives. He is the Mighty One, and He will save us. Our Father knows what is best for us. His truth will guide us throughout our lives, and it will lead us safely home. All we need to do is follow the solid Word of God!

Rose Joseph Thomas

March 20

The Broken Sword

*And take the helmet of salvation, and the sword of the Spirit,
which is the word of God.*
—Ephesians 6:17, NKJV

If you are acquainted with martial arts, you may have heard of the Japanese art of swordsmanship called *iaido*. This art is much more than simply learning how to draw a sword quickly and replace it in its scabbard. Preparation involves many years of developing both mental and physical fitness. It is about the ability to maintain a high state of awareness and how to quickly draw your sword in response to a sudden threat or attack. It may sound simple, but daily practice is the only way to achieve perfection. There would be no way to cultivate this readiness if one had a damaged or broken sword. The outcome would be disastrous.

As I thought about swords and preparation, I was reminded of the sixth chapter of Ephesians, where the armor of God is listed, and the sword is identified as the Word of God. Paul tells us that we must "take up the whole armor" in order to "be able to withstand in the evil day, and having done all, to stand" (Ephesians 6:13, NKJV). We are not fighting against normal human flesh and blood. Wrestling with spiritual enemies and rulers of darkness is no easy task. Most of the equipment listed—helmet, shield, breastplate, and shoes—protects the body from attack. However, the sword is the primary offensive weapon with which to charge against the enemy and defeat him.

I am reminded of another passage that states,

> Let the high praises of God be in their mouth,
> And a two-edged sword in their hand,
> To execute vengeance on the nations,
> And punishments upon the people (Psalm 149:6, 7, NKJV).

There are people who believe that only the Old Testament is relevant today. Then there are some Christians who believe the New Testament should be their only scriptural focus. In effect, they are going into battle with a broken sword. They are not fully equipped and will face a tragic outcome.

The two testaments are both needed if we are to be ready to do battle with a two-edged sword. Jesus is foreshadowed in every book of the Bible, and we need to study the Bible daily, as a whole, to be fully prepared for battle with the satanic enemy.

As we are confronted on every side by evil, let us be sure to study all of God's Word, praising Him for the victorious power it contains.

Karen M. Phillips

March 21

Do Not Give Up on Your Dream

I can do all things through Him who strengthens me.
—Philippians 4:13, NASB

Several years ago I decided to begin my dissertation journey and achieve my academic objectives. I started out enthusiastically and anticipated success over the next two years with God's help. I did great with the preliminary courses, but then, due to personal setbacks, I was unable to complete my doctoral program as planned. I had an ABD (all but dissertation) experience. My doctoral journey appeared doomed due to a broken relationship, becoming a single parent, and other challenges. All these difficulties negatively impacted my faith in God.

I prayed earnestly for God to intervene and lead me through the crucible and setbacks I faced. Due to human nature and the wavering of my faith, I often felt like quitting on my heartfelt goal. Then I asked God for forgiveness for doubting the plans He had ordained for me. I thanked Him for the strength He gave me daily to press on with my dissertation journey, even as it took me down winding roads of challenges and discouragement. It was difficult to keep going through a failed marriage, lack of support, negative criticism, and single parenthood. I experienced even more difficulty with the coming of COVID-19 and the loss of my parents.

I fed upon God's promises, including, "Do not be afraid or discouraged because of this vast army. For the battle is not yours, but God's" (2 Chronicles 20:15, NIV). Some years later I was favored with a second chance to complete my dissertation program through the mercies of God.

Even so, the completion of my dissertation was not without challenging issues. Through them all, I held on to my faith in God, and though sometimes I felt overwhelmed by the cares of life, my tenacity to continue was strengthened by prayer and supplication, which provided the strength I needed to continue.

I want to encourage you to build resilience and trust God in the face of adversity. When you are facing your own crucible while pressing on to reach your goals, pray for strength and claim His promise: "The Lord will fight for you; you need only to be still" (Exodus 14:14, NIV). He is faithful to His promise. I successfully reached my goal and attained my doctoral degree. What He did for me, He will do for you.

Marine E. Bryan

March 22

Hope Amid Adversity

*"Be strong and courageous. Do not be afraid or terrified because of them,
for the LORD your God goes with you; he will never leave you nor forsake you."*
—Deuteronomy 31:6, NIV

I had always hoped someone would come forward and purchase our vocational nursing school. Several people had inquired, hoping to acquire the school for free. I asked the Lord if it was His will for us to just give it up and walk away with nothing. What about all the start-up expenses, time, and intellectual effort expended in meeting the academic requirements needed for approvals? Then a sweet Voice said, "Wait patiently; there is better yet to come."

But instead, adversity came! COVID-19 dramatically affected our enrollment and instructional methodology, which resulted in financial depletion. Amazingly, we survived but struggled financially moving forward. We found being able to survive amid adversity was God's way of fulfilling His promise that He would not fail or forsake us.

As we wait and hope for the right person to buy the school, we are courageously moving the school forward, training vocational nursing students who will eventually work in the health care field and make a difference in the world. I am reminded of the following statement: "Hope is a powerful force that can drive us to overcome even the most difficult of circumstances. It is the belief that things can get better, that we can overcome adversity, and that a brighter future is possible. . . . Hope gives us the strength and resilience to keep going, to keep fighting, and to keep believing in ourselves and each other."*

Knowing God is in every detail of our lives, we placed our trust in Him, and we gained peace—for God is in control. He will fulfill His promise: " 'For I know the plans I have for you,' declares the LORD, 'plans to prosper you and not to harm you, plans to give you hope and a future' " (Jeremiah 29:11, NIV).

My prayer for each one of us is that we will keep trusting and hoping in the Lord, even amid adversity, for adversity can shape us and make us strong and courageous.

Edna Bacate Domingo

---

* Sumit Khade, "Hope: The Power to Overcome Adversity," LinkedIn, March 13, 2023, https://www.linkedin.com/pulse/hope-power-overcome-adversity-sumit-khade.

March 23

Clothed in His Righteousness

I delight greatly in the LORD. . . .
*For he has clothed me with garments of salvation
and arrayed me in a robe of his righteousness.*
—Isaiah 61:10, NIV

My oldest daughter loves to garden. Each spring her deft fingers infuse life back into our winter-worn garden. She selects each plant with care, methodically prepares the ground for planting, and deposits the plants exactly where she wants them. When she is home from her studies abroad, our garden is always filled with colorful blooms. Early one winter morning she dashed into my bedroom and showed me a picture she had taken on her phone of a lily that was still blooming in our garden. The time for blooming was over. But there, in the far corner of our decaying garden, surrounded by dead leaves, was the lily with its bright orange bloom.

For the next two weeks, the lily stood firm and resplendent despite the onslaught of the icy winter days, defiantly making a statement: in the midst of decay, there is life. Caught up in admiration over the beauty and fortitude of the lily, contemplating the source of its strength, and remembering God's promise in Matthew 6:28–30, I found a spiritual application. Consider the lily, how God cares for it and gives it strength to withstand the battering of the elements. He promises to do that and more for us.

There are times, however, when we forget God has "fearfully and wonderfully made" us in His likeness and has beautifully adorned us (Psalm 139:14, NIV). We are radiant symbols of hope that God has strategically planted just for this purpose. Like the lily, we can stand strong, elegant, and courageous even when surrounded by the harsh realities of life. When burdens threaten to crush us and giving up seems our only option, God sends messages of hope and reminds us He has not abandoned us.

Our lily eventually took its place among the dead plants, but its message is immortalized within me. In the winter of our lives, we can find hope in Christ. The One who took the time to beautifully design the flowers clothes us in His righteousness and displays us as symbols of hope for others to see. Thank You, God, for doing for us "exceedingly abundantly" more than we can ever ask or imagine (Ephesians 3:20, NKJV). We are filled with gratitude and praise.

Joan Dougherty-Mornan

March 24

Keep Blooming

"See, I am doing a new thing!
Now it springs up; do you not perceive it?
I am making a way in the wilderness
and streams in the wasteland."
—Isaiah 43:19, NIV

My orchid made me a proud plant mom. Its flowers bloomed for fifteen weeks. The friend who had given it to me instructed me not to throw it away after it finished blooming. "It will rebloom," she said. So I continued to nurture it.

How long will it take? I wondered. I was expecting the period of dormancy to be several months or even a year. However, within two months, I saw something new. *That must be a new root; it is too soon for a spike*, I thought, remembering the first time I became excited to see a new spike—only to realize it was a root.

Days later, I beamed with excitement after discovering the new growth was shooting upward. "It is a spike!" I shrieked. The timing worked out perfectly since my friend was going through a tough time.

I took a picture of the new growth and texted her yet another lesson I had learned from my orchid. "Many people throw away the orchid once it's finished flowering. Thinking that it has served its purpose and is now dead, we give up on the plant. But not so. In fact, you taught me this." My text continued, "When this plant stopped flowering, I kept watering it and continued giving it the sunlight it needed to grow. And guess what? It is growing a new spike. My dear, you may feel down. Things may seem to be at a dead end but do not give up. Keep persevering. He makes all things new."

God longs to make a positive change in our lives. In our darkest times, He assures us He will do the impossible, make "streams in a wasteland" (Isaiah 43:19, NIV)! The compassionate Gardener refreshes and sustains us. He wants to do something new within us. "Therefore, if anyone is in Christ, the new creature has come: The old has gone, the new is here!" (2 Corinthians 5:17, NIV).

One day God will make everything new. "Then He who sat on the throne said, 'Behold, I make all things new.' And He said to me, 'Write, for these words are true and faithful' " (Revelation 21:5, NKJV). We serve a God of new beginnings. His Word gives us the confidence that once we trust in Him, we can look forward to a brighter future.

Kimasha P. Williams

March 25

When Flowers Bloom at Night

Bless the Lord, O my soul,
and all that is within me,
bless his holy name!
Bless the Lord, O my soul,
and forget not all his benefits,
who forgives all your iniquity,
who heals all your diseases,
who redeems your life from the pit,
who crowns you with steadfast love and mercy,
who satisfies you with good
so that your youth is renewed like the eagle's.
—Psalm 103:1–5, ESV

I am privileged to own a few tropical *Cereus* cactus plants. Some refer to this plant as the queen of the night. It is also known as a night-blooming cereus and an orchid cactus. This unique species blooms once a year and only at night. One evening, as the shadows lengthened and the night darkened, I observed, with utter delight, the succulent petals beginning to unfold. Simultaneously, a delightful jasmine-like fragrance perfumed the night air.

As the evening progressed, the petals slowly, inch by inch, began to open. Around midnight, the waxy white petals had fully opened in all their splendor, exposing a golden-yellow interior. It was beautiful! At full bloom, the petals spread wide and radiantly, and then gradually, they began to fold and close. By the first sign of dawn, the last petal had closed, and the entire bloom hung limp. One night of glory in which it had enjoyed a few hours of magnificence before it returned to its original, unassuming pre-bloom posture.

Like the night-blooming cereus that blooms in the dark, God sometimes calls on us to bloom in the most difficult, darkest times of life. If we can learn to trust Him in the dark, we will be able to smile, give an encouraging word, and tell others of His love and care when they experience their own dark moments—and He receives all the glory.

We represent Jesus to others in our lowest, darkest valley experiences as much as in our mountaintop experiences. If, in spite of our pain, they can smell the sweet fragrance of God's love, peace, and long-suffering through us, we will have exuded the sweet-smelling perfume of an indwelling Savior. When Jesus abides within us, we can be at peace during adversity.

When we reflect on how God has led us, how He had provided for us, and how He has sustained us, we can truly say that God has been good to us, in the sunshine and the shadows, on the mountain and in the valleys, and in all seasons of our lives.

Gloria Barnes-Gregory

March 26

Up, Up in the Sky

Trust in the LORD with all your heart;
do not depend on your own understanding.
Seek his will in all you do,
and he will show you which path to take.
—Proverbs 3:5, 6, NLT

Never before in my life, and never since, have I sat on a ledge like that. My feet had no place to stand, and the closest place where I could put my feet on solid ground was almost three miles (five kilometers) away. Yes, 15,000 feet (4,572 meters) separated my feet from where they were dangling and solid ground. With that knowledge, I should have been petrified with fear.

But it was something quite different from terror that I felt. I was excited. It helped that I was not sitting alone on the ledge. In fact, the other person and I were like one at this moment. We were so tightly attached it was hard to breathe. He gently but firmly pushed my head toward his shoulder and told me to cross my arms across my chest and close my eyes.

He leaned forward, and at that moment, we both, as one, plunged into the enormous space that separated us from the solid ground below. It was perfect bliss. When I opened my eyes, the view was spectacular. I saw a lake, mountaintops, seashore, villages, trees, and clouds. After about a minute of this adrenaline-infused free fall, the tandem skydiver pulled a cord, and we were thrust upward. What a rush! So exciting!

We were no longer hurtling toward the ground, our faces flapping in the wind. Now we found ourselves peacefully, gracefully coming down with the open parachute stretched out above. If only we could slow down this moment and make it last longer!

In order to enjoy this experience, I had to make the decision to trust my tandem jumpmaster and the pilot. I felt assured that they were highly trained and very experienced. I was literally placing my life in their hands. The memory of that experience—the excitement I had felt—kept a smile on my face for days. Even now, years afterward, it still warms my heart.

Oh, that I would trust my Lord Jesus so completely. To be so connected to Him that we are one! How would that impact my journey on this earth? May we all move through life with peace and grace, firmly connected to our Savior.

Danijela Schubert

March 27

Trusting God in the Dark

Trust in the Lord with all your heart,
And lean not on your own understanding;
In all your ways acknowledge Him,
And He shall direct your paths.
—Proverbs 3:5, 6, NKJV

After I had completed college, it was time for me to enter the working world. I was so excited to be going on this new venture called independence. But independence was not as easy as I thought it would be. I found myself among thousands of young people looking for work. I sent out more than a hundred job applications, yet days turned into weeks which turned into months, and it became so frustrating. I became depressed. As I cried through the long nights, I wondered whether God could hear my prayers.

One day my mother saw me sitting in the dark. "What's wrong? Why are you sitting in the dark? Are you sick?" she asked. When I responded, "No," she turned on the light and sat down beside me, and we began to talk. Mothers are like counselors: they listen, give constructive advice, and motivate their children. After we had talked, I asked her to pray for me.

No one should ever have to feel like this. Have you been in a similar situation and felt depressed? This experience taught me that being upset with the world and with myself did not make the process of gaining employment any easier or faster.

As I prayed, the Lord revealed these verses to me: "Now faith is the substance of things hope for, the evidence of things not seen" (Hebrews 11:1, KJV). "So I say to you: Ask and it will be given to you; seek and you will find; knock and the door will be opened to you. For everyone who asks receives; the one who seeks finds; and to the one who knocks, the door will be opened" (Luke 11:9, 10, NIV).

I know it is not easy when someone says, "Be patient; everything takes time." This is especially hard to hear if you are anxious to start your life. God asks us to cast all our cares upon Him (1 Peter 5:7). He is the Burden Bearer, the Great Healer, and our Provider. He has our future in His sights. Do not give up. Stand firm, and leave it in the hands of God. Thanks be to God, I did find employment, and I am forever grateful to the Almighty for His goodness toward me.

Novalee Sherman

March 28

Decisions! Decisions!

For we walk by faith, not by sight.
—2 Corinthians 5:7, ESV

I graduated from college with a degree in communications and a minor in computer science. My first major job interview was as a news anchor for WVTM in Birmingham, Alabama, United States of America. The news director told me I was not on-camera material, but he loved my writing and wanted me to write the news. I did not know whether I was devastated by his comment or just happy I had been offered a job.

More job offers came in, and then I received a call from New York to work as a junior producer for the Children's Television Workshop, also known as *Sesame Street*. Life was good!

I sat down and looked over both offers. In my excitement, I never even looked to see what the salaries might be. I did not care. I was already daydreaming about living in New York. The salary offer was on the back page in very fine print. The local television station offered $15,000 a year. The New York job offered $13,000.

After I explained all the details to my parents, I tried to convince them the New York job was more prestigious, and I would be a New Yorker! My dad reminded me that my clothing bill for the previous year was about the same as what they were offering. He wanted to know how I planned to pay rent, eat, and buy clothes on $13,000. And my plans could not include his money. I was not happy. My parents suggested I pray about this decision.

There was no way I could live in New York on that salary. So, after much prayer, I accepted the local television writing job. At least I could live at home rent-free—a great motivator. I was also able to start freelance writing for the local newspaper and a magazine.

Every day we make decisions that place us on different paths. It is up to us to trust that when we give our decisions to God, He will never steer us wrong. It has been thirty-one years since I made the decision to become a writer. God has taken me through several corporate jobs, tech-support jobs, and finally, into education. But it is writing that has fueled me in the last several years. God has used my writing to become my new ministry. So, for anyone facing decisions, trust God and walk in faith. Money is not everything. Weigh all your options and pray. Lesson learned.

Paula Sanders Blackwell

March 29

A Teenager's Wake-Up Call

Hear, ye children, the instructions of a father, and attend to know understanding.
—Proverbs 4:1, KJV

I knew from an early age that education was important, but there was something I had not yet grasped—the importance of striving to be better than average. In my early years of school, I was an average student. I always passed my classes, but I was not driven to exceed my tendency to be an average student. I did not try to improve my learning skills. I felt it was all right to be average, and I was happy to just pass my classes and move on. I realized that my parents cared a lot. Every parent-teacher conference would end with my mom or dad telling me about the importance of being more than average.

This attitude changed when I entered middle school. I had a great relationship with my teachers, and I slowly started to take my parents' advice seriously. My relationship with education went from "I am doing this because I am supposed to, and I will get in trouble if I do not" to "I am doing this because I want to be successful. I want to be proud of my work." I stopped relying on my mom to light a fire under my feet to keep me motivated. Instead, I began lighting the fire myself. My hard work did not go unnoticed. I was consistently on the principal's Honor List, drafted into the National Junior Honor Society, and received an NAACP award. It made me feel great.

In high school, I have validated myself academically through God and the teaching of my parents. I have consistently received distinguishing honors. I have also completed two college courses already. As I became more independent and focused on my education, my parents no longer needed to keep looking over my shoulder and lecturing me about grades. They trusted me and knew that if I had a slipup, I would immediately figure out how to do it better next time. As a senior getting ready for college, I thank God for this wake-up call. I believe I now have two of the most important skills needed to help me through my college experience: self-motivation and self-determination. I will need them to reach my goal of becoming a medical doctor.

I thank God that I listened to my parents and received my wake-up call to do better in school before it was too late.

Ricki-Lee Riley

March 30

Praise the Lord

Praise ye the LORD. *Praise God in his sanctuary:*
praise him in the firmament of his power. . . .
Let every thing that hath breath praise the LORD. *Praise ye the* LORD.
—Psalm 150:1, 6, KJV

I attended the baptism of a young adult friend. The event had the perfect backdrop of a rustic farm nestled in lush rolling hills. The place was surrounded by timberland, and the majestic trees lent an atmosphere of serenity that was reflected in the faces of everyone gathered there. The breathtaking waterfront scenery included geese and swans floating on the water. Chairs were neatly arranged, and cool breezes caressed us like gentle hugs from heaven, reminding us to savor each passing moment while acknowledging that eternity was just around the corner. We sat during the service, and then some got up and positioned themselves in places where they could take photos.

We all witnessed the amazing power of God as the birds worshiped Him and acknowledged the induction of one treasured soul into His kingdom of grace. Throughout the service, the geese cackled appropriately when we said "Amen" and were silent when we were. As the pastor and my friend waded into the water, the birds swam to the farthest edge of the lake.

When the service ended, the geese returned to the middle of the lake and began a chorus of cackling "songs." Everyone looked on in amazement! It was as if unseen hands were controlling their beaks. Immediately, I recalled Jesus' words: "I say unto you, that likewise joy shall be in heaven over one sinner that repenteth" (Luke 15:7, KJV).

That experience was a tangible representation of Jesus' love and power. I will never forget the unspoken acknowledgment from the birds that a special transformation had taken place. When they praised God in their own way, it reminded me that He cares deeply for each of us.

Often we fail to recognize the deep significance of someone's decision to follow Christ. We can easily get distracted by their seeming indifference toward things we are familiar with, such as appropriate dress, adornment, and diet. May we always remember the Bible tells us man looks on the outside of a person, but only God can see what is inside the heart (see 1 Samuel 16:7).

Father, help me to keep my focus on things of eternal value rather than choosing to criticize and condemn.

Florence E. Callender

March 31

Red Rocks and Rattlesnakes

Out of Zion, the perfection of beauty,
God has shone.
—Psalm 50:2, NASB

I love to hike, and the experience of being out in nature is one I crave and cherish. There is so much beauty in this world.

One warm summer day, my husband and I met up with his friend Chris for a five-mile hike in Zion National Park, Utah, United States of America. The azure-colored sky was laced with puffy white clouds. There was a slight breeze, and the sun was high. Chris is a talented and creative musician, and his love for God is exhibited in all his musical arrangements. While my husband scanned the trail for rattlesnakes, I enjoyed the hike and being out in nature. I noticed Chris continually commenting on the various colors of the rocks, how they changed from pink to red to gray and sometimes white along one cliff wall. He saw the greenery of the trees contrasted with the deep-blue sky and the multicolored rock walls, observing their God-given beauty. Although we had hiked this trail before, I had never appreciated it as Chris did. His perspective inspired me to open my mind further to the beauty of God's creation that still exists in our broken world.

The trail ended at a beautiful double arch rock formation draped in beautiful shades of red, pink, and black, brilliantly reflecting the sunlight. Chris stepped into the arch and began to sing a song he wrote called "Our Faith Will Rise." His perfect pitch voice echoed off the surrounding walls and brought me to tears, reminding me of the immense love of our Savior. Our God not only created breathtaking scenery but also gave each of us marvelous talents designed to bless Him and others. What an experience!

This simple five-mile (eight-kilometer) hike reminded me to look up and see the wonders that exist in our world. I enjoyed this experience in a fresh, new way, using all my senses. I heard the birds chirping. I smelled the freshness of the trees and the dampness of the creek. I saw the vibrant colors of the rocks towering above us. But most of all, it was a reminder to thank our heavenly Father for giving us the gift of His love and the promise of eternal life. It was an experience I will never forget. And guess what? I never saw one rattlesnake! Praise God!

Judy Casper

April 1

The Keeper

*The LORD is your keeper;
the LORD is your shade on your right hand.*
—Psalm 121:5, ESV

God's creation is amazing! There are so many lessons we can learn from the creatures God has made. Have you ever kept a tortoise as a pet? They do not bark or fetch, and they are not cuddly, but some people simply love them. Maybe this is because they have such interesting personalities. These reptiles have personality characteristics that are common not just to themselves but to all turtles. Like humans, they are quiet, shy, and gentle. They are also intelligent and are able to recognize and form a bond with their keepers. We could learn a thing or two from them!

Tortoises are cold-blooded and need to bask in the sun every day to raise their body temperature and maintain optimal health. We need to bask daily in the presence of God's Son for optimal spiritual health. We do this when we spend time with Him. Through prayer, devotions, Bible study, sharing our testimonies, and witnessing, we form a precious bond with the One who created us—our Keeper.

We should always cherish our "feeding times." We need nourishment if we are to grow into strong, mature daughters of God. Jesus reminds us, "I am the living bread which came down from heaven: if any man eat of this bread, he shall live for ever" (John 6:51, KJV). As we feed on God's Word, He prepares us for heaven and the new earth, where we will live with Him forever.

Sisters, the Keeper encourages us to "walk by faith, not by sight" (2 Corinthians 5:7, ESV). Of course, there will be tough times, but it does not matter what we are up against. We can trust Him. Take time to know who He is, what He can do, and where He is leading. He knows everything. His Word declares, "You are a tower of refuge to the poor, O LORD, a tower of refuge to the needy in distress. You are a refuge from the storm" (Isaiah 25:4, NLT). When Joseph was thrown into prison, when he needed refuge from the storm, we read, "The LORD was with Joseph, and shewed him mercy, and gave him favour in the sight of the keeper of the prison" (Genesis 39:21, KJV). Like Joseph, we have a Keeper who is able to do the same for us.

Our Keeper knows us. He loves us at all times. He knows when something is wrong, and He promises that if we will "draw nigh to God, . . . he will draw nigh" to us (James 4:8, KJV).

Juliet L. Lucas Languedoc

April 2

Blessing

*But even the very hairs of your head are all numbered.
Fear not therefore: ye are of more value than many sparrows.*
—Luke 12:7, KJV

Her name is Blessing, and she is the most adorable Doberman mix that I know. "A dog named Blessing?" you ask. Indeed, let me tell you her story. All my life, I have loved and been loved by dogs, and while my husband is not quite as passionate about them, he has ensured that I am always surrounded by my four-legged besties. Before Blessing's arrival, my two other dogs were aging, and we sensed the sad but inevitable truth of death. Both were older than my son, and we enjoyed watching him grow up with them. He, too, lamented the fact that his companions would soon be gone and repeatedly asked for a new puppy. Although my desire for a puppy was ever present, I wondered how, with my very busy schedule, I would be able to care for one. What I really wanted was a canine bundle of joy as similar to my old dogs as possible. I knew I was likely wishing for too much, and although I could not ignore the longing, I thought surely it was too much to ask God!

One day, while overseas, my husband called me and said excitedly, "Shana, guess what? Our friend has pups, and she is willing to give us one!" I was shocked. First, my friend's dog was an older dog, and we had long given up hope she would ever have pups. Second, she was our "granddaughter." But the pups would be just what I had wanted, similar to my old dogs!

Despite the seemingly great news, I thought, *God, I don't know how I will care for this dog, but if it is Your will, let it be.* Two months later, a noisy, rambunctious bundle arrived. I named her Blessing because I believed her to be an answer to prayer. God would answer more than one prayer regarding His Blessing. Days after she arrived, despite being vaccinated, she fell ill with parvovirus. Regardless of the veterinarian's best efforts, I was given no guarantee she would survive. Again, I prayed, and God answered. Today Blessing is almost three years old and a continuous source of happiness to my family.

Friend, today, no matter what the situation is, whether big or small, take it to God in prayer. Remember, if God values sparrows, nothing is too small or difficult for Him!

Shana Cyr-Philbert

April 3

Big Enough With God

What shall we then say to these things? If God be for us, who can be against us?
—Romans 8:31, KJV

I love my morning walks. I get to enjoy beautiful scenery and greet my neighbors, and I see many animals along my route, both wild and domesticated. I often talk to these animals, although most of them merely give me strange looks or run away as fast as they can!

However, I have an especially fun relationship with two little Yorkies who live about a mile from me. I named the first one Molecule because he was so small. He would occasionally come out and bark at me, and I always sweet-talked him—for all the good it did me!

One day I walked by his house and discovered he had a sister, whom I named Atom, because she was even smaller than Molecule. However, her size did not deter her at all. She was much more ferocious than Molecule, even coming out into the street and baring her teeth at me.

If I saw my two little dog friends, it was a good day. They did not realize this, but I was happy to see them, and they were happy to bark and "scare" me off.

I eventually met their owners, and they assured me that the smaller dog (actually named Hope) would be a menace to everybody if she weighed more because she was not afraid of anybody. Her brother, Hunter, has remained more laid back.

One day, as I walked toward their house, I saw a woman approach with a large dog, many times Hope's size. Seconds later, Hope came rushing out, barking like crazy. I was concerned for her safety and relieved to see the woman holding her dog back so he would not get too close. I explained that Hope, no doubt, thought she was the same size as the larger dog. Luckily, nothing bad happened, and Hope was left with her illusions of hugeness.

I began to think about Hope's bravery and realized that I could be like her. No, I do not intend to start chasing large dogs, but I have realized that I am a match for anything or anybody as long as I have God on my side. After all, anyone who is with God is in the majority. Each of us is big enough for whatever comes as long as we stay close to Him.

Thank You, Lord, for being there for us so that we can handle any problem that comes our way!

Robin Widmayer Sagel

April 4

A Place of Utter Delight

*God saw all that he had made, and it was very good. . . .
Now the LORD God had planted a garden in the east, in Eden;
and there he put the man he had formed.*
—Genesis 1:31; 2:8, NIV

Have you ever asked for clarification at the close of your morning's meditation and paused to allow the Spirit to summarize your time together? What single thought have you taken with you into a new day? One day I found myself wondering about the Garden of Eden, specifically, *Why did God find it necessary to add this special garden in the east?* "Although everything God had made was in the perfection of beauty, and there seemed nothing wanting upon the earth which God had created to make Adam and Eve happy, yet he manifested his great love to them by planting a garden especially for them. . . . This beautiful garden was to be their home, their special residence."*

As I sat pondering this insight into the Creation story, the Holy Spirit spoke. "My child, because of My great love for you, I prepared this beautiful spot for you. The woods, the fields, the lawns, the animals, and the birds, even the waterfall and the fish, are all for your enjoyment.

"Before you were born, I saw you here: excited at the sight of the deer; silent at the song of the birds; laughing at the frenzy of the goldfish; delighted with the flowers, especially the dandelions in the spring; awed by the giant elm, the tasseling corn, the wide-open skies.

"I saw also your heartaches, your frequent tears, your loneliness, and your hurt; how you found strength in being alone in your cathedral. Child, I planned this for the happiness I knew you would find spending time in My creation. Wherever you may travel, there is truly no place like home—this special place I have prepared for you. Other places have their uniqueness, their beauty, despite the many reminders of the horrors of sin—the jagged mountains, the deep canyons, the steamy jungles, the frozen polar caps. But for you, a garden."

My takeaway for today: Father, thank You. I truly have no desire to be or go anywhere else! Really. Truly. Thanks. How about you, my sister in Christ? What will be your takeaway from the time you spend with your Lord this morning? And how will you respond?

Sharon Okimi

---

* Ellen G. White, "The Great Controversy: Chapter Two; The Creation," *Signs of the Times*, January 9, 1879, 2.

April 5

ASK and ACTS

"Keep on asking, and you will receive what you ask for. Keep on seeking, and you will find. Keep on knocking, and the door will be opened to you."
—Matthew 7:7, NLT

During one of my morning devotions recently, I was meditating on Matthew 7:7 when I saw a prayer acrostic I had never noticed before. I saw the ASK prayer, a method Jesus introduced over two thousand years ago in the Sermon on the Mount: Ask, Seek, Knock. Perhaps you, like me, have been praying the ASK prayer daily for many years without realizing it.

I knew of the ABC prayer—Ask, Believe, Claim. And over twenty-seven years ago, while reading Dorothy Eaton Watts's book *Prayer Country: A Tour Guide to the Wonders of Prayer*,* I came across the ACTS prayer.

The acrostic ACTS stands for Adoration, Confession, Thanksgiving, and Supplication. This acrostic has been such a blessing to me over the years. It has helped me to focus on adoration of God each time I pray. Over the years, I have developed A–Z names of adoration for God, beginning at the first of each month. It helps me to remember to always confess and ask for forgiveness and restoration. Thanksgiving is generally a part of my prayers, but the thanksgiving in the ACTS prayer makes me focus even more. Supplication—asking for our needs to be supplied often takes up most of our praying—but the ACTS prayer helps me to keep the balance between asking and thanking.

I pray the ACTS prayer in my private devotions and in my daily joint devotions with my husband, where we share and pray one prayer. I also use it when I pray in public settings. My middle-school students enjoyed using the ACTS prayer when I introduced it in my classroom. It has also been a great blessing in women's ministry prayer sessions. It helps the group stay focused and listen to one another as prayer is offered.

I invite you to try the ACTS prayer on your prayer journey. Share it with your spouse, children, friends, prayer partner, and prayer groups. May your prayer experience grow stronger as you continue on your prayer journey with the ASK and ACTS prayers! Pray on, my sisters!

Claudette Garbutt-Harding

---

* Dorothy Eaton Watts, *Prayer Country: A Tour Guide to the Wonders of Prayer* (Boise, ID: Pacific Press®, 1993).

April 6

A Reason to Worship

For the LORD is great, and greatly to be praised: he is to be feared above all gods.
—Psalm 96:4, KJV

Each Sabbath we go to church and lift our voices in praise to God in prayer and song. But what is our reason for worshiping God? The word *worship* comes from the Old English word meaning "worth-ship." We apply it to the action of human beings as they express their respect and praise to a God *who is worthy*.

The psalmist writes, "Worship the LORD with gladness; come before him with joyful songs" (Psalm 100:2, NIV). This is what we normally think of when we think about worship. We come to church to give God worship and honor. But how many times have you come to church longing to be filled, only to leave feeling just as empty, perhaps even more so, than when you came? What happened?

I remember back in the 1980s, my husband and I were young in marriage yet full of zeal to serve the Lord. My husband was an elder, sang in a young-adult choir, and worked with Adventist Youth. I was in charge of the children's divisions and worked with the Adventurer Club. Yet, with all we were doing, I felt empty. Why?

You see, my worship of God was only corporate. I worshiped God when I came to church, yet I did not take the time to worship God at home. The vitality and genuineness of corporate worship depend, to a large extent, on the vitality of our individual worship. If I am not worshiping God daily, I have nothing to contribute to the corporate worship experience. Worship is not limited to one day a week; it is a daily experience. Each day we need to come into the presence of God and worship Him.

If we want our lives to be centered on God, we must remain focused on our Creator at all times in all circumstances. To do this, we must live in an attitude of worship—something we can and must cultivate if we are to live a victorious Christian life.

Worship is a joyful experience! Our purpose for being is to worship God and bring glory to His name. The psalmist put it so nicely in Psalm 96:4. We worship because God is worthy of our praise, seven days a week.

Heather-Dawn Small (deceased)

April 7

My Clivia Blessing

*Behold, I stand at the door, and knock: if any man hear my voice,
and open the door, I will come in to him, and will sup with him, and he with me.*
—Revelation 3:20, KJV

Spring! A time of mixed blessings. Along with the warmth and sunshine comes an increase in pollen and allergies. For many, it is a time of headaches, hay fever, itchy eyes, sinus problems, and a lot of Kleenex. And then there are the clivias.

On the edge of our porch, opposite the front entrance to our home, stands a sun-splashed spot that is filled with the most beautiful yellow clivias. Right now, they are in full bloom.

When I originally planted the clivia, I considered the most appropriate spot, taking into consideration the shade and movement of the sun. I did not even think about the added blessing of its position opposite my front door. Now, whenever I open the door, I am greeted by a delightful splash of yellow against the beautiful green backdrop of my flower garden. It is such a gift to me, directly from the hand of my Creator, and it serves to remind me that He not only takes care of my needs but also delights in giving me something beautiful to look at—just for the sheer pleasure of it! What a wonderful Savior! I am continually awed by the love of my God for me.

As I consider the placement of the clivia in my garden, it makes me stop and think about where I position God in my life. Is He front and center of all I do and see? Or do I keep Him tucked away and out of sight, only to be taken out on Sabbath? Or when I want something? If I place Jesus in the center of my life, I will be blessed daily by the beauty of His presence. If I remain constantly connected to Him, my character will ultimately be transformed into His likeness, and I will naturally spread His joy and love to all those around me.

Jesus told His followers that if they would "seek first his kingdom and his righteousness . . . all these things" would "be given" to them as well (Matthew 6:33, NIV).

So how is God positioned in your life? As Christ's followers, let us give Jesus pride of place in our lives. Daily communion with Him is an important factor that will transform our lives, for it is by beholding that we are changed (see 2 Corinthians 3:18, KJV). By opening the door of our hearts to God, we enable Him to work in our lives.

Throw the door of your heart wide open to Him today!

Dawn de Grass

April 8

The First, the Last, the Most, and the Biggest

"Follow Me, and I will make you fishers of people."
—Matthew 4:19, NASB

"Put out into the deep water and let down your nets for a catch."
—Luke 5:4, NASB

For over twenty-five years, I held a special title for catching the first, the last, the most, *and* the biggest when Jon and I went fishing. It was always fun to boast about my title, which I did often and rather gleefully, but truth be told, the only reason Jon did not hold that title was because he was busy baiting my hook and cleaning my fish! It was a family joke, and it is a memory that brings me joy and continues to speak volumes about Jon's character and his love for me.

We had a lot of fun over the years. Some of the best times were when we were first married and had a fourteen-foot-long wooden skiff we would take out. It was small, which made it quick and easy to take over to Knudsen Cove and launch into the wild blue yonder for the day or the weekend. We would save up so that we could split a hamburger and have hot chocolate at Clover Pass, or more often, we would pack a lunch. It did not matter if it was raining; in fact, we always fared better on rainy days. They sometimes make for better fishing.

This brings me to this thought: Jesus said in Matthew, "Follow Me, and I will make you fishers of people" (Matthew 4:19, NASB). And in Luke, He said, "Now go out where it is deeper, and let down your nets to catch some fish" (Luke 5:4, NLT). I would not have caught any fish—let alone, the first, last, most, and biggest—if Jon had not said, "Let's go fishing," and taken me out into the deep water where the fish were in great abundance.

Today I am a different kind of fisher because I answered the call to follow Jesus and learn to fish His way. Now it is about letting Him take me out into the deep water because He knows all about who to fish for and when, where, and how to fish for them. All I have to do is follow Him, and He will bait my hook. Best of all, He cleans and sorts my fish!

At the beginning of the day, I love the thrill of heading out for an adventure with the One who loves me most, and at the end of the day, it is my prayer He will be well pleased, just like Jon was, as He looks at our catch.

Tawny Sportsman

April 9

Snorkeling Warnings

And though the Lord *has sent all his servants the prophets to you again and again, you have not listened or paid any attention.*
—Jeremiah 25:4, NIV

I love snorkeling! I first started snorkeling at Catalina Island, California, United States of America. I was hesitant at first, but my sister let me borrow her gear, and I was hooked! Later, we went to the grocery store to buy frozen peas because someone told us that the fish love to eat them. The cashier warned us not to let the bag of peas touch the water because the fish could see it and would go for the whole bag. I thought he was half joking, but I decided to humor him and hold the bag of peas outside of the water with my right hand while I fed the fish with my left.

I enjoyed seeing all the fish as they flocked to me, especially the orange garibaldi, which is our state fish. After a while, my right arm grew tired, and I reasoned that the cashier may have indeed been joking. He was not! No sooner had I let the bag touch the water than a huge fish with serrated teeth came up and bit my right index finger, trying to get to the whole bag of peas! My screams were muted by my snorkel mask as I frantically swam back to shore with one hand out of the water. Suddenly, my right arm was not so tired as I went into flight mode.

While snorkeling and enjoying the beautiful fish once more the next day, I did not notice I was swimming away from the shore. I was so engrossed in the beauty around me that I was not paying attention to the direction I was swimming. Suddenly, I felt someone tug on my leg, and I turned around and saw a stranger. I thought he was just trying to flirt with me, so I swam away even faster. Well, he swam faster still, following me, and grabbed my leg again. I turned around and looked at him again, agitated. He pointed toward a huge boat that I was headed straight toward, and then he turned around and swam toward the shore. I headed back to shore as well and sheepishly thanked him. Though I had been slow to recognize the help God had sent me, I was glad He used this man to keep me from danger.

Will you pray with me that God will help us to recognize when someone has come to warn and keep us from danger, whether it be physical or spiritual? Let us pray that we, too, may be conduits of His love to warn others away from danger.

Mary C. D. Johnson

April 10

"Daddy, Timmy's Crying!"

"I will never fail you. I will never abandon you."
—Hebrews 13:5, NLT

When I was a child, our family would take a summer vacation on beautiful inland lakes in Michigan, United States of America. My father was an avid fisherman. My brothers and I were eager to help him, and we could not wait to swim. I loved hanging out on the dock near the daddy I adored as he baited his hook, cast his line, and patiently waited for the first hungry fish to take a nibble. Our excitement was great when he snagged a fish. With a little more time and effort, there might be enough fish for supper.

I was seven years old, the eldest child, and the only girl with three younger brothers. One lovely morning I went to the dock with Daddy and Timmy, my two-year-old brother. Under the azure-blue sky, the sun sparkled like jewels on the clear water. It was the perfect day for an outdoor adventure. I walked up and down the dock and played in the shallow water with Timmy while Daddy fished. I looked in Dad's tackle box and admired his patience as he waited for an unsuspecting fish to hit the line. In my childish curiosity and intrigue, I lost track of Timmy. When I finally turned to look for him, I could not see him anywhere. I searched the dock again and then glanced down. There was Timmy, sitting on the sand, completely under the water, and he was crying soundlessly!

I called out, "Daddy, Timmy's crying, and he's under the water!" Evidently, Timmy had silently climbed off the dock, and there he sat, in need of rescue. I did not know what to do, but our daddy did. He lifted Timmy out of the water and held him close. "You're OK. You are safe now, and I will stay right with you," he comforted.

Sometimes I find myself in deep water. I do not know how I got into this mess, and I seem to be having a difficult time finding my way out. I do not know how to save myself from myself or the dangers of this world. But just as little Timmy had a father who loved and rescued him, I have a heavenly Father who watches over me. No matter what I have done, I know I can cry out to Him, trusting He will never leave me. He will always be by my side. Will you join me and call out to Him today?

Carolyn J. H. Strzyzykowski

April 11

Forging Ahead

I have fought the good fight, I have finished the race, I have kept the faith. Finally, there is laid up for me the crown of righteousness, which the Lord, the righteous Judge, will give to me on that Day, and not to me only but also to all who have loved His appearing.
—2 Timothy 4:7, 8, NKJV

I felt delighted when the Alberta Conference in Canada decided to lift the heavy restrictions associated with COVID-19, following local government guidelines, and announced we would have camp meeting in person. Every summer our denomination held camp meeting for nine days, offering programs and activities for all ages. The highlights, though, are the Sabbaths when guest speakers were invited to share the Word.

The camp meeting theme was "Forging Ahead," and the picture under the caption showed three people in a boat rowing and a fourth one looking ahead through a spyglass. They seemed to be moving through unknown territory, but they forged ahead, nonetheless. Similarly, in the midst of war, fires, floods, mass shootings, and high gas and food prices, we continue to forge ahead.

When my husband and I arrived at the camp meeting grounds, we were pleasantly surprised to see so many people. It made my heart glad to be free to worship and fellowship in the country, away from the demands of life. As I surveyed the familiar campground, I recognized some things had remained the same as we had left them a few years before. As I got closer to the main auditorium, I noted something new: a beautiful garden of prayer. I renamed the tranquil space the Garden of Eden, though it likely paled in comparison. The family who had created the space had taken much care to plant the right flowers and shrubs in the perfect spot. The benches were strategically placed to allow for quiet moments of prayer or to visit with others. The fountain in the middle soothed the soul as the water flowed gently into the basin. Couples and friends took pictures while others chatted and prayed to their heavenly Father.

I could not help but reflect on what heaven will be like. Paul reminds us that "eye has not seen, nor ear heard, nor have entered into the heart of man the things which God has prepared for those who love Him" (1 Corinthians 2:9, NKJV). I cannot wait to see what God has prepared for us. Let us join hands and hearts as we forge ahead to the kingdom.

Sharon Long

April 12

Miracle Garden

And my God shall supply all your need according to His riches in glory by Christ Jesus.
—Philippians 4:19, NKJV

I gazed at our backyard garden with awe and gratitude. It was summertime, and our trees were extraordinarily abundant with fruit. We had guavas, bananas, persimmons, papayas, star fruit, lemons, and many more—a sight uncommon in a big city such as Los Angeles, California, United States of America. Different varieties of organic vegetables grew lush and bountiful as well. Harvesting our own produce was very convenient and safe during the height of the pandemic, when access to supermarkets was constrained and risky. The garden was truly a blessing, especially at a time when my immune system was compromised. I remember telling my husband, "Look! There's my natural medicine right in our backyard."

My husband, Bonn, and my daughter Victoria were also blessed by the fruits of their labor. For Bonn, gardening is a source of strength, peace, and joy. He attributes his good health to spending hours tending to the garden. And Victoria enjoys harvesting kale leaves to prepare her special salad.

We were gratified to share our bountiful harvest with family and friends. We would fill bags with fresh fruits and vegetables and deliver them to the front doors of our friends. Then we would follow up our deliveries with a phone call or text message. Everyone always responded with such gratitude.

It is not only the food from the garden that brings me joy. Occasionally, I love to walk in a garden situated on a hill, and traversing the garden's forty-nine stairs helps to meet the need for physical exercise. The times spent quietly in prayer and meditation under the shade of the lemon and pine trees are so refreshing and provide food for the soul.

God wants us to be not only physically healthy but also spiritually nourished. Just like a garden, our inner self needs to be cultivated, fertilized, and guided by the Word of God. John writes, "Beloved, I pray that all may go well with you and that you may be in good health, as it goes well with your soul" (3 John 1:2, ESV).

God is always looking for opportunities to connect with us if we will only listen and respond faithfully. I believe that our backyard "miracle garden" was all a part of His grand plan and promise to sustain and prosper us.

Clody Flores Dumaliang

April 13

Lessons From the Master Gardener

The LORD God took the man and put him in the Garden of Eden to work it and take care of it.
—Genesis 2:15, NIV

I enjoy gardening. On many summer mornings, I sneak out of the house before anyone else is up to see what new and exciting thing is happening in my backyard garden. Are the tomato plants standing a bit taller today? Are the zucchini blossoms adding a pop of sunshiny yellow to the beds? What pesky critters are trying to chomp on my young seedlings? What about the pole beans? Are they finally climbing the poles, or are the rebellious little rascals trying to grow along the ground?

Gardening teaches so many lessons about a loving Savior and our relationship with Him. In the garden, we are confronted with life "at the bone." Here we see that seeds shallowly planted can be eaten by birds, and a heavy downpour can wash away the potential for life. Young plants must battle bugs and the elements in order to survive, and wayward young plants often require a gentle nudge to lay hold of the support stakes necessary for their growth.

In the garden, I have grieved the loss of plants eaten by critters that did not tend to them. And I have chosen to replant, to start all over again, recognizing that my part in the process is to sow, water, and cultivate. God is the One who does what I cannot—He alone can breathe life into dead places.

Is it any wonder that the first work God gave Adam was to tend the beautiful Garden of Eden? An all-powerful God who does not need any help from us at all invited Adam to be a gardener. Fascinating, isn't it? I like to think that in giving Adam this work, God was handing him the gift of a curriculum for life. In gardening, Adam would learn the value of working with his hands. As he diligently cared for young plants, he would learn to fulfill his role as a parent and guardian. In tending the Garden, he would develop a greater appreciation for food, for life, and for the earth; consequently, he would become a more diligent steward of it all. But more than any of these lessons, God gave Adam, and us, a treasure that nurtures our spirits.

Gardening reminds us that, like the plants we care for, we ourselves are under the care of the Master Gardener—God Himself.

Kathy-Ann C. Hernandez

April 14

The Struggle With Scorpions

"For the Son of Man came to seek and save those who are lost."
—Luke 19:10, NLT

A couple of girlfriends and I work out in the mornings in my detached garage. We call it boot camp. At least, that is what it could have been called a few years ago. Now it is more like a gentle workout for middle-aged, and beyond (*cough, cough*), ladies desperate to regain the twenty-year-old physiques they enjoyed in yesteryear—all without killing their joints. But I digress.

Because I live in the country, we are often "visited" by insects. My approach to any creepy-crawlies that have mistakenly ventured inside is to squish them. It is a sorry, not-sorry relationship. Unfortunately for them, they have ventured where they do not belong, and there is no turning back. However, one lovely lady in our exercise crew has a different approach. Her heart is beyond tender for all God's creations. The other day she kindly scooped up the perpetrator, which happened to be a scorpion this time, on a piece of paper and delivered it safely outside, where it could live the rest of its natural life in sunshine and freedom. Mind blown, I know.

This is such a beautiful illustration of our life with God. When we venture outside of where we were meant to be, Satan and his homies are more than happy to squish us. He is sorry, not sorry. But I am thrilled to report that our amazing God has a heart bigger than even my lovely insect-loving friend, even though I know that is hard to fathom.

Our Lord scoops us up from the unfortunate choices we have made that have left us in squish-happy places and delivers us back to life in the sunshine. Life in Him is unfathomable grace and unending love. Mind blown, I know!

So, the next time you start to beat yourself up for acting like a scorpion, please do yourself a favor. Just stop. Accept God's full forgiveness. Allow His tender embrace. Trust Him to carry you out of whatever situation you find yourself in. Admittedly, this is oftentimes a process that gives us a chance to exercise patience. And then allow Him to assist you into the better plan He has waiting just for you. You will thank me later.

Mary K. Haslam

April 15

All Yours—Take Them!

"Not by might nor by power, but by my Spirit," says the Lord Almighty.
—Zechariah 4:6, NIV

One summer afternoon I flew from Huntsville, Alabama, to Miami, Florida, both in the United States of America. My flight was delayed many times, so I arrived early in the morning the next day.

When I approached the welcome desk at the rental car office, weary and worried, the young attendant told me that my car was no longer available. Instead, there was a Mustang convertible that I could have for the same price as the inexpensive car I had originally rented. It was a "great upgrade and a fantastic deal for me as a regular customer," he enthused with a smile. He seemed quite certain that I would be delighted to drive such a fast car.

I had never driven a Mustang, and the extravagant, white two-door convertible felt strange to me. With great trepidation, I drove the few miles to my hotel, where the attendant was quite impressed with the beautiful car.

As I struggled to maneuver the car through the six-floor parking lot, I worried about having an accident. In the end, I decided to park it and catch an Uber ride back and forth to my work assignment the next day. The fancy car would stay in the garage until I turned it back in safely.

Before I fell asleep, my mind turned to the decision to park and leave the car in the garage. I felt convicted it had not been a wise decision. I thought about instances when I had a wonderful opportunity made available to me, yet I always followed the futile, safe path. God promises freedom, but frequently, I choose fear. He offers abundant life, but sometimes I prefer the enemy's lies. Many times I obsess over my faults instead of receiving God's forgiveness. The sovereign and omnipotent God wants to give me the best, like the Mustang in the garage, but I reach for less. Often, I think I do not deserve the Lord's blessings, and I need the Holy Spirit to remind me that I owe everything to Christ alone.

If you struggle to accept and receive the gifts God has for you, I pray you will take hold of them by faith in the One who has paid it all for you. If God is pointing you to a path that seems out of your league, walk boldly toward His purpose for you. God has blessings and favors for you, my sisters. Look for them. Claim them. Enjoy them—they are His gift to you!

Rose Joseph Thomas

April 16

Checkout Time

Pride goes before destruction,
a haughty spirit before a fall.
—Proverbs 16:18, NIV

It is Thursday and the last day of the month. My primary monthly income is a Social Security check, which is normally received between the first and third of the month. I live on those funds in addition to whatever other gifts God provides via family, part-time employment, gifts, or other avenues. Now I had just enough food for three days, including a free loaf of bread from the thrift shop, and some drinking water. I was sure that everything, except the water, would last until my Social Security check arrived. I was right. The drinking water lasted until this morning.

Last night I had begun to search for ninety-seven cents with which to buy a gallon of water. I found sixty cents—a quarter, two dimes, and three nickels. Then I found enough pennies to complete the amount needed. I kept praying that I would find a quarter so I would not have to go into the store with *all* those pennies.

It was then I realized that my pride was very much alive. I was ashamed to go into the store and count out thirty pennies in order to pay for the gallon of water. I was ashamed of my pride, ashamed of being ashamed. God's Spirit gently reminded me, "None of this is about you, Helen! The battle is between God and Satan." God had promised to meet all my needs, so why was I worried or ashamed? Satan had tested me, but now God would be glorified.

After seeking forgiveness, I went into the store, got my water, and slowly, at the self-checkout, I inserted each coin into the slot. As I left the store, I remembered that checkout time for our Savior had not been an option. Peter reminds us, "He was chosen before the creation of the world, but was revealed in these last times" for our sake (1 Peter 1:20, NIV). The decision to die for the sins of humanity was settled before the foundation of the world. Having become sin for us, He bore our shame on the cross. He bore my pain and my shame. There is, therefore, no justification for pride.

Thank You, Father, in Jesus' name, for Your love and Your commitment to transform us frail human beings into the image of Your Son. Thank You for taking away my sinful pride. Amen.

Helen O. Byoune

April 17

Worthy to Be Praised

"Worthy is the Lamb who was slain to receive power and riches and wisdom, and strength and honor and glory and blessing!"
—Revelation 5:12, NKJV

I am reading *Messiah*, by Jerry D. Thomas, and the following quote struck me to the core of my heart and soul: "When we finally understand, we will throw our crowns at His feet and sing, ' "The Lamb who was killed is worthy to receive power, wealth, wisdom and strength, honor, glory, and praise!" ' (Revelation 5:12)."* What a sense of awe this brings toward our Jesus, who went through the wilderness of temptation for you and me.

What a realization that Jesus placed Himself where I should be, yet He did it without sinning or worshiping Satan! He had me on His mind. He had you on His mind. Because He loved us so, He chose to use the words "It is written" during His temptations because His love for His Father and for us was greater than anything Satan had to offer Him (Matthew 4:4, 7, 10, NKJV). However, it was a price He felt: "After Satan fled, Jesus fell to the ground exhausted and nearly dead. The angels of heaven had been watching the battle, watching their beloved Commander as He suffered to make a way for humans to escape. He had survived the test greater than any that humans could endure. Now those angels brought Him food and water along with a message of His Father's love. They assured Him that heaven rang with joy over His victory."†

As I contemplate those scenes in my mind's eye, I realize that the only hope for us is, like Jesus, to stay connected to our Father and grab hold of Him through our imaginations, through Bible seeking, and through time spent with Him. We must take His hand as He extends it toward you and me. He reaches out to us and says, "I love you. I have saved you. You are Mine. I chose to go to the cross for you. I cannot imagine living through eternity without being close to you." I choose to grasp His hand, and I invite you to do the same as He brings you into His incredible embrace, where you will find love and safety. Accept the gift of His grace, for He is worthy to be praised!

Mary H. Maxson

---

* Jerry D. Thomas, *Messiah* (Nampa, ID: Pacific Press®, 2003), 83.
† Thomas, 83.

April 18

For Love of You and Me

"There is no greater love."
—John 15:13, NLT

A friend posted a photograph of his little girl; it was taken at the moment she realized Jesus had died for her. The spontaneous image showed her pain at Jesus' suffering, and as I lingered on the image, memories filtered through my mind of when six-year-old me experienced a similar moment.

On a warm Sunday afternoon, as my family napped, I slipped off my bed and headed for the living room. I was bored yet wide awake, so taking a nap was the last thing on my mind. I was fully aware of the need to be quiet when I noticed the large Bible sitting on a small bookcase. Curious, I picked it up and carried it to the sofa. The Bible belonged to my mother and was beautifully illustrated with images of old paintings. As I carefully turned the pages, stories I had heard in Sabbath School unfolded before me. Noah was building the ark as people stood around and mocked his faith. Then came the animals filing two by two inside the huge boat. I turned the page, and a brilliant rainbow shimmered across the sky.

I saw baby Moses hidden in a woven basket while Miriam stood among the river reeds close by. I loved that story! David, the shepherd boy, gazed up at the giant in front of him, his sling in hand. That story did not end well for Goliath. I turned the pages until I saw Baby Jesus in a manger. Wise men knelt in colorful robes and offered Him gifts. Then Boy Jesus, surrounded by teachers and scribes, sat in the temple, gently shining light into darkened minds, even as His parents frantically searched for Him. I turned the pages quickly and saw water turned to wine, raging waves silenced and still. Then there He sat, with children gathered about Him. One on His lap rested her head against His chest, and I longed to be that little girl.

When I saw Him in Pilate's court, stripped and whipped, I stopped. I knew how this story ended. When He fell under the weight of the cross, a stranger bent low to lift His load. As Calvary filled the page, my eyes swam with tears, for I knew then He had died for the love of me. My tears spilled as my heart stilled. No one had ever loved me like Jesus! No one would ever love me like Jesus! That moment set the trajectory of my life. He has my heart.

He died for the love of you, too, and soon He will return to take us home.

Karen Pearson

April 19

The Teardrop

Jesus cried out in a loud voice, . . . "My God, my God, why have you forsaken me?"
—Matthew 27:46, NIV

The painting drew my attention as soon as I took my seat in the large college-campus church.

I had seen the painting many times but had never really paid close attention to it until that moment when I noticed something I had not seen before. The painting depicted Jesus hanging on the cross, but the detail I had missed was a single tear making its way down the anguished face of our Redeemer. My mind immediately pictured a wind-swept Golgotha—the place of the skull—burdened with three heavy crosses. We often talk about the blood our Savior shed, the crude crown of thorns on His brow, and the cruel nails driven through His flesh. But the sight of that lone tear falling down His bloodied cheek startled me.

I had never given much time to thoughts of a weeping Savior and the mental and emotional anguish that lay behind that tear. Jesus endured beatings, mockery, and the horrendous crucifixion; it is impossible for us to ever imagine the agony Christ endured as those iron spikes were driven through His hands and as the cross was raised and thrust into the ground. With His body deeply lacerated and bleeding, the spotless Lamb of God was lifted up for all the world.

What unimaginable agony He endured at the wrath of Satan and the apparent separation from His beloved Father. His quivering lips trembled as He gasped, "My God, my God, why have you forsaken me?" (Matthew 27:46, NIV). Surrounded by the forces of evil in that terrible hour, Jesus could not discern His Father's face and was tempted to think He had been abandoned. And He endured it all because of His love for us and His trust in His Father's love.

An inspired writer wrote, "When men and women can more fully comprehend the magnitude of the great sacrifice which was made by the Majesty of heaven in dying in man's stead, then will the plan of salvation be magnified, and reflections of Calvary will awaken tender, sacred, and lively emotions in the Christian's heart. Praises to God and the Lamb will be in their hearts and upon their lips."* Truly! What love is this!

Cordell Liebrandt

---

* Ellen. G. White, *Lift Him Up* (Hagerstown, MD: Review and Herald®, 1988), 43.

April 20

Take This Cup From Me

"Please take this cup of suffering away from me."
—Luke 22:42, NLT

Jesus, the Master Teacher, taught His disciples a new way to pray. But He did more than teach them to break away from the forms into which they had fallen. He painted a portrait of God as a Father with the words "Our Father." How the disciples must have grappled to grasp the panorama unfolding before them! Elohim *is our Father! And we are His adored children!*

The disciples had forgotten the Father's love. It had been buried beneath the minutia of human-made requirements for centuries. Jesus came to change that, and in Love's ultimate gift, a blood-soaked cross was raised and thrust into the soil, and the Lamb of God was sacrificed for all. But before He went to Calvary, Jesus went to the Garden of Gethsemane—a place the disciples recognized as one of His favorite places to pray. On this night, however, there seemed to be a desperation, a raw urgency in Jesus' need to pray. Suffering immeasurable agony, their Master asked them to pray. And they did—until they fell asleep. They never noticed His blood dripping onto the ground where He lay stretched out in agony. As He writhed in pain, a new prayer was wrung from His heart: "Father, . . . please take this cup of suffering away from me" (Luke 22:42, NLT).

In that one agonized sentence, Jesus revealed how to pray from a place of desperation and pain. We are so familiar with the gentle rhythm of the Lord's Prayer. We teach it to our children. We give it melody and sing it in worship. We cling to it when walking through the valley, and we rejoice that one day, His kingdom, power, and glory will last forever!

But in the Gethsemane prayer, Jesus shows us how to pray when life has crushed us. In asking for the cup of suffering to be removed, the honesty of Jesus' cry teaches us that we can be just as honest. We can safely come before Him in brokenhearted, openhearted pain and pray our imperfect, impertinent, inappropriate prayers to the One we call Father.

Without the Gethsemane prayer, there would have been no victory cry of "He is risen!" on Resurrection Sunday. When we are broken by pain, let us pray like Jesus and trust ourselves to the love of our Father. Authenticity can form the bridge between our brokenness and surrender. Lean into Him today. He is only a heartbeat away.

Karen Pearson

April 21

God of the Hills and Valleys

*I am the Lord: that is my name: and my glory will I not give to another,
neither my praise to graven images.*
—Isaiah 42:8, KJV

There is a story in 1 Kings 20 that I find fascinating. Ben-Hadad, the king of Syria, went to King Ahab of Israel, demanding his silver and gold as well as his prettiest wives and his children. Knowing he could not win a battle against Syria, King Ahab agreed (1 Kings 20:1–4). Ahab's acquiescence made Ben-Hadad bold. He sent another convoy of messengers to tell Ahab that his servants would visit Israel the next day and would strip it of everything that Ahab found appealing (verse 6).

This second threat made Ahab angry, and for what was probably the first time in his life, he spoke out courageously. He refused to agree to the more stringent terms, which then made Ben-Hadad angry. A battle ensued in which Ben-Hadad and the thirty-two kings with whom he had joined forces were trounced by the seven thousand men in Ahab's army.

You would think Ben-Hadad had learned his lesson, but no. The following spring he returned with an army the same size as the previous one. His servants had convinced him that the only reason the Israelites had won before was that their God was the God of the mountains. They were convinced that He would not be able to defeat them if they fought the Israelites on the plains. The God of Israel proceeded to prove that He was the God not only of the mountains but also of the valleys. My friend, this story reminds us that God is Sovereign over every problem or situation in our lives. He is not surprised by the things that happen to us. Neither is He threatened or defeated by them. But when we do not bring our problems to God, we rob Him of the opportunity to prove His dominance over all things. Let us remember that the God we serve is all-powerful, all-knowing, and all-present. Let us lay our burdens at His feet, trusting that He will take care of them.

Father, thank You for the reminder that You are the God of the hills and the valleys. Today I want to lay at Your feet all that troubles me, trusting that You are able to give me the victory. In Jesus' name, I pray, amen.

Aminata Coote

April 22

Praise God

Be anxious for nothing, but in everything by prayer and supplication, with thanksgiving, let your requests be made known to God.
—Philippians 4:6, NKJV

From first to last, we are to praise God. Two stories from the Bible come to mind that highlight the benefits of praise. First is the story of a choir leading an army into battle. Judah was under attack by enemies, and when King Jehoshaphat was informed, he turned to God in prayer. He began his prayer by recounting God's power, then reviewed God's previous workings, and ended with a request for help. When he had finished praying, God sent a promise through a Levite, and the service ended with songs of praise. The next morning Jehoshaphat told his people that since God had already promised them victory, they would have the choir lead the army! "Now when they began to sing and to praise, the LORD set ambushes against the people of Ammon, Moab, and Mount Seir" (2 Chronicles 20:22, NKJV). Do you see the correlation between praise and victory?

The second story is from Acts, when Paul and Silas were in prison in Philippi. At midnight, they "were praying and singing hymns to God, and the prisoners were listening to them. Suddenly there was a great earthquake" (Acts 16:25, 26, NKJV). I cannot help but see connections between this story and an episode found in John Bunyan's *Pilgrim's Progress*. In Bunyan's allegory, two characters, Christian and Hopeful, are trapped in the dungeon of Doubting Castle. One evening, rather than bemoaning their fate, they start singing hymns and praises to God, which results in Christian remembering that he had a key called Promise that could aid them in escaping. After discovering the key grew or shrank to meet the various-sized chains and doors, they had a brief discussion on why they had not remembered the key beforehand. They realized they had remembered after they had started singing praises. Christian says, "God's word commands us to 'rejoice always,' and 'in all things to give thanks.' If we had obeyed, instead of looking at our circumstances and feeling sorry for ourselves, we would have used the power of promise long ere this."* In everything, do not be anxious, but pray with thanksgiving!

Melinda Ferguson

---

* John Bunyan, *The New Amplified Pilgrim's Progress*, adapted by Jim Pappas Jr. (Shippensburg, PA: Destiny Image, 2005), 257.

April 23

Blessings of the Ordinary

In every thing give thanks.
—1 Thessalonians 5:18, KJV

"Who makes your bed?" This question from a visitor came out of the blue. I am in my nineties, and I live alone. I have no family close by, and I do not have household help, so I answered her question, "I make my bed." She then asked, "Well, who washes your sheets?" Once again I responded, "I do. Though I do not wash them on a washboard or hang them on the line."

I thought about it later and about how different things are now from when I was young. When I was a child, my mother was left with four daughters and her mother to care for, and she had no way to earn a living. It was during the Great Depression, and jobs were hard to find, but through the help of longtime friends, Mother found a job cooking the noon meal at a country school. It meant moving out of town and giving up electricity, indoor plumbing, and running water. Everything, including the sheets, had to be washed on a washboard and hung on a clothesline. The water source was a spring at the bottom of a hill, and water had to be carried up the hill in buckets. But we had a place to live, food to eat, and each other!

At the end of the school year, a better job opened up, and we moved back to some, but not all, of the conveniences we had learned to do without. At least, we had electricity, a better water source, and a telephone! Then even better times came when Mother remarried. A local bachelor businessman had been an admirer since their youth, and when circumstances brought them together, it led to a happy marriage and the birth of a fifth daughter.

We moved into town and finally had all the conveniences that we had missed, including a bathroom! A wringer washer replaced the washboard, and we had running water instead of buckets, but everything still had to be hung on the clothesline until automatic dryers became available.

Now, we have conveniences we never dreamed of back then. But one thing has not changed—my bed still does not make itself. I am thankful I can still do it. My automatic washer and dryer take care of my sheets. I give thanks often for the many blessings we so easily take for granted, and I am reminded of one of my favorite promises: "Casting all your care upon him; for he careth for you" (1 Peter 5:7, KJV). Even when you are in your nineties!

Mary Jane Graves

April 24

Jesus Did Care

*"Are not two sparrows sold for a penny?
Yet not one of them will fall to the ground outside your Father's care."*
—Matthew 10:29, NIV

I have always suffered from breathing problems because of my nose. As I grew older, the problems became worse, so I decided to see a specialist. He discovered that the air passage in my nose was very narrow and crooked. When I lay on my back to sleep, I could not breathe normally and would end up breathing through my mouth, resulting in a very dry throat. My physician made an appointment for surgery.

I was scared and worried, but the doctor assured me it was a minor surgery and not serious. I asked my church to pray for me on that day. I called my friends and family and asked them to pray for me. At noon, I was wheeled to the operating room, and the doctor told my husband that he would be able to see me in my room after the surgery. I prayed all the way!

After the surgery, I woke up with terrible pain in my throat, and I was not in my room but in the intensive care unit (ICU). I found out later that my husband had looked for me from about an hour after surgery until he eventually found me at 7:00 P.M. in the ICU. I wondered why I was there instead of in my room.

The doctor told my husband that after the surgery, he and the anesthesiologist were talking when the anesthesiologist turned his head toward me and noticed I had stopped breathing. The anesthesiologist immediately reinserted my breathing tube, but I had lost consciousness for a couple of seconds. I praise God for taking care of me. He got the attention of the anesthesiologist in the middle of the conversation. He probably tapped him on the shoulder. If he had noticed my breathing later, I might have died.

When I think of being in the hospital, I truly thank the Lord for extending my life. Now I fully surrender my whole being to Him. God still has a plan for me, and I will praise Him as long as I live.

Sisters, each one of us is precious in God's sight. We do not need to worry, for He is still in control. Let us be women God can use according to His purpose.

Loida Gulaja Lehmann

April 25

Sing Along With Me

Praise Him with trumpet sound;
Praise Him with harp and lyre.
—Psalm 150:3, NASB

On the first day of school, as parents lined up, ready to drop off their little ones, I noticed a woman I knew. She struggled with a big, strong boy who tried to free himself from her hold. I remembered Esther because I had taught her daughter a few years earlier. I greeted her, and she asked, "Is Sam in your class?" I checked my list and saw his name. She was so happy. As she handed Sam to me, she told me he was unstable. I did not understand what she meant, so I told her that boys are typically very active.

Later that day, we learned he was autistic, and because he needed a personal aide, he would be transferred to another school in a few days. After a week, during which all I did was struggle to keep Sam safe, we heard he was not going anywhere. We would have him all year. Why? His mom phoned everyone working on the transfer and told them she wanted to keep her son in Ms. Mabel's class. Period! Why? Because she wanted me to teach her son.

Sam was in school every day on time. I noticed how he calmed down during naptime when I played a lullaby and turned the lights down. *Praise the Lord!* I said in my heart, for we were not allowed to talk about God in class. I wanted to shout, "This is an answered prayer!" The struggle with Sam continued. It got to a point where we had to tie bells to the doorknob to alert us when he tried to run outside. He was so fast and energetic, but the music at naptime calmed him down and became the tool God used to keep him calm for ninety minutes each day.

Over the course of the school year, we noticed Sam had stopped trying to run away as often. He learned to sit still and listen to rhymes and read-aloud books on the radio. At the parent-teacher conference, his mother said, "I told everyone my son would be OK in Ms. Mabel's class." All I knew was that it was not my abilities but God's! Music did wonders for Sam, and by God's grace, prayer, and music, we made it through the year. And I have to admit to shedding a tear the day Sam left my class.

My friends, the angels love to sing to God in heaven. Let us sing, too, for music has the power to soothe our troubled hearts. So, sing along with me, and let us praise the Lord!

Mabel Kwei

April 26

A New View

*"What do you want me to do for you?" Jesus asked him.
The blind man said, "Rabbi, I want to see."*
—Mark 10:51, NIV

The story of blind Bartimaeus always tugs at my heart. Here was a man at the roadside, making his way in life by begging—not a desirable existence. One day he learned Jesus would pass by. I believe Bartimaeus had heard of Jesus' heart of compassion for the marginalized and of His many miracles. Hope filled his heart, and Bartimaeus wondered, *What if Jesus cares about me too?* So, Bartimaeus began to muster the courage to engage Jesus as He drew near.

When Jesus was within hearing distance, Bartimaeus called out, "Jesus, Son of David, have mercy on me!" (Mark 10:47, NIV). As he cried out, he was shushed by people who thought he did not matter. He was used to being ostracized by others, but today he kept putting himself out there. "Son of David," he called louder, "Have mercy on me!" (verse 48, NIV).

He then heard the words that brought healing to his soul: "What do you want me to do for you?" (verse 51, NIV). Jesus not only heard him but also responded. Wow!

The blind man courageously appealed, "Rabbi [my Master], I want to see" (verse 51, NIV).

"Your faith has healed you" (verse 52, NIV), Jesus affirmed, and immediately, Bartimaeus received his sight. What a beautiful, teachable moment. Not only did Jesus embrace and heal Bartimaeus but the community also saw his value to Jesus. He gave them a new view as He gently revealed their spiritual blindness. By asking, "What do you want me to do for you?" Jesus modeled the importance of dignifying the man's needs rather than minimizing them.

As I considered Bartimaeus's story, I recalled a situation that occurred shortly after I arrived at Christian Record Services for the Blind. I went to the airport to meet a friend who was blind. I was unsure whether I should offer to guide or if she would prefer to navigate with her cane, a guide dog, or perhaps echolocation, as some people who are blind prefer. So when we connected, I asked the simple question, "Is there anything I can do for you?" That is how I learned she would like to hold the back of my elbow as I led her.

Jesus wants us to turn to Him too. He is ready to respond, "What do you want Me to do for you?" Sometimes He answers as we wish, and other times, He offers something better. But He is always there and listens with a heart of love. Let us turn to Him today.

Diane Thurber

April 27

Joy Will Come in the Morning

Consider it pure joy, my brothers and sisters, whenever you face trials of many kinds, because you know that the testing of your faith produces perseverance. Let perseverance finish its work so that you may be mature and complete, not lacking anything.
—James 1:2–4, NIV

I was privileged to care for my mother, who had dementia. She then developed Parkinson's disease, and we faced many challenges through this difficult journey with its seemingly never-ending descents. My mother went to sleep in Jesus in September 2015 at ninety-five years old.

Through this experience, I learned many invaluable lessons. Although I had always loved my mother, I learned to show it more than I had before. I learned patience, empathy, compassion, humility, and tolerance. I am still learning anger management and forgiveness. Additionally, I have been the grateful beneficiary of genuine friendship and generosity.

My most important gain, however, has been my spiritual pruning. Sharing my thoughts with fellow Christians (invaluable therapy!) left me encouraged and blessed. At times, when the crucible heated up and I felt cornered, I asked God, "Why?" I refused to believe, like Job's friends, that our loving Father was punishing my mother. As I cried out to Him, prayed more earnestly, and even argued with Him at times, my prayer life deepened and matured. Each crucible moment reminded me of my dependence on God, and I became more resolute to serve Him.

While saddened to have lost her and that she had to suffer to teach me, I rejoice that her suffering is over and that I have had the wisdom and flexibility to learn these lessons. I now strive, with God's help, to be a better person so her suffering will not be in vain.

Yet questions linger in my mind. *Was this for my mother's benefit? Or did God see the road I was headed down and use this experience to draw me back? If so, shouldn't I have been the one to suffer? Was my experience simply to prepare me to help support others experiencing similar trials?* With the help of God, I will be caught up in the air to meet Him, and these will be the first questions I will ask Him.

If you are walking through a similar experience, please know you are not alone. And always remember, "joy comes in the morning" (Psalm 30:5, NKJV).

Cecelia Grant

April 28

An Act of Humility

"Do you understand what I have done for you?"
—John 13:12, NIV

Washing my aged father's feet brought me deep spiritual healing. This act of humility on my part was the same action Jesus performed with His disciples as a demonstration of how to be a good servant and a reminder to be one. At the ripe old age of ninety, my father no longer remembered a lot of things due to the ravages of Alzheimer's. But I had harbored much guilt in my heart over the hurt I had caused my father many years before.

I left home as a teenager to get out on my own because I wanted to make my own decisions about how to live my life. I thought I was grown enough to make good choices away from the watchful eyes of my Christian parents. However, I made the mistake of entrusting my life to a man who did not have my best interests at heart. When he learned that I was pregnant, he immediately insisted I have an abortion—something that was illegal at that time. A close friend who believed in Christ counseled me against having an abortion. I listened to his wise counsel.

My mother insisted I return home, against my father's wishes. He was very disappointed when I returned and brought shame to the family. How could he, a preacher with a pregnant, unwed daughter, lead a flock when his own child had strayed so far?

Now, as a grown, responsible adult, I poured warm water into a basin and lovingly washed my father's feet in reverent respect. A lot of grace went into this act of humility. God had graciously given me this opportunity as a way of apologizing to my father for the disregard I had shown toward some of the biblical teachings he had tried to pour into the lives of his children so they could have a rich spiritual relationship with the Lord that he loved and served.

My son, now fully grown, has been a blessing to our family. He was a good caregiver to his stepfather and his grandfather in their later years. He spent quality time with them, meeting many of their mental and physical needs when they were no longer able to do so for themselves.

One day I hope to wash my son's feet. I want to let him know how much I appreciate his service to our family. As with my father, doing so will be an act of humility—an acknowledgment of God's gracious love and mercy.

Fartema Mae Fagin

April 29

Let Him In

Trust in the Lord *with all your heart;*
do not depend on your own understanding.
Seek his will in all you do,
and he will show you which path to take.
—Proverbs 3:5, 6, NLT

I watched his little legs propel him forward; his eagerness to cross the busy street was plain to see. He paid no attention to oncoming traffic, and his tail shook his body as he strutted confidently across the street, unaware of the dangers around him. Lucky for him, the car that had just turned the corner and was heading for him was driven by an alert and considerate driver. This driver, seeing the little pup happily and foolishly crossing the street with no care for or knowledge of the danger he was in, slowed to a crawl and gave him enough time to get safely to the other side of the street. I watched him from my parked car. He was a cutie indeed, and he seemed to smile with contentment at his great accomplishment. As he disappeared safely into a yard, I smiled, realizing his innocence and cluelessness regarding the dangers he had just escaped.

While driving home, I thought about this little four-legged creature as the lessons he had just provided came to mind. How many times have I run headlong through life, intent on my own agenda? How many times had God's guardian angels saved me from perils that I had created by my own actions? So often, we are guilty of making decisions and choices in life without consulting the Author and Finisher of our faith. It can be easy to notice this type of behavior in others—in my daughter and granddaughter—but do I recognize the habit in myself?

The wise man says in our text for today that if we acknowledge God in all our ways, He will direct our paths. Oh, that we would follow this counsel and allow God to direct our decisions, even the ones we think are inconsequential. Our God longs so deeply to be a part of our lives, and we fool ourselves by thinking He is too busy to be interested in our daily lives. When we fail to seek Him for wisdom in making the little decisions, we neglect to turn to Him for the big ones. That is how we run into danger, sometimes knowingly but often unknowingly.

My friends, let us not give our guardian angels unnecessary work. Let us acknowledge God in every aspect of our lives, seeking Him for wisdom as we make each decision. Let us do it today, and He will take us safely through.

Greta Michelle Joachim-Fox-Dyett

April 30

The Immeasurable Cost

"Father, glorify Your name."
Then a voice came from heaven, saying, "I have both glorified it and will glorify it again."
—John 12:28, NKJV

> In the cross of Christ I glory,
> Towering o'er the wrecks of time;
> All the light of sacred story
> Gathers round its head sublime.

These lyrics belong to the beautiful song "In the Cross of Christ I Glory."* The song looped through my mind as I prepared this devotional entry.

Every one of us has a story. Our decisions primarily shape our story—decisions such as what we want and how we will work to make it happen, the decision not to listen to spiritual counsel, and deciding that our bodies are our own and not treating them as the "temple of God" (1 Corinthians 3:16, NKJV). These are a few examples of some bad decisions we may make. Experiencing the immediate and long-term consequences of bad decision-making often leads to bouts of mental anguish and troubled times.

A powerful antidote to bad decision-making is learning to forgive. Receiving God's forgiveness, forgiving myself, and forgiving others are crucial to recovery. When we pray this simple prayer, "Father in heaven, teach me to pray," the breakthrough begins. His Word teaches us how to pray. Here are three things I have found helpful: First, never make God a lesser priority. He must be our number one. Second, we should be humble and recognize how blessed we are. We have so much when we could easily have so much less. And third, be grateful and remember the times we have had less.

Prayer is a lifestyle. Let us not use it merely as an emergency contact. God wants us to experience so much more than living from emergency to emergency.

Make no mistake about the cost of Calvary, where salvation was freely given, the love of God manifested itself, and our loving Jesus died so we may be forgiven. If we are faithful, we will soon live with Him eternally in glory. My friends, what a cost! There is no greater love!

Edna Thomas Taylor

---

* John Bowring, "In the Cross of Christ I Glory," 1825, public domain.

May 1

Simplifying Life

He also brought me out into an open place;
He rescued me, because He delighted in me.
—Psalm 18:19, NASB

*Commit your works to the L*ORD*,*
And your plans will be established.
—Proverbs 16:3, NASB

Several years ago, toward the end of winter, our daughter said, "It is now time to simplify!" She had a house ready for us to move into. At the time, my husband was seventy-two, and I was two years short of seventy. We graciously accepted her offer and listed our house for sale. It did not take long for depression to overtake me at the thought of having to leave my flower garden, fruit trees, and the elegant home where we had raised our children. It had been home for twenty-six years!

One morning at breakfast, I sat facing the window and saw the peach trees in full bloom. The magnolia trees were sprouting their buds and would soon be filled with flowers. Immediately, I said, "Thank You, Lord, for here I am feeling depressed as I look back, but You are giving me a better hope for the future." Ellen White writes, "It is now that our brethren should be cutting down their possessions instead of increasing them."* We should rather stop clinging and be joyful. Letting go is the answer. In truth, simplifying our lives is a form of spiritual cleansing. It softens the heart with gratitude, helps with being sensitive to the needs of others, and makes the world a better place.

God's Word, our standard for truth, admonishes us, "Lay not up for yourselves treasures upon earth, where moth and rust doth corrupt, and where thieves break through and steal: But lay up for yourselves treasures in heaven, where neither moth nor rust doth corrupt, and where thieves do not break through nor steal: For where your treasure is, there will your heart be also" (Matthew 6:19–21, KJV). And King Solomon wisely counsels, "Above all else, guard your heart, for everything you do flows from it" (Proverbs 4:23, NIV).

Now is the time to simplify. Let us let go of our many possessions—and cling to Jesus instead and to the promise He gives us of a better hope for the future!

Edna Bacate Domingo

---

* Ellen G. White, *Counsels on Stewardship* (Washington, DC: Review and Herald®, 1940), 59.

May 2

Just a Little Backpack

Bear one another's burdens, and so fulfill the law of Christ.
—Galatians 6:2, NKJV

Last May I was blessed to hike the Grand Canyon from rim to rim—something I have always wanted to do. It is over twenty-five miles of amazing scenery, steep ups and downs, and all the challenges that a desert canyon can bring in late spring in Arizona, United States of America.

We started off at about four o'clock in the morning and were joined by at least a hundred other brave hikers who had the same mission in mind—to reach the other side before dark. We made a beautiful, spiraling parade of headlamps down the side of the canyon through the wee hours of the morning. After taking a side hike to Ribbon Falls, we made it down through the floor of the canyon during the hottest part of the day, experiencing temperatures of nearly a hundred degrees. We took frequent breaks, refilled our water bottles at filling stations, and pushed on. The heat was starting to affect me, though, and I had not been able to eat much for hours. Then I made the mistake of putting a vitamin-based powder into my water. At the last stop before the final steep three miles, I started to feel extremely nauseated. My legs were cramping, and I had to stop every few hundred feet. My friend patiently waited with me while her athletic husband took her son up to our exit point at the top of the North Rim, which was still about a mile ahead of us.

Every step that I took required more energy than I could muster as I fought off heat exhaustion and more nausea. Right then, my friend's husband reappeared and offered to take my backpack, a seemingly simple thing as it weighed only a few pounds. But for me, at that moment, it seemed like an angel had come and given me wings! What was normally a small burden to bear felt like the weight of the world because of all the other challenges I was facing. Having someone relieve me of it made all the difference, and I was able to push forward to meet my husband, who was waiting for me at the top.

I was reminded how the little things that we do for people may not seem like much at all, but they might just be the things that allow them to tackle the much bigger things that they are struggling with. Let us look for even the little things to lighten someone's load. It might just make all the difference!

Nicole Mattson

May 3

God Is in the Details

For his eyes are upon the ways of man, and he seeth all his goings.
—Job 34:21, KJV

I was only twelve years old when I left the church. The years passed quickly, and at the age of seventeen, I started a computer programming course on Saturday mornings. The classes were held just in front of the Seventh-day Adventist Church. Seeing the church again, I felt a little nostalgic and started to miss my childhood.

I picked up my Bible and started to read Genesis. The story of Joseph moved me, but when I read Joshua, I could not accept how a God of love could order the killing of everyone, including women, children, and even animals. I stopped reading. I thought I was better than God!

Months passed. One day I decided to clean my house. There was a closet in which my father kept the church literature. Sitting on the floor, I picked up all the books and magazines and started to organize them. One book caught my eye. Its cover was blue—my favorite color. I decided to read it. It was called *Patriarchs and Prophets* by Ellen White. After I had finished reading it, my mind opened, and everything was clear. I finally understood that God is love. Despite my new understanding of God's love, I did not go back to church.

There was a dance in town, and some friends and I planned to go. I needed a new outfit. Although I favored wearing pants, a beautiful blue dress on display in a store window caught my eye. I fell in love with it, but I knew it was too expensive for my father to buy. I came up with a plan. I told him that if he would buy the dress for me to go to the dance, then I would promise to go to church the following Sabbath. He agreed. That night at the dance, the Holy Spirit was at work in my heart. I did not feel like dancing. The Holy Spirit was opening my eyes, and I began to see the futility of my lifestyle. The allure of the world's pleasures was broken. The following Saturday I kept my word and went to church, and I never stopped going.

I am amazed by how God works in such a personal way. Twice He used my favorite color to get my attention. No detail of our lives is unimportant to God. Whatever you may be living through at this moment, my friend, I know that the God who created the universe knows every detail of your life, and He is working to draw you closer to His heart of love.

Isabel Cristina de Almeida

May 4

Run to Jesus

God is our refuge and strength, a very present help in trouble.
—Psalm 46:1, KJV

My friend Betty gave me great advice one day when I felt far away from God. She said, "When you have strong feelings pulling you away from your trust in God, *run* to Him in prayer, read His Word, and find fellowship with other believers."

Betty spoke these words at a time when I was struggling with discouragement and depression. It felt like God had abandoned me. But Betty reminded me that God has promised He will never leave us nor forsake us (see Hebrews 13:5). He is always right by our side, no matter where we are, no matter how we are feeling.

But still, waves of despair threatened to overwhelm me. My emotions were pulling me further away from God's presence. That is when Betty's straight talk helped me to remember Bible truth and allowed me to choose faith over my feelings.

Because we believe in God, the enemy will try to lead us astray and make us feel far away from God by whatever means he can find. Getting us to trust how we feel over what we clearly know to be biblically true is one of his sneakiest attacks. He tries to convince us that we are too far gone to turn back to God. But that is a lie. The Bible reminds us that God is always waiting to welcome us back home with open arms. In fact, He runs to us and meets us on the way, just like the father of the prodigal son.

When we feel the woes of this world are too overwhelming, we can open our Bible and claim Jesus' promise to us: "I have told you these things, so that in me you may have peace. In this world you will have trouble. But take heart! I have overcome the world" (John 16:33, NIV). When we feel like we are buried in our sins, far beyond God's reach, His Word says that God's mercies are new every morning. Great is His faithfulness (see Lamentations 3:22, 23)!

When it feels as though our sins are too numerous for God to forgive, the Bible tells us that "as far as the east is from the west, so far has He removed our transgressions from us" (Psalm 103:12, NKJV). If you are in the depths of despair, just remember the Savior will never let you go. Run to Jesus! He is your refuge and strength. Trust yourself to His love.

Alexis A. Goring

May 5

The Value of Forgiveness

Have mercy upon me, O God, . . .
According to the multitude of Your tender mercies,
Blot out my transgressions.
—Psalm 51:1, NKJV

Our general understanding of forgiveness is that it is a process whereby we have a change of heart toward someone who has hurt us. In the legal field, the word *forgiveness* is synonymous with such words as *pardon, absolution, exoneration,* and *mercy*. However, the offender must admit their wrongdoing and is often required to pay a fine and/or accept restrictions before they will be granted forgiveness by the civil or criminal justice system.

Not so with Christ, our Advocate and Savior. He stood in the breach for us sinners. He paid the sin price on Calvary so we can stand before God the Father as clean and sinless.

When it comes to forgiving our fellow human beings, we lack the ability, and even the desire, to forgive and forget, unlike the father in the parable of the prodigal son (Luke 15:11–32). When the father saw his son coming some distance off, his only hesitation was to make sure this was truly his lost son. The boy was most likely unkempt, thin, and dressed in beggars' clothes—unrecognizable to most but not to his loving father, who immediately forgave the young man's foolish and wanton behavior. He ordered that his son be fully restored to his rightful position in the family, clothed him in the finest garments, gave him the ring bearing the family's insignia, and organized a welcome-home party.

While this is sometimes a difficult lesson for siblings and others to process, it is a lesson that Christ intends each of us to learn. Unlike earthly justice systems, God's abundant mercy and grace toward us know no bounds. He wipes the record clean and gives us a fresh start. No wonder King David could write about the joy of forgiveness (see Psalm 32). David is an example of someone who sinned greatly, repented sincerely, and lived to enjoy the extraordinary blessings of God's forgiveness.

My friends, the act of forgiveness is a greater blessing to the one who forgives than the one who is forgiven, even when there is no reconciliation. Do you need to forgive someone as sincerely and completely as God has forgiven you? He will help you. Ask Him today.

Avis Mae Rodney

May 6

Divided Attention

"A son honors his father, and a slave his master. If I am a father, where is the honor due me? If I am a master, where is the respect due me?" says the Lord Almighty.
—Malachi 1:6, NIV

Sometimes I find myself treating God the same, or even worse, than the way I resent others treating me, especially close family members.

I woke up this morning annoyed, sad, and ready to retaliate against a family member for a repeated offense. While I had been away traveling, I had expected that a specific family member would give me their time and undivided attention during our phone conversations. However, that is not what happened. What I got instead were short calls punctuated with lots of interruptions.

As I started my morning worship today, my mind was busy multitasking. While part of my thoughts was tuned into having my devotions, at the same time, another part of me focused on forming a retaliation plan against the guilty party. When I began to sing a song that was meaningful to me, I found myself misreading certain words. My mind was all over the place. When I realized what was going on, I made an extra effort to sing the song, but I failed repeatedly to get it right.

Then God spoke these words to my heart: "You have been complaining of not getting the undivided attention you longed for from family members, but here you are, doing the same thing and not giving Me your full attention during your worship time."

This was such a powerful wake-up call. I took a moment to repent and thanked God for His love and patience toward me. I also expressed gratitude to Him for allowing me to experience the lack of attention, for I could now see and acknowledge my behavior toward Him.

My sisters, I know that many of you will identify with me in this story, or at least, the part where my mind was all over the place during my devotions. So, I want to challenge you: will you join me and purpose in your heart to give God your undivided attention when you approach Him in worship? Let us also search our hearts the next time someone hurts us and ask God if there is a deeper spiritual lesson He wants us to learn.

Thank You, Lord, for extending Your grace and mercy toward us. You are awesome!

Evelyne Izeogu

May 7

A Few Minutes

"Then the kingdom of heaven shall be likened to ten virgins who took their lamps and went out to meet the bridegroom."
—Matthew 25:1, NKJV

After spending a week in Toronto, Canada, seeing old friends, visiting my high school, and enjoying the many attractions the city offers, my family was ready to go home. It was a sunny day and a great day for flying. We knew our departure time and what time we needed to be at the airport. We were only five minutes from the airport, and we did not anticipate any problems.

We woke up that morning with time to spare. There was just one more thing we had to do before we started to pack. I am too ashamed to tell you what that one more thing was. It is embarrassing because now, in hindsight, I know that it could have been avoided. Needless to say, what we thought would be an easy task did not go as planned. In the end, we left the hotel later than we had expected and had to navigate our way through an unfamiliar airport. You see, although I had been to Toronto several times before, I had never needed to drive. Someone picked me up, drove me around, and dropped me off. Not this time.

This time I had to learn to navigate Toronto for myself. Instead of going straight to terminal 3, we found ourselves at terminal 1 and had to take the tram over to terminal 3. This cost us valuable time. We hurried to the check-in desk only to learn that we had missed the boarding call by a few minutes. Oh no! The plane was still there, but we were not allowed to get on it. In all our years of travel, this had never happened to us. It really stung!

This experience reminds me of the story Jesus told about the ten virgins. Five had extra oil and went to the wedding feast. Five neglected to make preparations. "When the foolish virgins reached the banqueting hall, they received an unexpected denial. The master of the feast declared, 'I know you not.' They were left standing without, in the empty street, in the blackness of the night."* The parable offers a word to the wise: be ready. This was a hard lesson to learn because we missed our flight, but I am certain it will not happen again! My friends, let us not miss out on that final boarding call. A few minutes late could cost eternity.

Dana M. Bean

---

* Ellen G. White, *Christ's Object Lessons* (Washington, DC: Review and Herald®, 1969), 406.

May 8

Grateful for Small Blessings

"Whoever can be trusted with very little can also be trusted with much, and whoever is dishonest with very little will also be dishonest with much."
—Luke 16:10, NIV

In everything give thanks; for this is the will of God in Christ Jesus for you.
—1 Thessalonians 5:18, NKJV

As I sat quietly relaxing on the compound of the City Hall and Arts Centre in Hamilton, Bermuda, I learned a humble lesson on doing what I can with what I have, where I am.

If you are curious to know who my teacher was, I would have to tell you that it was some local birds. The timing was perfect because the groundskeeper was tending the lawns at the city hall, and the water sprinkler was on.

It had been a hot summer day, and the birds took the opportunity to get a cool shower from the sprinkler. There was still plenty of water left for them to cool their thirst. Watching this scene unfold before me taught me many things. While we might well need to aspire to greater things, we owe it to ourselves to use whatever is available to us in the present moment. If we are not able to use what we have now, what guarantee do we have that when greater blessings are poured out, we will have the capacity to handle them and realize the real value of the opportunity? If we can be grateful for the small blessings, then when larger blessings come our way, we will be able to receive and accept them.

So, today, my dear sisters, what small blessings are you ignoring while you wait for bigger blessings? Are you ignoring the fact that you have loving family members who care for you while you wait to start your own family in the future? Are you aware that you have enough in the pantry to make a delicious meal while you wait for funds to go shopping at the grocery store? And could it be that you are ignoring the fact that you are actually in a good job that allows you religious liberty to worship, even though you desire a promotion or a better job?

God watches to see how grateful we are for the small blessings He sends our way. Are we fully enjoying His favor today and trusting Him to send the greater blessings when He sees fit? Let us give Him thanks for everything, and He will take care of tomorrow.

Althea Y. Boxx

May 9

The Burden Bearer

*Praise be to the Lord, to God our Savior,
who daily bears our burdens.*
—Psalm 68:19, NIV

It was a day like any other when I met one of my former colleagues while walking downtown. I greeted her, and we exchanged some pleasantries and shared some old memories. She gladly remembered my faith, and encouraged by her good memories, I invited her to visit our church the next Sabbath. She came, and though she seemed to enjoy the service, she never came back.

Some years later, our paths crossed again. While we were busy catching up, she took me by surprise when she asked me, "Do you remember when I came to your church, and you asked me if you could hold my baby for a while? At that moment, I felt like a huge burden had been lifted from my shoulders as my baby passed from me into your arms! It seemed as though all my burdens were lifted up by an Omnipotent Power. How much I enjoyed that moment!"

I was amazed to hear her words, and I felt humbled by such an unexpected affirmation. I admitted sincerely I could not remember that gesture, even though I really love children, especially babies. It has always been a joy to cradle them in my arms, to feel their softness and the coziness of being close to them. After a while, as we continued to chat, my foggy memory recalled her holding a baby boy in her arms but nothing more.

"I still vividly remember that feeling of unprecedented deliverance of my burdens," she repeated. "And it was you who made me feel so relieved."

I told her that I did not even remember doing such a thing, but I took the opportunity to share with her that God, who loves her very much, had used me to extend His love toward her.

If the simple act of holding a tired mother's baby had exerted such a mighty influence, we would do well to daily follow the counsel to "find time to comfort some other heart, to bless with a kind, cheering word someone who is battling with temptation and maybe with affliction. In thus blessing another with cheering, hopeful words, pointing him to the Burden Bearer, you may unexpectedly find peace, happiness, and consolation yourself."*

Our Burden Bearer invites us to follow His example and bless others with His love.

Viorica Avrămiea

---

* Ellen G. White, *Our High Calling* (Washington, DC: Review and Herald®, 1961), 64.

May 10

The Certainty of God's Plan

*Your eyes saw my unformed substance;
in your book were written, every one of them,
the days that were formed for me,
when as yet there was none of them.*
—Psalm 139:16, ESV

Memories of the events on the day my son Jordan was born still send a shiver through me. His delivery was normal, without any complications. After the nurses were finished with him, they brought him to my room and placed him on my chest. He did not eat much, and after a while, we both fell asleep. Before I drifted off, I felt impressed to pull up the rails on the bed, so I did.

I am not sure how long I slept. I remember opening my eyes, feeling confused, and thinking, *Where is Jordan?* He was no longer on my chest. *The nurse must have taken him*, I thought, even as my panicked mind raced while my eyes searched the room for answers. The icy chill of fear hit me when I realized the room held no answers. Suddenly, I sensed, rather than heard, a voice say, *Look over the left side of the bed.* My heart froze with terror. There he was—caught between the rail and the bed, dangling from his blanket as it slowly unraveled. In a daze, I felt myself slide off the bed onto my knees and slip my hands under his tiny body. I caught him before his blanket had fully unraveled. He was sucking on his thumb, still fast asleep, oblivious to the danger around him and unaware of how much Heaven was focused on him at this moment. Between fervent whispers of "Thank You, God" and grateful tears, I gently wrapped him back in his warm cocoon and held him close until the nurse came to take him to the nursery.

Fast-forward to this past winter. Jordan is thirty years old today. I have watched him grow and mature into a remarkable young man and have not missed a chance to tell him that God was present at his birth and wants him to live. God planned his existence before he was conceived, and his life is filled with God-designed possibilities. Surely, God was in my hospital room that day, as He has always been in our lives; He made it clear that He has a plan for Jordan.

Some would say what happened in my hospital room that night was pure luck. But I say the sequence of events was too precise to be mere coincidence. Only He knows the value of those whom He creates for His purpose, those for whom He died and now lives. He is God, and He has a plan for everyone! What is His plan for you today?

Joan Dougherty-Mornan

May 11

Mama's Legacy

*Do not neglect to do good and to share what you have,
for such sacrifices are pleasing to God.*
—Hebrews 13:16, ESV

One bright Sunday morning on the beautiful island of Jamaica, when I was about ten, my mama was busy in the kitchen, humming her favorite song as I helped her. When the food was ready, she arranged the dining table in typical English fashion, adding a beautiful cloth napkin—a setting fit for a king. I was a bit confused. Were we having company for breakfast? If so, I hoped it was one of my aunts because I knew my cousins would also be coming.

When everything was ready, she went outside, and I followed, wondering where she was going. Some ladies who lived nearby also wondered and asked, "Miss Rema, where are you going?" She just smiled and said she would be back soon. I tagged along behind her.

Mama went up and down the street, searching for someone. Eventually, she came upon a dirty, ragged homeless man. We children were afraid of him, though he never seemed to notice us. He was lost in his own world. Mama bent down and said something to him. When she was done, he got up, straightened himself up, and proceeded to follow her. I stared in shock! Where was Mama taking this dirty homeless man? Straight to our home!

The neighbors scattered in fright as she took him inside, sat him down at the dining table, and waited on him. She served him roasted breadfruit, ackee, and codfish. She poured him a cup of hot Milo tea and gave him a bowl of fresh fruit. He ate his breakfast and asked for seconds. When he was finished, he sat still for a few minutes, then quietly stood up and left. Mama hummed her song while she cleared the table and washed the dishes. A few of the ladies at the door asked, "Miss Rema, you're keeping the dishes that the homeless man just used?"

With her radiant smile, she answered, "And why not? He is God's child, isn't he?" Then she came out and sat in her chair on the veranda as if nothing out of the ordinary had happened.

Mama's legacy lives on in the lives of her children as we fulfill the Lord's commission, "Inasmuch as ye have done it unto one of the least of these my brethren, ye have done it unto me" (Matthew 25:40, KJV). My friends, may we all share the love of Jesus with others as we wait for His return! Happy Mother's Day!

Jannett Maurine Myrie

May 12

The Invisible Door

*For the angel of the Lord is a guard;
he surrounds and defends all who fear him.*
—Psalm 34:7, NLT

When I was a little girl in Rio Grande do Sul, Brazil, I had an experience that strengthened my faith and confirmed that God's promises never fail.

We were a large family, and because of scarce resources and financial hardship, my mother sent me to work in another family's house, taking care of their children and helping with the household chores. In this way, I was able to afford to go to school.

My boss developed some liver issues due to heavy drinking, so the family called in some people to perform a ritual at the house to get rid of the health problems and the evil forces causing them. They met together in the living room, and then each of them walked through every room in the house as they performed the strange ritual, claiming it would take the evil away.

When they came toward the kitchen where I was washing dishes, they could not enter. Three times they tried to walk into the room, and all three times they fell back as if they had hit a glass door.

One of the men told the lady of the house that there was a greater spirit in the kitchen and that they were not allowed to enter while I was there. She then made me move to another room, and they were finally able to walk into the kitchen. Even though I was too young and innocent to fully understand what had happened there that day, I wondered why, after such a clear demonstration of God's power, my employers did not ask about my God instead of submitting their family to a lesser power.

As I grew up in the knowledge of God, I felt so grateful because I knew He had sent His angels to protect me from Satan's forces that day, even though I had not known to ask Him for His protection. I cherish this special promise: "If you remain faithful even when facing death, I will give you the crown of life" (Revelation 2:10, NLT).

Aren't you glad you follow this loving God? He promises that if we remain faithful, whatever the cost, He will send His angels to be with us. Our God is faithful, and His love endures forever.

Eva Cleonice Kopitar

May 13

A Perfect Example

Then the LORD *said to Satan, "Have you considered my servant Job? There is no one on earth like him; he is blameless and upright, a man who fears God and shuns evil."*
—Job 1:8, NIV

Everyone remembers the story of Job and the expression *the patience of Job.* I have read the book of Job many times, but I gained a new perspective just recently. The third quarter Sabbath School quarterly for 2022 focused on the theme "In the Crucible With Christ," and Job's experience was an obvious example that was included. As I reread chapters 1 and 2 of Job, something new jumped out at me. It was God who mentioned Job in His conversation with Satan, and He was boasting about Job! I wondered whether God would ever have reason to boast about me. That sobering thought led me to examine Job's life more intensely. I wanted to see the attributes that God admired.

First, God admired Job's lifestyle, which prompted Him to claim there was "no one like him on earth" (Job 1:8, NIV). Job was one of a kind. He did not follow the trends of his era, and he was content to pursue a close relationship with God, even though that made him very different from others. In God's sight, Job was unique; he stood out.

God admired Job's blameless life and his upright standing in the community. What a distinction to be considered blameless before God! Job met all of God's criteria while upholding God's principles and requirements, and he demonstrated his fear of God through his love and obedience. Job deliberately turned away from evil because he understood that evil was diametrically opposed to God and would negatively affect their relationship.

Satan countered by claiming Job's perfect life was a facade—an act in response to God's blessing. But even after Job lost everything, God observed, "And still he holds fast to his integrity, although you incited Me against him, to destroy him without cause" (Job 2:3, NKJV).

I want to be like Job: unique, blameless, and upright, a daughter of God who loves Him and turns away from evil. I want my God to boast about me. Sisters, wouldn't you like our heavenly Father to boast about you? Let us strive to know God as Job did, to follow Him and walk in obedience. May we be unique, blameless, and upright women who fear God and turn away from evil.

Valerie Knowles Combie

May 14

Carjacked!

*Though I walk through the valley of the shadow of death,
I will fear no evil;
For You are with me.*
—Psalm 23:4, NKJV

One Friday afternoon around noon, I left the office where I worked as a candidate attorney to consult with a client at the Goodwood prison. I tend to be directionally challenged and always use Google Maps to help me find the court. I climbed into my car, grateful it was Friday.

I drove, following the directions, oblivious to the fact that Google had chosen the shortest route to the court—a route that would take me through the notorious and extremely dangerous Nyanga township. Suddenly, I found myself in a very peculiar situation. I was stuck between a taxi stand and a row of shacks. The cars in front of me were not moving, and there were taxis everywhere. While trying to figure out the predicament I was in, I heard banging around my right ear. A brick broke the driver's side window. It happened very quickly, and I became dizzy.

Dazed and still trying to figure out what was happening, I saw a hand reach through the broken window, then another hand holding a gun. Two young men pulled me out of the car without a word and took my keys and my cell phone. I did not resist. I raised my hands and told them to take everything. One tried to get into the car but realized he would not be able to drive away due to the congestion. They panicked and quickly walked away with my keys and phone.

Though they had gone, I was alone without any way to leave, while a crowd of people stood around staring at me as if I had come from another planet. I knew I was still in danger. Then I saw a man who caught my attention. His eyes looked so kind and peaceful. He looked straight at me and said, "Sissy, there are your keys. Pick them up and go." I looked at the ground, and there were my keys, a few feet from the car.

I quickly started the car and noticed those kind eyes still looking at me. "Thank you," I said. He nodded and said, "Go!" Suddenly, the road cleared, and I headed to the police station for help. When I was in the valley of death, God came through for me. Through this stranger—this angel?—I felt God's presence and knew I was not alone. I do not know what valleys you are going through, but be comforted, sister, for God is never far from those who trust Him.

Deborah Matshaya

May 15

Never Alone

*"The Lord himself goes before you and will be with you;
he will never leave you nor forsake you. Do not be afraid; do not be discouraged."*
—Deuteronomy 31:8, NIV

After the passing of my husband of over fifty years, I keenly felt the loss of his companionship. On my morning walks, I sang songs, such as "O Let Me Walk With Thee" and "I Must Have the Saviour With Me." The lyrics not only eased my loneliness but also expressed my need for God.

One morning I went to Bangkok, Thailand, which was about 93 miles (150 kilometers) from the university where I taught. A private company provided van services to the school and charged 30 Thai baht for the drive from the campus to the station in Muak Lek and an additional 100 Thai baht from Muak Lek to Bangkok.

On my return journey, I found the waiting room at the Bangkok station unusually empty. I walked directly to the Muak Lek counter to purchase my ticket, and the lady looked up, smiled, and asked, "For two people?" Surprised, I glanced around and, seeing no one else, answered, "No, just one." I paid the fare, proceeded to the van, and took one of two empty seats behind the driver. Just before departure, the driver came through to take a head count.

I stated, *"Michan"* ("Mission," as the school was known) and gave him my fare. A puzzled look crossed his face as he looked at the money and walked to his seat. He returned after a minute and said, *"Ajarn* [Teacher], to Michan is thirty baht."

"Yes," I replied. "I gave you thirty."

"For two people, sixty baht."

I looked around to see whether there was anyone from the school whom he could have mistaken as my companion. I found no familiar face. "I am one person, one passenger," I clarified. Along the way, he picked up more passengers. No one took the one seat beside me. I wondered why.

I shared the story later with my daughter. "Oh, Mom," she exclaimed, "you should have paid for two passengers. Who knows? It could have been your angel they saw."

I agreed. It was a slow realization for me, but on that day, God used a ticket vendor, a van driver, a van full of passengers, and an empty seat to teach me that He will always be with me.

Bienvisa Ladion Nebres

May 16

Wrong Assumptions

"Do not judge by the outward appearance, but judge with righteous judgment."
—John 7:24, NASB

I wore many hats while our children attended Christian schools located on a college campus near our home. As their chauffeur, I dropped them off at the elementary school or academy, allowing myself a few moments to reach my office on campus. Afternoons and evenings became more of a challenge. Leaving my work, I picked up our children and then raced home to cook the evening meal while monitoring homework and music practice and doing laundry. Many afternoons and evenings included the extra commute back to the campus with a wait for band, orchestra, and chorale practice, plus editorial work on the school paper. Somewhere in an already hectic schedule, I was also the bookkeeper for my husband's business, a seamstress, and a homemaker.

One evening our commute proved to be out of the ordinary. We stopped at the only gas station on campus to refill my car's nearly empty tank, and I asked our oldest son to put gasoline in the tank for me. What a relief that he was old enough to help in this way. I could finally relax for a few moments! I saw our son go into the station to pay the attendant and then noticed in my rearview mirror that a car had driven up behind me. Assuming we had finished filling our tank, I decided it would be thoughtful to allow the next vehicle to fill up as well. Quickly moving my car forward, I felt a hard jerk from the rear end of my vehicle. Looking into my rearview mirror again, I was shocked to see the gas hose flying into the air, spewing gasoline everywhere!

The owner and several other men realized I had not completely pulled the hose from the gas pump, and they raced to hook up the hose and wipe up the gasoline. About twenty years later, I heard about a similar situation on the national news, but the results were much worse: the hose had broken from the gas pump, causing a serious fire.

How could I have caused such a serious chain of events? Simple! I had assumed something without all the facts. Such assumptions can be dangerous. God has warned us, "Do not judge according to appearance" (John 7:24, NKJV). We cannot read the human heart, so how can we make assumptions about another's life issues? Following God's word of caution could save someone's life and reputation.

Dottie Barnett

May 17

Lessons From Babies

God chose things despised by the world, things counted as nothing at all, and used them to bring to nothing what the world considers important. As a result, no one can ever boast in the presence of God.
—1 Corinthians 1:28, 29, NLT

While living in South Korea as a missionary for almost thirteen years, I was blessed to have three grandchildren. For the first time, I experienced what my mom said was one of two pleasures she received in her later years—serving the Lord and the joy of being a grandmother.

One day I was keeping my little Jo'Elle, who was less than two years old at the time. She was bilingual and spoke English and Korean. She decided to wear my toaster cover on her head, thinking it was a hat; she called it a hat in Korean. It was so cute and funny, and I told her mom, my daughter, all about it. We had a good laugh over it, and then my daughter explained to me it was not a toaster cover. Now it was my turn to be shocked. I had purchased it, thinking what a great job I had done, coordinating everything in my kitchen with the exact fabric and print.

Me'Chelle said, "Mom, that is a tissue-box covering." Then we both had another laugh. It was my turn to have made a mistake. It had started with a baby thinking she was wearing a hat, then to me thinking I had bought a toaster cover, only to be corrected and told I had bought a tissue-box cover. Isn't it funny how God uses a child to teach us lessons in life?

I am reminded of the many stories in the Bible about a child who was given responsibility at a young age. For instance, Josiah became king at eight years old and was responsible for leading an entire nation. For thirty-one years, he did his best to lead his people back to God. The Bible records that he did what was right in the Lord's eyes and walked in the ways of his ancestor David, not deviating from it even a bit to the right or left. The story is found in 2 Chronicles 34.

Long before Josiah, Solomon wrote that "even a child is known by his doings, whether his work be pure, and whether it be right" (Proverbs 20:11, KJV). Yes, even children can teach us important lessons in life.

Let us remember we can all learn and gain wisdom by listening—sometimes, even from the mouths of babes.

Bessie Russell Haynes

May 18

The Wrong Turn

All we like sheep have gone astray;
We have turned, every one, to his own way.
—Isaiah 53:6, NKJV

We climbed into the van in a hurry, hoping to make it in time for the hour of worship at the Waterman Seventh-day Adventist Church. It was Labor Day weekend, and we were in Loma Linda, California, United States of America, visiting family and hoping to meet some college friends at church. Before we left, we were given directions to turn left on Wier Road and then continue until we reached Waterman Avenue, where the church is located.

As we drove on, Weir Road was nowhere to be seen. Somehow, we had taken a wrong turn. In the rush to leave, no one had listened carefully to the directions. Perhaps each of us thought the other was paying attention. Nevertheless, we kept driving, hoping we would eventually reach Waterman Avenue.

After a few minutes of wandering (this was before the days of GPS devices), we called for directions to Waterman Avenue and the church. Thankful for the convenience of cell phones, we eventually made it to the church, albeit fifteen minutes late!

We are all traveling. Our destination is heaven. Sometimes we take the wrong turn, but we still keep going, confident that somehow, we will eventually find the right avenue.

Have we missed an important piece of information because we were not paying attention or depending on somebody else to listen to the instructions while we were preoccupied with trivial matters of this world?

Taking the wrong turn has many consequences. We waste time and energy and become frustrated. Some may enjoy the fleeting pleasures on the way, but now is the time to turn back, for we cannot be late for our appointment with God.

Have you taken the wrong turn in your life's journey? Look for directions from a reliable GPS—the Bible—and the map to salvation. The psalmist writes in Psalm 119:105, "Thy word is a lamp unto my feet, and a light unto my path" (KJV). Use the "cell phone" of prayer and connect with the One who not only knows the way—He is the only Way. Jesus said, "I am the way, the truth, and the life: no man cometh unto the Father, but by me" (John 14:6, KJV).

Evelyn Porteza Tabingo

May 19

Our Identity in Christ

"I will be found by you," declares the Lord.
—Jeremiah 29:14, NIV

"Diane, twenty ladies from the church are going to a ladies' night out event sponsored by a Christian radio station. One lady canceled. Do you want to go?" my friend Karen asked one January. We do not see each other often, and it sounded like a good time to connect.

I asked, "What are they doing at this ladies' night out?"

She shared, "It's a dinner, and there will be speakers from the radio station."

I took a leap of faith and said, "All right, sign me up!"

At the event, one of the speakers shared a story about a day when she was hurting and feeling lost. She sought out a bench in a quiet place. As she journaled, she found a passage she liked in Jeremiah 29:12–14: " 'Then you will call on me and come and pray to me, and I will listen to you. You will seek me and find me when you seek me with all your heart. I will be found by you,' declares the Lord." (NIV). She emphasized the phrase, "I will be found by you." It made her think about who she is in Christ. She started a list of identity statements. Then she shared what she found that day: I am found; I am yours; I am loved; I am made pure; I have life; I can breathe; I am healed; and I am free. It reminded me of the importance of knowing who we are in Christ.

Many years ago, while working in Women's Ministries at the local conference level, I learned that it is helpful to write these statements out. It is a good exercise to erase the negative tapes that play in our heads—things we have heard from others who think they know who we are. If we know who we are, we can have confidence in God's purpose for us.

For example, in Christ, I am not condemned (Romans 8:1).

In Christ, I am made alive (Ephesians 2:5).

This is a good thing to do in our own personal worship time. As we read God's Word, He will help us discover our identity in Christ Jesus. Try it today. Write out: "In Christ, I am _____." As you read from your Bible, ask God to show you how to fill in the blank. Before long, you will know exactly, from His Word, who you are in Christ.

Diane Pestes

May 20

God Called Me Home

He hath sent me to heal the brokenhearted.
—Luke 4:18, KJV

I was born into a Christian home with loving parents who taught me the ways of God. I fell in love with Jesus, and at the tender age of eight, I wanted to get baptized. That was considered too young, so I had to wait until I was twelve years old. I was a very independent and confident child, so it did not matter that I was different from the rest of the children at school. I loved the Lord, and that was all that mattered to me. My mother, bless her, invested in me and sent me to piano lessons. I played for the church, and this gave me purpose.

My relationship with Jesus grew as I spent time reading and studying the Scriptures along with the Spirit of Prophecy. Jesus used me to bless the church through singing, playing music, teaching Sabbath School, and speaking on Women's Days. It was a joy and a delight to serve my Jesus. I was active in the youth programs, attended youth camps, visited many churches, and extended my circle of friends. My relationship with Jesus grew strong over the years. I learned to trust Jesus with everything in my life, and my life goal was to become a schoolteacher.

I met a handsome young man, and we were married and blessed with two beautiful boys. Though they are now grown men, they are still the joy of my life. I continued to serve the church for many years.

But the enemy had been silently sowing seeds of doubt in my mind for a long time. I left the church and vowed never to go back. How did that happen? Overwhelmed with struggles at home, at church, and at work, I sank lower and lower. It was a very painful time. While I wanted Jesus, I did not want the church. As I drifted, the Light of Jesus became dimmer, but it never went out. I continued to sink into the depths of despair until . . .

Jesus called this prodigal to come home. Someone, prompted by the Holy Spirit, sent me a video on the Sabbath. It reminded me of who I am and to whom I belong. I am a child of God and belong among His people. I no longer stand at the front of the church to inspire and encourage, but He has placed in my heart the desire to reach one soul at a time. He has sent me to heal the brokenhearted. As Jesus reached out to me, I now reach out to others. The work is the Lord's. In humility, I trust Him to work within me and through me day by day. What a Savior!

Jennifer Billings

May 21

An Epiphany

And God said, Let there be lights in the firmament of the heaven to divide the day from the night; and let them be for signs, and for seasons, and for days and years: and let them be for lights in the firmament of the heaven to give light upon the earth: and it was so. And God made two great lights; the greater light to rule the day, and the lesser light to rule the night: he made the stars also.
—Genesis 1:14–16, KJV

I woke up early one morning to pray, and while in prayer, my mind was drawn to reflect on the power of the sun, which had just begun to pierce the eastern sky in all its glory and splendor.

The sun pierces the darkness and provides light so that I do not have to grope and stumble in the dark. It makes it possible for me to find my way along a path. The sun's rays provide warmth for plants and animals and are vital for healthy growth and development. Sunlight enhances photosynthesis, which is necessary for plants to produce food. It is an essential link in the food chain. We certainly could not live without the sun.

Just as we cannot live without sunshine, we cannot live without God's Son. He was the One who called it into existence. The *Son* created the sun for the benefit of all His creatures. He lives in heaven but is a very present Friend through the ministry of the Holy Spirit. He said of Himself, "I am the light of the world: he that followeth me shall not walk in darkness, but shall have the light of life" (John 8:12, KJV).

The Son can penetrate down to our very bones and marrow. Even the smallest, seemingly innocuous pebble in my heart He points out as sin. If left unchecked, it will grow, multiply, and before long, consume me.

The Son helps us to expunge these character traits through the illuminating power of the Holy Spirit. Through His power, we can become new creatures in Christ Jesus. Old things are passed away, and everything is become new (see 2 Corinthians 5:17).

As we bask in the warmth and light of the sun, may the Lord help us to appreciate and experience the transforming power of the Son. "So if the Son sets you free, you are truly free" (John 8:36, NLT).

Kollis Salmon-Fairweather

May 22

Not of This World

"In him we live and move and exist."
—Acts 17:28, NLT

What does it mean to be a woman of God? It seems these days that being a Christian is almost taboo. The world we live in is constantly changing, developing and accepting new, ungodly ideologies almost daily. As a young woman growing into adulthood, trying to figure out who I am and my place in this world can be frustrating. It can get overwhelming.

Peer pressure is real. I feel the push and pull to do the opposite of what I know in my heart God has called me to do. We all want to belong. It is always a temptation to do what everyone else is doing so we can fit in.

I have had my share of being reckless and making poor choices. I have had a taste of being immersed in the secular world. But I am learning daily that these are not the things that a woman of God should be doing. And while the world tempts us to have some fun, the reality is that the world does not satisfy in any way at all. Living in and of the world is a constant struggle that leaves us always searching for more. It is true that this world is not our home. We will never feel entirely fulfilled living here.

God has placed women in this world for a special purpose. As each of us is unique, one of a kind, God calls each of us to a unique purpose. He has created some women to be homemakers, wives, mothers, and givers. Some He calls to serve as missionaries at home or abroad. Others He calls to be doctors, teachers—the callings and the gifts are endless.

It does not matter what He calls us to do because being women of God has more to do with who He calls us to be—His daughters. He wants us to see and understand that we are called to reflect Him and be His light in a hurting world. Being women of God means He calls us His own, and we are beautiful in His sight.

Being women of God means understanding that we are not called to conform to the standards of this world. Ours is a greater calling: "For we are His workmanship, created in Christ Jesus for good works, which God prepared beforehand that we should walk in them" (Ephesians 2:10, NKJV). As women of God, we find our greatest joy in loving and serving our Savior!

Erin Lambillotte

May 23

Those God Honors

"For those who honor Me I will honor."
—1 Samuel 2:30, NASB

God has no reason to honor humanity. It almost feels blasphemous to consider such a thought, yet when we reflect on the myriad ways He has honored humans, it is pretty amazing. He left heaven to endure this sinful earthly experience. He hung on a shameful, painful cross for a wretch like me. He showed mercy to the ungrateful Israelites and softened His heart upon hearing Moses' plea. He honors our simple requests and needs and even fulfills our wants as He sees fit. It has been so amazing to witness the miraculous way He has honored my two children.

It so happens that, unlike me, both of my children are athletically inclined. One day my nine-year-old son came home from school and informed me of a baseball league he wanted to join. We visited the office, signed up, and then realized that most of the practices and games were scheduled for Saturdays. Flashbacks kept surfacing of kids whose parents failed to put them in activities, fearful that they would be unsuccessful because they would not participate on the Sabbath. Not a few of these kids have lived with regret and even resentment because they felt they had "missed out on life" for being an Adventist.

I distinctly recall Pastor Aswin Somasundaram's discussion with me before my baptism. He told me that being an Adventist is not about what you *cannot* do but about what you *can* do!

I spoke to the coach and told him that my son would still join and benefit from the activities on any other day but the Sabbath. Well, the first few practices were on Tuesdays and Thursdays, and then the first game was scheduled for Sabbath, of course. *It rained all day*, and the game was postponed to the following Tuesday.

It is unbelievable but true that most of the games and practices that year were rescheduled to a weekday or even Sunday, and my son was able to participate in most games. He was grateful that God did that for him. He is now in high school, and on his first day on the team, he spoke to his coach and explained he would not participate on Sabbaths. It was amazing how the coach respected and appreciated his standing up for his beliefs. How vital it is to teach our children that when they honor God, He will honor them.

Caren Henry Broaster

May 24

Coming Out of Isolation

Not forsaking the assembling of ourselves together, as the manner of some is; but exhorting one another: and so much the more, as ye see the day approaching.
—Hebrews 10:25, KJV

The last three years have been challenging. After COVID-19 came into our lives, everything changed. We had to shut down our face-to-face ministry and go online. Sabbath School for kids disappeared. The Sabbath services went viral. Sabbath potlucks and fellowship were a thing of the past. The faces of individuals changed. Every smile was covered by a mask. People were often unrecognizable, except for their eyes. We greeted each other from six feet away with a nod or air fist bump. Gone were the warm hugs and handshakes on Sabbath morning as we greeted friends that we had not seen for a week. Individually, we became isolated from our sisters and brothers.

I am single and live alone with my two cats. After three years of being isolated, it has been difficult for me to get back into the habit of getting up early on Sabbath morning, getting dressed, and driving to church. I had gotten into the habit of going for a brisk Sabbath walk and coming home to watch church on my television. I did not dress up for three years. I did not have to drive to church on Sabbath morning or Wednesday night. I became really comfortable watching church in my pajamas in my bed with my snacks. I know I am not alone in this. Perhaps you have also experienced the same thing.

It has been challenging for me to change my habits after three years. I like a comfortable church. But we are admonished by Paul to come together and worship and not neglect gathering together with one another. He urges us to love and encourage each other, especially as we see the day of the Lord approaching. And if you are paying attention to the news, you know the day is approaching quickly.

I encourage you today to come out of isolation and worship with others in the house of the Lord while it is still day. The New Living Translation renders Hebrews 10:25 this way: "And let us not neglect our meeting together, as some people do, but encourage one another, especially now that the day of his return is drawing near."

Eva M. Starner

May 25

Tears

You keep track of all my sorrows.
You have collected all my tears in your bottle.
You have recorded each one in your book.
—Psalm 56:8, NLT

I will never forget traveling to Minsk, Belarus—one of the oldest cities in Europe—with its charming cobblestone streets and the beautiful Svislach River in the background.

My connection with Minsk happened when I visited the Island of Tears, an amazing memorial set up in 1988 to commemorate the Belarusian soldiers who died in the Union of Soviet Socialist Republics' nine-year war in Afghanistan (1979–1988). The heart of the memorial is the chapel, with its haunting figures of grieving mothers, sisters, and widows shedding tears together as they remember their loved ones lost in the war. I stayed there for a while, thinking about those mothers and their pain. I reflected on the tears I have shared with women who experienced similar trauma.

When words fail, tears flow. Tears have a language all their own—a tongue that needs no interpreter. Most often, they appear when our souls are overwhelmed with feelings that words cannot describe. Maybe this is how you feel today, and this is OK. But here is good news. Our God takes notice of every tear. David wrote, "You keep track of all my sorrows. You have collected all my tears in your bottle. You have recorded each one in your book" (Psalm 56:8, NLT). He also wrote, "The Lord has heard the voice of my weeping" (Psalm 6:8, NKJV).

A teardrop on Earth summons the King of heaven, who takes note when hard times cause us to become full of tears. The times when you feel embarrassed or disappointed are turned into moments of tenderness with Him. He never forgets the crises in our lives where tears are shed. He understands, He feels, and He cries with us. What a comforting reality that is!

Jeremiah was so grieved that his people persisted in rebelling against God that "the weeping prophet" became his nickname. Even so, God selected Jeremiah to be His voice at the most critical time in Israel's history. And God also can use you and your tears as His voice.

If you have tears today, remember two things: God keeps track of all your sorrows, and "weeping may last through the night, but joy comes with the morning" (Psalm 30:5, NLT).

Raquel Queiroz da Costa Arrais

May 26

Turn Right at the Intersection

*Whether you turn to the right or to the left,
your ears will hear a voice behind you, saying, "This is the way; walk in it."*
—Isaiah 30:21, NIV

Some time ago, I was driving to the public library, but I was not 100 percent certain on which street it was located. I was coming from a different direction than usual, so I was uncertain of the way to get there. I put the address in my GPS and proceeded to follow its instructions on the best way to reach the library. As I was driving, I discovered it was taking me to a location I was certain was *not* the library. Now, I can be directionally challenged sometimes, but this fact does not prevent me from ignoring my GPS on occasion. Nevertheless, in this case, I went to the location it gave, grumbling at the GPS all the way there.

When I arrived at the destination, I discovered it was the senior center, not the library. I drove into the parking lot but did not see any sign for a library, just the senior center. I informed my GPS that it was wrong, turned around, and drove to where I knew the library was located.

I was so proud of myself when I found *Public Library* displayed in bold letters across a beautiful, old stone building. I parked my car and smugly walked up to the entrance of the building. That is when I saw another sign. In the window, a colorfully lettered sign read, "The library is now at the senior center."

I had been so certain I was on the right path. The first few signs even told me that my thinking was correct. But the voice in my car was telling me to head in a direction that made no sense to me. The final sign confirmed for me that the GPS had been correct all along.

Sometimes God gives us directions that make no sense to us. Everything in our environment is clearly telling us to go one way, but God is giving us different directions. It is especially puzzling if God has led us down a certain path before, and now He is advising us to change direction. He can see something we cannot. He is present and relevant in our lives now.

How much time and aggravation I would have saved by believing the GPS directions the first time! How much time and aggravation could we save by believing and following God's directions the first time?

Annette M. Barnes

May 27

Facebook Revelation

*"Then the virgin will rejoice in the dance,
And the young men and the old together;
For I will turn their mourning into joy
And comfort them, and give them joy for their sorrow."*
—Jeremiah 31:13, NASB

While scrolling through the Facebook page of one of my friends, a new revelation came to me. But let me backtrack a bit.

A new position was advertised in the office after my senior leadership position in the church was made redundant. I was told that an amazingly organized person had been chosen for the new position. In my distress, that rubbed against me. Although this process was very painful for me, I was intentional about doing the right thing. I made sure there were flowers waiting for her at her desk on her first day of work. I had written down a detailed list of all the work processes she would need to access. I answered all the questions she had, both during the handover and afterward. I listened as we sometimes used our lunch break to walk and talk, all the while feeling pained by this transition. As time went by, I had selfish thoughts: it should have been me who was in her place and doing things she was doing. Every time I saw her or passed by her office, I felt a small pang in my heart. So, my heart and my head were not in agreement. I kept praying.

Back to the pictures I saw on Facebook. They were of her visiting different countries as a senior administrator in the church. She is enjoying her work and is well accepted in her new role. She is the first female to hold this position in this territory. And then it dawned on me! If my role had not been made redundant, she would not have been willing to take a senior role. She would not have been preparing for the opportunity the Lord had now given to her. It is because I was no longer in that role that a younger, capable woman had opportunities no other woman had before her. And because of her, many other women will have a door opened to serve in senior church positions in the future.

Finally, my heart and my head are in the same place. It was worth the pain, and I can now rejoice at the thought of what future opportunities have been made possible. If you are in the middle of sorrow, I pray that you will remember that God will turn it to joy, just as He promised!

Danijela Schubert

May 28

Radical Love

*The lines have fallen for me in pleasant places;
indeed, I have a beautiful inheritance.*
—Psalm 16:6, ESV

The unknown fills the soul with anxiety. *What is next?* I asked myself, even as I cried out to God for an answer.

I had just received my nursing degree and passed the board examination to obtain my license, but I had no way to pursue my dream career in this country. *Why did God allow me to come this close but not close enough?* I thought in desperation. My mind was so clouded by my own anxious thoughts that I could not hear His calming voice, reminding me of how He had provided for me in the many challenges I had experienced throughout my student years. Every single time. And now that I was faced with even more challenges as a new graduate, why would things be any different?

We tend to ask Jesus to change our situation, not realizing that He often allows us into difficult circumstances in order to change us. I had a great job offer pending acceptance that had been graciously extended three times already. Without the work permit I desperately needed, I would never be able to accept the position. Only a miracle would allow me to receive it before the deadline. As I wrestled in prayer, it finally dawned on me—I was praying for the wrong thing. The moment I realized that I should be praying for peace instead of an answer to my dilemma, everything changed.

Finally, the deadline arrived, and after spending time with God, I exchanged His peace for all my worries. I checked the progress of my status. It remained unchanged: the case was taking longer than expected. I trusted that it was God's will because He had something different for me.

Later that same day, I opened my mailbox, and to my surprise, I found a letter approving my work permit. Everything had fallen into place. At first, I said it was just in time, but in reality, it was in God's perfect time. He truly wants the best for each of us. He loves us because we are daughters of the King of kings! We have a beautiful inheritance waiting for us. In every trial we encounter, God will see us through because of His radical love for us.

Luisamaria Navarro

May 29

But I Cannot Stand the Sight of Blood!

Be still, and know that I am God.
—Psalm 46:10, KJV

In college, I never considered studying anything related to the health field. After all, I could not stand the sight of blood or even a simple wound. Instead, I chose to study journalism. I lived in Venezuela, and I wanted to graduate by the time I was twenty. But my dream fell apart after my family and I had to immigrate to the United States of America due to the political issues we faced. I was almost done with my studies! I had just one semester left to finish, and it hurt so much. However, I was certain I would be able to complete my degree once we were established in our new country.

Time flew by, and I just worked and worked and worked. I had a boyfriend, and I built dreams of my future with this guy. But God had another plan, and that dream also fell apart. During my grieving time, I discovered that I had cancer. I was devastated. Even though I always enjoyed a sincere relationship with God, I realized how much I needed to surrender all to Him. After I told God I was willing to accept His will and do anything He wanted me to do, He reassured me with the promise, "Be still, and know that I am God" (Psalm 46:10, KJV).

After renewing my relationship with Him, I discovered that He wanted me to be a nurse. "But wait, Lord," I prayed. "I cannot stand the sight of blood! Why nursing?" Silence. "OK, God. I accept Your will, but I need You to give me a stomach that will tolerate anything and the mental capacity to study anatomy, chemistry, pharmacology, and all those difficult subjects."

When I accepted God's plans for my life, He introduced me to the love of my life, who is a nurse. God has since called him to be a pilot, and to make a long story short, we were married four years ago. God called us to study aviation and nursing at Andrews University in Michigan, United States of America, to prepare us to be missionaries and to introduce our Savior to those who do not know Him. God has given me a strong stomach (and nose) and the capacity to pass my classes with As and Bs. All credit to our awesome, loving God. How I praise Him! I am now a junior, and I love the health field!

God can use "bad" things in life, like a trampoline, to propel us toward His highest dreams. If He can do that for me, He can do it for you!

Monica Torrealba

May 30

From My Diary

The Lord knows how to rescue the godly from trials.
—2 Peter 2:9, ESV

Saturday

The locals in Montevideo, Uruguay, have a hike known as Tres Cruces—Hill of Three Crosses. It is designed as a Via Dolorosa—the journey Jesus took on His way to Calvary. There are fourteen crosses along the trail, each depicting a section of the Crucifixion story. At the top, three huge crosses are dotted with relics and prayers.

Though I am still really ill, this was the week my beautiful family of roommates wanted to go. Of course, it was! Hauling myself up the mountain, I cursed God. Hiking is usually my favorite activity but not that day. That day I was dead. As we rose in elevation, I could barely breathe. I threw up once. My fingers turned white from lack of oxygen. I wanted to go home.

Then, there in front of me, the cross. Tears welled up in my eyes, and I turned so the others would not see. There I stood, complaining about the blandest problems known to man when I belonged to the Savior of the world. In my tired, feeble state of mind, I realized I had not been giving my all to God. I saw my sins, the jealousy, anger, impatience, gluttony, lust, laziness—everything I had submitted to during the difficult week. How foolish. To let hard days separate me from the love of my life, my Lord and Savior Jesus Christ. I prayed a prayer of sorrow and asked forgiveness as I let His love wash over me. He was in charge, not me.

Today

I rolled my ankle on the way down from Tres Cruces. But that is not going to stop me. Even if this week is worse than the last, I will let God be in charge. Next week we are doing an eight-hour hike up to the La Laguna shelter. The goal is to raise money and awareness for the Venezuelan refugee crisis. I am going to go. Despite the weakness I currently feel, I am praying that God will give me the strength to go on. I know He will.

My friends, how easily we lose sight of what truly matters. Let us pray for one another and also for the needs of those around us. While we struggle through a tough week, for them, their nightmares last much longer than a week.

Sophia Jaquez

May 31

Professional Development for Marriage

And we all, who with unveiled faces contemplate the Lord's glory, are being transformed into his image with ever-increasing glory, which comes from the Lord, who is the Spirit.
—2 Corinthians 3:18, NIV

For over thirty years, I was involved in education at various levels. I taught in public schools and in Adventist church schools, including one-teacher schools and at the academy level. I also taught education classes at a self-supporting college. During all those years, the one thing that remained consistent was the need to grow—to learn and be prepared to be my best at whatever I did. As part of that growth experience, I attended professional development (PD) classes.

Following the death of my husband of twenty-nine years from COVID-19, I met and married Jim. He had come from a very unpleasant divorce, while I, on the other hand, came from a long life of relative peace in my marriage. All marriages require adjustment, regardless of age and circumstances, and for us, it became apparent that we had a lot of growing to do. I discovered a number of excellent videos on YouTube produced by Focus on the Family. These videos covered essential topics for helping produce a thriving marriage. As I watched them and even got my husband to watch some with me, I realized I was basically doing professional development for marriage.

Professional development is essential not only for teachers and married couples but also for Christians. While professionals in the field of education conduct the PD for educators and professionals in marriage counseling share their expertise on marriage, who do we look to for our PD on becoming better Christians? I think we all agree with 2 Corinthians 3:18 that beholding Christ is the best way to become more like Him.

Unless we actively pursue personal time with God and spend time in His Word, we will never grow. It is not enough to want to become more Christlike if our eyes are not focused on Christ moment by moment. It is not enough to pursue wishful thinking. We have to actively pursue beholding Christ. There are wonderful resources available for watering the garden of our spiritual life. These can serve as our PD for becoming the Christians God wants us to be. I pray we will take 2 Corinthians 3:18 to heart and be intentional in our desire to be like Christ.

Sharon (Clark) Mills

June 1

The God Who Hears

Be careful for nothing; but in every thing by prayer and supplication with thanksgiving let your requests be made known unto God.
—Philippians 4:6, KJV

One Tuesday my alarm reminded me of my church's weekly midday prayer time, and I joined the conference call. Soon after, my prayer partners Ann and Gail chimed in. Ann led out by identifying several prayer requests that had been shared by others—some in our church and others from our local university. Then we proceeded to share our own requests. When it was my turn to share, I mentioned that I was praying to resolve a matter that had been dragging on with the Internal Revenue Service (IRS). Ann petitioned the throne on my behalf.

After our prayer time, I went on to do my part to try to resolve my situation. I searched online to find a contact number for the IRS and proceeded to make multiple calls but to no avail. I scoured the web to find other contact numbers, searching for a chance to speak with a representative—the automated system was not helping! Eventually, I found a number that allowed me to speak to an actual person and not a machine! What a relief to finally be transferred to someone who could explain what was happening with my particular tax filing.

My testimony today is that we should never underestimate the power of prayer. My sisters prayed on my behalf, and God delivered on that very day, only hours later. He directed me to the exact number I needed to call and helped me connect with exactly the right person who could take care of my situation. I was then able to acquire the supporting documents I needed to resolve the problem.

My sisters in Christ, pray about everything because God hears and answers our prayers. Sometimes we get the answers right away, and sometimes we do not. But we can be confident that God hears, and He will answer. You may have been praying over many things or a few; you may have been praying for ages or a moment; your situation may be simple, complex, or dire but never lose hope. Continue to pray because our heavenly Father can and will deliver. Never underestimate the power of prayer. Take some time to find a prayer group or a trusted prayer partner and pour your heart out in prayer. We serve a God who hears!

Taniesha K. Robertson-Brown

June 2

A Miraculous Gift

*"Call to Me, and I will answer you,
and show you great and mighty things, which you do not know."*
—Jeremiah 33:3, NKJV

The Bible says that God loves to give us the desires of our heart if we ask Him. In Trinidad, the requirement for renting a house was one month's rent in advance and $100 as "reward" money. This reward was essentially to thank the owner for renting the house. As I studied my Bible, I could not find any verse where God required such things, so I purposed in my mind not to pay a reward. I determined to trust the Lord to make a way for me to obtain some land. I told Him that even if it was a little house made of rough boards, I would appreciate it.

I kept on praying and never gave up trusting that God would answer my prayer. I held on to God's Word. "Therefore be patient, brothers and sisters. . . . [As] the farmer waits for the precious produce of the soil, being patient about it" (James 5:7, NASB). As I went about my daily tasks, I prayed to the Lord about my need. I prayed through promises, which included, "If we hope for what we do not see, through perseverance we wait eagerly for it" (Romans 8:25, NASB). I continued this endeavor for five years. Then something strange happened.

One Sunday morning my husband went to purchase the newspaper and returned with a friend whom he had not seen in years. I cooked a delicious meal and invited our guest to join us, along with my brother-in-law. After lunch, my husband's friend began sharing plans the government had for ex-service members. From the discourse, I learned that land was being given to ex-service members in the Maracas, Saint Joseph Valley, Trinidad, to cultivate and build homes for their families. This sounded great to me!

My husband and brother-in-law immediately completed the application, and after they had done so, the visitor left, and we never saw him again. I have often wondered about that incident. I believe it was providential. Well, those applications were sent off in the mail the next day, and ultimately, my husband's application was accepted, but my brother-in-law's application was denied. That year twelve ex-service members whose applications had been approved received their portion of land. My friends, let us persevere in prayer!

Sheila Johnson (deceased)

June 3

God Answers Even Simple Prayers

"If you believe, you will receive whatever you ask for in prayer."
—Matthew 21:22, NIV

Costco Wholesale is a huge store that is usually crowded, especially on the weekends. To avoid the crowds and long checkout lines, I like to go on a weekday in the late morning or afternoon.

One beautiful spring day I decided to go to Costco and get my bulk supplies for the home. As usual, I went in the early afternoon. I always stock up on almond and soy milk and get a case of twelve cartons each.

Before heading to the milk aisle, I always pray to find someone willing to help me carry the heavy milk cases and put them inside my shopping cart. After praying, I went to the aisle where the cases were and was very happy to see a nice gentleman standing right in front of the milk cases. Immediately, I asked him if he would help me put the two cases in my cart. He kindly agreed and placed them inside the shopping cart. We chatted a bit, and I shared with him a small inspirational tract that I always have in my purse. He graciously took it and thanked me.

When I finished shopping and was leaving the store, I prayed again that God would send someone to help me lift the cases into my car trunk. As I walked toward my car, I saw a young man and his two little sons walking in front of me. We recognized each other because he worked in my office complex. I asked him to help me put the cases in my car, and he helped me.

It turns out this same young man had previously helped me some months ago put the milk cases inside my car trunk. It was such a coincidence to see him again after all that time—at just the time I needed his help. He mentioned that he remembered helping me before.

I was so amazed and grateful to God for hearing my simple, humble prayer to find help at the right time when I needed it. Nothing is too small to bring to God in prayer.

My dear sisters, please remember that our great God wants to help you no matter what your problems or needs may be. He is always there, and He loves to have us turn to Him for help. Let us always place our faith and trust in Him.

Stella Thomas

June 4

Beauty for Ashes

*"To console those who mourn . . . ,
To give them beauty for ashes,
The oil of joy for mourning,
The garment of praise for the spirit of heaviness; . . .
that He may be glorified."*
—Isaiah 61:3, NKJV

Our first pregnancy was so exciting. I loved being pregnant! Although the nausea and vomiting, not so much. My doctor put me on medication, and it helped. I had no idea what was in store for us, but I was so looking forward to meeting our first baby. I could hardly wait!

At sixteen weeks, we had our first ultrasound and discovered we were having a baby boy. Everything looked fine. At twenty weeks, my blood pressure became elevated, but my family doctor was not too worried about it. Around twenty-three weeks, I felt extremely tired and wondered when I would start to feel my baby move.

By Sabbath afternoon, I was feeling awful, so we went to the emergency department. As I was almost twenty-four weeks, which is the age of viability for babies, they transferred me to the Grey Nuns Community Hospital in Edmonton, Canada. When they did an ultrasound, they found our baby was very small for his gestational age and that I had developed preeclampsia. I was transferred again, and how we prayed!

I was put on bed rest as we tried to help our baby put on more weight ahead of what would be an early delivery. We learned from the specialists that the blood flow through the umbilical cord was compromised, and they told us that baby Micah would not make it to full term—he had to gain more weight as soon as possible. After delivery, he would be in the neonatal intensive care unit, and they could give us no sure answer as to his prognosis. We were devastated. We prayed so hard for a positive outcome.

At our next ultrasound, they could not find a heartbeat. The perinatal specialist came to tell us our baby had died. I was induced and had nineteen hours of hard labor. Our son Micah Basil Baird was stillborn on July 3, 2010. We were devastated. The grief stole my breath. I almost lost my faith. Friends and family rallied around us, praying for us and offering support.

One year later, our rainbow baby, Alyssa, was born. Jesus gave us beauty for ashes. And when He returns, we will see Micah face-to-face. Oh, how we look forward to that day!

Noella (Jumpp) Baird

June 5

Let Not Your Heart Be Troubled

*"Let not your heart be troubled; you believe in God, believe also in Me. . . .
I go to prepare a place for you. And if I go and prepare a place for you,
I will come again and receive you to Myself; that where I am, there you may be also."*
—John 14:1–3, NKJV

John Bunyan, author of *Pilgrim's Progress*, knew something of heart troubles, having lost his first wife, the mother of his four children. He also spent twelve years in prison for preaching without a license. While he was rotting in prison—wait, he did not rot in prison! He wrote *Hearts' Ease in Heart Trouble* in prison. Based on John 14:1–3 ("Let not your heart be troubled"), *Hearts' Ease* offered God's promises and comfort for suffering, loss, and sorrow.

I found a kindred spirit in Bunyan's writings because great sorrow struck our family when I was a young mother. My husband, our thirteen-year-old son Tony, and our eleven-year-old son Joey lost their lives in a plane crash. Gone were any illusions about trouble and suffering only happening to others. This did not fit with any of my plans, hopes, and dreams. I was going to marry a nice man, have a dozen red-haired sons, and drive an Audi. It never occurred to me that I could face terminal illnesses, addictions, divorces, financial failure, or the death of people I love.

How could my heart not be troubled in a world full of such troubles?

I waited by the phone as search and rescue combed the mountains of Alaska, looking for the small plane. We did not have to wait forever, although it seemed like it. My own brother, a pilot, delivered the excruciating news: "There are no survivors." Our two youngest children, who were home with me, pressed onto my lap, the three of us forming the tightest, hottest speck of excruciating agony in God's whole gigantic universe. *Does He know? Does He care?* flashed through my mind. And almost instantaneously, the answer followed: *Yes, He knows; yes, He cares.* My sorrows are His sorrows; my grief is His grief; my loss is His loss; and Jesus, too, will not see my family until the resurrection.

As one with us, He endured our sorrows, troubles, and pain. He carries us, keeps us, provides for us, and comforts us. He is ours, and we are His. The One who says, "Let not your heart be troubled," is with us. Always.

Pat Arrabito

June 6

Like a Toad

*"For I know the plans I have for you, declares the Lord,
plans for welfare and not for evil, to give you a future and a hope."*
—Jeremiah 29:11, ESV

I was out on my usual morning walk when a slight movement on the sidewalk caught my attention. Looking closer, I saw it was a toad.

The ones I had seen before were mostly fat, slimy looking, and potbellied, with protruding eyes reminiscent of the frog prince of fairy tales. This one was emaciated and dehydrated, with a rather deflated belly, weakly hopping along the cement sidewalk with no sign of water or vegetation in sight.

Feeling sorry for the poor animal's plight and pushing aside the many stories I had read about poisonous frogs, I attempted to nudge the pathetic little bundle into a small bag I always carry with the intention of looking for a verdant patch into which to release it. To my consternation, the more I tried to "save it," the more it tried to hop frantically away from my efforts, probably seeing me more as a predator than a help.

My thoughts went to our own frequent reactions along the sidewalk of life. We often become emotionally and spiritually emaciated, weakly plodding along with no sure sight of verdant pastures for repose and failing to see the Lord's outstretched hand of help. We struggle like the toad against the very One who desires more than anything to save us.

"He who took humanity upon Himself knows how to sympathize with the sufferings of humanity. Not only does Christ know every soul, and the peculiar needs and trials of that soul, but He knows all the circumstances that chafe and perplex the spirit. His hand is outstretched in pitying tenderness to every suffering child. Those who suffer most have most of His sympathy and pity. He is touched with the feeling of our infirmities, and He desires us to lay our perplexities and troubles at His feet and leave them there."*

Dear friends, whatever you are struggling with, hear the words of the Master: "Come to Me, all who are weary and burdened, and I will give you rest" (Matthew 11:28, NASB).

Jessy Quilindo

---

* Ellen G. White, *The Ministry of Healing* (Mountain View, CA: Pacific Press®, 1942), 249.

June 7

God's Way

*Wait on the LORD: be of good courage,
and he shall strengthen thine heart: wait, I say, on the LORD.*
—Psalm 27:14, KJV

Before retiring, I had big intentions of settling in the country. My desire had been to enjoy country living, breathing fresh air and growing most, if not all, of the food we would consume. As the years passed and health issues arose, the idea of country living became less desirable. I allowed my thoughts to focus on the "what-ifs." What if we got sick and could not get to the medical facility necessary to provide the medical care needed? What if a section of the road was destroyed due to flooding? What if the electricity failed? Many thoughts occupied my mind, but the topmost thought was about having to drive on a curvy, dark country road in the rain.

Sadly, I allowed thoughts instilled in my mind by Satan to divert me from God's plan, and I settled for something less. We made the transition to Georgia, United States of America, when we were in poor health, but we stabilized quickly. I was unhappy with where we had chosen to live. I started to look at land for sale. I found at least three tracts of land, but each time I thought the property was within reach, a problem would arise, and it would become unavailable. I had pretty much given up hope when, one early spring morning, I felt impressed to drive into the country in another county to see whether I could locate land for sale.

After driving for some time, to no avail, I headed home. Then I noticed a "For Sale" sign, almost out of sight, in the ditch. I contacted the seller, but the price was $5,000 more than I wanted to pay. When I asked about a reduction, they immediately reduced it by $5,000 without me even mentioning how much I was willing to pay. I knew God had orchestrated this entire scenario.

As I reflect on the path taken in acquiring this land, I must acknowledge that it was God's intervention that made it happen, despite the obstacles in my previous attempts to purchase land. My friends, never lose hope! Be persistent despite difficulties when you know it is God who is leading you. "Trust in the LORD with all thine heart; and lean not unto thine own understanding. In all thy ways acknowledge him, and he shall direct thy paths" (Proverbs 3:5, 6, KJV).

Mary Head Brooks

June 8

Preservation Power

*I will lift up mine eyes unto the hills, from whence cometh my help.
My help cometh from the LORD, which made heaven and earth.*
—Psalm 121:1, 2, KJV

One night, as my younger sister was driving home from a long trip, it began to rain. But this was no ordinary rain; this rain would cause a flash flood. My sister had been driving on the back roads and, at this point, was only ten minutes from home when the car came to a halt and water rushed in. This young black woman found herself stuck in an area filled with neighbors who were not typically known for being kind to those of darker hues. She was alone, with no cell service, in a thunderstorm, and no help in sight—or so she thought.

A man who lived in one of the surrounding houses came out to help. He tied a rope around a tree and then to himself in an attempt to rescue her. Though a valiant effort, it did not work. My sister, unable to swim and short in stature, became increasingly scared. She had no idea how she would make it. Thankfully, the man did not give up. He carefully guided her and told her what to do to keep the car from being swept away.

He then encouraged her to open the sunroof and climb onto the roof of the vehicle. This instruction was critical, as the pressure of the water had prevented my sister from opening any door. In hindsight, had she waited even two more minutes, the car would have died before she could open the sunroof, leaving her trapped inside. Now on the roof with rain, thunder, and lightning all around her and still out of contact with family, my sister saw another car coming toward her. Fortunately, the waters prevented a collision. And thankfully, the kind stranger who had been so helpful already did not leave the drivers. In fact, he was instrumental in helping search and rescue to locate them.

As I listened to the story, I marveled at God's power to preserve. My sister could have drowned, been struck by lightning, been killed in a collision, or been harmed by a person with ill intentions. But God sent a resourceful stranger right on time! It is easy to wonder where God is in our difficult circumstances. But God truly is our Helper. When you find yourself feeling scared or helpless, I encourage you to reflect on Psalm 121 as a reminder of God's preservation power.

Jesseñia Robinson

June 9

Encourage Each Other

And when they give the book to one who cannot read, saying, "Read this," he says, "I cannot read."
—Isaiah 29:12, ESV

Young Vasantha was illiterate. She could not even sign her own name. Whenever she went to the market to buy groceries, she was cheated by unscrupulous shopkeepers. She felt she was more of a hindrance than a blessing to her family. More than anything, Vasantha longed to learn how to read and write. She was determined to do so.

Her first experience in literacy class was very embarrassing. She knew absolutely nothing. She could not recognize even a single letter or word. To reassure her, I placed my hands around her and said, "Vasantha, don't worry. You will read one day." I encouraged her to keep attending class every day. The Literacy Center offers more than learning how to read and write. Students are taught how to do simple arithmetic and other skills, such as preparing healthy meals and making wire baskets, paper flowers, and embroidery. They can also attend health talks and exercise classes. These activities encourage the women, and it is wonderful to watch as they become more hopeful and begin taking an interest in life.

One day Vasantha mentioned she was waiting to be asked to read the Scriptures in church and how much she would love to sing like other women. Once again, I encouraged her to pray about it and to trust in the Lord for His wisdom. At the end of the year, by God's grace, Vasantha was able to read the Word of God. All praises to Him!

Once she became literate, she joined the government-sponsored Women's Self-Help group in her village. She thrived, eventually becoming the leader of that group. In that role, she often goes to the bank, where she signs for the salaries of her group members. The bank manager was amazed to see the transformation in this once shy young woman. Vasantha credits God.

I am grateful for the role I was privileged to play at the Literacy Center. I give all the glory and honor to the Lord for shaping Vasantha into a wonderful mother, a blessed wife, and a valuable member of society. We are blessed whenever we help make a difference in someone's life. Is there someone who needs your help today?

Premila Masih

June 10

Daughters of Inheritance

"For I know the plans I have for you," says the LORD.
"They are plans for good and not for disaster, to give you a future and a hope."
—Jeremiah 29:11, NLT

If you are like me, you love a good story. Tales of people making decisions that challenge the status quo fill us with admiration and hope and inspire similar actions in others. Recently, I read a story about five courageous sisters who made me appreciate Jeremiah 29:11 in a new way.

In Numbers 27, a man named Zelophehad died, leaving no male to inherit his property. According to the law, his family line would end, and his five daughters would have no right to the property. The sting of injustice brought the daughters of Zelophehad to the tabernacle. As they stood before Moses, they boldly presented their petition: "Why should the name of our father be removed from among his family because he had no son? Give us a possession among our father's brothers" so his name will not die out (Numbers 27:4, NKJV).

In other words, "Our father did not have sons, but we are here. Don't we count?"

When Moses brought their case before the Lord, He honored them in a way that would protect them. God instructed Moses to give them the property and their father's inheritance as if they were male heirs. But God went further. In this precedent-setting case, God established an innovative law that could be known as the Daughters of Zelophehad Amendment. If a man died without a son to pass his inheritance on to, his daughter would receive it. If he had no daughter, then the inheritance would pass to his brother and so on to the next male in line. This amendment in the law provided for women who would otherwise face a difficult future.

Just as God provided for Zelophehad's daughters, we can believe God has a future for us. Many Bible promises show that God cares about our welfare. Is there a circumstance in your life that seems impossible to you? Have you been praying for God to move a mountain? Then remember these five courageous women, and go boldly to the throne of grace, and ask.

Dear Father, thank You for reminders of Your love for us. Sometimes we are not brave, we are not courageous, and we lack the faith to ask. Forgive us for limiting what You want to do for us and through us. Help us to be bold and become instruments for Your mission. Amen.

Sherma Webbe Clarke

June 11

Ruffled but Not Uprooted

Let your roots grow down into him, and let your lives be built on him.
Then your faith will grow strong in the truth you were taught,
and you will overflow with thankfulness.
—Colossians 2:7, NLT

Last winter, as I drove through my neighborhood, I noticed many of the trees had lost their leaves. This was not the first time I had noticed it; however, for some unknown reason, I was now intrigued as to why this happened. After searching the internet, I learned the main reason was to conserve energy for survival during the cold, dry winter temperatures. Instead of expending energy to protect their fragile leaves, trees shed those leaves in order to survive the season. *Wow!* I thought. *Instead of perishing during that trying time, trees choose to let go of the very thing that gives them beauty!* After all, what is a tree without leaves?

Are you going through a difficult time right now? Are you experiencing a cold and frigid season in which you are losing "leaves"? The very things you thought gave you beauty, meaning, and purpose in life? Have you lost your job, property, possessions, a close relationship, a loved one, or your health? Sometimes, sisters, God allows us to lose our "leaves" to give us a better understanding of the things that really matter. Sometimes He permits us to go through difficulties to give us renewed purpose and vision that help to build our character—a character we will take with us when He returns to bring us to our heavenly home.

James admonishes us, "Consider it pure joy, my brothers and sisters, whenever you face trials of many kinds, because you know that the testing of your faith produces perseverance. Let perseverance finish its work so that you may be mature and complete, not lacking anything" (James 1:2–4, NIV).

Although you may be facing a difficult situation, I encourage you to stay rooted and grounded in Jesus Christ. Through a life of prayer and Bible study, discover that He is our true Source of strength, energy, comfort, and everything we need to survive. He has the ability to restore everything we have lost and give us more—so much more. He will help us bloom and flourish in this life and the life to come.

Yes, stay grounded and rooted in Christ. Be blessed!

Sacha Clarke

June 12

Pinpoints of Light

"Arise, Jerusalem! Let your light shine for all to see.
For the glory of the Lord *rises to shine on you.*
Darkness as black as night covers all the nations of the earth,
but the glory of the Lord *rises and appears over you."*
—Isaiah 60:1, 2, NLT

As of this writing, I am in quarantine for the second time. The first time was precautionary. This time I am not so sure. I am awaiting the results of the PCR test for COVID-19. The symptoms are mild, so I may just have an extreme case of sinusitis. The fear and despair coursing through me, however, have left an acrid taste in my mouth. COVID-19 summons feelings of trauma, loss, uncertainty, and emotional discord.

Enjoying time alone is one thing, but having to isolate from family, seeing them from a distance in your own home to keep them from harm's way, is something else entirely. Today I struggled. I love having my family in my space.

While I felt lonely and despondent at that moment, I knew I was not alone. I was not without hope. God does not abandon His children to the darkness. He was right beside me, sending precious signals of His presence. It shone in the one ripe guava on the tree and sparkled through the young man at the medical center who offered me his chair. God showed Himself in the messages I received from loved ones. I heard Him reminding me of His love in the songs and hymns of the Sabbath that evening. He promised me He would not stop the work He has begun within me.

"Are not five sparrows sold for two pennies? Yet not one of them is forgotten by God" (Luke 12:6, NIV). He watches over every sparrow. He sees when they fall. Not one goes unnoticed by Him. How much more will He watch over me?

Sisters, God reveals Himself in unexpected ways during our darkest moments. There are pinpoints of light if we look for them with the eyes of faith. "Turn your eyes away from that which is dark and discouraging, and behold Jesus."* He will show us the way to find strength, hope, and joy as He dispels the shadows and shines His light into our hearts and minds.

Greta Michelle Joachim-Fox-Dyett

---

* Ellen G. White, *Selected Messages*, bk. 2 (Washington, DC: Review and Herald®, 1958), 399.

June 13

The Unlikely Toolbox

For . . . the body is not one member but many.
—1 Corinthians 12:14, NKJV

I was teaching the Sabbath School lesson when the study had us take a closer look at 1 Corinthians 12:14–20. There were quite a few odd looks as I pulled out a toolbox and opened it. We looked at all the normal tools one usually finds in a toolbox. Then I spoke to the women in the class and asked, "What do you use when you need to tighten a screw on a cabinet, and you don't have a screwdriver?" They all answered, "A butter knife!" Right answer!

I continued, "And what do you use when you don't have a hammer to drive a nail into the wall?" Again, all the ladies got it as I pulled one of my high-heeled shoes out of the toolbox. The men in the class were a little befuddled.

OK, so back to the lesson. The screwdriver and butter knife are both capable of performing the same task. They just look a little different. An old, timeworn butter knife with some dents in it is not a shiny-handled screwdriver. If given the choice, which one would you pick first? The same with the hammer. A person feels pretty powerful with the knowledge of how to sling that hammer so that it hits the nail on the head the first time. So why would I settle for using my worn-out heel in hopes of hitting my mark?

Paul says in 1 Corinthians 12 that all members of the body were designed for a purpose—to meet a need. And the same holds true for the members of the church—all members, not some members. So think about this for a moment: God's people do not all look the same. They do not all function in the same manner or have the same ideas about how to accomplish a task. God expects us to help those who are not as "shiny" or "powerful" to do their part in the Lord's work. Though they may fail or falter at the start, though they may miss the mark on their first attempt, we can encourage them to use and grow their talents and skills for God.

Do you feel like a shoe or a butter knife? Be encouraged, my friend, for there are many ways to work for God. Make yourself available to be used by Him, and He will put you to work. Regardless of whether you are a bright, shiny hammer or a worn high-heeled shoe, in the Master's hands, you will be the best person for the job!

Victoria M. Shewbrooks

June 14

Learning How to Walk

Now to Him who is able to protect you from stumbling,
and to make you stand in the presence of His glory, blameless with great joy,
to the only God our Savior, through Jesus Christ our Lord, be glory, majesty,
dominion, and authority before all time and now and forever. Amen.
—Jude 24, 25, NASB

I partied my way through high school as a rowdy, boisterous girl who loved to laugh with friends. And I imbibed in my share of weed and wine to help that happen. A religious conversion at nineteen turned the wild-child me into a pin-straight, prim-and-proper young lady whom my friends could no longer recognize. When two of my best friends from high school came to visit, they stared at me, confused, and wondered, "What have you done with Jennifer?"

I will admit that I came across as pretty austere and joyless. The truth was, underneath the severe exterior brewed a fear of falling back into my old ways. While I believed that God had forgiven me for my past, I also believed He now left it up to me to straighten myself out. This belief may have been reinforced by my childhood experiences with a strict father who, although he placed high expectations on me, found it difficult to cultivate a close relationship.

When I first learned to walk, I knew two things: One, that Mommy and Daddy believed I could; otherwise, why were they wildly waving their arms and cheering on the other side of the room? Two, I knew that if I fell, they would scoop me up in their arms, set me upright, and cheer me on as I tried again. Now imagine yourself, child of God, learning to walk. God stands on the other side of the room, cheering for you. You take a few steps, then stumble. He picks you up, sets you upright, and you try again. Now imagine yourself one day running right into His arms.

In reality, our heavenly Father walks alongside us. He wants us to know the impossibility of reaching those ideals in our own strength. He does not expect us to reach those standards as a means of obtaining righteousness; rather, He wraps us in His righteousness at the outset. Jesus' gift of His righteousness transforms us. We serve Him with joy—no longer desiring anything that would separate us from Him. And when we fall, He scoops us up in His arms, sets us on our feet, and walks alongside us. He knows we will ultimately walk without falling.

Jennifer Jill Schwirzer

June 15

Fathers

*Because you are sons [and daughters],
God has sent the Spirit of His Son into our hearts, crying out, "Abba! Father!"*
—Galatians 4:6, NASB

Jairus trembled as he laid a tender hand on his daughter's fevered cheek. He knew with certainty that if he did not act at once, his daughter would die. Quickly, he turned and walked out of the room, out of the house, and down the street. Pushing through crowds, he frantically looked for Jesus. Finding Him at last, Jairus threw himself to the ground and begged, heedless of the stares, the whispers, and the raised eyebrows. He did not care. All he could see was the face of his daughter as she lay in agony on her bed. Jesus was the answer and the focus of all his hopes.

Another father watched for Jesus as he held his son tight. The tormenting demon often threw his son to the ground in a seizure. He had found the disciples, and in desperation, he pleaded with them to help. But on this day, only Jesus could save. Anxiously, the father waited, unaware of the miraculous events transpiring on a mountaintop, clinging desperately to a thread of hope. When this father spotted Jesus returning to His disciples, he boldly interrupted, begging for help! Decorum and propriety could not come between this father's need and Jesus. Not even his lack of faith. He would confess and beg for enough faith if only his son could live.

What beautiful hearts these two fathers had—their children were uppermost in their minds. They were willing to risk all and spend all to see them whole again! And like those earthly dads, our heavenly Father looked upon us, His children, stricken with the ailments of sin and twisted by sorrow and grief. His heart ached. We were separated from Him by misunderstanding, our own choice, and a cruel enemy. So our heavenly Father sent His only Son into the world to show us His heart, to live and to die for us. The Father placed all His hope in Jesus too. Think of it! The Father bent over His only Son, broken and bleeding upon the cross. In the act of giving up His only Son, He hoped to save the children He formed with His own hand. This is our Father. Dad. Abba. He is the One we can run to when we are needy or when we hurt. We can trust His heart like no other. After all, He was willing to spend everything and risk everything to bring us peace and healing through His Son. What a wonderful Father!

Jodi Scarbrough

June 16

In Heaven, No More . . .

"He will wipe every tear from their eyes."
—Revelation 21:4, NIV

Have you ever felt that life on Earth is consumed by competition? It exists in every facet of life: sports, politics, education, entertainment, and advertising.

As early as the Garden of Eden, competition showed up. Eve was presented with the dilemma of having to decide: *Should I believe God or this serpent?* We know what she chose, and it has been downhill ever since. The entire human race became bent. But, a loving Creator immediately put into place a plan of rescue and restitution—the only One who could unbend the bent.

I think of two little friends who were chatting about their fathers one day. My brother Timmy was one, and his next-door neighbor, Tommy, the other. At one point, the conversation began to warm up a bit as each boy extolled his own father's achievements. Needless to say, it became a contest to outdo one another. In the heat of the moment, Timmy began to sense he was losing the battle. Frantically racking his brain for something to match or exceed the glowing accomplishments of Tommy's father, Timmy finally came up with this pitiful boast: "Well, my father has more bent nails than your father!"

More bent nails. Certainly not the greatest prize-winning achievement to brag about. And yet there is a lesson that can be drawn from this desperation-driven youthful offering.

No one can boast of more bent nails than our heavenly Father. All His earthly children—every last one—is a bent nail. And there is no one more qualified to straighten out a bent nail than He is. Think of Saul, the bounty hunter, out to murder Christians, who became Paul, perhaps the greatest Christian evangelist ever. Remember those "Sons of Thunder," James and John, whose stormy natures were gentled under the influence of their Friend Jesus.

A day is promised when all things will be made new. Revelation 21 and 22 paint a breathtaking portrait of what is in store. Forever, there will be no more tears, sorrow, crying, death, or pain, nor sin of any kind (see Revelation 21:4). And best of all, there will be no more bent nails!

Christine B. Nelson

June 17

Faith in the Dark

*So the woman conceived and bore a son.
And when she saw that he was a beautiful child, she hid him three months.*
—Exodus 2:2, NKJV

A few months ago, my mother, father, and cousin tested positive for COVID-19. My brother and I nursed them while at home, taking precautions. What we thought would last a few days, however, carried on for weeks. As my cousin recovered, my father and mother became weaker by the day until my father was hospitalized and put on oxygen. Both my parents had high blood pressure, so we were not sure they would survive. One evening I could not pray but only had tears running down my cheeks. As I turned the pages of my Bible, searching for some encouragement, I came across Exodus 2:1, 2. The background of this story is that the Israelites were in Egyptian bondage, and the king ordered his people to drown the Israelite baby boys in the river. He wanted to control the number of Israelites because he saw them as a threat to his kingdom.

One brave Jewish woman, however, took the risk of hiding her baby son for three months. Every single day Jochebed found a way to hide baby Moses, unsure when her secret would be discovered. Her focus was not on what would happen next but on taking care of her son and ensuring he was safe. She did this for three whole months until she could not hide him anymore, but she never gave up. In verses 3 and 4, we are told that she made an ark of bulrushes, asphalt, and pitch into which she placed the baby and set it among the reeds by the riverbank (NKJV). She then instructed his sister to watch over him. What determination!

To cut my long story short, I determined, like Jochebed, to do everything in my power to take care of my parents while trusting their future to God. Every single day we served them and prayed for them, and by God's grace, my parents eventually recovered.

In life, we will encounter challenges that seem to have no solution. But like Jochebed, even though the future seems dark, we can pray and work with determination and faith in God. He is with us, and He has promised never to leave or abandon us (see Hebrews 13:5). " 'For the mountains may be removed and the hills may shake, but My favor will not be removed from you, . . .' says the Lord who has compassion on you" (Isaiah 54:10, NASB).

Precious Chitwa

June 18

Homeless, Yet Homeward Bound!

For the eyes of the Lord are over the righteous, and his ears are open unto their prayers: but the face of the Lord is against them that do evil.
—1 Peter 3:12, KJV

Jesus saith unto her, Said I not unto thee, that, if thou wouldest believe, thou shouldest see the glory of God?
—John 11:40, KJV

The situation made absolutely no sense whatsoever! How could God allow it to happen? This was no ordinary crucible, and there were times when she felt numb in every respect. Rejected, despised, abused, betrayed, and ridiculed, she felt lost and alone. Was she so unworthy that she deserved this fate? In her car "home," she began her devotions as the morning rush-hour traffic sped by. *Why am I even worshiping Him,* she wondered, *when it seems as if He has abandoned me?*

Then she remembered the encouragement she had received from a friend some months earlier, telling her not to give up on God, even though her prayers did not seem to be on the answered list. On its heels followed the memory of her two spiritual brothers, Joseph and Job. As she contemplated their lives, she realized what they had in common despite enduring immense suffering: their steadfast determination to serve God. They had decided to trust His loving care, no matter what. With her mind fortified and her spirit strengthened, she completed her devotions with renewed hope that God would see her through this ordeal.

That same God, in His mysterious way, used that someone to start a miraculous chain of events. She got off the streets and found a job. Like an eagle mounting up higher and higher, she learned to wait upon the Lord. He had not forsaken her, and she had not given up on Him. Without a roof over her head and without a job, with miserable comforters and false accusers, her faith had been tested and proven. Now she knew beyond any doubt that regardless of circumstance, God was her Redeemer, her Father, and she was His child.

What are you facing today, child of God? Are your fears overwhelming? God has you in His sight. He has not abandoned you. He says to you now, "Be still, and know that I am God: I will be exalted among the heathen, I will be exalted in the earth" (Psalm 46:10, KJV).

Cloreth S. Greene

June 19

Exodus

"But as for you, you meant evil against me; but God meant it for good."
—Genesis 50:20, NKJV

It has been very difficult being in a strange country over the past seven years, without family assistance and not having the means to support myself. I have jokingly called it my Egypt-wilderness experience. There have been times when it seemed I would be consumed by fear and anxiety. I lost hope in God and decided to take matters into my own hands. As a result, I have been scammed, abused financially, manipulated, and abandoned several times over.

In hindsight, this all occurred because I lost faith. I prayed but never waited for God's answer. I thought He would not forgive me. I sinned in direct defiance of His laws, and as a Christian, I should have known better. But God, in His lovingkindness, does not hold our sins against us if we genuinely repent. I was reminded of Psalm 25:6, which says, "Remember, O Lord, Your tender mercies and Your lovingkindnesses, for they are from of old" (NKJV).

I continued to struggle. Whenever I thought things were looking up, it lasted only a few years before I was at rock bottom again. When I finally realized there was nothing I could do in my own power, I cried out to God:

> To You I will cry, O Lord my Rock:
> Do not be silent to me,
> Lest, if You are silent to me,
> I become like those who go down to the pit (Psalm 28:1, NKJV).

My faith had to be transformed into action. It had to be more than just a concept that I studied in a Sabbath School lesson. Not until I let go of the reins could God take control of my situation. And then the impossible became possible with God! In my time of distress, I turned to my Creator and Friend. With prayer and fasting, I was given a renewed sense of hope that my situation would change. And although I did not know how, I praised God for the victory. For two years, I worshiped aloud in my apartment, dancing like David and Miriam. I thanked God for what He was about to do. I sensed deep in my spirit that a change was coming.

"And we know that all things work together for good to those who love God, to those who are the called according to His purpose" (Romans 8:28, NKJV). God is faithful, and He loves us with an unending love. I am now settling into a new chapter in my life, continuing to grow in faith. Never lose hope! If He could rescue me, He can rescue you!

Kimberly M. H. Henry

June 20

The Pressure of Third Base

"Come to Me, all who are weary and burdened, and I will give you rest."
—Matthew 11:28, NASB

I recently shared a message about God's overwhelming love that I would like to share with you. While trying to express the depths of God's love for the audience, the image of a baseball game popped into my head. Now, mind you, I am not a sports fan; however, when God desires to share His love, it does not matter what analogy He chooses to use!

Imagine a player on third base with another team member up to bat. Everyone's focus is on the runner on third base. The ball cracks against the bat, and now the pressure is on to make it to home plate. The crowd is chanting, "Run!" as the umpire watches intently to see whether the player will make it to home plate.

As I spoke, God showed His love for me in this analogy. He is the One standing at home plate, rooting for you to come home. You can do it! The angels are in the crowd, chanting, "Come home! Run! You can make it!" At that moment, getting around the bases of life seems so daunting. You are weary. Exhausted. Totally unsure that you can make it. But as you listen to the chanting, you feel renewed energy coming from somewhere. A boost of rejuvenation from seemingly nowhere floods your body. You begin to run, and as you do, a glimpse of home plate catches your eye. You know it means victory! The image takes over, and now you are running with every ounce of power and passion within you.

Your heavenly Father is at home plate, and you hear Him say, "Come home, all who are weary and heavy laden, and I will give you rest!" You can hardly get there fast enough! You are now within inches of home plate. Then you hear the word *safe*! You are home!

The angels erupt in praise as they cheer from the stands. Tears fill your eyes. Though you feel utterly spent, you are victorious! You made it home!

Whatever bases you find yourself navigating through at the moment, no matter how far away home plate seems, and no matter how weary you are, know this: it is because of God's great love that you can successfully make it to home plate and victory. Keep running with Jesus, and victory is certain! You will hear the words, "Well done! You are safe. Welcome home!"

Sabrina Crichlow

June 21

Leftover Love

Live a lover's life, . . . a life Jesus will be proud of.
—Philippians 1:9–11, *The Message*

Not quite six months ago, I lost my husband of almost twenty-six years, although we had been soulmates for the better part of thirty years. Every day I hear, in the recesses of my mind, snippets of Jim's wise, caring counsel: "Always keep the top half of the gas tank full." "Use all three of your mirrors so you don't back into my truck *again.*" Jim Sutton was a big man with a big heart who lived life to the fullest and was happiest when sharing Jesus. On top of that, he always made me feel like the planet's most beautiful and cherished wife. And then he was gone.

During a phone call with my grief counselor, she suggested I would eventually have to redirect—repurpose, if you please—the love I still had for Jim but could not bestow until resurrection morning. Frankly, I did not care for this thought, yet I began praying that God would show me what to do with the "leftover love" weighing painfully on my broken heart. I wanted to heal. Then, in my Bible reading one morning, God gave me the solution to this conundrum, couched in Paul's words to the Philippians: "So this is my prayer: that your love will flourish [Really? That can happen even *after* Jim's death?] and that you will not only love much but well. . . . Live a lover's life, circumspect and exemplary, a life Jesus will be proud of: bountiful in fruits from the soul, making Jesus Christ attractive to all" (Philippians 1:9–11, *The Message*).

Soon after, I took myself on a Sabbath retreat to my back deck, where I spent the day in prayerful study. I wanted to discover what a widow living "a lover's life" looks like and what that had to do with healing. During my retreat, God led me to some thoughts that provided clarification:

> The thrilling secret beyond all suffering is that even—*especially*—in that place of suffering, we can become God's gift to others. [. . .]
>
> [. . .] Our hearts may be busted and bruised . . . but I just keep repeating the healing secret of what to do with your own broken heart: *give it away, because this is how you begin to heal.* [. . .]
>
> [. . .] In being the gift of healing for someone's brokenness, we receive a gift of healing for our own brokenness. [. . .]
>
> So here's to being the gift. [. . .]
>
> Here's to the beginning of a new journey.*

And I wished myself a bon voyage.

Carolyn Rathbun Sutton

---

* Ann Voskamp, *Be the Gift: Let Your Brokenness Be Turned* Into *Abundance* (Grand Rapids, MI: Zondervan, 2017), 5–7; italics in original. Ellipses in brackets indicate omitted content; those not in brackets appear in the original.

June 22

Upside Down

"Behold, I am going to do something new,
Now it will spring up;
Will you not be aware of it?
I will even make a roadway in the wilderness,
Rivers in the desert."
—Isaiah 43:19, NASB

I am not sure what possessed me to plan a most unlikely excursion for my fifteen-year-old grandson and my seventy-eight-year-old self. (A secret ingredient perhaps in our veggie nachos at the new Tex-Mex restaurant in town? Or, more likely, my upside-down existence since my husband Jim's death six months before that still clouded my thinking.) In any case, Zion and I signed ourselves up for a four-rope zip line adventure in Georgia's nearby mountains. By the time zip line day arrived, four family members, ranging in age from eleven to seventy-eight (yeah, me), had gotten involved. And the adventure had expanded from four to seven zip lines. Actually, I originally signed up as a spectator, but the slick-talking zip line manager at the front desk convinced me I would be safe, even in my elderly "condition." And that is how I found myself sporting a bright-yellow helmet and an unflattering seat harness.

Then, the zip line festivities began. Though I whooped in support of my family members whizzing down the first four lines (I always went last), I would hold my breath, cling to the safety line, and squeeze my eyelids tightly shut on my own terrifying rides. Before our ride down the fifth (and longest) line, the guide suggested some might like to zip-line upside down. I stifled a scornful laugh at his preposterous suggestion. Then my three family members actually did it! So I began to self-commune: *Carolyn, you just lost your soulmate of thirty years. What could be worse than that? Being upside down on a zip line cannot be any scarier than the uncertainty and loneliness you have been carrying around.* "What's that flip-over maneuver again?" I asked the guide. Soon I was zipping down the line upside down. When I opened my eyes and looked "up," I saw a forested pond "above" me. When I looked "down," my elevated feet appeared to be walking across the sky. I was living a metaphor. The location of the earth and sky had not changed, but my perspective had. For suspended and whizzing with me through thin air, God was doing "something new," something healing. Euphoria? No, more like conviction. Though recently widowed, I now knew I would survive the ride ahead in my new upside-down world.

Carolyn Rathbun Sutton

June 23

God's Timing Is Perfect

God is our refuge and strength,
A very present help in trouble.
—Psalm 46:1, NKJV

The year 2020 was a year that most of us would rather forget, but then how can you forget a year that never was? At least, that is how it felt with COVID-19's isolation and closed restaurants, schools, and churches. Then there were the masks! It would be hard to forget the masks. Looking back on it, that year was quite eventful for us, though not in a good way. In June, my husband was put on steroid medication that sent him, two days later, into atrial fibrillation (A-fib) for the first time. His heart was shocked back into rhythm in the emergency room.

In late October, my husband and I came down with COVID-19. My case was mild compared to his. He ended up with pneumonia and was hospitalized. While there, he went into A-fib again and was moved to the ICU (intensive care unit). His hospital stay lasted eleven days. We had planned a trip to California to visit our youngest daughter and her family but had to cancel the night before, with boarding passes already issued, because my husband had another A-fib episode.

In November, a number of our family traveled to Mexico on vacation. On their return, our daughter had an emergency appendectomy, and our granddaughter's gallbladder needed removal. Our precious three-year-old great-grandson was rushed to the hospital and then transferred by ambulance to a pediatric ICU with a diagnosis of type 1 diabetes. The father of our granddaughter's mother-in-law passed away, and she had to fly home to be with family.

Here is where we can see God's hand through it all. If we had taken our planned trip, we would not have been available to help when it was desperately needed. What if our daughter's appendix had ruptured, our granddaughter had her gallbladder attack, our little great-grandson had diabetes symptoms, or the precious father had died while they were in Mexico? God providentially held all of this back until they arrived back home in America. What if we had taken that trip and my husband went into A-fib on the plane?

While God did not cause or prevent these things from happening, He knew what needed to be done to ease the circumstances. We never know what is around the corner, but by faith, we can know God will be there to see us through.

Sue Anderson

June 24

All My Help Comes From the Lord

I will lift up mine eyes unto the hills, from whence cometh my help.
My help cometh from the LORD.
—Psalm 121:1, 2, KJV

Several years ago, I was admitted to the hospital with excruciating pain in my left side. Initially, they thought it was a urinary tract infection, but after an abdominal ultrasound, they discovered I had a kidney infection. Then I heard the comforting voice of the Holy Spirit: "Dawn, pray your way to victory." Right there and then, I knew my only source of survival and help would be in praying to the Lord. I learned to pray when I did not feel like praying. Psalm 121 became my daily affirmation. I worshiped the God of heaven in the hospital room—weak, battered, and ravished by pain and fever. For the next seven days, I was treated with seven different antibiotics, but instead of improving, my condition grew worse.

On the eighth day, the doctor walked into my room, held up a bottle, and said to me, "This is the best antibiotic on the market to treat kidney infection; there is no other like it." A second scan revealed that my kidney had started to form abscesses on the exterior. It was Sabbath when they performed surgery to drain the abscess and obtain a specimen. After that, the sample revealed I had methicillin-resistant *Staphylococcus aureus* (MRSA), a type of bacteria that is extremely difficult to treat because it resists most antibiotics.

The medical team was astonished because five previous specimens were negative for MRSA. With the correct diagnosis, I was given vancomycin—one of the few antibiotics to treat this superbug. The infectious disease doctor told me that he had never had a case of MRSA affecting the kidney in which the bacteria had remained undetected in the blood. He said he could only hypothesize that it was present, and my body fought it.

Five days later, the fever was gone, and I was released from the hospital to a rehabilitation facility to continue my recovery. It took nearly ninety days for my complete healing. Whenever I reminisce about the difficult journey with MRSA, I am reminded I am now closer to God and am growing in Him. I am eternally grateful to Him for not only giving me a second chance at life but also teaching me that prayer is the source of victory.

Dawn M. Johnson

June 25

No, Never Alone

Fear thou not; for I am with thee: be not dismayed; for I am thy God: I will strengthen thee; yea, I will help thee; yea, I will uphold thee with the right hand of my righteousness.
—Isaiah 41:10, KJV

I was heading home to Huntsville, Alabama, United States of America, after a short visit with my sister, Lynn, and her family in Virginia, United States of America. Hugs and goodbyes were exchanged, and I was in the car, singing along with the cassettes I had packed for the almost eight-hour drive home. I had decided to take an unfamiliar route to avoid the mountain and heavy interstate traffic.

The cool, clear early morning air, the beautiful landscape, and the uncluttered road made the drive just perfect—that is, until I hit what I thought was a patch of dense fog that slowed me down considerably. The scenery disappeared, and so did the road! I could not see outside the car. I literally dropped to a crawling pace because I was unfamiliar with the road and had no clue how long I would remain in the fog. I prayed, cried, and listened for the slightest sound to indicate that I was leaving the road. Talk about fear! *But what was that?* I heard the Lord say, "Fear thou not; for I am with thee: be not dismayed."

"OK, Lord," I whispered. "You drive."

I do not know how long I was in that fog, but it seemed like an eternity. And since I had taken the road less traveled, I was alone. I would have to inch my way through the fog or wait for it to dissipate. But I trusted God would bring me through it—and He did! Just as quickly as I had hit the fog, it lifted like a curtain. The view was even more beautiful. My tears quickly dried as I sang with a clearer perspective the rest of the way home.

Life is like that, isn't it? We are scurrying along, taking on our daily challenges until we hit dense fog. The death of a loved one, a broken relationship, a financial deficit, a wayward child, or a health crisis close in around us. We feel boxed in. Powerless. Alone.

My friend, we are never alone. The Promise Keeper has assured us of His presence, His comfort, and His wisdom. "O what peace we often forfeit"* when we try to work things out ourselves and fail to trust Him. The fog is Satan's FEAR: False Evidence Appearing Real. It is a favorite tactic of his. But God has everything under control. He holds us in the palm of His Hand. *Thank You, Lord, for Your abiding presence always.*

Kaven Ible

---

* Joseph M. Scriven, "What a Friend We Have in Jesus," 1855, public domain.

June 26

The Perfect Plant

Seeing in the distance a fig tree in leaf, he went to find out if it had any fruit. When he reached it, he found nothing but leaves, because it was not the season for figs. Then he said to the tree, "May no one ever eat fruit from you again." And his disciples heard him say it.
—Mark 11:13, 14, NIV

Do you have a garden? I have attempted to grow tomatoes and peppers in my backyard. It is a bit of an adventure. One year I had plants that grew lovely tomatoes and peppers. However, just before harvest, something (a squirrel or chipmunk, I suspect) came and enjoyed my produce. But they did not just take a tomato and eat it. They took one bite out of each tomato and each pepper and left the rest of the fruit on the vine to rot. A maddening scenario.

The next year I acquired a pepper plant. This time I decided to keep it safely indoors. It grew tall, with beautiful leaves. It was a lovely plant. But no fruit. I even kept it over the winter, and it grew into a beautiful, lush plant with shiny leaves. The second year it produced one very tiny pepper. It did not even look like much of a pepper, just a small green ball.

And I wondered, *Though the plant itself fared so well in the house, why did it produce virtually no fruit? Isn't the purpose of a pepper plant to produce fruit? Not just look pretty?*

So I put it outside where there was a possibility for squirrels and chipmunks to pilfer the fruit before it was harvested. That year it produced peppers. I watched it carefully and tried to keep the enemies of my harvest away, and I came away with an actual crop of peppers! The plant had finally fulfilled its purpose, albeit looking a bit worse for the wear.

Gardening is not easy. Living in the environment where we produce fruit is not easy. But when we isolate ourselves, we do not produce the fruit God meant for us to bear. We become like the fig tree—beautiful but with no fruit—and our potential is unfulfilled. If we are not out in the adventuresome world where we are designed to be, we cannot generate the fruit God has prepared to produce through us. Neither can we gather the fruit God has sent us to harvest.

Just as fishermen catch fish, Jesus called His disciples to catch people. And just as we harvest fruits and veggies, Jesus calls us outside our comfort zones to find people ready for harvest—people who are ready to commit their lives to God. Sometimes, we even find them in our own backyard.

Annette M. Barnes

June 27

God Has a Plan

"For I know the plans I have for you," declares the LORD,
"plans to prosper you and not to harm you, plans to give you hope and a future."
—Jeremiah 29:11, NIV

Life was tough while growing up in the rural countryside of Jamaica. I grew up with two siblings but without a father in the home. We often lacked basic needs—clothes and shoes, food and running water. Nevertheless, I grew up happy and had high hopes and big dreams for my life. I dreamed of attending college and having a professional career, getting married by the age of twenty-five and having four children, traveling the world, and living in a mansion. That is what a successful life meant to me. I wanted the life I did not have growing up.

Not until I reached my twenties did I realize life has a way of throwing curve balls at our dreams. From sickness and broken relationships to near-death experiences, I experienced it all. Yet, through it all, I learned to pick up the pieces and keep trusting God. Through the storms of life, I learned these four lessons:

First lesson: God has a plan. He wants us to know Him and love Him above all earthly possessions. God desires to give us eternal life, and that is better than gaining the entire world.

Second lesson: Material things do not indicate success, though some are necessary in life. Everything I sought was only temporary in the light of eternity.

Third lesson: God can heal us from the pain and disappointment of life. He is the God who heals, and He is ready to help us. He does not hold grudges because of yesterday's failure.

Fourth lesson: God is enough; therefore, I am enough. Though we were made for relationships, they should not come before our relationship with our Creator.

Unfulfilled dreams and broken promises can sometimes get in the way of trusting and believing God, but we can find peace and comfort in knowing God has a plan for us. His plans are always the best. I have accomplished all my dreams and plans, except I am still single and have no children. Even though I desire the latter, I know I am complete in Christ. One day I will be made whole when I see Jesus. I will shout and sing a hallelujah song. My trials will be over. I will have completed the journey and rest safely at home with Jesus.

Dawn M. Johnson

June 28

God Knows

*Even before a word is on my tongue,
behold, O Lord, you know it altogether.*
—Psalm 139:4, ESV

Growing up, I never imagined myself as a teacher or professor. I always dreamed of being an architect, which I did and enjoyed until my husband and I decided to move to the United States of America so he could study to become a pastor. To make a long story short, after fourteen years at Andrews University, my husband and I returned to Brazil as theology professors with our doctorate and master's degrees, ready to teach religion to university students.

The first year of teaching was challenging, learning how to deal with students, the system, and class preparation. There were many rough days, but one stood out as especially hard. The students seemed indifferent and defiant. It seemed my teaching was making no difference. To make matters worse, the online platform I used for this class was not working properly.

The next day I seriously considered whether I should continue as a religion professor or transition back to architecture. I prayed, asking God to send me some encouragement because the situation had become very difficult. In that particular class, I was teaching about a Christian worldview. The goal of this class was to explore the controversy between Jesus and Satan. Later that day, I gave the students an exam.

After finishing the exam, a student asked to talk with me. She wanted to let me know she had begun the semester as a non-Adventist, even though her entire family was Seventh-day Adventist. But after reading the assigned chapters of *The Great Controversy*, she realized that everything now made sense in her life. She also mentioned how my classes had helped her to further understand the world. She said she had chosen to become a Seventh-day Adventist. She was experiencing conversion!

I was in awe. My heart was full of joy and gratitude to God for two reasons. First, a young woman understood the great controversy and its implications for her life and decided to be part of the Seventh-day Adventist Church. Second, God had heard my silent prayer and used this student to show His love and care for me. How I love being a professor of religion! And this same God wants to show His love and care for you!

Carina Prestes

June 29

Rough Water

*Then he got into the boat and his disciples followed him.
Suddenly a furious storm came up on the lake, so that the waves swept over the boat.
But Jesus was sleeping.*
—Matthew 8:23, 24, NIV

Have you ever been on a ship in the middle of a storm? Well, I have! My husband and I traveled to Guatemala for an evangelistic campaign. At the end of the campaign, the hosts took us sightseeing around the country. One sight was Lake Atitlán. This lake is notable because, at certain times of the day, the tide gets rough, and it becomes quite difficult to navigate.

I would never shy away from taking a boat ride on a lake, and so we did just that. Heading back to the boat to start the return trip, I felt somewhat apprehensive when I noticed that the men who were crewing the boat had begun to put on their life jackets. They had not done so on the previous trip. Then they instructed us to put on our life jackets and to place some additional cushioning on our seats. Feeling uneasy, I prayed to God, asking for His care. We never imagined what we were about to experience!

As we started to cross the lake, the waters churned, and the ship bounced unsteadily atop the waves. We had to be careful not to strike our heads against the roof of the boat. It hurt every time the ship was slammed by the waves or tossed about on the fierce waters. More frightening was the sound of the boat moaning against the pressure of the waves. It seemed the ship would break into pieces at any moment. How grateful we were to God that He brought us safely through the surrounding storm.

When I read Matthew 8:24, I think of the disciples and how, like them, we try to fight the storms of our lives on our own. We become terrified, helpless, and are about to give up, just like the disciples that night on the Sea of Galilee. Where is God? He is right there. Our Savior waits to hear us say, "Lord! Save us. Lord, help me. I can do nothing more on my own. I am sinking, Lord. This problem is too great, and my strength is failing me."

At that moment, He will rise to calm the storm that threatens to destroy us. Let us not wait until the last moment when divine help is right beside us. Call on Him, and watch to see what He will do on your behalf.

Damaris Prieto

June 30

When the Storms Come, Why Fear?

"Fear not, for I am with you;
Be not dismayed, for I am your God.
I will strengthen you,
Yes, I will help you,
I will uphold you with My righteous right hand."
—Isaiah 41:10, NKJV

A vicious thunderstorm with tornado-like characteristics pummeled the region where I live in Maryland on the East Coast of the United States of America. I had entered a shopping mall to buy a couple of items only a few hours before this life-altering event, so I was totally unaware of the weather alerts warning everyone to take safety precautions and find shelter. I left the mall, and because there were no signs of impending danger, I decided to drive to a nearby store for a few items I still needed. Within minutes, I drove into an ominous thunderstorm of epic proportions. A darkened sky, falling trees, crackling lightning, pouring rain, forceful winds, poor visibility, and traffic jams surrounded me. I cried out to God, "Am I going to be OK, Lord?" I was unable to determine my beltway location or find my way home, unaware that God was with me. You see, moments later, God opened my eyes, and I saw the next exit was my homeward-bound exit. What a relief!

I had begun to sing "Almost Home" when a short distance ahead of me, a fallen tree blocked the road. *Oh no! How will I get home?* I tried a different route, which ended the same way. My soul cried, *How do I get home?* After a third attempt to find a way forward was blocked by another fallen tree, my heart's cry was, *Will I ever get home, Lord?*

I drove to the parking lot of a nearby high school to wait it out. Suddenly, I noticed the traffic seemed to be moving steadily. A quiet voice within me urged me to try again. As I made the turn onto the road that would lead home, I saw a car behind me turn around and drive away. Paralyzed by fear, I stopped the car. Fear had blinded me from seeing that the fallen tree now blocked only one lane.

Suddenly, I heard a loud voice say, "It's OK!"

I repeated to myself, "It's OK." But still I did not move.

The voice sounded again, more urgently than before. "It's OK!" My entire being jolted into action as I realized I was truly homeward bound. What a night of rejoicing that was for me! In my angst, anxiety, and fear, God was closer than any other. He whispered, "Cynthia, I will never leave you nor forsake you. I am always with you."

Cynthia Best-Goring

July 1

Bristles

*"For nothing is concealed that will not become evident,
nor anything hidden that will not be known and come to light."*
—Luke 8:17, NASB

This morning, after finishing my breakfast, I went to the sink to rinse my dishes. I put the plate under the water and began to run the kitchen brush around the plate.

We use the kitchen brush, which usually stays behind the sink, to scrub the dishes before they get washed. The brush has a handle and bundles of bristles stuck into the head of the brush, seven rows wide by eight rows deep. Each of the fifty-six bundles has about twenty-five individual bristles in it. (Yes, I counted them!) The outside bunches are a bit worn in places. The bunches are placed rather close together to guarantee a good solid brushing, but there are still empty places in between the bunches of bristles.

The usual practice is to rinse the dishes and then set them aside until they get washed. After I had gone around a couple of swishes, I saw an earwig crawling across what I was rinsing. I had not seen it when I picked up the brush or the plate. I had not noticed it when I started rinsing the dishes. But it came out and made itself known to me.

I wondered how many nasty things I have hidden in my nice Christian lady "bristle brush." I have my church membership bunch. There is also my devoted wife bunch, my tithe bunch, my faithful church-attendance bunch, and my teacher bunch.

But I also have some bunches that are a little worn. One of them is my patience bunch. It can show up when I am really stressed because I sometimes forget to let Jesus be in charge. Another one is my self-sacrificing bunch because sometimes I do not want to give up my wants and desires to yield to someone else, so I get a little worn down trying to "be nice," as I know a child of God ought to be.

But what concerns me is the thought of what I might have hidden deep in my "good" bunches of bristles. Is it so well hidden that most will never see it? Have I hidden it in my heart rather than hiding God's Word? All the undesirable feelings, thoughts, and actions were washed away when I was baptized, and if I want them to stay gone, I need to keep God's Word hidden in my heart. Do you have any "earwigs" hiding in your bristle brush?

Summer Stahl

July 2

Clean Hands

Whatsoever thy hand findeth to do, do it with thy might; for there is no work, nor device, nor knowledge, nor wisdom, in the grave, whither thou goest.
—Ecclesiastes 9:10, KJV

As the weather warmed up, the nursing-home facility granted brief scheduled outside visits for their residents to reunite with family and loved ones. A pandemic was running rampant in the world and had taken its toll on the population, especially the elderly and vulnerable who were residents in health care facilities. Restrictions, in accordance with the Centers for Disease Control and Prevention guidelines, were in place so that everyone would be safe.

One staff member reported that due to staffing shortages, sometimes the residents tried to help one another. This practice could have contributed to the spread of the virus in such crowded and understaffed facilities.

I had a scheduled visit with an elderly family friend. Nita seemed happy to see me as we engaged in lively conversation. She had an earlier visit with her nephew, who left her with a bag of her favorite candies. She shared the miniature Reese's Peanut Butter Cups with me. I complimented her on her beautifully manicured nails.

One young male staff member approached me with an extended hand in a friendly gesture. I refused to extend my hand in return. The spread of the pandemic had caused fear and panic to the point that many felt uncomfortable with even as simple a gesture as a handshake.

"My hands are probably the cleanest hands in this place," he said and then gave me a big smile. I still refused to extend my hand. As my visit continued, I learned that the young man's role at the facility was the "diaper man." He was responsible for changing the diapers of residents who needed this type of service. "Whatsoever thy hand findeth to do"—this young man was the designated "diaper man" and had no qualms about it. It was just a part of his job duties as a team member at the care facility.

Nita and I concluded our visit and I went on my way. Several months after my visit with her, she passed away at the age of ninety-two. Nita was a hardworking woman who loved the Lord, nature, and her fur babies. She now sleeps, awaiting the Second Coming of Jesus.

Fartema Mae Fagin

July 3

From His Eye View

"Look at the birds of the air; they do not sow or reap or store away in barns, and yet your heavenly Father feeds them. Are you not much more valuable than they?"
—Matthew 6:26, NIV

One summer day, as I was busy in the kitchen, I looked out the window because something caught my attention. Right there in front of me was a beautiful hummingbird, looking at me through the window as if to ask for some sweet water to refresh itself on the hot summer day.

As I contemplated the amazing colors of this tiny bird and its ability to remain in the air, I stood amazed. It left as suddenly as it had arrived. I had only a few seconds to watch, but it was enough to leave me with a feeling of awe at God's amazing creation. I stood there, reflecting on the wonder of God's ability to make such complex designs, combine colors in such unique ways, use physics and engineering I do not even understand, and put together such a tiny and beautiful creature. Those few seconds of awe reminded me of the verse that says God cares about birds, including those that are not so unique nor as beautiful as hummingbirds, such as sparrows.

While on a recent trip to a women's retreat, I remembered this encounter with the hummingbird as my plane took off and the ground faded into the distance. From that altitude, there was no chance of seeing a person, much less a tiny bird. As I thought of how God looks down from His heights and cares about the birds—the tiny, the common, the special, and the unique creatures that fly over our heads and fit in our hands—I again felt in awe of His love. If God, from much higher than the cruising altitude of my flight, could see a tiny bird and care about its life, would He not see me? Would He not care about my worries and concerns as He says He does? Would He value me as much as that tiny bird I cannot even see from my plane window?

I know that God cares, even when I do not feel it or when it is hard to believe because there is no evidence. From my seat in the sky, I cannot see the birds, but I know they are there because I have seen them in the past. Likewise, I have seen God's care for me in the past. And I have His Word and assurance that He will never fail His promises.

Lord, as I continue to trust Your Word and grow in faith, remind me to look with awe at Your creation and know You care about me. Help me to live out this assurance in my life.

Nilde Itin

July 4

Paws, Claws, and Know-It-Alls

Live in peace with everyone.
—Romans 12:18, NLT

When one has a community of cats with unique temperaments in the neighborhood, there will be conflicts. Needing several good hunters to reduce the rodent population that was destroying our garden, we adopted four young cats. We were happy they remained socially comfortable in their new home with us, although my twelve-pound Zimba pouted for a few days.

One dark night, without warning, peace and security vanished from our deck when an uninvited guest appeared. Let me call him Boss. He stood proud and tall. His badge of authority was a two-inch scab on the side of his cheek. His dirty yellow coat gave evidence of a bad-hair day. I immediately knew Boss was trouble! His agenda was to dominate. Without provocation, he would stalk the gentlest cats, attacking with a shriek and a bite or slash of his claws! Boss always left behind an intimidated and injured cat with less fur than when he had found it. Very likely, Boss suffered great deprivation and abuse in the past, never having been nurtured and loved as had our integrated cat family.

Are we not all like Boss at times? Many of us have been dropped on the back roads of life, starving for love and emotional security. On the prowl, some seek those they can intimidate. Often, claws are hidden discreetly within sarcasm, unsolicited advice, or a critical spirit. Such attacks in life leave one feeling confused and wounded.

Should we meet someone like this in our community, church, or workplace, how do we maintain the Spirit of Christ and avoid being wounded personally?

Immediately, pray for the mind and heart of Christ. Next, practice the art of graciousness, for Romans 12:18 tells us to "live in peace with everyone" (NLT). Step back and allow them to give their opinion without interruption. The next step is the most difficult. Keep your emotions and tone of voice under control! Never allow yourself to be pushed into a negative or defensive mode. Finally, remember the wise words of C. S. Lewis: "To be a Christian means to forgive the inexcusable, because God has forgiven the inexcusable in you."*

Dottie Barnett

---

* C. S. Lewis, *The Weight of Glory* (New York: HarperCollins, 1980), 182.

July 5

Expect a Miracle

Then Peter said, "Silver and gold I do not have, but what I do have I give you: In the name of Jesus Christ of Nazareth, rise up and walk."
—Acts 3:6, NKJV

The man, whom I will call Benjamin, could not walk. He had never been able to walk, had never taken a step in his life, and he must have awakened that eventful morning with absolutely no idea that this day would be any different from all those that had preceded it. He was wrong.

Benjamin was carried by someone to the Beautiful Gate, as he was every morning, and deposited there to beg for money. It would not have crossed his mind to ask for anything more, as money was his perceived need. Healing—an impossible thing—was not likely to have been on his radar at all.

Peter and John were passing by on their way to the temple. They saw him; he saw them and asked for money. Oh, Benjamin! How I would love to have been looking on during those next few minutes. Benjamin was about to be the recipient of a miracle unlike any most had ever seen before or dreamed of.

After commanding his full attention, Peter informed Benjamin that he had no money, but what he did have, he would gladly give. "Get up and walk," he said. And Benjamin did.

Lame from birth—can you imagine? But there was no learning curve for Benjamin. He was told to walk, and he walked. No tottering about, no falling down, and no time needed to learn things like balance and direction and speed and coordinating arm and leg movement. In fact, we are told he leaped (verse 8). What a view that presents to my mind's eye!

We, too, awaken each morning to a new day filled with infinite possibilities—some that we have thought of and hoped for and some that have never occurred to us. Just think what God is capable of doing for us and what He will do for us if we let Him.

On the last morning of Benjamin's paralysis, he did not dream of putting himself to bed that night. Neither do we know what is in store for us on any given day. Let us be prepared for the unexpected.

In fact, let us expect a miracle.

Carolyn K. Karlstrom

July 6

Coney Island Miracle

The angel of the Lord encamps around those who fear him, and he delivers them.
—Psalm 34:7, NIV

It was a beautiful day in July, perfect for an outing. My husband and I decided to take our children—four-year-old Etisha and three-year-old Jaime—to the amusement park on Coney Island, New York. We invited a family friend to come along.

The children's excitement upon learning that they were going to Coney Island was exhilarating, to say the least. Shrieks of joy filled the air. The thought of riding a train added to the excitement.

When we arrived about an hour later, we decided to take the children on a few rides. We walked around for a while as we enjoyed the sights and sounds of Coney Island. Then came the time for the special treat of an ice cream cone—a moment of sheer pleasure for the children. While they waited to be served, they admired their surroundings. Many vendors displayed their wares of beautiful things just waiting to be bought.

Suddenly, the question was asked, "Where is Etisha?" Our world came to a halt as the search began. Panic and desperation immediately followed this question.

My husband and our friend went in opposite directions in search of our daughter. I stayed at the ice cream parlor just in case she returned. During those crucial moments, I prayed for God's protection over her, trying to avoid the negative thoughts that vied for my attention.

God heard my prayer. Etisha had wandered off as she was admiring the beautiful things all around her. She told us she realized she was lost, and then she heard a voice that said, "Go back the other way." She obeyed. It was then she saw her dad running toward her with open arms. She was safe. God sent His guardian angel that day to protect a little lost girl.

Sometimes we wander away from the loving care and protection of our heavenly Father. We are distracted by all the "beautiful things" around us. Yet our Father is constantly watching over us and whispers, "Come back."

May we not only hear but also listen to the still, small Voice that says, "This is the way; walk in it" (Isaiah 30:21, NIV).

Merita E. Joseph-Lewis

July 7

Turning Point

Therefore, if anyone is in Christ, he is a new creation; old things have passed away; behold, all things have become new.
—2 Corinthians 5:17, NKJV

Thursday, July 7, 2005, is a day that is etched in my memory. I had arrived in London on March 1 with a two-year working holiday visa, as many Australians were doing at the time. Living in a suburb north of London, I commuted into the city via the underground so I could work at a large tertiary hospital. I awoke to my normal morning alarm on July 7 but decided I needed to snooze the alarm for another five minutes in bed. Strangely, I never heard a subsequent alarm and slept in. *Oh no!* I thought, *I'm going to be late for work!* I rushed about to get myself ready and bolted out the front door, walking briskly toward the train station, hoping I would get there on time.

At the station, the platforms were uncharacteristically full of people. Then I heard an announcement that officials had suspended train operations. At a public pay phone, I called work, explaining that I had no way to get there. As I walked back home, I passed a shop with television sets in the window. What I saw on the screens shocked me! I saw emergency vehicles and personnel, mangled train parts lying across the tracks, human bodies covered up, and carnage everywhere! I did not fully understand and rushed home to turn on the television news. At the same time, I grabbed my mobile phone, which I had inadvertently left behind in my dash for the train not long before. I had eighty-one missed calls, including international calls from my family back home. Then reality hit. The very train I normally took to work each day had been the one blown up! I began to weep uncontrollably. The undeniable truth was that God had intervened to save my life.

Only recently, after straying from my Christian upbringing, I had reluctantly begun to attend church with my two housemates. Though I still had doubts about God, He, in His mercy, would find a way not only to draw me back to Him but also to show me that He cares for me, has a purpose for my life, and wants to give me a hope and a future (see Jeremiah 29:11). That day, seventeen years ago, will forever be a turning point in my life. I can boldly say, "I have found my way back to God." He has blessed me in my career and personal life in ways I could never have imagined. He cares for me. I hope you know He cares for you too!

Jenny Rivera

July 8

Near-Death Experience

"What is the price of two sparrows—one copper coin?
But not a single sparrow can fall to the ground without your Father knowing it."
—Matthew 10:29, NLT

When I was a little girl, I lived with my aunt and uncle and studied in a little school some distance from their home. My uncle took me to school every day on his bicycle before continuing his ride to work. In the evening, after school, he brought me back home on his bike. He did his part in educating me, and I did mine.

One rainy day my uncle rode me to school and continued on to work, as usual. I was chagrined, however, to find the school empty; we had not been aware it was a holiday. I did not like the idea of waiting there alone for so many hours. Since my uncle would not return for me until late in the afternoon, I decided to walk home. I tossed my schoolbag over my shoulder, picked up my water bottle, and headed home.

Somewhere along the return trip, though, I sensed someone was following me. Turning to look behind me, I spotted a man with a gunnysack in his hand. He appeared to be taking purposeful strides toward me. My little heart skipped a beat, and I picked up my pace. When I next glanced over my shoulder again, I realized the stranger had also picked up his pace and was staring intently at me. I started to run, my heart in my mouth. The roadway on which I traveled was deserted. One more glance revealed that the man behind me was running as well, closing the gap between us. Panic threatened to overcome me. Then I looked ahead of myself, down the road. My uncle's house seemed to have appeared out of nowhere! Could it be I was there already? It was almost as if some unknown power had airlifted me to safety just in the nick of time!

I reached home and the safety of my uncle's family. When I was out of the stranger's view, I breathed a great sigh of relief and looked heavenward. I could literally feel the protecting presence of God all about me. That incident assured me that God has a plan for each one of us. In fact, the Bible tells us, "Before I formed you in the womb I knew you; before you were born I sanctified you" (Jeremiah 1:5, NKJV).

Rita Das

July 9

Lemon Meringue Pie

*But speak thou the things which become sound doctrine:
that the aged men be sober, grave, temperate, sound in faith, in charity, in patience.
The aged women likewise, that they be in behaviour as becometh holiness,
not false accusers, not given to much wine, teachers of good things;
that they may teach the young women to be sober,
to love their husbands, to love their children.*
—Titus 2:1–4, KJV

On the Monday after Mother's Day, the companies located in our office building decided to have a barbecue. The potato salad, along with everything else, was very tasty! One of my coworkers decided to get a slice of lemon meringue pie for dessert. She cut a very small sliver of pie and took small bites. I mentioned that I do not particularly like the meringue, but I love the lemon. (Lemon meringue happened to be my mother's favorite pie.) My colleague responded that she had never had lemon meringue pie before! Shocked, I exclaimed, "*What?*" Then, the remaining two coworkers seated at our table said the same thing. They had never tasted lemon meringue pie!

I was speechless for a minute, and then a dose of reality hit me! I said, "Oh, yes, you are only in your twenties." They responded with, "Yes, we have a lot to learn!" I then realized how my seventy years of life experiences could influence the young women I associate with either positively or negatively. And I do have the responsibility, as a Christian, to ensure that my life tells them a story that is both loving and redemptive.

In my role as a supervisor, I often share my knowledge and expertise regarding processes, policies, and procedures. I asked myself, *When an ex-employee emailed me with some unkind, unrepeatable words, was my reaction acceptable to my onlookers? When my coworker was in tears, had I looked the other way? Does it matter when we share what we did over the weekend?*

The goal and responsibility of a Titus 2 woman is to train younger women in biblical, measurable, Spirit-empowered, love-based living. I never thought that lemon meringue pie would open my eyes to the measure of influence my life as a Christian has on everyone I meet.

I pray that both you and I will continue to be the kind of examples that lead others to the Jesus who loves us all.

Sylvia A. Franklin

July 10

Encourage One Another

I am sending him to you for the express purpose that you may know about our circumstances and that he may encourage your hearts.
—Colossians 4:8, NIV

When reading my women's devotional book each morning, I often pause to thank the Lord for my sisters in Christ who make these books possible. Yet, despite all the years I have read these books, I did not fully appreciate them until the COVID-19 lockdowns took away my physical interaction with loved ones. During that time, the story of Elijah also took on new meaning for me. He, too, was isolated at one point in his life (1 Kings 17:2–7). Even so, God provided for the prophet's needs: fresh water from the brook Cherith and a daily supply of bread and meat, delivered by ravens each morning and evening. God provided for me in my isolation as well.

In one devotional book* I read during this time, some authors shared their struggles with losing family members, the grief that followed, and how the heavenly Father had guided them through these painful uncertainties. Other sisters shared about God's protective covering when they and/or family members traveled on the streets and highways of life. Still others shared about the wonder of God's great and marvelous creation. One devotional especially stands out in my mind. In her written piece, the author stated how God looks out for women in special ways. She lists women who suffered but were cared for by God. The author reminded me that where there is no struggle, there is not much life, strength, spiritual muscle, or a trophy or crown.[†]

Some devotionals that fed my soul also launched me into deeper Bible study and dialogue with the Lord. One such piece reflected on heaven's gates of pearl (Revelation 21:21). Pearl develops from a protective coating formed when certain mollusks are in danger. It seems that we, too, must experience hardship—and God's provisions—on our way to our heavenly home. This gave me pause for reflection for the entire day and beyond. I thank you, sisters in Christ, for recording and sharing your walks with God. God allowed you to be both my company and my comfort during a very challenging time!

Jasmine E. Grant

---

* Carolyn Rathbun Sutton, ed., *Covered and Carried* (Nampa, ID: Pacific Press®, 2021).
† Sutton, 253.

July 11

Seek Wise Counsel

Let the wise listen to these proverbs and become even wiser.
Let those with understanding receive guidance.
—Proverbs 1:5, NLT

From the time I was twelve and upward, I attended a small country church. The members of that church family were nurturing, caring, and loving. Recently, I was reminiscing with a childhood friend who also attended that church. We both agree that our experiences there influenced our lives positively and were instrumental when we made major decisions. The adults from church spent time with the young people, often joining us in a variety of social activities. We never felt intimidated when approaching these adults to seek advice on some topic. We valued the perspective of wise, dependable, and informed adults above that of our peers.

For this reason, I had difficulty reconciling the circumstances and decisions of King Rehoboam in 1 Kings 12. I was baffled that he would seek advice from his inexperienced peers on such an essential matter as ruling a kingdom instead of consulting those with greater depths of wisdom and experience. Also, how ironic that Rehoboam actually rejected counsel from the older men who had previously advised the wisest man who ever lived—his father, Solomon. The elders counseled Rehoboam to deal kindly with his people. Upon the advice of his younger friends, he did just the opposite. Rehoboam considered the advice from the inexperienced to be more valuable than that of the older men.

The older men had seen the fulfillment of King Solomon's prayer during his reign after he petitioned God for "an understanding heart to judge Your people, that I may discern between good and evil" (1 Kings 3:9, NKJV). They knew that God gave Solomon exceeding "wisdom . . . understanding, and largeness of heart" (1 Kings 4:29, NKJV). Had King Rehoboam followed in the spiritual footsteps of his father, he would have experienced the same benefits that came from his own father's counsel: "A wise man will hear and increase learning" (Proverbs 1:5, NKJV). Unlike Rehoboam, let us learn to seek wise counsel from the wise.

Dear Lord, please help me seek and accept instruction and gain wisdom from Your Holy Word. I pray this in Jesus' name. Amen.

Annette L. Vaughan

July 12

The Transformative Power of Humility

When Abigail saw David, she quickly got off her donkey and bowed down before David with her face to the ground. She fell at his feet and said: "Pardon your servant, my lord, and let me speak to you; hear what your servant has to say."
—1 Samuel 25:23, 24, NIV

David was an outcast, working on a voluntary basis as a protection force for a wealthy businessman whom he had never met. After a period of protecting the rich man's holdings, David thought it was time to be "paid" for his services. So he sent his men to Nabal, the businessman, to ask for provisions. Nabal curtly refused and accused David of being a nobody. The stage was set for conflict. Furious, David vowed to kill Nabal. Nabal's resourceful wife, Abigail, heard about the situation and decided to intervene to avert disaster. As you read the story in 1 Samuel 25, note three valuable lessons Abigail models for conflict resolution.

First, Abigail was humble in her interactions with David. With more than an abundant supply of provisions for David's men, she fell on her knees and first apologized for her husband. Though she was the wife of a wealthy landowner, she was self-effacing and soft-spoken. Today humility is a characteristic often ignored in our egotistical society. However, the Bible counsels, "Humble yourselves in the sight of the Lord, and He will lift you up" (James 4:10, NKJV).

Second, Abigail affirmed God's role in David's life. She reminded the future king that God was leading in his choices, saying, "The Lord has held you back from coming to bloodshed" (1 Samuel 25:26, NKJV) and "my lord fights the battles of the Lord" (verse 28).

Finally, Abigail protected David's reputation in God's work. She suggested he not do anything that would impact his good name and that God would deal well with him (verse 31). Humble, encouraging, and protective. Wow! What an approach to conflict resolution!

Think about your last argument. How might these tools have been useful to you? How might these tools be useful to you in the future? What if we were humble and apologized *first*? How can we be more respectful of God's role in the lives of others? How can we better practice humility in our interactions with others, respecting their rights more than our own?

Lord, help us apply Abigail's selfless principles in all our relationship challenges.

Edith C. Fraser

July 13

How Rude

And the servant of the Lord must not strive;
but be gentle unto all men, apt to teach, patient.
—2 Timothy 2:24, KJV

What a morning! My friend accompanied me to the auto body shop to get my passenger sideview mirror stabilized in its holder. We got to our destination about ten minutes before my 11:00 A.M. appointment. The warehouse windows and doors were still closed. After we waited a while, a man appeared. "Are you the one my brother said would be coming to see me?"

I nodded a yes, feeling relieved. Greeting him by name, I said good-naturedly, "Your brother said the price for the job is sixty dollars." He nodded as I continued, "Do you think that's a little steep?"

He examined my unstable mirror, which I had been holding in place with tape, and began pushing, pulling, twisting, and turning it.

Trying to be helpful, I asked, "Would you like me to take off the tape?"

His thunderclap of a response dumbfounded me. "Don't tell *me* what to do!"

I immediately apologized.

He continued, "I've been hearing the word *sorry* all my life." Walking off, he exclaimed, "Fix it yourself!"

Ten minutes elapsed. He returned, white puffs of smoke exiting his nostrils. When he headed toward my car door's mirror and said, "Let me look at it," we flew out of his path.

The mechanic maneuvered the mirror and then asked me to operate the inside motor switch. Next, he got a pinch of paste and touched it to the back of the mirror, which held it fast in its holder. The mechanic urged me to purchase a tube of this paste, which was sold only to dealers. His service charge was sixty dollars for labor plus a hundred dollars for a tube of fixative paste. I decided not to purchase the tube of glue.

Since coming to the repair place, I had had to bite my tongue several times, but I always decided that was the best choice.

The man suddenly asked, "Do you attend the same church as my brother?"

I told him we were the same denomination but met with a different congregation.

Later, when sharing with the mechanic's brother about our encounter at the auto shop, he chuckled and commented, "Usually he is not like that."

I was grateful that we had kept silent, as Jesus did when confronted with anger and rudeness. May Jesus be our example every day in the face of unprofessionalism and disrespect.

Pauline A. Dwyer-Kerr

July 14

Can I Forgive Myself?

*"The L*ORD*, the L*ORD*, a God merciful and gracious, slow to anger, and abounding in steadfast love and faithfulness."*
—Exodus 34:6, ESV

A friend told me of the night terrors his deceased wife had on occasion. She would wake up panicked that she was going to hell because she had an abortion as a teenager. It broke my heart that in her Christian walk, she never fully understood the love of Christ and the depth of His understanding and forgiveness. I assured my friend that Jesus loves us, He knows our troubles, and He understands the powers and principalities we are fighting, and if we repent and ask for forgiveness, He always forgives us. Assuredly, she was forgiven, but did she ever forgive herself?

As I heard myself reassuring my friend, a still, small Voice said, "What about you? What about the things in your life that you have not forgiven yourself for?" That caught me by surprise. I did not expect that. But through counseling another, I realized that I also need to forgive myself and fully accept the forgiveness offered by Christ. It is one thing to know that God forgives you; it is another to turn that burden over to Christ and finally forgive yourself. When I realized I had been withholding forgiveness from myself and let it go, I felt the weight of the world fall off my shoulders. How I wished my friend's wife had been able to experience that before her death.

I am so thankful for a God who loves us enough to carry our burdens and cast our sin "into the depths of the sea" (Micah 7:19, KJV). Our God is the Source of all mercy. His name is "merciful and gracious" (Exodus 34:6, ESV). He does not treat us according to what we deserve. "He does not ask if we are worthy of His love, but He pours upon us the riches of His love, to make us worthy. He is not vindictive. He seeks not to punish, but to redeem. Even the severity which He manifests through His providences is manifested for the salvation of the wayward. He yearns with intense desire to relieve the woes of men and to apply His balsam to their wounds."*

Is there something for which you need to forgive yourself? Bring it to the Savior, and lay it at His feet. It is a needless load, too heavy to bear. I pray we allow Jesus to tend our wounds.

Jo Shuck

---

* Ellen G. White, *Thoughts From the Mount of Blessing* (Mountain View, CA, Pacific Press®, 1956), 22.

July 15

A New Beginning

*And looking at them, Jesus said to them,
"With people this is impossible, but with God all things are possible."*
—Matthew 19:26, NASB

The most profound experience for me as a Christian took place when I was eighteen years old while I participated in a devotional program with my church. The program consisted of forty days of prayer and reading the Bible. At that time, I was studying chemical engineering in Peru, and my goal was to become an engineer. But sometimes God's plan for our lives is different from ours. He has a better plan. One morning, as I was on my knees praying, I cried out to God, "Can You take away all the pain from my heart? Please help me forget the trauma I experienced during my childhood. Help me, Lord!" God answered and took away my anger and healed my pain from the sexual abuse I had endured, and He helped me forgive the brother who abused me. In return, I told God, "I want to serve You, Lord. You have forgiven me and given me the opportunity to start a new life!"

For two years, I asked God for direction. Then, one day during my personal devotions, I found an answer in Luke 5:1–10. As a result, I decided to study theology after completing my chemical engineering degree and become a fisher of people for God. Shortly after I earned my theology degree, God opened a new door and gave me the opportunity to earn a master's degree in geology in the United States of America.

Before I left Peru, my brother asked me for forgiveness. I assured him that I had already forgiven him and that I prayed relentlessly that he would meet Jesus and follow Him.

God restored my life, and by His grace and love, He healed the deepest wounds from my heart! I was like a trampled flower on the ground, but Jesus found me and gave me new life. He is making me more compassionate, resilient, determined, generous, and persistent. My dedication to Him continues to grow stronger. Through the education God miraculously provided, despite the adversity I sustained in childhood, and through the God-given victory and healing I have received, I intend to help broken children and women find healing. I want to serve God and praise Him forever! My friend, God is always there to heal and give us a new beginning! With Him, everything is possible!

Raquel Bendita Larico

July 16

Not Alone

*"So do not fear, for I am with you;
do not be dismayed, for I am your God.
I will strengthen you and help you;
I will uphold you with my righteous right hand."*
—Isaiah 41:10, NIV

I have to go; I cannot stop crying," I told my supervisor. I do not remember how I got home or even seeing the road. All I remember from those moments was walking into my bedroom, falling on my knees, and crying my heart out to the Lord. My marriage of sixteen years had ended. I could not believe it. I had no idea how I would keep going, let alone how I would keep it together. But I knew that I had to find a way for my children—my twelve- and ten-year-old sons.

Doubt flooded my mind. I cried until it hurt. "Why, Lord? How did this happen?" I begged for answers. "What is going to happen to my children? How am I going to make it?" I closed my eyes and rested my head on the foot of the bed. It felt like I was resting on the Father's chest.

In the silence, I heard Him say, "I am here. I have always been here. I've got you. I promise that you are not alone."

At that moment, I felt His embrace, and peace filled my heart and mind. Then I remembered the promise Jesus gave to His children through all ages: "I am with you always, to the very end of the age" (Matthew 28:20, NIV). It was true! He had been with me during the sixteen years of my marriage, and He was with me when it ended. We can trust His promises. I knew He would be with me until the end!

It has been almost twenty years since that wonderful encounter with my Lord, and I still remember how it felt as though it were yesterday. When life gets tough, I remember the promise He gave me that day: "I've got you. . . . You are not alone."

You may be feeling lost and alone today. My friend, Jesus' promises are true. He is always by your side. If you are crying your heart out to Him, for whatever reason, just remember that He has been there for your every tear and every sorrow (Psalm 56:8, NIV). He is always by your side; He's got you! Hold on to His hand, and do not let go. No matter what the situation or problem you are going through, He is never far away. Trust Him. Hold on. You are not alone.

Mayra Rivera Mann

July 17

The Power of Prayer

*Pray at all times in the Spirit, and with this in view,
be alert with all perseverance and every request for all the saints.*
—Ephesians 6:18, NASB

When I was growing up, I heard the claim that every woman has an overwhelming desire to become a mother. I have always loved babies and admired moms packing their babies into strollers and taking them for walks. I longed for the day I would also become a mom, but I chose to get married after I had finished my schooling. Thankfully, my husband-to-be was patient enough to wait for me. So, at twenty-nine, I got married and imagined life would unfold according to our plans and timing. Our dream life of raising four children would now become a reality.

Not so! We had taken life for granted and did not realize even conception required God's green light. We thought He would just flow along with our plans, and all would be well. Well, God had a different plan. The months turned to years, and the years to almost a decade, and still no pregnancy. We followed all the advice and sought medical treatment to conceive but to no avail. As the years went by, the frustration intensified, and we struggled to watch other parents rearing and loving their children. Thankfully, our merciful Father provided us with nieces and nephews to babysit and love like our own, even to this day.

When my parents experienced a traffic accident and could not attend church, my dad begged us to go to the altar and pray on his behalf. God knows our every need and desire even before we ask, and that particular Sabbath, when we stepped into the church, a head deacon invited us to participate in a special prayer ceremony in which petitions were written and inserted in a prayer box. We both wrote out my dad's request and also added our request for a child. We later shared how we had poured out our hearts to God, and throughout the service, I was like Hannah, who went up to the tabernacle and prayed with great weeping (1 Samuel 1:10).

While we still sought medical assistance, this time our son was conceived and born nine months later to a very grateful family. We formed a big circle at the hospital and offered prayers of thanksgiving. Two years later, God doubled His blessing, and a beloved daughter was born to us. My friends, let us keep trusting and knocking like the persistent woman in Luke 18:1–18.

Caren Henry Broaster

July 18

Remembering

*And he said unto me, My grace is sufficient for thee:
for my strength is made perfect in weakness. Most gladly therefore will I
rather glory in my infirmities, that the power of Christ may rest upon me.
Therefore I take pleasure in infirmities, in reproaches, in necessities, in persecutions,
in distresses for Christ's sake: for when I am weak, then am I strong.*
—2 Corinthians 12:9, 10, KJV

What was that question that I was about to ask? I wondered. I could not remember but made a mental note to ask my daughter. Perhaps she would remember. Two days later, I still had not seen my daughter, but I remembered I had wanted to ask her something. But what was it? I asked my husband, but he could not remember either.

This made me fearful. *Why can't I remember things like I used to?* My mind played out various scenarios, none of them good. Would I end up in a facility, not knowing anyone, not even my dear children, grandchildren, or even my great-grandchildren, just as my parents and in-laws had?

The fear became entrenched. *What can I do? Who will take care of me?* This great fear is one that seems to happen to many people as they grow older. The questions! Can I forestall this loss-of-memory problem? Can I will my brain to perform better, or will I slowly become so forgetful that I do not even remember that I am forgetting? Then I asked myself, *Can I, like Paul, take pleasure in my infirmities, in reproaches, in necessities, in persecutions, in distresses, for Christ's sake? Am I able to do that now? Do I have the faith necessary to carry me through these aged years?* In 2 Corinthians 12:10, we read Paul's words, "When I am weak, then am I strong" (KJV). I feel very weak now. Does that mean that I am strong?

I have no answers. At this time, the doctors, philosophers, and ministers have no answers either. There are pills that can be used to help, but how will I know when that will become necessary? *Lord, I cannot do this on my own.* Only God can step in, calm my fears, and help me lead the life He has chosen for me. *Lord, help me realize that Your grace is sufficient for me and that Your strength is made perfect in weakness, just as You promised. And that will be enough for me.*

Avonda White-Krause

July 19

Growing Old

Now also when I am old and greyheaded, O God, forsake me not; until I have shewed thy strength unto this generation, and thy power to every one that is to come.
—Psalm 71:18, KJV

Growing old is not for the fainthearted. Psalm 71 is a prayer for the aged. The writer understood the challenges of aging and wanted God to favor him with strength. I understand the old man's desire because I remember, not long ago, the last time I did a spur-of-the-moment cartwheel flip in my backyard. As I was turning in midair, I wondered if I had the strength to complete the move. But praise God, I landed safely on my feet and did not break a wrist or leg. However, my brain had a serious discussion with my body as it chastised it for making such a quick decision without considering the consequences of breaking a bone. Both my mind and body agreed: no more dangerous moves in the future!

The writer of Psalm 71 wanted everyone to know God's power. He declares,

> O Lord, you alone are my hope.
>   I've trusted you, O Lord, from childhood.
> Yes, you have been with me from birth;
>   from my mother's womb you have cared for me.
> No wonder I am always praising you!
>
> My life is an example to many,
>   because you have been my strength and protection.
> That is why I can never stop praising you;
>   I declare your glory all day long (verses 5–8, NLT).

As we grow old, we can still show God's strength. And as we become weaker, we can still proclaim how good and strong God is. Let us not lose heart as we grow old. In the later decades of life, we can still faithfully give our service to God. Many seniors volunteer their time and energy to help feed the poor. Some are involved in distributing diapers to needy mothers. Whatever God is calling us to do, we should do it with all our might. Remember, God is greater than our age, and age is only a number.

Lord, as we grow older, let us still serve You faithfully. When we grow weak, help us to show others Your strength. Through our wrinkles, let others see the joy on our faces that comes only from You. Lord, even when we begin to move more slowly, let us still move for You. May we gladly do Your will until our last breath. So long as we are on this earth, let us live according to Your purpose, for Your glory. In Jesus' name. Amen.

Yvonne E. Ealey

July 20

Finding Peace

"He who would love life and see good days. . . . Let him seek peace and pursue it."
—1 Peter 3:10, 11, NKJV

As women, we are often inundated by societal factors of gender bias, patriarchy, and traditional roles ascribed to us. Are we able to find peace among the various challenges that pose threats to our emotional, physical, and spiritual well-being? While raising four young children amid the constant hustle and bustle of this journey called life, I found that achieving, practicing, and maintaining peace seemed elusive and impossible. I often felt alone, frustrated, tired, and hopeless. But when I began to share my feelings and experiences with family members and close friends, I realized how similar our stories were.

I began to explore an essential question that ultimately changed my life. How do we find this state of tranquility and calm known as peace? Imagine being in a state in which nothing that this life can throw at you will take away your peace. Have you ever experienced this peace that transcends all understanding, or are you still searching for it?

One of my favorite Bible verses states, "Do not be anxious about anything, but in every situation, by prayer and petition, with thanksgiving, present your requests to God" (Philippians 4:6, NIV). Each morning before sunrise, I find peace through my conversations with God. My closet provides a quiet place for these moments. Resting from routine activities during the Sabbath hours also intentionally helps me to attain peace of mind, body, and spirit. "Great peace have they which love thy law" (Psalm 119:165, KJV).

We are "fearfully and wonderfully made" (Psalm 139:14, KJV), and God has created systems within us that allow us to know beforehand when a crisis is building so that we can maintain our peace. Providing awareness to those around us and having important conversations with the individuals closest to us are important. We must remember to live our lives *in* Christ and to place our hope and trust in Him. God does not promise us a life free of pain and hardship, but He does provide the strength to endure any struggle. "And the peace of God, which transcends all understanding, will guard your hearts and your minds in Christ Jesus" (Philippians 4:7, NIV). My prayer is that we will experience the peace God grants us in our day-to-day living.

Eleasia Charles

July 21

Just a Little More Time

Draw nigh to God, and he will draw nigh to you.
—James 4:8, KJV

When my dog Blessing arrived, my first priority was her safety. Although my other dogs were old, they were jealous and territorial. A big wooden fence was constructed around her cage to ensure she remained out of harm's way. On weekdays, she was only let out into the yard at night, and soon, she was used to playing fetch and "come get the shoe" before our bedtime. As she grew bigger and was able to stand up to her rivals, she was permanently allowed out of the cage. How she enjoyed her newfound freedom and demonstrated her ability to chew up shoes, toys, and everything in sight! Despite being a perfect combination of stubborn, bossy, and demanding, her loving nature has continued to win everyone's hearts.

While her training was unintentional, Blessing's favorite time to play is at night. She has a knack for pushing the front door open with her mouth and popping a shoe—or anything else—into her mouth so that we can fetch them from her. This is an exhausting task for most of us since she is so fast. Her other favorite game is to give hugs, which are often unexpected and can be unsafe now that she is almost as tall as I am when she stands on her hind legs.

One of her most unforgettable attributes is her longing to spend more time with me. After being told that she needs to leave the balcony or lie down after giving one of her long hugs, she will look up at me with her sad brown eyes as if to say, "Just a little more time, Mommy, please?" Needless to say, she almost always succeeds in getting her way.

As I think about the relationship between my four-legged friend and me, I wonder whether God ever longs for us to know that He also asks, "Can you spend just a little more time with Me today?" What keeps us from doing so? Do the cares of the day drown out the quality time that my heavenly Father wishes to spend with me? Am I robbing myself of spiritual blessings by not allowing myself to bask sufficiently in His presence?

Today, as you start your day, be intentional about setting aside some quality time to spend with the God who loves you with an everlasting love. If you "draw nigh to God, . . . he will draw nigh to you" (James 4:8, KJV).

Shana Cyr-Philbert

July 22

God Cares for Our Every Need

Cast all your anxiety on him because he cares for you.
—1 Peter 5:7, NIV

My friend Elizabeth shared with me this touching experience. One day, after she finished some grocery shopping, Elizabeth came out of the store with her grocery cart and headed toward the parking lot. She went to the area where she usually parked her car but could not find it. My friend continued to walk up and down the parking lot, looking for the car. Just then, a kind gentleman noticed her predicament and offered to help her find the car by using the car-locator button with her key. He then helped her look around the parking lot, but he was also unable to locate the car.

By now, Elizabeth was tired, frustrated, and worried. She stopped and earnestly prayed, asking God to help her find the car soon. After Elizabeth had finished praying, she went to search another area of the large parking lot and was finally able to find her car. For some reason, Elizabeth had inadvertently parked in this section and forgotten she had parked there. My friend immediately thanked God, happy and relieved to have found her car.

As she was about to take the groceries out of the shopping cart, a young man came and offered help. Elizabeth was so glad because her back hurt after pushing the cart all over the parking lot. After he had loaded the groceries, she reached into her purse to give him a tip, but he refused and said that he was happy to help her. Elizabeth thanked God for a second time, grateful to Him for sending this young man to help her.

When Elizabeth got into the car, she noticed a flyer had been placed on her window. My friend got out, removed the flyer, and read these words on it: "Just to remind you that God loves you!" She had tears of joy after reading those words and felt reassured that God was looking after her and that He would always love and care for her. For the third time, Elizabeth praised God for the wonderful ways in which He had taken care of her that day and brought her safely home.

My dear friend, you can always trust and depend on our loving and caring God. Nothing is too small or too big for Him to take care of on your behalf. You can go to Him with whatever problems, trials, and sorrows you may face in life, and you will find He is always there. Sometimes He helps in unexpected ways. Just keep trusting in Him. Always.

Stella Thomas

July 23

Perfect Peace

*"You will keep him in perfect peace,
Whose mind is stayed on You,
Because he trusts in You."*
—Isaiah 26:3, NKJV

God had come through for me in many ways during the weeks preceding December 2019. I had witnessed miracle after miracle at every turn. From the applications for my master's degree through the admissions process to the start of my studies, everything seemed to be going well until I hit a bump with a mandatory bridging module that would be crucial in determining my graduation in subsequent years.

I had struggled with Sabbath classes and examinations throughout my undergraduate years. I had been ridiculed at every turn. Most importantly, it was the one major condition I had prayed over while deciding on my master's applications while God worked out the admissions. I was so certain we had those bases covered with my new university until the bump with my bridging module. As part of the module, a graded team project had been scheduled over a weekend. Either I participated in it, or I would forfeit the class that year and have to take it the following year. The icing on the cake was when my professor mentioned that particular project was always scheduled over a weekend, so if I took it the next year, it would probably still not work out for me.

I felt so disheartened that I cried a heartbreaking sob as I wondered why I had to deal with this again. However, I remembered just how much God had come through for me on several occasions. Those memories brought a sudden flood of peace that overwhelmed me. I clearly remember reiterating to the professor that I would still be unable to make it for the project, and I left the rest to God. He kept me in perfect peace, stilled the storm, and provided an alternative to the project in the most unlikely way. I did not need to drop the module, and neither did I have to take it the next year. I was able to write a research paper in place of the project, and I still finished with my cohort. God ended it beautifully, as He always does, in His own time.

I pray you also experience Him in ways that continue to increase your faith in Him. As He did and still does for me, I hope you experience His perfect peace, which surpasses every understanding, while He works it all out for you. Amen.

Kristeena Daniella Abbey

July 24

With Jesus in the Storm

He said to them, "Why are you afraid, you men of little faith?"
Then He got up and rebuked the winds and the sea, and it became perfectly calm.
—Matthew 8:26, NASB

Have you ever thought about which day you would choose to spend with Jesus while He walked on Earth if you had the chance? And why exactly would you choose that particular day?

Let us do a quick exercise. Read the story from the Bible, then close your eyes, imagine the scene, and then imagine yourself there. What do you hear? What are people saying? Do you see Jesus? What is He doing and saying? Linger in that moment. Concentrate on the images. How do you feel in that situation? Now, let us snap back to the present moment. How do you feel now? You may think this is a strange exercise, but I want you to ponder the emotions you felt. Because when we are with Jesus, He changes our lives and turns everything around for good.

The story of Jesus calming the storm comes to my mind. It is a good story to use with this exercise. After a tiring day, Jesus and His disciples got into a boat and began to cross the lake. There were other people who also followed them in boats.

A terrible storm began. The disciples tried to keep the boat afloat by bailing out water as fast as they could—just like us, with our problems, trying to work them out on our own. Though they forgot that Jesus was with them, He was still there.

When they realized their efforts were in vain, they remembered Jesus. The solution was right in front of them, and they cried out, "Master!"

Can you imagine that moment? Jesus rises with peace on His face and commands the sea to be still. The waves cease, and Jesus asks the men, "Why are ye fearful, O ye of little faith?" (Matthew 8:26, KJV).

That is the day I would like to be with Jesus. What a powerful reminder of the many storms of life I have had and how I tried to solve things with my own intelligence and strength, but it did not help. This story reminds me that Jesus is there, in front of me, waiting for me to ask Him for help. I can almost hear Him say, "Ceci, why are you afraid? Don't you have faith?"

Let us turn to the Creator of the winds and waves, who alone can calm the storms of life and bring us peace.

Cecilia Nanni

July 25

Brain Tumor

[She] who dwells in the secret place of the Most High
Shall abide under the shadow of the Almighty.
—Psalm 91:1, NKJV

"You have a brain tumor," the doctor announced. I was dumbfounded. Not me. I am the raw vegan exercise junkie who spent decades helping others with health. In an instant, my world was turned upside down.

Maybe you know what it feels like to have the entire trajectory of your life changed in an instant. Anyone who has been there or is there now knows exactly what I mean. With a single phone call, conversation, or unexpected event, the life you thought you were living turns out to be a complete mirage. So what do you do in times like these?

First, let us start with what you do not do. I speak from experience. Do not hide. Do not become bitter. Do not hate. Do not blame. Do not fear. Do not doubt. Do not lose hope. Do not self-destruct. Do not become paralyzed. Do not despair. Do not forgo crying loud, long, hot, snot-coming-out-of-your-nose tears. And for goodness' sake, do not weaponize your pain onto others. All of these are carnal responses to a spiritual opportunity to grow, win, overcome, forgive, live, love, laugh, learn, teach, mentor, comfort, heal, seal, and reveal Christ. No, no, my dearest sisters in Christ, *you are not alone*. So please do not act like you are or as if what you do in response to what is happening in your life affects only you. Your response to this will make or break not only you but also many more. So here is the secret sauce that helped me.

It is Psalm 91; that is the key. She who runs into "the secret place of the Most High shall abide under the shadow of the Almighty" (verse 1, NKJV). It is during these times—times when we need more strength—that the One who has "all might" steps right in and provides us with cover while He works with our situations. Release your burden, and run under the safe shadow of His wings. View your life storm from there—where it is dry, safe, and warm. Nothing and no one can harm us there. There we will find peace and calm assurance. There we can claim His promises. Be hugged. Be loved. Let us talk more in glory over tea. God did a miracle in my life as I embraced this approach. I would love to hear how God completes His good work in you (Philippians 1:6).

SanDia Waller

July 26

Heal Me, Lord

Heal me, O Lord, and I shall be healed;
Save me, and I shall be saved,
For You are my praise.
—Jeremiah 17:14, NKJV

Have you ever prayed and asked God for healing? I cannot count all the times in my life I have faced illness and asked God to heal me. The illness could be a bad cold, back pain, or cancer. I believe most of us have asked God for healing. How does God answer our requests for healing?

Jeremiah tells us that when we cry out to God for healing, we are healed, and as a result, we give Him praise. But I seem to recall a number of times in my life when I cried out to God to heal me, and I was not healed. Is Jeremiah lying? Did I not pray the right way? Was there something I needed to do in addition to praying? For years, I struggled with God's seeming "no" answers to my prayers to be healed. Was I not worthy? And if not, how could I become worthy?

And then one day, as I read through several Bible verses that have to do with God healing us, the thought came to mind that God did heal me but not in the way I expected. You see, I forgot to ask for and then accept God's will. My asking for healing did not include God's will, only my will to be healed.

In 1985, I was first diagnosed with rheumatoid arthritis at the age of twenty-seven, and I prayed for healing. I spent many hours in the Bible and in prayer, asking God and pleading with Him to heal me. I was young. Too young to be dealing with debilitating arthritis. I had a two-year-old daughter. I was only six years into married life. This could not be happening to me. So I prayed like the importunate widow (Luke 18:1–8) for healing. The pastor and elders anointed me, but healing did not come in the way I asked.

Our God is so wise. He alone knows our future and what is best for us. He did heal me—not in body but in mind. I found joy in Jesus during a very painful time in my life. He healed my sadness and gave me hope and the ability to see my situation and life in general through His eyes of joy. It took me a few years to realize that God had indeed healed me. But when I did, I rejoiced. Yes, I was still in pain, with swollen and painful joints, but I had peace and joy inside. I saw God using my situation to connect me with my sisters who were in pain, whether physical or emotional. My friends, God does heal!

Heather-Dawn Small (deceased)

July 27

God Cares About the Little Things

"What is the price of five sparrows—two copper coins? Yet God does not forget a single one of them. And the very hairs on your head are all numbered. So don't be afraid; you are more valuable to God than a whole flock of sparrows."
—Luke 12:6, 7, NLT

My neighbor Cheryl is such a classy woman. She carries herself with poise and grace. She also wears an intoxicating perfume. I always knew when she had been in the hallway because her perfume lingered for hours. One day I asked her the name of her perfume, and she said, "It is Chanel." I thought to myself, *I need to get some Chanel too.* But then I thought, *Why do I want to smell like someone else?* I prayed and asked God to show me what my signature scent should be.

As I faded off to sleep, I heard a voice say, "Thierry." The next morning I saw a perfume advertisement on my YouTube feed. The perfume's name was "Angel." And the designer of the perfume? Thierry Mugler.

The previous anecdote might seem random, but it was a timely reminder for me. You see, for some time, I had been very anxious about writing the first chapter of my dissertation. It felt overwhelming because I needed more resources for my problem statement. But where to find them? Then I came across an article written by a man named Thierry, and it gave me the additional information I needed to write the first chapter. Just like that! God answered two prayers in one swoop. I also discovered that Angel perfume was made with patchouli flowers. These blossoms are a beautiful lavender color—my favorite color.

We so often forget that our God cares about the little things in our lives. More importantly, God cares about our fragrance. What perfume are we leaving behind everywhere we go? Do we leave behind the scent of excellence or carelessness? Do we smell like positivity or negativity? Faithfulness or murmuring? Do we leave behind the scent of inspiration and hope?

My friends, remember that "we are a fragrance of Christ to God among those who are being saved and among those who are perishing" (2 Corinthians 2:15, NASB). We want not only to be like Christ but also to be the fragrance of Christ in the world. Let us be intentional about spending time in His presence. Let us linger long with Him until His fragrance permeates our lives and sweetens the atmosphere around us wherever we go.

Raschelle McLean

July 28

Guerrillas!

"Be strong and of good courage, do not fear nor be afraid of them; for the Lord your God, He is the One who goes with you. He will not leave you nor forsake you."
—Deuteronomy 31:6, NKJV

The barrel of a machine gun was just inches from my face. To the left was another, and another to the right. I met the gaze of the person aiming at me, and to my surprise, it was a woman! But her eyes did not look like human eyes; they were more like a wild animal's—haunted and pursued. "We are going to fill you with holes like a colander!" She was not teasing.

I was traveling by bus in Guatemala, returning to university after Christmas. Waiting for the bus that early morning, the passengers talked agitatedly about the guerrilla revolt. "Did you hear they captured nine gringos this week? They killed them all!" They eyed my blond hair.

The arrival of the bus spared me from answering. We all boarded, huddled together, resigned to the long trip ahead. When dawn broke, we were in territory disputed by the guerrillas. Suddenly, the bus jerked to a halt. *Guerrillas!* I saw them through the windows, appearing out of the jungle foliage, heavily armed. Oh, how I wished I was any color but white and blond. I whispered a one-word prayer: "God?"

They ordered us off the bus, and as I jumped out the back door, a shout rang out, "Gringa!" Three guerrillas ran at me, beating me, insulting me, and promising death. I could not join the rest of the passengers, so I turned back toward the bus door. A tiny old lady stood in the doorway, hunched over from her long years. I held up my arms, "Come, I'll help you down." Her eyes were filled with terror, but she allowed me to lift her down, and she scurried over to join the other passengers. Next came a mother with small children, then another old woman. With nobody else left on the bus, I had no choice but to turn around and face my captors. But their expression had transformed; their eyes were wide, jaws slack, surprised. Without a word, they motioned for me to join the others. Eventually, we were released and continued our journey.

I do not know whether they saw an angel or were just surprised that a gringa helped others without regard for their weapons and threats. I only know I am alive today because God saved me. He was with me through the valley, and He will do the same for you. His promises are true!

Diane Duncan de Aguirre

July 29

Miraculous Deliverance

*The angel of the LORD encampeth round about them
that fear him, and delivereth them.*
—Psalm 34:7, KJV

The Southwest India Union workers were excited to be part of a Holy Land tour a number of years ago. My husband, our younger son, and I were among the forty-eight members of the tour group. My husband had to attend the General Conference Executive Committee's Annual Council meetings immediately after the tour, so his plan was to fly from Egypt to the United States of America. One of our friends from America requested tramadol, a pain-relieving medication for his wife who suffered from arthritis.

Our first flight took us to Jordan, where we spent two days sightseeing. Then we proceeded to Israel, where we spent another two days. Our last destination was Egypt, where our tour bus reached the border in the evening. At the border, during the baggage check, they found the tramadol in my husband's bags. We had no idea it was illegal to bring it into the country. My husband was arrested and kept in police custody.

What a terrible day! We could not believe it, nor could we do anything about it. After the baggage check was finished, everybody returned to the bus except my son, me, and the tour leaders. We stayed with my husband. When the police insisted we board the bus, my son declared that he would not leave Egypt without his father.

The first thing I did after checking into the hotel was to call some friends who were in the tour group and pray with them. The next day we left for India, but my son stayed, and our church in Egypt took good care of him. I am so thankful for our worldwide church family!

Once I arrived home, I asked my neighbors to join me in prayer. Every day I skipped one meal and prayed, trusting God would take care of the situation.

While in prison, my husband faced some challenges, but despite the hard times, he ministered and shared God's Word with the other prisoners. I believe God had a purpose for him to be in the prison. All praises to Him! Almost four months later, he was released. The judge declared him innocent, ruling that he was carrying medicine, not drugs. Oh, how we praised God for this miracle! Friends, the "angel of the LORD" still surrounds, protects, and delivers His children today. Place your trust in Him. He who promised is faithful!

Kochuthresia Selvamony

July 30

A True Witness

Be not a witness against your neighbor without cause,
and do not deceive with your lips.
—Proverbs 24:28, ESV

A truthful witness saves lives,
but a false witness is deceitful.
—Proverbs 14:25, NIV

Years ago, I met a new church member at a potluck. We sat across from each other and were introduced by mutual acquaintances. We began an interesting conversation about technology. However, the tone of her voice sounded confrontational to my ears. I shrank back into my chair and began a silent conversation with the Lord. "Do you see this, Lord? This person does not seem to like me, and we just met. Surely, I have not had time to offend her." Then I became aware of a couple of people at the table who seemed to be shrinking into themselves, trying not to draw attention. I realized that this new member had been given a false picture of my character, and she believed it without taking the time to get to know me.

Today much is heard about false narratives. And this has led me to wonder how false narrators can influence so many people. Is it their position in the church or community? Their wealth? Their attractiveness? Their persuasiveness? Lucifer held a prominent position in heaven, and his influence led to one-third of the heavenly host being cast out of heaven. Several cult leaders have led followers to their destruction. How many friendships have we missed because we believed someone's false narrative? How many people have missed heaven because they did not give Christ a chance? They listened to false narratives about His character rather than seeking a relationship with Him.

How should we deal with false narrators? "Be kind to one another, tenderhearted, forgiving one another, as God in Christ forgave you" (Ephesians 4:32, ESV). Let us follow Christ's example and strive to be faithful and true witnesses for Him.

Happily, as the years passed, the new member mentioned earlier did give me a chance. Our subsequent interactions revealed my true character. She now greets me as a sister in Christ. Praise the Lord!

Barbara Burris Neequaye

July 31

The Advocate

My little children, these things I write to you, so that you may not sin.
And if anyone sins, we have an Advocate with the Father, Jesus Christ the righteous.
—1 John 2:1, NKJV

Most people—particularly law-abiding citizens and faithful believers, be they Christian, Jew, Muslim, or other—will never see the inside of a courtroom. For the unfortunate ones accused of having committed an infraction against the law, the courtroom is where legal battles are fought.

My experience has led me to conclude that, in many ways, our earthly courtrooms are modeled on the heavenly courts. Here in Canada, we have the accused in the "prisoner's box"; the prosecutor is on the right, and the defense counsel is on the left of the counsel table. Spectators are seated in the body of the courtroom. Court staff, including the court reporter (who is there to record all that is said), sit on the right, and the clerk of the court sits on the left. The clerk of the court's main function is to assist the presiding judicial officer, who is the highest-ranking person in the courtroom. Much deference is given to the judge. Everyone stands upon the judge's entry, and no one sits before the judge is seated, and only after being instructed to do so by the clerk of the court.

Everyone has an advocate when they appear before the court. Those who are unable to retain a lawyer of choice may be assigned one by the state. Occasionally, an individual will choose to represent themselves. However, they do so often at their own peril. In the heavenly courts, no one is at risk of a lack of legal representation. All sinners have access to the same Advocate: Jesus Christ, the supreme Advocate. The heavenly records show that we broke the law when we sinned. God's judgment requires our death as punishment, but Christ steps forward, pleads our case, and presents His grace and mercy as the pardon for our transgressions of the law. Most importantly, His redemptive service is totally free of charge.

The ancient philosopher Socrates is credited with this observation regarding the duty of earthly judges: "To hear courteously; to answer wisely; to consider soberly; and to decide impartially." However, we are painfully aware this is often not the case. Many people do not receive fair and just treatment under earthly legal systems. Let us give thanks for the fact that our true Advocate is Christ Jesus, the righteous One, and that God is the only true and just Judge. Thank You, Lord!

Avis Mae Rodney

August 1

Wonderfully Made

*I praise you because I am fearfully and wonderfully made;
your works are wonderful,
I know that full well.*
—Psalm 139:14, NIV

I will never forget the time I went in for a routine exam with my dentist (we will call her Dr. B). She is well informed and very skilled. Before starting the work on my teeth, Dr. B noticed something she thought might indicate a problem.

When I smile wide, the gums above my upper teeth show. Apparently, this does not measure up to the acceptable standard of beauty for a woman. My dentist recognized it as something she considered to be an imperfection. She told me that she "could fix it."

Dr. B explained that in order to fix my smile, she would first have to break my jaw. She would then work to reconstruct my mouth to remedy the problem. That was all that was needed in order for my gums not to show when I smiled.

When she said she would start "fixing" me by first breaking my jaw, I cringed. Sadness flooded through me as I thought of all the women in the world who undergo plastic surgery, Botox treatments, and other man-made procedures to "fix" what they think is wrong with their appearance.

You may have seen these real-life situations in before-and-after shows focusing on appearances: the man who went from "fat to fit" has now become desirable to women around the world; the "ugly duckling" who has been transformed into the world's ideal of a beautiful "swan" and is now someone all men want to marry. Sadly, these days, even children are not exempt from being judged and pursuing the world's standard of beauty.

Wanting to look and feel attractive is innate for most of us mere mortals. But destroying how God made us to change ourselves into what the world considers beautiful is never a good idea. The Bible says that we are made in God's image. We are "fearfully and wonderfully made" (Psalm 139:14, NIV). The Maker of the universe loves us just as we are!

We are God's masterpieces. So, let us not allow the world to convince us we need extreme surgery to attain its standard of beauty. We are *wonderfully* made!

Alexis A. Goring

August 2

The Quiet Strength of Meekness

"Blessed are the meek, for they shall inherit the earth."
—Matthew 5:5, NKJV

I remember when my mother bid us goodbye to travel to the United States of America to improve her life and make a way for us. It must have been two or three o'clock in the morning when we children said goodbye to her before climbing back into bed. In my eleven-year-old mind, it would be only a short while until we would be with her again. And though we communicated constantly and had a close relationship with her over those years, it would be twenty-seven years until we would live together again in the same space.

At different periods throughout this almost three-decade wait, I often asked the ineludible question, "How long?" There were many difficulties and disappointments along the way, but I eventually had to learn to wait in meekness until the time had come. *Meekness* is an attitude of willing submission to God without resistance.

In a world where everyone wants to be dominant, there is a special call on the lives of God's daughters to be meek. God is pleased when we wait on Him to make things happen for us. This is our surety as women. When we are treated unjustly, unkindly, or indifferently by others and are tempted to retaliate, be meek. When we have been praying for a prodigal child for decades, an issue of blood, a husband, a promised child of our own womb, or a thorn in our flesh that persists, be meek.

To those who abide in meekness, Christ has promised so much more than we can imagine, both now and when He returns. You see, that attitude of quiet surrender when the tough times unsettle us is an unconquerable force that will refine us like nothing else! All of us are waiting, enduring, hoping, and experiencing a lot, but our true beauty lies in the submission with which we choose to walk daily despite our circumstances.

Sister, how meekly have you been waiting? Will you join me in repenting for our lack of meekness, for murmuring and resisting when we should have been trusting? Let us ask the Holy Spirit to give us a spirit of meekness that will truly reflect the beauty of Christ's character in us, for "a meek and quiet spirit . . . is in the sight of God of great price" (1 Peter 3:4, KJV).

Lleuella Morris

August 3

Last Person on the List

Do nothing out of selfish ambition or vain conceit.
Rather, in humility value others above yourselves,
not looking to your own interests but each of you to the interests of the others.
—Philippians 2:3, 4, NIV

It was my birthday, and my colleagues at work had organized a lunch celebration for me. They always tried to arrange for such events to be surprises, but they never surprised anyone. Everyone knew that sometime during their birthday week, the staff of nine women and one man would come together to celebrate. We were almost like a family.

Although it was not usual to give gifts during birthday celebrations, for some reason, the staff thought it would be good to give gifts on my birthday. With input from colleagues, a coworker prepared a poster to present to me. It listed in vertical order most of the roles they perceived that I played in society: Daughter, Wife, Mother, Sister, Aunt, Friend, Colleague, Citizen, and others. At the bottom of the list was the word *Person*. The colleague presenting the gift told me that the staff wanted me to keep the poster in my office as a constant reminder of the message they wanted to convey. She acknowledged that the order in which the roles were listed did not have anything to do with my performance in each category, except for the last one, as they believed that I tried to be the best in whatever role I played.

She said their message to me was related to the last role on the list: Person. According to my colleagues, I placed myself last on my list, and their wish for me was that I would work to move *Person* to the top of the list.

I have to admit that I was honored to have been perceived as an unselfish person. But I was, and still am, comfortable with being last on my list. That is the example Christ has left for us, as outlined in Philippians 2:5, 6. While there are some circumstances in life that require us to pay attention to ourselves so we can better serve others, as Christian women, we do not have to think about the notion of making self first all the time.

When we get to heaven, no one will regret not placing themselves first on their list. There is no shame in being last. After all, Jesus reminds us that "the last will be first, and the first last" (Matthew 20:16, NKJV).

Evelyne Izeogu

August 4

Trying to Make Sense of My Life

Trust in the Lord *with all your heart;*
do not depend on your own understanding.
Seek his will in all you do,
and he will show you which path to take.
—Proverbs 3:5, 6, NLT

Sometimes things happen in our lives that do not seem right at all. I do not know about you, but I wonder why. "Why me?" On those days, I just want to run and hide and get away from the world, but I cannot. So, instead, I go for a walk, most often at night when no one can see me crying or upset. And that is where I talk with Christ about what is going on in my life. You see, I have a hard time with people who lie and also with people who are unkind to others who are less fortunate. This is especially true of people who treat children with disdain and hatefulness. Children are a gift from Christ, and they are only children for a little while. If we do not treat them with love and kindness, we will lose them, and they will not want to follow Jesus but will go in the wrong direction and follow Satan.

So, on one of those walks, I asked the Lord to talk with me and give me a sign that He was near and could hear me. Some really cool things have happened since then. I felt the desperation leave, and happiness flooded my soul. I felt the anger leave as joy entered.

As I walk around the campus where I live, God has shown me many different nighttime animals: a very big toad, a fruit bat, and a small owl that watched me and did not fly away as I rounded the corner. God pointed out the moon and many awesome stars. My nightly walks ground me and help me in my daily walk with Christ.

When life does not make sense, it is mostly because we do not understand our circumstances. Remember, Solomon tells us *not* to lean on our own understanding because our understanding is limited. We do not get to see things from God's perspective. We do not get to see God's plan and purpose in our lives from the beginning to the end. That is why we must simply trust that God has a plan and a purpose for everything we encounter. If we acknowledge that God is with us in the good times *and* the bad times, He will see us through.

My prayer for each of us is that we will trust God with our lives and have the faith to live as Jesus wishes us to. We can, in His strength, even when life does not seem to make sense.

Nancy Mattison Mack

August 5

Where He Leads Me, I Will Follow

Trust in the Lord with all thine heart; and lean not unto thine own understanding.
—Proverbs 3:5, KJV

When we made the choice to follow Jesus all the way, it meant letting go of all self-sufficiency and replacing it with complete trust and dependence on Him. It also meant we would face many crucibles.

My family's spiritual journey consisted of many answered prayers and blessings that reassured us of God's leading. Nevertheless, our faith was severely tested and tried. Financial loss was one crucible we faced. My husband and I both lost our jobs, but we endeavored to focus on Jesus, whose loving-kindness and provision for our family were consistently proven. Our dependence on Him resulted in relocating thousands of miles across state lines.

Though we trusted His will, we found ourselves questioning His plan. After relocating, the affordability of our children's Christian education became a challenge. While Christian education always means a financial sacrifice, the cost was now double what we had previously struggled to afford. Following the recent completion of my graduate degree, I felt the overwhelming need to become certified for advanced practice registered nursing to help cover tuition and revive our financial freedom. But my timing was not in sync with God's timing.

Though I relapsed into self-sufficiency, God's love, mercy, and provision remained constant and comforted me. Our children were successfully enrolled in Christian education while we searched for financial opportunities. A few weeks later, we were granted funding for the education of all three children—funding that was available to them each year until the completion of high school. The balance owed was only 17 percent of the combined tuition. This was such an abundant gift from God, far more than we expected.

Sometimes we question God's directions and often run ahead of Him instead of trusting His promise to care for us. If I had been granted certification at the time of my pursuit, our family would have been denied funding because the qualification process was based on income.

We often become frazzled or distraught when our desires do not align with God's will for us. But if we fully submit ourselves to His will, we find His plans far exceed our own.

Thessamar Moncrieffe

August 6

A Teacher's Prayer

*"The student is not above the teacher,
but everyone who is fully trained will be like their teacher."*
—Luke 6:40, NIV

School begins today. I am excited for the new year. My classroom is ready, and so am I. As I sit behind my desk, awaiting my students, I pray.

"Good morning, Father! Thank You for this brand-new school year. Thirteen lively boys and girls will enter my classroom this morning. Several are returning students, but a few are first-time students at this school. A handful will be excited to be back, to be learning new things. Most will think it's another boring year in school (their thoughts, not mine). Some will work hard at their studies and do well. Others will work even harder and will still have a hard time. But all of them will walk through my doors as Your children.

"I pray that You will give me the ability to alleviate the new-student jitters. Show me how to motivate and spark the interest of the disinterested learners. Please make this an anything-but-boring school year. Father, I need the energy to keep up with the live wires and the calmness to reach the quiet ones. Provide me with the wisdom to know how to get through to the student who is having difficulty understanding his math assignment. Equip me with a brain that can come up with ideas to help a student figure out what to do for her science project. Most of all, Father, please give me Your love for these children. Help me to see them through Your eyes. Help me to recognize when a student has had a rough night and no sleep. Help me to be a friend to the lonely child on the playground. Give me the patience to explain a concept for the fourth time to the one who does not understand what he is doing. Give me the words to encourage the child who is frustrated because he has done the same problem five times and come up with five different answers—all of which are wrong. Give me a listening ear, a watchful eye, and a soft but commanding voice. I ask for Your light to shine through me so that my students see You when they look at me. Thank You, Father, for hearing and answering my prayer. Amen."

And now, I hear the murmur of voices in the hallway. I smile. Let the learning and the fun begin! It is going to be a great year!

Kathy Pepper

August 7

The Augusts of My Life

*"Forget the former things;
do not dwell on the past.
See, I am doing a new thing!
Now it springs up; do you not perceive it?
I am making a way in the wilderness
and streams in the wasteland."*
—Isaiah 43:18, 19, NIV

I was born in August, and the month was always a joyous time during my childhood. Every year I looked forward to wonderful festivities. When I was eight, I spent a fun-filled summer in Germantown, Ohio, United States of America, chasing cows while visiting the Taylor and Wright families. I was afraid to fly home to Newark, New Jersey, so my parents arranged a train ride for me. Looking out the window as the train rumbled from the countryside into the city and going to the dining car was such a treat! An angel disguised as a woman sat and talked with me throughout the entire trip. When I arrived home, the dining room table was decorated for my birthday celebration. It is one of my best birthday memories.

As an adult, however, the month of August has brought many sad and painful memories. I lost both of my parents, six years apart, in August. "It's me and You, Jesus," I said after my mom's death. Despite the pain, my relationship with Christ Jesus grew stronger.

Then, on August 1, 2011, I lost my son to suicide. No parent should ever experience such indescribable pain. As I grieved, I knew I needed God more than ever. Thank goodness, my daughter, friends, and family provided hugs and listening ears—when I felt like talking.

For consolation and self-care, I am usually out of town visiting family on August 1. This year was no exception. An extended family member was expecting her sixth grandchild on July 29. When the grandmother and I visited the past-due expectant mom, I hugged her tummy and said, "Aunt Mari is here now."

That night the dad called to say they were heading to the hospital. On August 1, 2022, their beautiful baby girl made her entrance into the world. I shed tears of joy for this memorable gift! My daughter said, "It is time to move from the grief and enjoy the new life that has been given to us." August 1 will always be a day of memories and a time for new beginnings.

Marialyce Fordham

August 8

A Mother's Love Is Matchless

*"Can a mother forget the baby at her breast
and have no compassion on the child she has borne?
Though she may forget,
I will not forget you!"*
—Isaiah 49:15, NIV

Mothers are gifts from God. With His hands and heart, He created mothers in His image to display unconditional love, tender kindness, and self-sacrificing love.

When my mother, Varadhamma, experienced bleeding in her old age, she was taken to the hospital, where she was diagnosed as having cervical cancer. Tears rolled down my cheeks, and I agonized through sleepless nights, trying to find ways to save her despite being in the final stage of the cancer. We gave her Ayurvedic medicine, but it was a burning fire to her, and she refused to take it. She did not want to be admitted to the hospital, but whenever she started to bleed, we took her immediately to the hospital for a blood transfusion. It was a great struggle. She was in Bangalore, India, while we were an hour away, in Hosur. Our son, Pavan, used to care for her needs, and our daughter, Punithain Oman, always inquired about her well-being and prayed for her. My husband counseled us to be courageous and trust in the Lord.

During the COVID-19 lockdowns, we were not allowed to travel from one state to another. At this, my mother stopped eating, only taking in some liquids. She slept all the time and quickly became dehydrated and anemic. We carefully moved my mother to Hosur to stay with us. She had been bedridden for about fifteen days when she suddenly began to gasp for breath. That night she passed away. She was seventy-eight years old.

Since the lockdown was still in place, the pastor and church officers supported us and allowed us to have her burial at Hosur Cemetery. We thank the Hosur family for their support and care. We thank God that we belong to His big family. My mother's love, hard work, smiles, and sincere spirit are sweet memories that often come to mind. We miss her terribly. Yet God's words comfort me. "As a mother comforts her child, so will I comfort you" (Isaiah 66:13, NIV). We understand God's love through the example of a mother's love. Yet His love is even greater. Mightier. Matchless!

Eshwaramma Peter

August 9

A Little Child Shall Lead Them

"And God will wipe away every tear from their eyes; there shall be no more death, nor sorrow, nor crying. There shall be no more pain, for the former things have passed away."
—Revelation 21:4, NKJV

On one of our summer vacations when my daughter, Mariana, was seven years old, she found a baby bird that could barely fly. She was so delighted, and she and her cousin, Daniel, spent the entire afternoon playing with the baby bird. It was a day filled with joy.

Nighttime came, and she carefully placed the little bird in a small box with some fruit for it to eat. The next morning she woke up very early and went running to see the little bird. She was devastated to find it had died during the night. She cried inconsolably, and so did Daniel.

After a while, she dried her tears and said to me, "Mom, let's pray."

I went into the room and closed the door, and we knelt to pray. After I had finished praying, we got up, and then my daughter looked at me and said, "You don't even seem to know how to pray." Out of the mouth of babes! But she was right. My prayer had been formal and impersonal.

"Let's pray again!" I said. We knelt, and I opened my heart to God. I told Him about the joy my daughter and nephew had experienced while playing with the little bird. How she had taken care of it, and the pain she was feeling because it had died. I talked about the return of Jesus and how much she would like to have the little bird back and play with it in heaven. After I finished praying, we got up, and she looked at me and said, "Thank you, Mom."

When she left the room, she was no longer crying. When she saw her cousin crying, she asked, "Why don't you pray too?"

To which he replied, "For what? Will the little bird come back to life?"

She responded, "I prayed," as if to say that talking to Jesus had made all the difference.

She went to the room and came back with a folded piece of paper. "Keep this for me, Mom," she said. "I want to give it to Jesus when He comes back." I opened the paper, and she had written, "Jesus, my little bird died."

Despite her age, she knew that prayer is not memorized phrases but the opening of one's heart to God. She understood the hope of the resurrection. May God help us to trust His love with the sincerity of a child's faith.

Isabel Cristina de Almeida

August 10

Mama's Prayer

*"Can a woman forget her nursing child
And have no compassion on the son of her womb?
Even these may forget, but I will not forget you."*
—Isaiah 49:15, NASB

My mom passed away a few years ago at the ripe old age of ninety-four. She was a tenacious woman, having graduated from university in the early 1940s on a full scholarship. She was an acknowledged beauty and possessed a remarkable musical talent. So, it is no surprise that she was a bit of a diva. A polite understatement would be to suggest she had a strong personality.

As a single mom for much of our childhood, she managed to keep house and home together, thanks to her education and fierce courage. We butted heads a lot, but I always admired her refusal to let anybody else define her life. Similarly, my siblings and I were all allowed to chart our own course without excess interference by our mother. She was there to support us, but she left us to work out our own way in life, even when she may have disagreed with our choices.

Her faith had been tested on many occasions through tough times. She always told us she prayed for each of our family members every day, a task I assumed, as the eldest child, upon her passing. When we cleaned out her house after the memorial service, we found a small stack of three-by-five-inch cards on which she had handwritten or typed texts that were meaningful to her. One of them really touched my heart. It was a special request to God on behalf of her children.

"O Lord, keep the circle of my little family unbroken when we stand before you on the Day of Judgment. Compensate for my mistakes and failures as a parent and counteract the influences of an evil world that would undermine the faith of my children. And especially, Lord, I ask for your involvement when my son and daughters stand at the crossroads, deciding whether or not to walk the Christian path. They will be beyond my care at that moment, and I humbly ask you to be there. Send a significant friend or leader to help them choose the right direction. They were yours before they were born, and now I give them back to you in faith, knowing that you love them even more than I do. Toward that end, I dedicate this day of fasting and prayer."[*]

And now, as I pray that same prayer for my adult children, I can feel the concerns Mama had for us. I invite you to make this prayer your own. There is power in a mother's prayers.

Linda Nottingham

---

[*] Adapted from James Dobson, "Introducing Children to Christ," Dr. James Dobson Family Institute, January 11, 2023, https://www.drjamesdobson.org/blogs/introducing-children-to-christ.

August 11

Closed Doors

*"For my thoughts are not your thoughts,
neither are your ways my ways,"
declares the* Lord.
—Isaiah 55:8, NIV

As I write, I am on the beautiful campus of Union College in Lincoln, Nebraska, United States of America, to settle one of my daughters in for her first year of college. Memories of my own first few days as a student are vivid. As a high school senior, my heart was set on attending Georgia Tech. The application form had to be requested and submitted by mail. I carefully placed the completed form in my backpack, securely behind the front cover of a large textbook, and took it to school for my school counselor to review. When I removed it, I froze. An ugly brown water stain marked every page. Every other item in my bag was dry. There was no explanation for it.

I sat on the bench outside my classroom and cried, praying for a miracle. A soft voice I had not heard before whispered, "It's not where you need to be." Dismissing the voice, I spoke to the school counselor, and she promised to call Georgia Tech and request a new application. The deadline came and went, and the reality that it may have been God's voice I had dismissed took root in my heart. So, I applied to Union College, where my twin sister planned to attend.

The week before classes were to start, we packed the car full and prepared for the long drive from Florida to Nebraska. Before leaving, we stopped by my aunt's house to bid them goodbye, and I went to her kitchen for water. Suddenly tripping over nothing, I grabbed the top of the refrigerator to steady myself and pulled down a dusty envelope with my name and a Georgia Tech return address. Through the endless hours of that long drive, I pondered the envelope and realized the school counselor had "accidentally" sent the application to my aunt's address. Discovering it just as we were starting out for Nebraska was God's way of reminding me He was leading my journey to Union College—the place where I did need to be.

Three decades later, as we prepared for my daughter's journey, a now well-known voice whispered, "Union is where she needs to be, and your journey paved a path for her."

Sometimes God closes doors to protect us and, at other times, to lead us to something better. And sometimes that better provides an opportunity to partner with Him as He carves new doorways for those who will follow behind us.

Melissa Martinez

August 12

Careless Words

*Gracious words are a honeycomb,
sweet to the soul and healing to the bones.*
—Proverbs 16:24, NIV

Several months ago, our congregation held an evangelistic series. A well-known evangelist came to town, and I looked forward to hearing him. However, before the meetings began, our pastor asked for volunteers to help with the children's program. So I decided to volunteer.

As I walked into the room that first evening and looked around, I noticed a mannequin dressed like someone from Bible times. It was Jesus. We were instructed to make sure that none of the children played on the stage near the mannequin during the meetings.

Finally, the children began to arrive. By the time we started, about fifty five-year-olds filled the room. We sang together, told stories, and enjoyed making crafts and eating snacks. As the meeting wrapped up and parents came to collect their children, I stayed behind to clean up. The few children that remained played quietly near the stage.

A little five-year-old boy walked up to the mannequin. "Is that Jesus?" he asked. We assured him that it was. Inquisitively, he reached out to touch Him. I did not realize how fragile the mannequin was. In a moment, at the lightest touch, it fell to the floor in pieces.

"Oh no, Ben!" someone called out. "You killed Jesus!"

Ben looked horrified and then burst into tears. He was inconsolable. The teacher who had spoken those careless words so quickly now realized what she had said as she witnessed the impact of her words. She hurried over to comfort the child. It was a difficult task to convince him that he had not really killed Jesus.

As God's children, we need to be careful of the words we speak. Though we may not intend to wound others by what we say, words spoken in haste can have a devastating effect on those who hear them. Our tongues should be used in uplifting and encouraging those around us, not in careless words or thoughtless gossip.

We are fortunate that our God is not as fragile as the mannequin. We can be confident that He will not fall apart when we reach out to Him in prayer. We can safely cling to Him. He will always be near to strengthen, guide, and provide the courage we need to finish the race.

Carey Pearson

August 13

Before We Ask

*"Until now you have asked nothing in My name.
Ask, and you will receive, that your joy may be full."*
—John 16:24, NKJV

Last week I was getting ready for Sabbath and the upcoming week and was organizing the money in my wallet to make sure everything was there and we were ready. I always hold on to any one-dollar bills I receive while shopping during the week. I like to plan ahead and have a goal in mind, and my top goal is always to give back to God, first and foremost. I like to have ten one-dollar bills for Sabbath to pass out a dollar to each child for the lambs' offering, and then the rest goes in the offering plate.

I counted out the ones I had in my wallet and noticed I was two dollars short. I looked up and said, "God, I'm two dollars short for tomorrow. If You could see fit to get me two more dollar bills, I would greatly appreciate it." Then I added, "Anything extra You give me before tomorrow, I will put in the jar for missions." We have an ongoing project at church where we collect change and bills to donate toward missions.

I knew the mail carrier had just come by our house, so I went out to get the mail. There was only one envelope in the mailbox. Enclosed was a letter from the Red Cross, asking me to fill out a survey on a recent experience I had with the fire department and the Red Cross coming out to install smoke detectors in our home. Along with the letter were two crisp one-dollar bills! I looked up and said, "You had this in the works before I even asked!"

God is so amazing in how He works. Before we ask, He is already working on an answer. It is so important to always ask God for our needs and then trust He will answer. When we ask, we also need to have faith that He will work out a way. He even provided me eight more one-dollar bills before Sabbath started, so those went in the jar for missions!

Sometimes the answer is not as immediate or easy as this one was, but God does answer! If not in this life, then He will answer when Jesus comes. Lift up your needs and the needs of others to Him in prayer. "I call on you, my God, for you will answer me" (Psalm 17:6, NIV). Then sit back and watch Him work!

Shannon J. Pigsley

August 14

Our Father Has Promised

"There is more than enough room in my Father's home. If this were not so, would I have told you that I am going to prepare a place for you? When everything is ready, I will come and get you, so that you will always be with me where I am."
—John 14:2, 3, NLT

Saturday nights at our home are considered movie nights. With my husband's busy schedule during the week and after a wonderful day at church, it is the best time for us to just pause, relax, and enjoy a good movie. Recently, we watched a movie based on a rescue worker who teams up with his ex-wife to find their daughter after a massive earthquake in California, United States of America. As we all know, with most movies of this nature, there is chaos, mayhem, and a lot of near-death moments, but the "good guys" usually survive the ordeal.

As I sat enjoying the excitement and critiquing all the things that were obviously impossible, well, except in movies, there was a point when the young lady was able to contact her hero father by phone. After he had expressed his joy to know she was alive and told of his love for her, he told her of a place he wanted her to get to and that he would meet her there and rescue her. With all the energy she could muster, she and her two new friends headed to the location her father had mentioned. At one point, though, it meant they would be going in the opposite direction of the crowd. One of her friends noticed and pointed it out to her. He asked why she would want to go one way when the crowd was heading in the opposite direction. Her reply hit me hard. She said it did not matter what direction the people were headed; her father had promised. So long as she followed his instructions, he would rescue her. And he did!

This sounds to me just like what God requires of us. He told us He would come back to rescue us from this world of chaos and mayhem with many deaths and near-death experiences. All He asks of us is to follow His instructions, and He will save us—even when following His instructions means going in the opposite direction of the crowd. We just need to remember and follow His guidance, and we will be saved. Despite those times when we feel like He is not coming back anytime soon, just trust Him. He loves us, and He is coming back to save everyone who has listened and followed His instructions.

Candy Monique Springer-Blackman

August 15

Look for the Waymarks

Set thee up waymarks, make thee high heaps: set thine heart toward the highway, even the way which thou wentest: turn again, O virgin of Israel, turn again.
—Jeremiah 31:21, KJV

Wanting to switch up my workout, I decided to go for a hike. I found a trail called Rainbow Mountain. As I began to work up a good sweat, I was surprised by how rigorous the hike was. The trail featured many large boulders on the path and hard uphill climbs. It was very unpredictable, and I was filled with anxiety about getting lost in the middle of that expansive park, especially as I wondered whether there were mountain lions in the area. However, the beautiful scenery calmed my fears.

The only thing that remained constant was the waymarks. I knew if I followed the path marked "Rainbow Mountain Path," I would not get lost. As I walked, I came to a fork in the road and noticed there were no more waymarks. I walked back and saw a sign that said "Private Road." Returning to the labeled path, I soon found my way back to my car.

My friends, we should look for the waymarks as we wait for the promise of Jesus' return. I am reminded of this beautiful hymn:

> Look for the way-marks, the great prophetic way-marks,
> Down through the ages, past the kingdoms four.
> Look for the way-marks, the great prophetic way-marks;
> The journey's almost o'er.
>
> Down in the feet of iron and of clay,
> Weak and divided, soon to pass away;
> What will the next great, glorious drama be?
> Christ and His coming, and eternity.*

My friends, Jesus is coming to take us home. Determine to look for the waymarks!

Raschelle McLean

---

* F. E. Belden, "Look for the Waymarks," 1886, public domain.

August 16

The Full Armor

*Put on the full armor of God,
so that you can take your stand against the devil's schemes.*
—Ephesians 6:11, NIV

I was awakened early in the morning, around five thirty, praying, "Lord, thank You for Your love." I knew then it would be a challenging day, and the Holy Spirit was preparing me.

A friend called with a series of questions about events happening in their life. We often talked about the complexities and direction of our paths. As we spoke, I shared that God has a plan for each of us. The question was asked why I thought a particular person in their life wanted to destroy them. I thought about that and whispered a prayer to ask the Holy Spirit to guide my response. The words came to me immediately: "Put on the full armor of God, so that you can take your stand against the devil's schemes" (Ephesians 6:11, NIV).

I shared that it was the evil one, working through their friend. The war between good and evil rages on. I warned my friend against becoming discouraged but rather to seek the promises of God—for that is where the answers can be found. My friend further admitted struggles with knowing who God is and how to accept His ways as a path to a better, more meaningful life. As I searched for memories of past blessings and answered prayers, my mind felt like a roller coaster, tossed and turned every which way. Silently, I continued to ask the Holy Spirit for calmness and stillness to clear my thought process. The inspired Word from Scripture came: "Cast all your anxiety on him because he cares for you" (1 Peter 5:7, NIV).

I admonished my friend to search for God in every facet of life, to look at current circumstances, and to complete an inventory of past experiences when grace and mercy had carried and supported them all along. We continued to talk for more than an hour, and I hoped the conversation was as refreshing for my friend as it was for me.

As our visit over the phone continued, an incident came to mind. A few years earlier, a situation had befallen me, and I was dumbfounded that it was happening to me. I recited what I had gone through and the support I received from others and shared it was that encounter that had led me to proclaim God as my personal Savior and Lord.

Debi Slack

August 17

Stand Firm

*Put on the full armor of God, so that when the day of evil comes,
you may be able to stand your ground, and after you have done everything, to stand.
Stand firm then, with the belt of truth buckled around your waist. . . .
In addition to all this, take up the shield of faith,
with which you can extinguish all the flaming arrows of the evil one.
Take the helmet of salvation and the sword of the Spirit, which is the word of God.*

And pray in the Spirit on all occasions with all kinds of prayers and requests.
—Ephesians 6:13, 14, 16–18, NIV

I was talking with someone about "truth." She said, "There is *their* truth, *your* truth, and *the* truth." I think the word *truth* has become culturally confused with perspective and opinion. I believe there is one truth, but if it disagrees with our perspective or opinion, we discount the evidence and adopt false narratives as fact. You have seen it as well. That is where lies often live—in perspective and opinion. Even facts do not get in the way of a person's delusion. All that is necessary is to trust the wrong person promoting a false narrative.

The Bible says it this way: "For this reason God sends them a powerful delusion so that they will believe the lie" (2 Thessalonians 2:11, NIV). There is truth, the Truth that sets you free, and the only way we can discern it is to pray and ask for it, to lay aside our predetermined ideas and seek with open heart and mind. We must examine the evidence for ourselves. Do not settle for taking anyone's word on it without proof. Jesus counsels us, "Therefore be wise as serpents and harmless as doves" (Matthew 10:16, NKJV).

This is a spiritual and mental battle. "For we do not wrestle against flesh and blood, but against principalities, against powers, against the rulers of the darkness of this age, against spiritual hosts of wickedness in the heavenly places" (Ephesians 6:12, NKJV).

With so much conflicting information from authorities who claim to be experts, it can be hard to discern what is true. I know. There is confusion everywhere, but as children of God, we do not have to live there. "Choose for yourselves this day whom you will serve. . . . But as for me and my house, we will serve the Lord" (Joshua 24:15, NKJV).

So, let us put our armor on, pray for discernment, and stand strong in the Lord.

Ann Trout

August 18

Jesus Has My Back

*In God I have put my trust, I shall not be afraid.
What can mankind do to me?*
—Psalm 56:11, NASB

For fifteen years, I had lived with intermittent neurological problems: a burning on my left arm and tingling in my fingers. An MRI revealed a cavernous hemangioma in my spinal cord at C4 and C5, the midsection of my neck. The lesion itself was not connected to any veins or arteries—an entity in and of itself that presented itself on the surface of my spinal cord.

At the time, those of us with this condition stood a 2 percent chance that the lesion could hemorrhage and render us quadriplegic. The concern was that a blood ring had already formed around the lesion, which suggested that it had leaked. So there was current damage to my spinal cord.

There are risks with any surgery, but I had the added risk of a 2 percent chance of paralysis that could be triggered by the surgery. The surgeons determined that my spinal cord would be monitored during surgery, and if it cooperated, they would remove the lesion. At the first sign of complications, the surgery would stop. The young doctor who gave me this news told me she had performed only four of these surgeries on the spinal cord, but she did them in the brain all the time. I thought, *Lord, don't You want someone more experienced to perform this surgery on me?* I felt I was in big trouble. So where do we go when in trouble? The Lord led me to these words, "In God I have put my trust, I shall not be afraid" (Psalm 56:11, NASB).

So there I was. The anesthesiologist commented that I looked a little edgy. I said, "A little."

She replied, "Well, you have an excellent surgeon."

I thought of Jesus. Those were my last thoughts until I heard myself say, "The bed is too short!" as they wheeled me into intensive care. I had slid down in my bed. The assistant surgeon told me later that he was amused by my complaint about the bed. It was a good sign because it meant I could feel my legs.

I had lain on my belly for an eight-hour surgery while they removed the entire lesion that had transected my spinal cord. The surgeon was indeed a skilled doctor, and the Great Physician, Jesus, had her back and mine as many prayed for my healing.

Friends, we can safely put our trust in God. He will always have our back!

Joan (Jo) Yelorda

August 19

The Helper Engine

"If you love Me, you will keep My commandments.

"I will ask the Father, and He will give you another Helper, so that He may be with you forever; the Helper is the Spirit of truth, whom the world cannot receive, because it does not see Him or know Him; but you know Him because He remains with you and will be in you.

"I will not leave you as orphans; I am coming to you. . . .

". . . But the Helper, the Holy Spirit whom the Father will send in My name, He will teach you all things, and remind you of all that I said to you."
—John 14:15–18, 26, NASB

"Mommy, why has our train stopped at this desolate station?" little Dhruva asked.

"They are waiting for the 'banker,' a helper engine that will attach to the back of our train to push it from behind and help the main engine pull the train up the hill," Mom replied.

"It will help our engine! Will we need it when we come downhill?" Dhruva inquired.

"When going downhill, they move the helper engine to the front of the main engine to help it brake. These engines are known as 'brakers,' " Mom answered.

We all experience ups and downs in life, and when we do, isn't it wonderful to know that God will send us a "banker" to lift us up and a "braker" to prevent us from falling? When we are in pain and feel discouraged, desperate, or overwhelmed when we face opposition and find ourselves deep in despair, God will rescue us.

He says, "Stand on your feet" (Ezekiel 2:1, NASB), but He does not expect us to do it alone. God will make it possible for us to stand by sending help. "The Spirit . . . set me on my feet" (verse 2, NASB). The Holy Spirit is our helper engine, and He will lift us up.

Likewise, when we sin and stumble in our faith, the Holy Spirit will guide us. He will teach us what to do. (See John 16.) And when we do not know what to pray for, the Holy Spirit intercedes for God's people "in harmony with God's own will" (Romans 8:27, NLT).

So, my friends, be strong and courageous, for our God will never leave nor forsake us (see Deuteronomy 31:8, NIV). The God who says, "I have written your name on the palms of my hands" (Isaiah 49:16, NLT), holds us in the palm of His hand and will bring us safely to our destination.

Suhana Chikatla

August 20

Tampering With Sin

*"May your hearts be fully committed to the LORD our God,
to live by his decrees and obey his commands."*
—1 Kings 8:61, NIV

Lying awake, unable to sleep, one night I could hear a train in the distance. My husband tells me the track is probably a couple of miles from our house, but in the stillness of the night, it is easy to hear. It made me think of our home in Saint Louis, Missouri, United States of America.

When we lived in Saint Louis, there was a not-too-deep woods behind our house and then a train track. We figured we could expect maybe three or four trains a day—we could live with that. We soon learned the double track was a major east-west track across the United States. Thirtysome trains traveled that track in a twenty-four-hour period. At first, we heard every one of them, day and night. But gradually, we got used to them, slept through the night, and barely noticed them during the daytime. When company stayed overnight, they would say, "Wow! We heard the trains in the night," and we would respond, "We didn't notice."

The trains and sinful tendencies in our lives have a lot in common. At first, we know that something we are thinking, reading, seeing, or doing is very wrong. But the longer we engage in the activity, the less evil it seems to be. The Holy Spirit's voice becomes less discernible.

Judas loved Jesus and desired to be with Him. He even felt a desire to change his character and life, and he hoped he would experience this by connecting with Jesus. But Judas did not come to a full and complete surrender. Because "his heart was open to unbelief, the enemy supplied thoughts of questioning and rebellion."*
It was a gradual downward course for Judas. Mrs. White says, "This will be the experience of everyone who persists in tampering with sin."†

When we were ready to leave Saint Louis and sell our house, the real estate agent told us we had to disclose the train tracks behind the woods and that it might take six months for the house to sell. Within three weeks, we had a buyer. "Oh," the man said, "I grew up by a train track. I will hardly notice." As we live in this sinful world, may we not become so conditioned to it that we "hardly notice." Our only safeguard is a close connection with Jesus.

Sharon Oster

---

* Ellen G. White, *The Desire of Ages* (Nampa, ID: Pacific Press®, 2005), 718.
† White, 720.

August 21

Know Your Conductor

For there is one God, and one mediator between God and men, the man Christ Jesus; who gave himself a ransom for all, to be testified in due time.
—1 Timothy 2:5, 6, KJV

Having a personal relationship with God is so important. I was reminded of this in a situation that occurred one early spring morning as I darted out of the house. I was headed to the nearby train station to catch the commuter train to go to work. It was essential to get this train because it was the last one for the day going to my job's location.

As my husband drove me to the station, I quickly read my devotional for the day. When we got to the station, the train was already there and getting ready to depart. As I rushed out of the car, the train began slowly pulling out of the station. When the conductor glanced out the door and saw me, he quickly radioed the driver to stop the train. That allowed me to board and find a seat. I was so appreciative of his kindness and continually thanked him and thanked God.

As the train pulled out of the station, my husband called me to say what an amazing thing had just occurred. He had never seen that situation happen before. I told him I had not either. Then I mentioned that the only reason it had happened was because I knew the conductor personally and had developed a nice camaraderie with him. It was easy to do because I saw him on the train every day as I commuted to work.

God is our heavenly Conductor. He knows us. He sees us every moment of our lives. How important it is for us to develop a personal relationship with Him, to meet with Him every day in Bible study, reflection, and prayer. Then, "when the enemy shall come in like a flood, the Spirit of the Lord shall lift up a standard against him" (Isaiah 59:19, KJV). When we are accused and lied to by the enemy, the Spirit of the Lord will raise a banner against him. Jesus will mediate on our behalf and stand up and say, "Stop! No further! I know her; she is covered by My sacrifice."

We are loved by our God, my friends. He is always there for us and loves us more than we can imagine. Let us take time to get to know our heavenly Conductor. We will never find a closer Friend than Jesus.

Raquel Gosling-George

August 22

Search Party

"For the Son of Man has come to seek and to save that which was lost."
—Luke 19:10, NKJV

My husband is part of a small local soccer group. Last summer they planned a picnic at the beach for the team and their families. We live an hour away from the beach, and being from the Caribbean, the thought of going to the beach filled me with excitement because it reminded me of my homeland.

Almost as soon as we arrived, the children wanted to get into the water. So, under the watchful eyes of my husband and me, our sons, six and two years old, headed for the water. The beach was very crowded.

My husband and I soon began talking with other parents who were also watching their children. As we visited with one of the mothers, I looked up and could not find my oldest son. "Where's Chalum?" I asked my husband. We both looked around but did not see him. He was not in the water or on the sand with the other kids. Frantic, I rushed to our vehicle, hoping he had gone back to it. He was nowhere to be found. Hurrying back to the water, I called his name, fearing he may have been carried away by the waves.

Panic set in as other members of our group came to ask how they could help. Soon small search parties were formed, and people went in every direction searching for Chalum. I knelt on the beach, paralyzed with fear, holding my younger son, praying to God to help us find Chalum.

A few minutes later, someone cried, "They found him!" And there he was, emerging from the crowd, holding the hand of one of the men who had found him. What a relief! Still on my knees in the sand, I thanked God with all my heart.

Sisters, that experience makes me think of the Savior who came as part of a search party to this world to look for you and me. Jesus Christ came to seek and save all who are hurting and dying without hope. I imagine God the Father as the head organizer of the search party. I see Jesus Christ, who went to Calvary's cross to redeem us. I see the Holy Spirit calling us, wooing us, and leading us into God's unfathomable love. The angels, too, cooperate with Heaven to aid us on our journey home. And once we have been rescued, we become part of a search party that seeks for the lost and helps guide them to safety.

Sacha Clarke

August 23

He Feels My Pain

*The Spirit of the Lord is upon me,
because . . . he hath sent me to heal the brokenhearted,
to preach deliverance to the captives, . . . to set at liberty them that are bruised.*
—Luke 4:18, KJV

*The Lord gives strength to his people;
the Lord blesses his people with peace.*
—Psalm 29:11, NIV

I am wounded. Brokenhearted. Betrayed. Will I ever be delivered from the restraints that have held me in mental and emotional captivity for so many years? Will I ever fully recover from this deepest, most intimate hurt? The abuse started when I was only seven years old. It began with only a small touch. I was just a child, innocent and trusting. I adored and loved my stepfather. However, his small touches grew into something dreaded, unnamed, and monstrous—and continued for six very long years. I no longer adore this person. At every family gathering, he is still there. I cannot bear to look at him.

If anyone had to look at me, they could not possibly know that yearslong childhood trauma lies buried within me, etched into every fiber of my being. I do not know that I have ever shared this deep pain this openly with anyone.

Perhaps you can relate, at least in part, to what I have shared. Perhaps you, too, need God's help to forgive and let go. Perhaps you need God's strength so you can pray for those who have hurt you. It takes courage to ask Jesus to work mightily in the life of someone who has injured or damaged you. And when the enemy of our souls taunts us with lies as he tries to resurrect that hurt from the past—or build on it—perhaps you also need Jesus to free you from the sting of unwanted emotions so that you can walk free.

So, even as I bear my burdens of grief and hurt, I remember I am not alone in my despair. These amazing words of comfort flood my mind: "The Lord is close to the brokenhearted and saves those who are crushed in spirit" (Psalm 34:18, NIV).

Tonight, Jesus, I am that crushed and brokenhearted little girl again. Only You know how desperately I hurt. That is why I trust my heart to the safety and healing love of my heavenly Father, who surrounds me with protective, comforting angels—and never wastes my pain.

Gail Dotski

August 24

When Old Things Pass Away

*Therefore if anyone is in Christ, this person is a new creation;
the old things passed away; behold, new things have come.*
—2 Corinthians 5:17, NASB

My personal story is a testimony of how God transformed the pain I suffered in childhood into a blessing. He caused the old things to pass away and filled my life with new beginnings!

My parents are wonderful, hardworking people, but neither of them had the opportunity or the means to receive a formal education. They both worked tirelessly to give my three siblings and me food, shelter, and an education. When I was a child, my mom said, "Raquel, you will study. You will go to the university; you will be different." I took her charge very seriously and worked diligently to honor her wish, while my parents sacrificed much to make it possible.

But suddenly, that goal seemed doomed when, at the age of six, I experienced an unspeakable ordeal that shattered my world and made it impossible to envision any future for myself. My oldest brother began to abuse me—a nightmare that lasted almost two years. To say that this situation devastated my life is a gross understatement. I felt so ashamed. I suffered in silence and could not turn to anyone for help. I felt guilty, isolated, abandoned, and rejected, and I had no self-esteem to speak of. Then something happened that changed my life.

One day our neighbors invited me to go to the Seventh-day Adventist Church with them. That visit brought me an unfamiliar joy and peace. I continued to attend that church where I felt hope and acceptance. I learned about God's love and forgiveness and discovered that I was a valued child of God. When I was fourteen years old, I gave my life to God and was baptized into the church. I dedicated my life to serving Him.

God found me at my lowest, most painful moment. He took away the old things—the shame, guilt, and fear from the past—and gave me a new beginning. He took away my pain and healed me! The Bible promises, "If anyone is in Christ, this person is a new creation; the old things passed away; behold, new things have come" (2 Corinthians 5:17, NASB). This promise is a reality in my life! My friend, He can give you a new beginning too. Just come to Him. He is waiting to make all things new for you.

Raquel Bendita Larico

August 25

Not by Any Means

*Now may the God of peace who brought up our Lord Jesus from the dead,
that great Shepherd of the sheep, through the blood of the everlasting covenant,
make you complete in every good work to do His will,
working in you what is well pleasing in His sight,
through Jesus Christ, to whom be glory forever and ever. Amen.*
—Hebrews 13:20, 21, NKJV

On a snowy Sabbath, we headed to church for the morning service. I was pleased to learn that Pastor Ron Nickerson, who is now retired, would be the speaker. As he started to speak, I realized he was talking about Uzzah, the Israelite who was struck down after reaching out to steady the ark of the covenant when the cart of oxen stumbled while carrying it (2 Samuel 6:1–7; 1 Chronicles 13:9–12).

I thought Pastor Nickerson was brave to preach about this particular story. I had heard this story since I was a little girl in Sabbath School, and it always made me feel uncomfortable. After all, it seemed Uzzah was doing something good by trying to keep the ark from falling, so why would a loving God, who was full of grace and mercy, not accept that?

The preacher mentioned the common ethics platitude that the end justifies the means. I was certainly familiar with this philosophy. I had seen it in action a number of times. I remember a supervisor telling me that he justified his mistreatment of workers because the end result was "for the best." However, I had witnessed the consequences of this practice and had lost a treasured coworker to suicide as a result. I wholeheartedly agreed that "the end justifies the means" was not a mantra for Christians and certainly not a directive from God. Then the preacher drew a conclusion that changed the way I view the story of Uzzah. He said this story is an example that the end does not justify the means. God's will is never accomplished by disobeying Him. While it was God's will for the ark to arrive at its destination, disobeying Him to get it there was not. As Christians, we must seek to follow God's will in all things.

So these days I am not only comfortable with the story of Uzzah but also find a certain sense of relief after having witnessed the "ways of man" far too many times (Proverbs 5:21, NKJV). *Today, Lord, let Your Spirit work in me that Your will may be accomplished through the means that You choose.*

Marsha Hammond-Brummel

August 26

Through It All

The LORD is close to the brokenhearted;
he rescues those whose spirits are crushed.
—Psalm 34:18, NLT

I had many ideals and ideas regarding the way I imagined my life would turn out. These included not remaining poor, not having children out of wedlock, and marrying a loving, lovable, and godly Seventh-day Adventist gent. We would work for the Lord and have six children. We would own a house in the countryside, with a small spring running through lush fields and gentle hills. I had many daydreams back in the day.

Reality struck. Life is certainly not a bed of roses. I suspect that I am not alone. As preteens, the dreams were to start our monthlies and begin wearing training bras. As teens, the dreams—in fact, earnest prayers—were to have one of the fine young men as an escort to the youth camp meeting dinner or the prom. As young adults, the dreams were renamed aspirations and were educational, professional, and financial. They also encompassed social growth and development, also known as establishing self as cultures dictate.

As maturing women, especially if unwed, marriage and children become the next focus of our prayers. We then become caught up with the needs of our children, who become the focus of our earnest prayers as we teach, train, and love them.

Our middle-age years can be filled with prayers on behalf of our husbands, homes, and marriages, which can sometimes face rough waters during this season. By the time we reach our sixties, our prayers erupt in earnest on behalf of our adult children who may have wandered far from their childhood faith. By our seventies, we are paying and praying for ill health that the stresses of our yesteryears have birthed.

It would seem a woman's life is filled with unending demands, distresses, and deficits were it not for God. He is our Peace, Balm, Healer, Helper, Comforter, Hope, Friend, Savior, and Lord. He remains with us always. He is faithful, and He cannot lie. He "is not slack concerning His promise" (2 Peter 3:9, NKJV). He will keep unto the end that which is committed to Him. Sister, "peace, be still" (Mark 4:39, NKJV). Unto Him who is able to do so much more than we could imagine or think, be all the glory (see Ephesians 3:20, 21, NKJV). In whichever season of life you find yourself, may you sense His presence now. He is near.

Keisha D. Sterling-Richards

August 27

Crucibles

Fear thou not; for I am with thee: be not dismayed;
for I am thy God: I will strengthen thee; yea, I will help thee;
yea, I will uphold thee with the right hand of my righteousness.
—Isaiah 41:10, KJV

At one time, I associated the word *crucible* with a high school chemistry laboratory. My understanding is deeper and different now. Having lived longer, faced challenges, and survived the many knocks and bruises of life, I now have a spiritual awareness of the word. It is more than a ceramic or metal container in which substances may be melted or subjected to very high temperatures. I see a crucible as God's righteous right hand upholding me in every stage of life, even when I do not realize it.

God is guiding and protecting me in my choices. The hot fire represents the various difficulties and trials that come upon me. All experiences in life are designed specifically to purify and transform our characters to become more like Christ. I am like the impure gold, defiled with sin. A wonderful promise is that God, our Creator, is always with you and me in every trial and situation. Whenever we find ourselves in the crucible, we are never alone.

We sometimes ask our Savior, *Why do You send trials our way, and why so many?* He reassures us that we are His children. He knows us and what is for our best good. He wants to grow us so that we reflect His character. Each fiery trial burns off the dross of sin in our character. By remaining faithful, we will come forth refined and pure, revealing the lovely reflection of our Savior. This is when others will see God in us.

After building a strong relationship with the Son, I no longer think about high school memories of laboratories when faced with a crucible but focus instead on God. I desire to be like Jesus, don't you? With that as our desire, let us wholeheartedly learn to trust in Jesus! No matter what challenges we may face, we can say, "In Him, I place my trust!"

Precious Father, we are Your children and admit we are sinners. Thank You for the crucibles and trials that come our way. Forgive us when we sin. May we remain faithful—in Your strength. May we grow to reflect Your character and be a part of Your kingdom. We love You and thank You for always loving us. Amen.

Yvonne E. Ealey

August 28

To Love and Respect God

Praise the LORD! I will give thanks to the LORD with all my heart,
In the company of the upright and in the assembly.
—Psalm 111:1, NASB

Great are the works of the LORD; they are studied by all who delight in them" (Psalm 111:2, NASB). *Delight* means pleasure of the mind and senses. Do we meditate until we feel pleasure in all that God does for us? Have we thought of all the wonders He gives us? Nature, our very breath, family, the ability to think? And do we think, as the psalmist does, about the characteristics of God and how He uses them on our behalf?

> He has caused His wonders to be remembered;
> The LORD is gracious and compassionate.
> He has given food to those who fear Him;
> He will remember His covenant forever (verses 4, 5, NASB).

God is gracious. He evaluates and judges with benevolence. He is compassionate and sad to see us suffer, and therefore, He seeks to alleviate our pain. He is sustaining. He strengthens us and remembers us and all that happens to us. How many things God does for us!

> The works of His hands are truth and justice;
> All His precepts are trustworthy.
> They are upheld forever and ever;
> They are performed in truth and uprightness (verses 7, 8, NASB).

God's works are faithful and just. His commandments are trustworthy; they are eternal, made in truth and righteousness.

Our goal as Christians is to follow God and become more like Jesus. And as we draw closer to God, we will become more like Him. As we do, we will naturally seek opportunities to share the gospel with others and will be more merciful, compassionate, and helpful. We will remember others, and this will influence everything we do in truth and righteousness.

The psalmist himself tells us how to achieve this: "The fear of the LORD is the beginning of wisdom; all those who follow His commandments have a good understanding" (Psalm 111:10, NASB). We grow in wisdom as we show great love and respect for God and His holiness.

If we want to know how to achieve all the above, we must love and respect God. Only in this way will we be able to intentionally follow all that He advises and asks of us and thus be a good influence on others.

Cecilia Nanni

August 29

Fifty-Two Cents

Be still, and know that I am God.
—Psalm 46:10, KJV

My car insurance payment was due. The rate had increased by $7.45 over the same period compared to the previous year. When I received a letter from my insurance company stating that because Americans were driving less due to the COVID-19 lockdowns, rates would be reduced by 11 percent nationwide, I shared the exciting news with my prayer partners. One of them responded, "Every little bit helps!"

A month later, I received another letter from the insurance company that stated the final amount due had been reduced to $663.10. The due date was three weeks later than normal. An extension! I lifted my hands to the Lord for His marvelous works and prayed, "Lord, thank You for providing for this need."

When I gathered my mail, I saw an envelope from the chief financial officer of the state in which I reside and work. It read, "This official letter from the State of Florida is to notify you that we believe you are the owner of unclaimed funds we have recovered and are currently holding on your behalf." I read further and noticed the funds were categorized as coming from two accounts—"wages, payroll, salary." The reporting entity was my workplace.

Again, I said, "Thank You, Lord!" I knew it would likely be an insignificant sum of money, but every little bit helps. The following Monday, after my prayer-line devotion and early morning walk, I dialed the number listed in the letter. Despite the wearisome telephone prompts and hold time, I was finally transferred to a customer service representative.

I told him about the letter I had received, and he informed me that the first account was for $415.58. The second, $247.00. He did a quick calculation and said, "You have a total of $662.58. I will send you a claim form right now; no return postage necessary."

"When can I expect the check?" I asked. He told me to give it ninety days. I was elated! How improbable is it that my local state employer would award those funds right then? I then needed only fifty-two cents to pay my car insurance! With my pink piggy bank held over my head, I vigorously shook out fifty-two cents. My friends, never stop praying. He hears!

Pauline A. Dwyer-Kerr

August 30

A Lesson on Grace

"So in everything, do to others what you would have them do to you,
for this sums up the Law and the Prophets."
—Matthew 7:12, NIV

It was Valentine's Day, and from my bedroom window, I could see a fresh coating of powderlike snow. After completing my devotions and other preparations for the morning, I ventured into the family room, where my husband sat, watching the news. Since this was Sunday, neither of us was in a hurry to do much. Then he said something that changed the course of the day. Vondell directed me to look out the kitchen window. I did not think much of the request, as I expected to see more snow from a different angle.

When I entered the kitchen, I lifted the shade over the sink and rolled back the curtain covering the patio door. Immediately, my hand went to my mouth. I had no words for what my eyes beheld. The one lone pine tree in our backyard had snapped during the night and fallen over into our neighbor's yard, destroying the awning on the patio, disfiguring the gutters, and mangling his boat. My appetite evaporated as anxiety took its place. Had anyone been hurt? Had the damage been extensive enough to make a portion of the home uninhabitable?

Immediately, I prayed, "Father, please let these people be all right."

Vondell slid on his boots and went next door. They were relatively new neighbors, and we rarely saw them. He spoke with the wife, as the husband was out, and she said they were fine. Later that evening, when Vondell spoke to the husband, he was told not to worry. They would be speaking to their insurance company in the morning. He already had a plan in mind to repair the damage and remove the fallen tree. Immediately, I lifted my hands in praise to God. Things might have turned out very differently. *Grace*—that is what I recognized this to be.

As we became more acquainted with this couple, we learned of their Christian faith and how they, too, had been the recipients of God's grace on many occasions. How good God is: when things seem the worst, He steps in and offers grace that we have neither earned nor deserve. Grace is something God gives freely. Grace is something we can share with others. Grace is love in action.

Yvonne Curry Smallwood

August 31

A Reluctant Rose Lady

Walk in the way of love, just as Christ loved us and gave himself up for us as a fragrant offering and sacrifice to God.
—Ephesians 5:2, NIV

As the second spring in our new home arrived, I found myself weeding and trimming twenty rose bushes. Yes, twenty bushes! Caring for so many bushes took more time than I had while working full time. I had intentionally chosen to have only two rose bushes at our previous home. As my hands worked in the soil and I felt the sun beating on my back, my first instinct was to grumble, as I had the previous year. Instead, I chose to notice each unique color combination of the tea rose bushes, since no two were alike, and heirloom varieties that flourished beside newer varieties. I started to visualize the original owner of this home as she chose each bush and lovingly arranged them in this large flower bed.

As I worked with my roses, I decided they were obviously meant to be shared, so I began taking cut roses to my office each week. My coworkers and our patients loved them and dubbed me "the Rose Lady." I soon found other opportunities to share them with ailing friends, church members, and even for a wedding! I remembered how I had dreaded the work of caring for the roses that first year and wondered what I would ever do with all those flowers. Now I was experiencing such joy as I shared them.

Today, as I knelt in my garden, working the soil and sweating in the sun, I remembered the dear older couple who had originally built this home. Sadly, they are both gone now. I thought of their old, gnarled hands weeding this very soil before me. Hands that were once young planted and cared for these roses. Now I am honored to care for them and use them to bless others. It is no longer a burden. It has become a labor of love.

As I finished patting the soil around each bush, I noticed a bit of blood on my thorn-pricked finger, reminding me of Jesus' nail-pierced hands. There was no reluctance on His part to come and save us. He never complained but loved us so intensely that He gave His life freely to save us. *Thank You for the fragrance of Your love, Lord. May its sweetness flow through me and bless the world.*

Judith Woodruff Williamson

September 1

The Cows Are Out

And as He was sitting on the Mount of Olives, the disciples came to Him privately, saying, "Tell us, when will these things happen, and what will be the sign of Your coming, and of the end of the age?"
—Matthew 24:3, NASB

This morning, after breakfast, I went to get dressed. But I was so tired and the bed looked so inviting, I lay down and just talked with God. My husband, who was outside, called me. The neighbor said the cows were out (translation: outside their fence). So he was going down to unlock the gate at the other end of our property. They could herd the cows off the road there, and then they could return to their pasture through our place.

Many years ago, we bought some land that originally had been part of a ranch, and after living near cattle, we know how to help get cows back inside the fence.

So I told myself, "Cows are out; better get dressed." It was a warning; if the cattle are out, there is no way to know what might be coming next. I might be needed to help move them. The rancher might be knocking at the door. A cow might even show up in the yard, as the gate at the end of the driveway is not usually shut. I did not know what might be coming, but I knew it was not time to lie in bed in my nightgown, feeling tired. It was time to get dressed and be ready.

What warning signs do you see that remind you to get ready for Jesus? And how do we get ready? Do we buy beans, bullets, and Band-Aids, according to "preppers" on the web? Do we sell everything and send our money to the mission field? Do we quit work and walk the streets of the city telling everyone, "Jesus is coming soon"? Do we examine every known sin and confess with weeping and mourning?

For me, it means buying more when things are on sale to help feed others because there will probably be some hard times before we get to the exceedingly hard times. But mainly, it means to pray more—for me, my family, the believers who are currently persecuted, and the unsaved. It also means increasing my Bible study, increasing my memory work, and sharing the Word wherever possible. And it means I must get out of bed and get busy.

What does "get ready" mean to you?

Summer Stahl

September 2

In My Father's House

*"Let not your hearts be troubled. Believe in God; believe also in me.
In my Father's house are many rooms. . . . I go to prepare a place for you."*
—John 14:1, 2, ESV

Like many mothers, I was anxious when my youngest son left home to go to college. My anxiety, however, was heightened because he was going to the United States to go to school, far from home here in Lusaka, Zambia. Because of the COVID-19 lockdown, he had done his first semester online, but now he needed to travel to America. Before his travel, he had applied for on-campus accommodation, as advised for international students, and was placed on a waiting list. We diligently checked the list to see whether he had been accommodated. I had joined all the webinar meetings for international parents to ensure we did all that was needed. One of these webinars was on accommodations for students. The instructor assured us that international freshmen would be given priority regarding housing.

On arrival in the United States of America, my son's registration and other orientation programs went well—except for the accommodation. He remained on the waiting list, and things appeared far from reassuring. Finally, a few days before his father was scheduled to return to Zambia, my son sent a desperate message: "Mama, this accommodation looks like it's not as easy as we thought. We need to pray." The message was followed by several sobbing emojis!

My mother's heart was crushed. I literally cried out to God and said, "Lord, help me! My son!" I was immediately impressed to send an email to the director of housing at the university, but the only response I received was an automated "I am out of the office." Desperation increased as I paced throughout the house. Within a few minutes, however, another email arrived from the director, asking for his details. I quickly sent those to her. She replied soon after, providing contact information for a person who offered him not one but two options for housing! My son was shocked at the speedy answer to our prayers, and he picked the first room he was shown. All this happened within thirty minutes of that first desperate cry for help. I thanked and praised God! It turned out that my son had erroneously been put on the wrong list. "In my Father's house are many rooms" (John 14:2, ESV). That day two of them were available.

Mukatimui Kalima-Munalula

September 3

I Asked God, "Why?"

*"For My thoughts are not your thoughts,
Nor are your ways My ways," says the Lord.*
—Isaiah 55:8, NKJV

I lost my mother on September 1, 2020. It was during a COVID-19 wave—a time when some people's faith in the Lord was being tested. The news on television and in newspapers headlined the growing number of deaths worldwide. Then life seemed to come to a standstill when lockdowns were put in place. Conditions worsened. No hospital beds were available for the sick, no ambulances were available to transport patients, no space was available for cremation, and burial grounds were full. People were living in fear because of the coronavirus.

My mom had to go to the hospital for her routine kidney checkup, and, unfortunately, she became infected with the coronavirus, likely from other patients. She was admitted to the ICU (intensive care unit). Although she seemed to recover well and was released from the ICU, her health began to deteriorate. My family and I were very concerned. Our church family faithfully prayed for her for several weeks. I had much faith, and I trusted that God would restore her to health.

Tragically, on September 1, my birthday, my brother called to tell me that our mom had passed away. Tears filled my eyes and rolled down my cheeks. I questioned God: "Why, God, why? Why didn't my mom live?" But then a still, small Voice spoke to me and said, "I didn't want your mom to suffer. I didn't want her to be in pain. So I took her in My arms to give her rest."

I had trusted that God would heal my mom. I had begged for a miracle. But no miracle happened. I accepted, however, that my mom's death was for her good because she was suffering and that God let her rest in His perfect time. I look forward, though, to when God will come the second time, and I will be able to see my mom and dad again.

"Then we who are alive and remain shall be caught up together with them in the clouds to meet the Lord in the air. And thus we shall always be with the Lord" (1 Thessalonians 4:17, NKJV). That is the blessed hope we have in Jesus.

Shaila Rao

September 4

Strength of the Son

"Now may the Lord's strength be displayed, just as you have declared."
—Numbers 14:17, NIV

The temperature had finally climbed above 0 degrees Fahrenheit; it was now 5°F (-15°C). Snow had fallen lightly during the night. But as I looked at the driveway on the east side of the house, I noticed that the snow was already melting. How could that be? The answer was the strength of the sun. Here, at five thousand feet elevation, the sun is very strong. One of the things we tell people who come to the mountains for the first time is to wear plenty of sunscreen and to drink lots of water because they are now closer to the sun.

The Bible talks about a different Son who also has great strength: "The Lord is my strength and my defense; he has become my salvation" (Exodus 15:2, NIV). In the Old Testament, David was in danger throughout much of his life, so it is not surprising that he would look to the Son for his strength. He certainly sang about that often in his psalms, or songs.

It was not just David, though, who sang about God and His strength. The introduction to Psalm 46 reads, "For the director of music. Of the Sons of Korah. According to *alamoth*. A song." And the verse that follows assures us that "God is our refuge and strength, an ever-present help in trouble" (verse 1, NIV).

As women, we tend to like Proverbs 31. Verse 1 indicates that this proverb was written by King Lemuel. Although we do not know who he was, the verse tells us he was taught these things by his mother. This poem is an acrostic, meaning that each verse in the original Hebrew starts with the successive letter of the Hebrew alphabet. The woman whom King Lemuel describes was amazing; she could do just about everything! "She is clothed with strength and dignity; she can laugh at the days to come" (verse 25, NIV).

Where did she get this strength? In much of Proverbs, wisdom is personified as a woman—wisdom that comes from God (Proverbs 1). So the book of Proverbs begins and ends with the woman of wisdom and strength.

Paul gives a good closing to this thought: "For the foolishness of God is wiser than human wisdom, and the weakness of God is stronger than human strength" (1 Corinthians 1:25, NIV).

Ardis Dick Stenbakken

September 5

Should I Board?

I can do all things through Christ who strengthens me.
—Philippians 4:13, NKJV

My husband and I headed to Boston Logan International Airport in Boston, Massachusetts, United States of America. I was flying to Puerto Rico on a tour to promote my new book and my recently released music CD. I was taking this trip solely by faith and was in constant prayer regarding the trip and the ministry.

My flight was delayed because of bad weather, and I had a connecting flight to catch. The gate agent assured me that he would check to ensure I would make my next flight before I boarded the plane. The flight was delayed two more times. Then the computer system went down, making it impossible to verify whether the first flight would land in time for the connecting flight, which was the only daily flight to my final destination.

After several hours, they called the passengers to board the flight. Would I have to spend the night in Newark, New Jersey? Was there an alternate flight? Should I just go back home? I had a radio interview and a concert scheduled for the next day. "I can't miss tonight's flight, Lord. You are my only hope," I said.

"Should I board?" I asked the courteous agent.

"Wait a moment," he replied, quickly realizing he had no way of checking.

I decided I would board, trusting in the Lord. I was confident that He would provide a way for me to reach my destination if we were not on time for the next flight.

When we boarded the first flight, it was actually time to board the second flight. When I finally arrived in New Jersey, I hurried from terminal A to terminal C. I felt weak, tired, and hungry, and my load was heavy (due to lack of experience in the travel business). Was my connecting flight still there? I steadily marched on. Finally, after almost an hour, I reached the gate at eight o'clock at night.

"We are delayed, waiting for a flight attendant and should be departing at about eight forty-five," the agent said.

Praise the Lord! What a relief! I had barely made it! No! We—the Lord and I—had made it! *Dear Lord, You are always on time. Thank You!*

Rhodi Alers de López

September 6

God's Promises

Be content with such things as you have. For He Himself has said,
"I will never leave you nor forsake you."
—Hebrews 13:5, NKJV

"Fear not, for I am with you;
Be not dismayed, for I am your God.
I will strengthen you,
Yes, I will help you,
I will uphold you with My righteous right hand."
—Isaiah 41:10, NKJV

This testimony was shared with me by Minnie Goldwire:

Praise the Lord, who promises: "I will never leave you or forsake you" (Hebrews 13:5, NKJV). His promises have been fulfilled many times in my life. In 1988, I was in the hospital because I could not walk, and I had severe pains shooting up my leg. I was given medication for the pain, but I had no relief. The pains would last about fifteen seconds, then stop. Many tests were performed, but the doctors could not find the cause. They finally gave up, figuring the pain was not real.

At first, I became discouraged and felt hopeless. I prayed to my God, telling Him that the doctors had given up on me. But He promised: "I will never leave you nor forsake you" (Hebrews 13:5, NKJV). I told God I could not take the pain any longer. I told Him I couldn't go on like this, and I asked Him to help me. I had prayed this before, and I thought His answer would come through medication and hospitalization. But my help came from the Lord. I was finally able to sleep that night, and I had only one slight, mild pain episode after that day. I praise God for healing me. Once the pain stopped, I was able to be rehabilitated to walk again. I serve a mighty God. He has never failed me, and He will never fail you. Always trust Him.

Praise God for Minnie's testimony. When things seem hopeless, remember that God will never leave those who have hope and faith in Him.

Minnie Goldwire (deceased), as told to Ruth Cantrell

September 7

Gone, but Not Forgotten ... Yet

*"Can a mother forget the baby at her breast
and have no compassion on the child she has borne?
Though she may forget,
I will not forget you!"*
—Isaiah 49:15, NIV

"Put your finger in a glass of water and pull it out. The hole that's left behind is how much you'll be remembered when you're gone." Grandpa said that many times when I was growing up. But even though I was taught not to contradict my elders, I think he was wrong. Grandpa has been gone for more than twenty-five years now, yet I still clearly remember him. I recall when he took me fishing and put up wooden swings and a tree house in his backyard for us kids. I remember watching him watering his flower wall every night, making popcorn, playing cards on the back porch, and doing so many other things.

Yes, I totally disagree with him. But wait—maybe I need to rethink this. My son, Jeremy, was nine years old when Grandpa died. Recently, I asked Jeremy what he remembered about his great-grandfather, and he told me two things. He recalled Grandpa helping him make a wooden boat. He could not figure out how to angle the nails, and Grandpa (who was a carpenter by trade) showed him how to do it. He also remembered Grandpa giving him a red wooden toolbox—a box Jeremy still has.

My daughter Katrina was three when Grandpa died. I also asked her what she remembered about Grandpa, and understandably, she did not have any clear memories of him. Mostly, she recalled that he always sat in the same chair in his living room.

Jessica, my youngest child, was not born until the year after Grandpa died, so she has no memories of him. And as that thought dawned on me, I realized Grandpa might be right after all. I have two grandchildren who have no memory of him either. To them, he was just an old man (their great-great-grandfather) who lived a long time ago. Although I remember Grandpa very well, I admit there will come a time in the not-too-distant future when there will be no one left on Earth who will remember the man I knew as Grandpa.

But wait—there is Someone who will remember him forever. The Lord says, "I will not forget you!" (Isaiah 49:15, NIV). And I am so glad He will always remember you and me too.

Kathy Pepper

September 8

A Legacy of Christian Education

Train up a child in the way he should go,
And when he is old he will not depart from it.
—Proverbs 22:6, NKJV

I grew up in a family in which my dad was the sole breadwinner while my mom was dedicated to taking care of the family. My dad worked as a medical technologist and microbiologist at the Subic naval dispensary in Subic Bay, Zambales, Philippines. Both my parents were advocates of Christian education, so my siblings and I went to church school in our hometown until fourth grade. Later, we attended boarding school at Philippine Union College (PUC), now known as Adventist University of the Philippines.

After I graduated from high school at PUC, I enrolled at the Manila Central University, College of Optometry. My mother was disappointed with my decision to study at a university that did not share our beliefs, but I assured her that I would not do anything that conflicted with the biblical teachings we had grown up with. For the duration of my collegiate experience, I never had to attend a class, a board certification lecture, or a licensure examination on a Saturday. I praise God for allowing me to share His love and my faith with others as I pursued my endeavor to become a board-certified and licensed optometrist in the Philippines.

I am grateful for God-fearing parents who instilled in my siblings and me a love for God and His Word. We were taught early in life that we serve a God who loves us so much that He gave His only Son, Jesus, to die on the cross, ensuring our salvation from sin. We grew up in a home where real joy was evident. We were taught to put Jesus first, others next, and ourselves last. We routinely had morning and evening family worship and were actively involved in church activities, which enriched our spiritual growth. Our parents frequently told us that we may not be rich in material things in this life, but Christian education is the legacy they can give us to prepare us for God's heavenly kingdom.

I am very grateful to my parents for the legacy of a Christian education, which we have passed on to our own children. We thank God for enabling us to send our children to Christian schools so that they can become God-fearing, loving, and responsible adults for this world and the world to come.

Rhona Grace Magpayo

September 9

The Importance of Forgiveness

Therefore encourage one another and build each other up, just as in fact you are doing.
—1 Thessalonians 5:11, NIV

One morning during my devotions, something I read triggered this question: When I see our brothers and sisters faltering, do I seek to guide and encourage them, or do I point out their faults and leave them feeling hopeless? After mulling this over for a while, I thought of a picture I have of Jesus and the sinful woman of John 8:3–11. As I reviewed the details in that picture—the "righteous" Pharisees, with the stones in their hands; Jesus writing in the dirt; and the dejected woman feeling certain that she is as good as dead—I thought, *What a scene! Such condemnation.*

Next, I thought of my many past transgressions and God's love toward me. *Jesus died for me as well as for that poor sinful woman,* I thought. *The least I can do is to seek to encourage others when they falter and not stand in judgment as the "righteous" Pharisees did, stone in hand and pointing out the sins of others.* I want to be like Jesus. He, without hesitation, forgave the woman and encouraged her to move on with her life. Jesus does not want us to constantly rehash our sins or the sins of others. We are to forgive ourselves, forgive others, and move on.

I remembered a best friend of many years who told me a story of forgiveness that humbled him greatly. His daughter overheard him talking to someone about her. After she confronted him about it, she said to him, "I forgive you." He said she has never once mentioned the matter since. When he told me that story, he was so choked up he could not continue. He had to end the call and finish the story in writing. He is so grateful for his daughter's forgiving heart.

I cannot explain to you my feelings upon hearing my friend's story because many years ago, he overheard me talking to someone about him. He could not forgive me. Our relationship broke up, and we did not speak to each other for eight long years.

That memory is helping me to learn to see the good in others and to forgive. It directs me to think of the many times I have offended others, but they forgave me. It inspires me to follow Paul's directive to "encourage one another and build each other up" (1 Thessalonians 5:11, NIV). I must do what Jesus did. He forgave the woman's sins and helped her move on with her life, guilt-free and grateful. As Jesus' disciples, we must understand the importance of forgiveness.

Jasmine E. Grant

September 10

Power in That Name

"Everyone who calls on the name of the Lord will be saved."
—Romans 10:13, NLT

I have heard many eloquent prayers in my life. I am ashamed to say this, but I have even been a little jealous of people who pray beautiful, humble, and soul-stirring prayers. One of my closest friends, Kennetia, fits into this category. I love to hear her pray, especially on my behalf! She prays with a sincerity that shows her love of interceding on behalf of others and knowledge of a person's need for a touch from our heavenly Father.

Some of the eloquent prayers I have heard were a little long. I know our Father hears them because they are from humble, sincere hearts. It is important to note, however, that God does not hear our prayers just when they are complex, intricate, and take hours to complete. (OK, I am exaggerating when I say "hours," but I think you understand what I mean.)

I have experienced many trials in my life. During most of those, I have spent much time praying, asking God for peace and resolutions to the situations I have found myself in. There was one time, however, when I needed God's protection and did not have time for a lengthy plea for help. I had lost control of my car while driving. I knew I was going to collide with the semitruck beside me and be killed. All I could do was yell, again and again, "Jesus! Jesus!" My mind was not focused on how to deliver an elegant prayer that would move the most seasoned Christian. All I knew was that I needed to be saved, and Jesus was the only One who could save me. And you know what? He did! Yes, I did get hit by that truck, but I walked away with only a few bruises and some pain. Hallelujah!

Romans 10:13 states, "For 'everyone who calls on the name of the Lord will be saved' " (NLT). Not only do I believe that with all my heart, but I have experienced it.

I do not know whether you appreciate hearing a powerful prayer as much as I do. I will say this, though: know that in times of trouble, you do not need a long, detailed prayer to get through to the Father. Always remember, there is indeed power in the simple, beautiful name of Jesus!

Elaine "Lainey" Lyons

September 11

Goatsbeard and Me

*Purify me from my sins, and I will be clean;
wash me, and I will be whiter than snow.*
—Psalm 51:7, NLT

I noticed the first yellow goatsbeard on Whale Cove Road about five years ago. It has blossoms similar to those of dandelions. When the bloom is done, seed parachutes appear. Breezes knock them off the stems, and they float around. The whole plant is attractive, but viewers need to beware.

I recognized the goatsbeard because this evil intruder had been a major enemy on my father's farm. As a child, I had been instructed to pull out every goatsbeard I found. I yanked this one out and continued my daily walk. *That's the end of this menace,* I thought. Was I ever fooled! Each summer I find a few more. They pull out easily, but they never give up.

Goatsbeard is a noxious weed and a heartless destroyer of good cropland. It creates havoc in pastures. I was delighted to see my neighbor cutting his pasture very short. This was done just as the goatsbeard blooms were beginning to become parachutes. Many goatsbeards will not flourish, thanks to him. I am doing my share too.

As I reflect on the destruction created by goatsbeard, I think of the sins in my life. Some are so glaring that they are easily spotted and yanked out, but much of my sin is not so easily removed.

We frequently hear careless words. Without intent, those words become part of our vocabulary. Those careless words escape our mouths. Despite regret, we cannot take them back. Unhealthful eating habits or insufficient exercise have negative effects on our daily lives too. Many a healthy body has been contaminated in this way.

Cutting our devotional time also clouds our spiritual walk. It is easy to skip the extra prayer time that we so desperately need. A late call to work, an unexpected visitor, or a telephone call can cause us to lose those precious minutes with God. Just like getting rid of goatsbeard, these slipups are very difficult to remedy. Fortunately, God never gives up on us. I pray every day that He will remove my personal "goatsbeards" permanently. Little by little, victory is coming. My reward will be a little corner on Hallelujah Square.

Patricia Cove

September 12

Amazing Grace

And the grace of our Lord was more than abundant, with the faith and love which are found in Christ Jesus.
—1 Timothy 1:14, NASB

When I attended middle school, my favorite teacher was Mr. Mendelson. He taught us science, and his classes were so interesting. We learned about the senses, the clouds, the microscopic world, and so forth. He was a fun teacher, and he also was a teacher we respected. Homework assignments were given each day, which were covered the next time in class. If a student did not bring in their homework, a mark was placed in his book for those who admitted it. A double mark was put in his book if he called on you to answer the homework question and found out then that you did not have your homework completed.

One day he asked the class to get out their homework. Taking out my loose-leaf binder and turning to the science section where my assignments were kept, I found, to my horror, that my assignment was not there. I looked and looked through all my subject sections, but I could not find it. *Where is it? Did I forget to do it?* It was obvious to everyone that I did not have my homework. While looking at me, Mr. Mendelson asked very kindly whether anyone did not bring in their homework. I felt so ashamed and embarrassed to admit that in front of the class. Well, Mr. Mendelson proceeded to go over the homework questions, and I continued to keep my head down, hoping he would not call on me. If he did, I knew I would fall apart and break down in tears. Thankfully, Mr. Mendelson did not call on me that day. Years later, after becoming a Christian and looking back at that event, I realized that grace was extended to me.

Jesus knows the right way to treat sinners. He is not out to get us or embarrass us, but through His grace and forgiveness, we are given the chance to do better. By His grace, we want to do better too. Just like that day in class, that grace motivated me to remember to do my homework each day. Mr. Mendelson knew his students well. He knew who the slackers were and who was trying, and he dealt with each accordingly. That is what made Mr. Mendelson a great teacher. How much more is the amazing grace that God extends to us! It is a reason to sing praises to our God. He will always be for us and never against us (see Romans 8:31).

Rosemarie Clardy

September 13

Reflection on a Day's Events

"And you will hear of wars and threats of wars, but don't panic.
Yes, these things must take place. . . .
". . . But the one who endures to the end will be saved."
—Matthew 24:6, 13, NLT

I woke up one winter morning, thinking it was another cold and cloudy day. Then I looked out the window. Awaiting my view was a beautiful gift from the Lord. Amid the dark clouds was a sliver of light—an incredible array of white, blue, and pink. I said, "Thank You, Lord, for letting me know that despite the cloudiness, the sun is pursuing its course worldwide."

The beautiful hue of white, pink, and blue illuminated by the sun piercing through was a reminder of God's promise to watch over His children, no matter the circumstances or the location.

War is brewing in one country, and people in other parts of the world are concerned about the fallout on their way of life. Thousands of Christians are caught up in the conflict, and our only recourse is to pray and plead with God to spare His children. As time passes, let us remember what the Bible told us about wars and rumors of wars. We need to realize that even if we are not personally suffering in that war, it could have been us.

The Bible also tells us that the devil is starting all the conflicts because he knows that he has "but a short time" (Revelation 12:12, KJV). We know that the Lord is in control, despite what we might wish to happen to those who instigate wars and evil deeds. We can be sure He will not let one hair of His children fall to the ground without His notice.

While contemplating the fast approach of the Lord's return, let us ask Him to help us trust in His infinite wisdom. As we wait patiently, let us ask Him to strengthen our faith and give us the needed resolve while praising and thanking Him for the good and the bad. This world is not our home, but the Lord sees fit that we live in it for a bit longer. He is the Master of the universe, and everything is under His control. His prophecies are sure.

Let us come confidently to His throne (see Hebrews 4:16), and intercede for one another while we await His return to take us to a better world where there will be no pain, death, wars, or rumors of wars.

Come soon, Lord Jesus!

Flore Aubry-Hamilton

September 14

The Invitation

May he [God] strengthen your hearts so that you will be blameless and holy in the presence of our God and Father when our Lord Jesus comes with all his holy ones.
—1 Thessalonians 3:13, NIV

I have been a pastor's wife for fifty-plus years now (yes, he still preaches almost weekly, gives Bible studies, counsels, leads in memorial services, and so forth). We are often invited to perform weddings, or at least, we are invited to them. As our culture has changed, small guest lists are more typical, and sometimes the pastor is not invited to a wedding if he is not officiating.

I think of the Communion service to which Jesus had invited quite a list of men (John 13:1–30). Matthew, the hated tax collector; Peter, outspoken and confident; Thomas, who had a difficult time believing; John, teachable but also hot tempered; Simon, the warrior Zealot; and even Judas, the traitor, was there. When I invite a group of people to my home, I try to put together those who have things in common and enjoy one another's company. But, consider Jesus' disciples: They all had been arguing over who would be the greatest in Christ's kingdom. Think of it: your guests arguing before they even arrived at your event. Should Jesus have been more selective in His invitation?

As I think about God's wedding feast (Matthew 22:1–14), I am so thankful we all are invited to attend. Our credentials, economic status, race, sex, geographical region, and qualifications will not matter. Jesus is the One who extends grace and pardon toward us; He qualifies us. It is all Him! We just need to know the Host and choose to be there. Our minds can barely grasp how special an occasion this will be. At the feast will be many we have known here on Earth—family, friends, and acquaintances. There will be others we have never met, but we had some influence on their lives.

Think of the missionary families you helped sponsor that you never met and the families they brought to Christ. Then there are the numerous ministries you donated to and prayed for. You may have written devotionals and other articles that have helped others in their walk with the Lord. What a reunion that will be!

I am planning on being there; how about you?

Louise Howlett Driver

September 15

No Kitchen

For I am persuaded, that neither death, nor life, nor angels, nor principalities, nor powers, nor things present, nor things to come, nor height, nor depth, nor any other creature, shall be able to separate us from the love of God, which is in Christ Jesus our Lord.
—Romans 8:38, 39, KJV

One of my former students, a very brilliant young woman, married the man of her dreams. He was equally brilliant. They had been in my class together.

In time, they decided to build a house. Finding a plot of land with highway access, they designed a floor plan that included a master bedroom with an en suite bathroom, a second bathroom, two offices, and a large gathering room. About to submit the plans to the building authorities, she noticed a glaring omission. They had no kitchen!

Frantic, she called a high school friend who now owned a construction company. Immediately, he and a crew member flew down to solve the problem.

Just as the kitchen is the hub of the home for our physical needs, likewise, the Word of God is the center of our daily spiritual needs. When Jesus came to Earth two millennia ago, He also alluded to this when He said, "I am the bread of life. He who comes to Me shall never hunger, and he who believes in Me shall never thirst" (John 6:35, NKJV).

Ellen G. White expanded on that thought: "Fill the whole heart with the words of God. They are the living water, quenching your burning thirst. They are the living bread from heaven. . . . And He [Jesus] explains Himself by saying, 'The words that I speak unto you, they are spirit, and they are life.' John 6:53, 56. Our bodies are built up from what we eat and drink; and as in the natural economy, so in the spiritual economy: it is what we meditate upon that will give tone and strength to our spiritual nature."*

As my students forgot an essential component of their home, so we must not forget our daily bread of life.

Glenda-mae Greene

---

* Ellen G. White, *Steps to Christ* (Washington, DC: Review and Herald®, 1977), 88.

September 16

A Perfectly Timed Phone Call

The LORD is good unto them that wait for him, to the soul that seeketh him.
—Lamentations 3:25, KJV

Sometimes we have disappointments, and our feelings are hurt by family, friends, or loved ones. When this happens, it usually cuts us deeply.

I have a loved one whom I have not seen in many years, but we were very close when we were younger. I frequently thought about her and longed for an opportunity to see her again.

I had a speaking engagement that was only two and a half hours from my friend's home, and I thought it would be a great idea to visit her after the engagement. I called her and left a message, saying I would be coming sometime in September. I did not tell her a specific day, suggesting she call me to determine the date and time. I planned to be in the area for a week, so I was hopeful we could work it out. The next day, early in the morning, I received a text from her, saying, basically, that she was busy the entire month and would not be able to see me. She did congratulate me on the speaking engagement, but she left it at that. My heart sank. I was so hurt that I cried to God, and I also talked about it with my husband. Then I let it go since it was no longer under my control.

Later that same day, I received a call from a young woman who used to be our Bible worker and a student when my husband and I worked at the Mission College of Evangelism in Oregon, United States of America. We have a great relationship, even though we might not see each other for years at a time. Her call was unexpected, but we talked for more than an hour and said how much we missed each other. I then told her about my speaking engagement, and she asked me where it was. It turned out that it was four hours from where she lived. She then said that she was willing to drive that long distance to see me. It was late at night, so we prayed together and then hung up, and I went to bed.

The next morning when I awoke, I realized what God had done. He had shown me that He cares about our disappointments and makes a way to reveal how much He loves us. It was His perfect timing for that phone call. He turned my hurt and pain into joy.

Elaine Buchanan

September 17

A Sense of Déjà Vu

*The angel of the L*ORD *encamps around those who fear him,*
and he delivers them.
—Psalm 34:7, NIV

One day my son Bert and I drove home after shopping and visiting with my mother. Restless, Bert started playing with the knobs and dials on the dashboard. A sudden blast of hot air hit us.

"Turn that off, please!" I insisted.

He did so. Then he started jiggling the radio knobs. First, the music was so low it was barely audible. Then he turned it so loud that I cried, "That hurts my ears!" I did not want a headache. We entered an area where radio reception was very poor. Loud static filled the air. I turned off the radio.

After about two quiet minutes, Bert started fiddling with the handles that opened the passenger car window and door. I pulled Bert back toward me. "Stay right here!" I insisted. "If the door flies open and you fall out, you could get badly hurt or killed!" Unfortunately, a four-year-old has a really short attention span!

The next time I looked, Bert was clinging to the door handle, and it suddenly flew open! I do not know how I managed to slow down enough to pull into a country store parking lot with Bert hanging tightly to the door handle. I grabbed his crisscross overall straps and pulled him back into the car. We sat silently, resting, as I struggled to regain my composure. I had strange feelings of déjà vu as if this had happened to us before. But it had not.

Then I recalled hearing a hair-raising story years before. Langdon Hudson, a biology professor, had told a similar story at a program at our church. The same thing happened with him and his small son, Larry—even pulling Larry to safety by his overall straps!

I made Bert ride in the back of our two-door Ford Custom after that. (Back in the late sixties, new cars had seat belts for adults but none for children. Child seats finally became available after our little Ann was born in 1971.)

In both cases, perhaps guardian angels held the boys' hands fast to the door handles. There may have been extra angels who saw to it that the roads were traffic-free during those moments. However they did it, we were deeply grateful! What a mighty God we serve!

Bonnie Moyers

September 18

The Teacup Miracle

*"Before they call I will answer;
while they are still speaking I will hear."*
—Isaiah 65:24, NIV

Have you ever felt like your life is upside down? That you are walking through darkness? That you are so alone that you are afraid?

That is exactly the way I was feeling. I was afraid of what could happen to me. I needed to be sure that God was by my side. I prayed and asked Him to manifest His presence in my life, but I was not sure how He could do that.

I love tea sets, but after a recent move, I was not able to find one of my favorite sets. I was disappointed, but finally gave up searching.

One day, when I was feeling especially sad and distressed, I opened one of my moving boxes, and there was the tea set I had been looking for. I was so happy to find it. I noticed, however, that this set had only three cups, and I needed four. I searched in the store where I had bought it and was told that pattern had been discontinued.

A week later, a box arrived by mail. I had not placed any orders, and I did not recognize the name of the person on the return label. My husband opened the box—and what a great surprise! Inside was a teacup that perfectly completed my set! There was also a beautiful handmade card in which the sender thanked me for the way I had helped her in her life.

God had chosen to show me His wonderful love and concern with a small gift that, for me, was a great miracle. God, who knows me well, had hidden something from me for a long time. Something that would serve to strengthen me at the perfect time.

Maybe today you are going through a difficult time in your life. God is willing to show you that He is by your side. He has not left you alone. He will find many ways to reveal His presence and His love for you. Perhaps you do not need a miracle to confirm God's love, but the Lord uses many ways to make known His tender care. He says to us: "Do not fear, for I am with you" (Isaiah 41:10, NIV).

Damaris Prieto

September 19

Teacups and Keys

*"I will give you the keys of the kingdom of heaven;
and whatever you bind on earth shall have been bound in heaven,
and whatever you loose on earth shall have been loosed in heaven."*
—Matthew 16:19, NASB

My teacup rack no longer holds teacups, not my preferred choice, but because of common sense. These days the rack is hung above a ceramic-tiled floor. I figured that one teacup rack filled with six china teacups and saucers, plus one ceramic floor below, might not mix well if a cup were to fall during a dusting session. So the teacups were moved into a cabinet with a glass front. They are still lovely to view, but they are now protected from smashing on the floor.

The pegs below the rack, though, still contain an assortment of antique keys. None of the keys were ever mine originally; they are simply ornamental. I have acquired them one by one. Some of the keys are large, almost bulky, while others are quite minuscule. Some belonged to my mother. Others were given to me because the givers knew that I have a fascination for old keys. I have wondered what each key unlocked. I do know the purpose of the so-called skeleton keys and a tiny diary key. Even those tease my imagination: what doors did the skeleton keys unlock, where and when they were used; what was written in the diary, and who did the writing.

Scripture tells us about keys—the keys of heaven that will be given to God's servants (see Matthew 16:19). A thorough study of Scripture reveals that the keys of the kingdom do not have the physical appearance of metal keys; rather, the term relates to the knowledge and acceptance of the gospel, the story of Jesus. They are wonderful, life-changing keys! If we accept and use what we have learned about Jesus, we have the desired keys to enter the kingdom.

To my understanding, this means that when we discover the gospel message, our hearts are unlocked and opened wide to Jesus as our Lord and Savior.

On Earth, we may open many doors and chests with keys of various sizes and shapes. We humans are known to lose our keys or get locked out of our homes because we are careless with their care. The keys to the kingdom of God, however, offer us the assurance of entrance to the Lord's heavenly kingdom, where we will live with Him forever.

One day we will actually see Jesus face-to-face. Imagine that day!

Betty Kossick (deceased)

September 20

Peacemakers

"Blessed are the peacemakers, for they will be called children of God."
—Matthew 5:9, NIV

Have you been caught in the midst of a tense situation or a heated disagreement in which individuals with different opinions are adamant about their position? Were you the one who could "pour oil on troubled waters"? Were you the one to take control of an out-of-control situation and defuse a potentially volatile occurrence?

Abigail is described in the Bible as "an intelligent and beautiful woman" (1 Samuel 25:3, NIV). She was the wife of Nabal, a wealthy but foolish man. When David and his men, who were fugitives at the time, came to Nabal's land seeking provisions and help, Nabal responded rudely and refused to assist them. David, angered by Nabal's response, was planning to take revenge by attacking Nabal's household.

Abigail, upon hearing about her husband's actions and understanding the dire consequences that could result from David's wrath, took it upon herself to intervene. She gathered food and supplies and went to meet David and his men. Abigail humbly and respectfully approached David, acknowledged his righteous cause, and sought forgiveness for her husband's offense. She acted as a peacemaker, preventing a potentially violent conflict and persuading David not to carry out his vengeful intentions.

David, moved by Abigail's wisdom and grace, commended her for her actions. "Praise be to the Lord, the God of Israel, who has sent you today to meet me. May you be blessed for your good judgment and for keeping me from bloodshed this day and from avenging myself with my own hands" (1 Samuel 25:32, 33, NIV). As a result, David did not carry out his plan to harm Nabal's household. Soon after, Nabal died, and David married Abigail.

In our fallen world, situations lead to violence, wars, and loss of life. We are called to be peacemakers, and the Bible promises that peacemakers "will be called children of God" (Matthew 5:9, NIV). We are to reflect God's character in our actions—in the church, our workplace, the community, our homes, and the whole world. Let us strive to be peacemakers by seeking reconciliation and promoting harmony, and we shall be called "children of God."

Estelle Baker

September 21

Help!

*"Call to Me, and I will answer you,
and show you great and mighty things, which you do not know."*
—Jeremiah 33:3, NKJV

While giving the devotional talk in one of the classes for my master's degree, a classmate of mine asked, "If God calls you to be the principal of your school, what would your response be?"

I answered hesitatingly, "Lord, equip me." The following day I received a letter from my education superintendent. My hands quivered as I learned of my appointment by the education committee as the new school head. Though hesitant, I accepted the call.

Oh, how I felt my lack of experience! I cried most nights and feared for what might become of the school under my administration. Holding my Bible, I read today's verse, and it gave me peace and hope. But when I remembered the heavy responsibility of planning for the opening of classes, I felt panic. I did not know what to do.

The Department of Education sent a memorandum to all public and private schools about holding limited face-to-face classes; the memorandum stipulated the preparations needed to be accomplished for resuming classes. Among the bulky requirements were two-door classrooms. This posed a great problem. With a little more than one hundred students, where would the school find the finances to support this requirement? In anguish, I poured out my heart to God and expressed my need.

There were times when I would stay in the school's prayer room for an hour and weep before God, and I felt His loving arms around me. I experienced peace despite the huge challenges. As approved by the school board, the mandate of the Department of Education would be followed despite almost empty coffers. I wrote letters to benefactors and claimed God's promise to provide. Thankfully, He honored my faith and provided for *all* our needs. Those I wrote letters to responded positively. The benefactors personally brought the needed supplies. A parent, not of the same faith, donated a substantial amount. We all rejoiced when, after the scheduled ocular inspection, the Department of Education approved our application for limited face-to-face classes. Today those two-door classrooms remind me constantly that God is faithful. Truly, He answers prayers.

Fe C. Magpusao

September 22

When Overwhelmed, Pray!

*"When you pass through the waters, I will be with you. . . .
When you walk through the fire, you shall not be burned."*
—Isaiah 43:2, NKJV

I was overwhelmed as I tried to slog through the corrections the city's planning committee had made to the drawings for a home garage conversion we had undertaken. The feeling of helplessness pressed together with the hopelessness of ever making sense of the jargon.

We took on this project after our daughter divorced and came to live with us. We have a very large garage that we had wanted to convert into living space for years, but it was not until recently that California law allowed us to do so. However, after receiving the document from the city, outlining at least five major hurdles for us to overcome, my faith began to falter.

At the height of my frustration, my daughter, Carmen, walked in and asked, "What's the matter?" When I showed her the documents, she simply answered, "You don't need to stress over this. I have a friend who knows people in the city who can help us with all this—and at good prices too!" I felt ashamed that instead of turning to prayer, where the real solution to my dilemma lay, I allowed uncertainty and confusion to overtake me.

In her book *Life Sketches*, Ellen White tells of a time when her husband, James, had to walk three miles and back in the rain to bring provisions. She wrote, "As he entered the house, very weary, my heart sank within me. My first feelings were that God had forsaken us. I said to my husband: 'Have we come to this? Has the Lord left us?' "* She could not hold back the tears "and wept aloud for hours"† until she fainted. The very next thing she writes is: "Prayer was offered in my behalf. Soon I felt the cheering influence of the Spirit of God, and regretted that I had sunk under discouragement."‡ How silly and inconsequential my little "crisis" seemed after reading this testimony from a mighty woman of faith! And how faith affirming to know that prayer lifted her—and can lift you—from the pit of discouragement.

Lourdes E. Morales-Gudmundsson

---

* Ellen G. White, *Life Sketches of Ellen G. White* (Mountain View, CA: Pacific Press®, 1943), 106.
† White, 106.
‡ White, 106.

September 23

Peace, Hope, and the Kindness of Friends

"For I know the plans I have for you," declares the Lord, "plans to prosper you and not to harm you, plans to give you hope and a future. Then you will call on me and come and pray to me, and I will listen to you. You will seek me and find me when you seek me with all your heart."
—Jeremiah 29:11–13, NIV

Because I was a stay-at-home mom, my husband and I depended solely upon his income. When he fell off the roof of a home he was renovating, losing the ability to work, we worried. Making matters worse, we had just moved into a new house with a large mortgage.

And then, one day, they came. One carried a fifty-pound bag of rice, another a bag of oats. Still others brought sacks of groceries, and finally, some handed us cards with cash and checks enclosed. Our friends had thrown a surprise housewarming party. Our friend Charlie gave us a $4,000 check, which paid our mortgage until my husband could work again.

God had moved upon the hearts of our friends to lighten our burdens. What if, instead, He had sent a text message, saying, "Sorry for your hardships. Praying for you"?

God knows that life is hard. He lived here for a time, and He suffered through the most painful experience a human can endure—death on a cross. Yet this God, who bore the ultimate pain, has empathy for our pain. And so, He sends us tokens of His love in the little things of life: that ray of sunshine on a tear-stained face, that perfect piece of fruit so sweet we cannot help but thank Him, and that random act of kindness from a stranger. Every earthly blessing is a message of love from God, signed with the cross of Christ. Those blessings fall upon the just and the unjust because God loves every one of us as His very own child. Think of three things you normally take for granted. Speak them out loud right now, thanking God for each one.

Dear Giver of all good gifts, not because we deserve these blessings, but because You love us, we receive them with open, grateful hearts. Help us step away from our constant striving for worthiness into the realm of gift receiving. Thank You for lending Your compassionate ear to our sorrows, Lord, for we have not always been compassionate to others. Thank You for hearing our prayers because we do not always hear others. Thank You for speaking hope into our lives, for we do not always speak hopefully to others. Help us to be more like You, Jesus. Amen.

Jennifer Jill Schwirzer

September 24

The Gift of Friends

[I] cease not to give thanks for you.
—Ephesians 1:16, KJV

"Shall I plug in your laptop?" Melissa asked as she helped me unpack at the location of our next presentation appointment.

"The cord is in the zipper bag in my carry-on," I responded.

"The bag is empty" were the next words I heard, followed by, "This is most disconcerting."

I laughed at Melissa's choice of words but stopped suddenly as they registered. The power cord was not in the zipper bag, and I was scheduled for a presentation in less than a week. And my laptop had only four hours of battery time left. "Dear God," I heard Melissa whisper, "You know where the power cord is. Help us remember."

We did remember. "I'll bet it's still sitting on the floor in Idaho," said Melissa, trying to sound cheerful. But we were now in the state of Washington—for the next five days.

The computer company indicated they would be happy to send out a replacement cord for a "ridiculous sum of money," as Melissa put it. The other problem was that it would arrive in ten to fourteen days. By then, we would be in yet another state!

"Dear God," I heard Melissa say again, "You know she has never forgotten her power cord before. Not in nearly one hundred years." (How I struggled not to laugh!) Melissa continued: "Please help us to think of another solution."

"Carol!" I heard myself saying. "I'll text and ask if there is any possibility that Carol could retrieve the power cord and ship it here overnight."

"She will!" cried Melissa. "You're lucky to have a friend like her!"

A couple of hours later, it was a done deal. Carol could get the power cord to me in time for my seminars—and at less expense than purchasing a new one.

The apostle Paul regularly thanked God for his friends and mentioned them in prayer (see 1 Thessalonians 1:2, 3). Genuine friends are gifts. Is there someone for whom you need to give thanks today? Over time, neglecting to do that could be most disconcerting.

Arlene R. Taylor

September 25

My Life on Paper

As far as the east is from the west, so far hath he removed our transgressions from us.
—Psalm 103:12, KJV

Do you have keepsakes from your past? I have several containers in my house that are full of interesting papers, baby books, reminders from when I was younger, pages torn from magazines that contain articles and stories written by my loved ones—and the list goes on and on.

Recently, I opened the containers to sort through them and give them a semblance of order. What fun it was to see letters written to my then fiancé the summer we were apart, the small Bible my husband received at his nurse's pinning, and my handprint in clay from when I was in first grade.

Closing the containers, I gathered up my diaries and journals and carried them downstairs to read through them. While holding these journals and diaries, the thought entered my mind, *This is my life on paper.* The concept startled me but carried a lot of meaning. The words I wrote, from when I was eleven years old until recently, speak about events that happened to me or others, along with feelings and emotions. My life—on paper.

Not everyone keeps a journal or diary. For some, it is stress releasing and therapeutic to write their thoughts down. For others, it is a chore that they would rather not do. My life on paper. What if I tear out a page that holds a memory of something I wish I had done differently? It is no longer in my journal. Is it now gone from my memory? If it would only be that simple. Handwritten and typed thoughts can be destroyed simply by erasing or deleting what was once there, even by burning the paper. But are those thoughts truly gone?

I am reminded of God, who is the perfect One to delete the parts of our lives we wish had never been "written." He has promised to delete them forever if we but ask Him. Satan desires to continue to keep us down with our past "life on paper," but we can choose to give those life happenings and regrets to God for His power to destroy, and He remembers them no more. Let God have your past. After all, He died for you!

Valerie Hamel Morikone

September 26

Hospitality

*Don't forget to show hospitality to strangers,
for some who have done this have entertained angels without realizing it!*
—Hebrews 13:2, NLT

As a young pastor's wife, I was very concerned about how I would fit into my new environment. Although I was a preacher's kid and had lived in numerous places growing up, I was not prepared to move to Mississippi in 1967. I had never lived in the South, and the adjustment was difficult. We had to move from our original house because the landlord sold it, and the only house available to us backed up to the city dump. On the evening of moving day, we had to drive fifty miles to attend prayer meeting at one of my husband's four churches.

One of the dear members looked at me as I walked into the church and headed to the piano, and she questioned my demeanor. I shared with her I was tired as we had moved that day and had driven fifty miles to the prayer meeting. She told me to come by her house before we left to go home. I thanked her and said we would stop by. Imagine our surprise to find a full meal prepared for us, and she packed up the leftovers and sent them home with us! What a blessing!

My other memorable experience with hospitality was after the birth of our first daughter. One of our members called to explain that she did not have the funds to buy a gift for our newborn. She offered instead to clean our house. Housecleaning was her profession. I welcomed the offer; I had a nine-month-old and a new baby, and my husband had torn tendons in his knee.

She came the next morning about seven o'clock. She cleaned, reorganized my pantry, cleaned my oven, and did laundry. She sang the entire time she was cleaning, and when she left at three o'clock that afternoon, dinner was on the stove! What an unforgettable gift!

Hospitality does not require fancy table coverings, silver, and crystal. It just means opening your doors and your hearts and welcoming people into your space. I have received many blessings across the years through opening our home and inviting people in.

Imagine what would have happened if Abraham had ignored the three men he saw traveling near his home? He entertained not only angels but also the Son of God! It was a God appointment! Do not miss your opportunity to have a God appointment.

Wilma Kirk Lee

September 27

Looking Back

*Wait on the LORD: be of good courage,
and he shall strengthen thine heart: wait, I say, on the LORD.*
—Psalm 27:14, KJV

In every thing give thanks: for this is the will of God in Christ Jesus concerning you.
—1 Thessalonians 5:18, KJV

Recently, I concluded that God is working through the various events that have transpired in my life and is weaving them together for my benefit. During that reflection time, I wondered about failed applications, unanswered emails, missed phone calls, illness, and ill treatment. I was able to see possible reasons why God permitted some things to happen, and I was grateful, but there are still those situations that I am unable to fathom why God permitted to happen.

When I look back at how God has changed many circumstances in my life, I am compelled to put all my trust in Him. He knows both the beginning and the ending of everything. So, my dear sister, you may be looking back on your life and wondering about a few things. You may be asking God about the husband you are hoping to find, the child you are longing to conceive, the degree or training you are dreaming of completing, or the home you are saving to buy, but you cannot seem to make sense of it all.

The challenge is that we may never understand all that transpires in our lives, but we can have the confidence that God is in the mix. This phenomenon challenged me the most when I was hospitalized some time ago. It was an extremely difficult time for me. When the incident occurred, I could not imagine a single possible reason why God had permitted me to be in the circumstances I was in. A few months after my release from the hospital, though, I saw God move in miraculous ways to change the entire trajectory of my life. Even more importantly, I believe that God used that incident to preserve my life.

No matter how difficult your circumstances, be confident that God has your best interests at heart and that He is working all things—yes, every good and seemingly not-so-good situation—for both your earthly and eternal benefit. So, when you look back, also remember to look up to God because He will see you through whatever circumstances you have to deal with.

Taniesha K. Robertson-Brown

September 28

Staying the Course

Being confident of this very thing, that he which hath begun a good work in you will perform it until the day of Jesus Christ.
—Philippians 1:6, KJV

It rained heavily that afternoon. CT and I needed to make a short stop just before getting into the town center. After making our delivery, we decided to take an alternate route to avoid the heavy traffic in the town center. We started on our adventure, thinking that we could find our way without assistance. We quickly recognized that we were on a route that did not seem familiar to either of us, and we did not have the help of a GPS.

We stopped on the side of the road for a moment and quickly made a call to ask for directions. Having received the information, we continued on our way. We drove much farther than we anticipated. At this point, we began to question our choice to drive this route, and the unfamiliarity generated some fear in us. CT, the driver who was my co-adventurer, asked me if I thought we should turn back and go the original route that would take us into the town center. I thought for a moment and then said, "Let's turn back."

CT then asked a question that had a potent message: "What if we are close to the exit and turn back now?"

I paused for a moment and then replied, "That's true."

We continued on. Shortly after, I spotted a familiar landmark and realized that we were about two minutes from the exit. Wow! Imagine if we had turned back! We both laughed, and we still smile each time we pass that exit and remember our adventure.

After getting home that day, I reflected on the profound question that CT asked. It reminded me that we are on a journey, and sometimes we feel like giving up. We feel defeated, fatigued, and depleted. The reality of the promise of Christ's return is taking longer than we anticipated. In reality, however, we are close to our eternal home, and we cannot give up now.

In these last days, we must press on! Jesus has promised to return for us, and His promise is sure! He has also promised to be with us until the very end (see Matthew 28:20). Amen!

Simone E. Johnson

September 29

Running the Race

Know ye not that they which run in a race run all, but one receiveth the prize? So run, that ye may obtain. And every man that striveth for the mastery is temperate in all things. Now they do it to obtain a corruptible crown; but we an incorruptible.
—1 Corinthians 9:24, 25, KJV

Have you ever had to study for a detailed exam? Preparing for a detailed exam can be compared to running a race. In a marathon, the runner spends much time preparing for it. This requires working out daily. The workout begins with warming up, stretching, and then daily practice runs. During this training, the runner's diet is also important. He or she eats nutritious foods, including lots of carbohydrates; drinks plenty of water; and gets adequate rest.

When preparing for a detailed examination, great effort is also required. The individual spends much time in daily preparation, even late into the night or during early morning hours. Good nourishment is also required. On the day of the exam, the individual should be well rested in order to reason out the answers to the questions.

I will take my board certification examination in brain injury medicine next month. As I write this devotional, I am anticipating passing the exam, as I have been rigorously preparing for this test. It is not a simple test. I will have to endure seven hours of testing time. Because the test is challenging, I have spent countless hours in preparation during the past few years. I prepared by reading suggested textbooks, taking notes, and doing practice questions.

I have also prayed that I would be prepared for the exam, recognize the answers from the information studied, and pass the examination. I have confidence that with the help of God, I will pass the test. Any worthwhile endeavor requires me to push myself. It also requires developing endurance and resilience.

How many of us are prepared for the second coming of Jesus? Are we spending countless hours in personal Bible study and witnessing for Him? In this world, we put much energy into striving for a corruptible crown; how much more time should be spent in attaining an incorruptible one?

Mirlande Jordan

September 30

Finishing the Race

*Do you not know that in a race all the runners run,
but only one gets the prize? . . . They do it to get a crown that will not last,
but we do it to get a crown that will last forever.*
—1 Corinthians 9:24, 25, NIV

As I listen to the news about the upcoming Olympics, I remember when I was with some children who were participating in a Special Olympics event. Because I worked for the Special School District in Saint Louis, Missouri, United States of America, we teachers accompanied these children so we could encourage them. They struggled because they were not necessarily athletic, and at times, they wanted to give up and quit. But with our encouragement and support, they continued to the finish.

One time my husband, Jerry, and I were in California, United States of America, when there was a multiple sclerosis (MS) walk in Pasadena. Having been diagnosed with MS many years ago, I had always wanted to participate in one of these walks. Jerry and I, along with our two daughters and two young granddaughters, decided to participate. There were hundreds of people walking, as this was the largest MS walk in the United States at the time.

The main thing I remember about that walk is all the encouragement I received along the way. There were stations set up offering water or juice, snacks, and encouragement: "You can do this!" "You are doing great!" "Keep going!" There were some rest stops, and I did take advantage of a few of those. But there was never one word of discouragement. Because of my family and all the encouragement, I did finish the three miles.

The Bible mentions several times that we are all in a race. Paul says, "Let us throw off everything that hinders and the sin that so easily entangles. And let us run with perseverance the race marked out for us" (Hebrews 12:1, NIV). He says we are in this race "to get a crown that will last forever" (1 Corinthians 9:25, NIV). So, just as I received encouragement for my walk, the Bible says we should encourage one another as we "see the Day approaching" (Hebrews 10:25, NIV). With encouragement from one another in our walk with Jesus, we will one day say along with Paul, "I have fought the good fight, I have finished the race, I have kept the faith" (2 Timothy 4:7, NIV).

Sharon Oster

October 1

He Was There All the Time

"So do not fear, for I am with you."
—Isaiah 41:10, NIV

I had no idea that my life was about to change. I was very involved in my career of teaching, working in the church, traveling, and taking care of my family. Then it happened. I received a call from my doctor, asking me to come to the hospital for a recheck of a recent mammogram.

Yes, they found a lump. I was stunned. Up to that time, I knew of no one in my family who ever had breast cancer. *God, please help me to process this. Don't let it be malignant.* My faith began to falter. I tried my best to hold on to His unchanging hand but felt overwhelmed. I asked my family and spiritual warriors to pray with and for me. The hospital scheduled a biopsy and indeed found cancer. I was stunned! *How can this be?* Yet God came through.

With prayer, I was able to completely depend on Him. He was just waiting for me to trust Him. He was there all the time. After lumpectomy surgery, a treatment plan began with four chemotherapy infusions and five and a half weeks of radiation. After treatment, I was never prescribed any additional medication. In fact, I was able to continue teaching that year.

Now, what is this? I am retired, and my health is great. I am busy, involved in church and in the community, and trying to follow a vegetarian diet. No stress in my life. Then it happened again: I received a call from the hospital to come in for a recheck of a recent mammogram. *Now, Lord, You were there before. My faith is stronger. So, I am totally depending on You.*

Tests revealed a lump in the same breast, and it was malignant again—twenty years later. I underwent a mastectomy. Can you imagine that? My resolve was strong, though, and I told God that whatever He chose to do with this situation, I would submit myself fully to Him. If this was a way to save me, so let it be. I was on medication for the next five years.

I can only imagine the day when I find myself standing before Jesus. I can only imagine when all I will want to do is worship Him. In His presence, there will be no more sickness. What a glorious day that will be!*

Vivian Brown

---

* MercyMe, "I Can Only Imagine," by Bart Millard, track 5 on *Almost There*, INO Records, 2001, compact disc.

October 2

The Rest of the Story

For my thoughts are not your thoughts, neither are your ways my ways, saith the LORD.
—Isaiah 55:8, KJV

My paternal grandmother died when I was attending college. I was angry with God, convinced she was not ready to die. I remember screaming a prayer one day, "She wasn't ready to die!" These simple words held an accusation: "God, You are not fair; my grandmother wasn't ready to die." No sooner had the thought crossed my mind than I sensed God's reply to my accusation. The impression came in a still, calm voice to my heart: *I decide when she is ready to die.* While I was recovering from the shock that the God of the universe had just spoken to me, a peace came over me. God had not addressed my grandmother's readiness or death. However, His declaration of sovereignty settled me. God is perfect in His timing and just in His decisions. I chose to place my trust in Him and have faith that all was as it should be.

Fast-forward twenty years. I am with my parents and sister, talking about my grandmother's death. My father tells us that during her last days in the hospital, all her organs began to shut down except for her heart. Her heart was beating strong as if she were trying to will herself to live. During this time, one of the hospital chaplains spoke to my father and uncle. He said, "Sometimes when a person is at the end of life, they will fight to live. They fight, not because they want to live but rather because they don't want to disappoint their loved ones by not fighting to live." The chaplain continued, "Sometimes the dying person just needs permission from loved ones to stop fighting so they can rest."

"And that's what we did," my father tells us. He and my uncle did just that. They went into my grandmother's room and told her that they would not be disappointed if she was tired and ready to stop fighting for life. A few days later, my grandmother died.

As I sat there listening to my father, all the missing "gaps" filled in. I realized that my grandmother had been ready to die after all. I also marveled at the wisdom of God. He could have defended Himself against my accusation of being unfair. He could have told me to call my father and have him explain my grandmother's end of life. But He did not. God told me what I needed to hear in order to grow in trust in His works—even when I could not understand them.

Carmalita Green

October 3

Thirteen Women Disciples

*Then He called His twelve disciples together and gave them
power and authority over all demons, and to cure diseases.
He sent them to preach the kingdom of God and to heal the sick. . . .*

*So they departed and went through the towns,
preaching the gospel and healing everywhere.*
—Luke 9:1, 2, 6, NKJV

The National Cancer Centre Singapore posted an announcement on Facebook: "Join us at the 5th International BRCA Virtual Forum on 13 August 2021 for the most up-to-date information on hereditary breast and ovarian cancer!" The announcement poster listed thirteen female doctors, along with one male doctor, who would be presenting. All fourteen are experienced medical physicians and faculty members at different medical universities. Indeed, they presented the latest research on hereditary breast cancer and ovarian cancer among young women.

I nicknamed the women doctors the Women Disciples. They reminded me of the twelve disciples whom Jesus appointed to continue His work with power and authority. His disciples were to have His power over demons, heal the sick, and preach the gospel as they went (Luke 9:1, 2, 6).

First, Jesus sent out His twelve disciples. Next, He sent out seventy disciples (Luke 10:1). Later, just before He ascended to heaven, Jesus promised they would receive power to be His witnesses to the end of the earth. Days later, in the upper room, the Holy Spirit anointed a whole roomful of disciples to preach the gospel, heal the sick, and cast out demons.

Today we, too, are Christ's disciples. Medical work is one of the ways to reach out to people before bringing the gospel to them. In following Jesus' example of meeting the needs of the people first, we can be medical missionaries for the Lord. Our medical missionary work can begin even at home. "A demonstration of the principles of health reform will do much toward removing prejudice against our evangelical work. The Great Physician, the originator of medical missionary work, will bless all who thus seek to impart the truth for this time."* The 1,000 Missionary Movement, among other initiatives, trains laypeople for this type of medical work.

If God calls you to this work, are you willing to answer the call?

Yan Siew Ghiang

---

* Ellen G. White, *Evangelism* (Washington, DC: Review and Herald®, 1946), 514.

October 4

Our Unexpected Transition

Now faith is the substance of things hoped for, the evidence of things not seen.
—Hebrews 11:1, KJV

It is hard to believe it has been thirteen years since we moved to Atlanta, Georgia, United States of America, in 2012 to be closer to family. This huge metropolis was certainly not a place we would have chosen for relocation at this stage in our lives. Our children, who wanted us closer to them, would never understand the daunting emotional stress of our move—the loss of home, friends, work associates, church members, neighbors, and community. They were young. We were seniors. "Lord, help us to adjust and make new friends" was my simple prayer.

The closest church to us, postmove, had over three thousand members. It was way too large for my liking, but we could get there without getting on the congested interstate. So, we arrived at Sabbath School early enough each week to claim our favorite aisle seats—row six from the back on the left. We reviewed names as we traveled to church and did our best to put names with faces so we could smile and speak with others before Sabbath School, during greeting time, and after church. The Wednesday evening service was also a great place to meet members. We learned that several members had relatives who lived in the Midwest, where we had lived for forty-eight years: Kansas City, Missouri; Kansas City, Atchison, and Leavenworth, Kansas; Denver, Colorado; and Omaha, Nebraska. We met others who knew at least one of our children.

I thought that perhaps other transfer and new members wanted friends as we did. With that in mind, the clerk, with approval, provided me with their names and phone numbers. I welcomed them to our church by phone, and we met them after the service. We invited them, along with others, to our home for a meal. This became an awesome Holy Spirit–led ministry that was such a blessing to us. We made friends for life. Hopefully, this ministry can be resumed soon.

One of the beauties of being part of God's family is being able to stay connected with friends—no matter where you live. Several of our Kansas City friends have relatives who live here in Georgia. Others have visited while on business trips. Some have come just to see us. Whatever the case may be, their visits have been a blessing. Our children were kind enough to invite us to move closer. We just had to put our feet in the Red Sea and let the Lord do the rest.

Shirley Sain Fordham

October 5

The Roaring of the Ocean

God is our refuge and strength, a very present help in trouble.
—Psalm 46:1, KJV

It was the longest ocean wave I had ever seen on the Pacific Ocean coastline. One continuous mass of white foam, without a break. I had come to this beach to still my thoughts, but my mind kept racing with the complexities of life: what to do, where to go, and what decisions would be the wisest ones to make. I tried to read to take my mind off myself, but that did not help. I tried to sketch, but the wonders around me kept distracting and averting my eyes.

The ocean was making itself known that day; it wanted to be heard. In all my days there under those massive palms, I had never heard such roaring. Finally, I decided to lay all my books down, sit up, and have a look. The massive wave stretched out for miles along the coast. One followed another. Each new wave swelling up from the pier produced a roar that did not let up. The sound seemed to be loud even inside my head. I wondered, *How can I think through all of this?* The roaring continued steadily for fifteen minutes. Then silence. A wonderful stillness and "deafening" silence but for only a minute. A new wave brought more roaring for the next fifteen minutes, followed by another brief silence. This sound pattern continued for the next hour. When those still, silent moments descended on me for an instant between the thundering of the next waves, I found myself thinking, *Oh, what peace! And I might not even have noticed it were it not for the roar that preceded it.*

That is when it hit me:

> God is our refuge and strength, a very present help in trouble. Therefore will not we fear, though the earth be removed, and though the mountains be carried into the midst of the sea; though the waters thereof roar and be troubled. . . .
>
> . . . God is in the midst of her; she shall not be moved. . . .
>
> . . . Be still, and know that I am God. . . . The Lord of hosts is with us; the God of Jacob is our refuge (Psalm 46:1–3, 5, 10, 11, KJV).

This is what I needed to focus on. It did not matter that my life events were roaring around me; God was still here with me. Whatever the situation, God can make a place of peace within me. I rejoiced that I would be all right. God knows about all the noise in our lives as well as the roaring interruptions. He silences them long enough for us to find Him.

Victoria M. Shewbrooks

October 6

The Struggle

And Enoch walked with God; and he was not, for God took him.
—Genesis 5:24, NKJV

As children of God, we all know it is important to have a daily relationship with God. We know that spending time in prayer and Bible reading each day is vital for keeping our spiritual lives healthy and growing. Yet how many of us can truly say we spend time with God daily? Not just time with God but unrushed time with God. I would answer, I try but do not always succeed.

The psalmist writes, "You will show me the path of life; in Your presence is fullness of joy; at Your right hand are pleasures forevermore" (Psalm 16:11, NKJV). We all want to spend time in God's presence, receive His joy, and follow the path He shows us. But how do we keep our appointment with God each day when life is so full and we are pulled in many directions by family, work, or friends? Yes, I can find time, but it is mostly rushed time.

When I think of someone who followed God well, I think of Enoch. The Bible says he walked with God and was so close to Him that God took him from Earth. Can you imagine the conversations he had with God? At one time, I envied Enoch. After all, what did he have to do? Most likely, his wife cleaned the house, cooked the meals, and looked after the children, so he could spend a lot of quality time with his Father. But is that a true assumption? Now, I think that like all men of his time, Enoch had to work to feed his family and provide for their needs, maybe in the fields or with cattle; the Bible does not say. But I am sure he did not sit idly each day just talking with God.

So how did he have such a close walk with God? Ellen G. White writes, "Brethren, pray at home, in your family, night and morning; pray earnestly in your closet; and while engaged in your daily labor, lift up the soul to God in prayer. It was thus that Enoch walked with God."* How do I find unrushed time each day to spend with God? I make sure I begin each day with prayer. I may not have time in the morning to study my Bible, but I will make time during my day to do that, whether during my lunch at work or in the evening before bed, when I remove all distractions and focus on Jesus. That time alone with God gives me great joy.

Heather-Dawn Small (deceased)

---

* Ellen G. White, *The Adventist Home* (Washington, DC: Review and Herald®, 1980), 213.

October 7

The Joy in Serving the Lord

And whatsoever ye do, do it heartily, as to the Lord, and not unto men.
—Colossians 3:23, KJV

Serving the Lord with all our hearts brings great joy. God Himself gives us joy as a token of His approval of what we are allowing Him to do in us. Understanding how privileged we are to serve the God of heaven, the Commander of angelic hosts enables us to humbly serve Him, whatever the cost. I especially love to see young people serving the Lord whenever they have an opportunity. I often pray for and encourage young people to give their time, energy, and talents to God's service. Of course, I have always longed to see this choice exemplified in the lives of my own young-adult children.

My son, fresh out of medical school, returned home to rest and make plans for the next stages of his life's work. I proposed that he consider accepting the call to serve at a little hospital in a neighboring country. This distant hospital was experiencing a serious need for another physician to join and relieve their severely overtaxed medical staff.

"I am willing to go, Mother," he responded. "However, there is a problem." Indeed, his service at that medical facility would be on a volunteer basis: no salary, no stipend, and only the provision for daily meals. My son wanted to serve God in a position that came with a salary. After all, he was just beginning his life's work. His concern was understandable.

"I understand your thinking," I assured him. "It is good to have at least a little salary to live on. On the other hand, remember that God promises to provide for our needs and is a rewarder of those who diligently seek and serve Him." On faith, my son decided to serve that little hospital. Though adapting to a new environment and work schedule was challenging for our son, we continued to pray for and encourage him. How grateful to God I am every time I hear my son enthusiastically share yet another positive story about his job at this hospital! Though he still receives no regular salary for his efforts, he experiences a holy joy that God gives him for his willingness to serve with all his heart.

Let us encourage our young people to give their best to the Lord, serving as missionaries wherever the need arises, even to the point of sacrifice. God will surely bless them with joy.

Omobonike Adeola Sessou

October 8

Fashioned With Love

"The Lord your God is with you,
the Mighty Warrior who saves.
He will take great delight in you;
in his love he will no longer rebuke you,
but will rejoice over you with singing."
—Zephaniah 3:17, NIV

I have a strange habit of naming my dresses. I refer to an elegant cobalt-blue dress with shimmering threads throughout as Big Blue. Another blue dress, shorter and with a halter-style bodice, is known as Little Blue. A dress I call Snowflake also resides in my closet, although I am more of a warm-weather lady. Then there is the Hot Mess dress that I added to my collection.

Hot mess describes someone who is disorganized or something that is in disarray, especially when the result has a level of charm, like my homemade dress. I had purchased several yards of fabric splashed with bright pink-and-yellow circles with large bands of vivid blue. I decided to make a dress from this fabric and chose a pattern.

Because I was sewing during shelter-in-place restrictions, I could not go to the store to buy lining fabric. Instead, I found remnants in my fabric stash—a turquoise piece and an olive-colored piece. Neither matched the dress's fabric, but I pressed on. Who would see the lining anyway? During a fitting, I realized the neckline was puckered. I resolved this mistake by adding elastic to the neckline to draw in the extra fabric.

When I tried on the finished garment, I laughed. I had not matched the large circles at the seams, resulting in a collection of half circles. When I considered the flaws—the mismatched lining, the altered neckline, the misaligned circles—I called it a hot mess dress.

Sometimes I feel as if I am a hot mess. I have flaws. At times, my words do not match my actions. Some days I am bright and cheerful, but often I fail to reflect Christ's character. Then God speaks to me, "I know you feel disheartened by mistakes. Follow Me. I will never fail you."

God formed man with His hands and breathed life into him. He blessed humanity with diversity in appearance, thought, personality, and talents. We are unique, and He can use our flaws for His glory. When you are tempted to focus on your mistakes and shortcomings, imagine our loving Father stopping you and speaking Zephaniah 3:17 into your experience.

Sister, you were fashioned by the Creator, and He delights in you.

Sherma Webbe Clarke

October 9

The Empty Oil Bottle

Now may the God of hope fill you with all joy and peace.
—Romans 15:13, NKJV

I had one last pan of patties to cook. Glancing at the bottle of oil, I could see I barely had enough to finish the job. I really did not have much to worry about, though, knowing the store was close by and I had the means to buy more.

I wonder what it must have felt like for the widow of Zarephath and her son (1 Kings 17): she had just enough oil and flour to prepare a small cake for each of them, and then they would slowly die of hunger. What a blessing she received when she accepted Elijah's word that there would be enough flour and oil to sustain the three of them until the rain came.

Thankfully, I have never been in the situation of having an empty flour pot. The word *empty* has quite a depth of meaning when pondering the dictionary definition. It means to contain nothing, to be hollow, deserted, forsaken, and meaningless.*

As we consider the number of empty stomachs around the world and the lack of food, the word *empty* indicates more than physical hunger. Too many lives are forsaken and deserted. Oh, may Jesus come soon and put an end to the suffering we constantly see around us. Jesus knows all who are running on empty today. He sees the lives that need filling with love and care and others who are lonely and low on energy and health. There are others struggling in despair with financial problems; some have had their homes burned or washed away, losing loved ones.

These things will cease when Jesus comes, but while we wait, He will help us reach out to connect with those we meet about us who need to be filled with encouragement. Each day we need to be renewed in the strength that comes from God so we are filled with His power to do His will. "But they that wait upon the Lord shall renew their strength" (Isaiah 40:31, KJV). If our spiritual life is running on empty, there is no way we can work efficiently for God. Pray and stay close to Him, for Satan will do all he can to snatch us from His hands.

I have shared my thoughts with you. Now I must go back to my kitchen to finish my cooking. As I do, I open a new, full bottle of oil, and I pray for each of you. May you feel the power of the Holy Spirit filling your lives with peace, hope, and joy today.

Lyn Welk-Sandy

---

* *Merriam-Webster's Unabridged Dictionary*, s.v. "empty," accessed February 21, 2024, https://unabridged.merriam-webster.com/unabridged/empty.

October 10

Strong Women

Strength and dignity are her clothing,
And she smiles at the future.
—Proverbs 31:25, NASB

The mental health industry now recognizes that mental health solutions are not found just in biochemistry but that solutions can also be strength based. In other words, individuals can access their own unique set of strengths to overcome problems.[*] Becoming a strong woman may take weeks, months, or even years to achieve as one moves from challenge to challenge and strength to strength since growing in strength is always a process in motion.

Becoming strong is a unique journey for each woman. At first, she may try to draw upon her weakness as she fights to overcome obstacles. She may feel the pain of apparent failure. She may lose focus at times and not see a clear solution to her dilemma. Yet she resolves to fight on. Over time, she realizes that where she was once weak and foolish, she is now growing in strength and wisdom. Throughout the entire process, she accepts her challenges and faces them, continuing to work for solutions and resolution.

You may wonder, *What is the* how *of this process? How is she enabled to become and remain strong?* The true source of *how* is usually found in her life practices: the time she spends soaking up the truths of Scripture, the way she applies them to her own life through thought and prayer, and the ongoing resolve to secure her faith in the Lord while on the healing journey.

We all have experienced pain, guilt, weakness, and other emotional challenges. These challenges are universal. God knows. He understands and prompts our hearts when it is time to change. He loves us too much to leave us burdened by guilt and sin. And He is the divine *how* for our change. His Word tells us, "My strength is made perfect in weakness" (2 Corinthians 12:9, NKJV). "Be strong in the Lord and in the power of His might" (Ephesians 6:10, NKJV). "I can do all things through Christ who strengthens me" (Philippians 4:13, NKJV).

By God's grace, provision, and strength, *I am that strong woman*!

Edna Thomas Taylor

---

[*] Carl Brun and Richard C. Rapp, "Strengths-Based Case Management: Individuals' Perspectives on Strengths and the Case Manager Relationship," *Social Work* 46, no. 3 (July 2001): 278–288, https://doi.org/10.1093/sw/46.3.278.

October 11

Alert and Praying

*And pray in the Spirit on all occasions with all kinds of prayers and requests. . . .
Be alert and always keep on praying for all the Lord's people.*
—Ephesians 6:18, NIV

I stared in awe. Every branch of every tree was incredibly weighed down with the heaviest snow I had ever seen! We pulled into the freshly plowed parking lot, strapped on our snowshoes, and started up the trail. The massive snowfall muted our voices in the complete stillness.

Thankful for the few people who had gone ahead of us, my husband led the way as we trudged toward the remote lake, enjoying the indescribable beauty and keeping *alert*. Hiking in deep, fresh snow means there are dangers not present at other times, including tree wells. A *tree well* is the area under a tree where there is not as much snow as the surrounding area. It is possible to fall headfirst into the "well" and be almost swallowed up by the snow around it. People have died in tree wells.

The Bible reminds me to be alert for the enemy seeking to swallow me in deep trials and temptations that can catch me off guard. I also need to be alert to the signs of the coming of Jesus. In addition to being alert, it is important not to walk alone in difficult terrain where great danger exists. And in the journey of life, how grateful I am for others who walk with me and help me stay alert to danger in my path.

Ephesians 6:18 reminds me that being alert includes prayer on *all* occasions and being a woman who *keeps on praying* for all the Lord's people! I have a group of friends I can ask to pray at any time. I have asked for prayer over family members, decisions, discouragements, health concerns, and much more!

If someone falls into a tree well, 90 percent of the time, they cannot get out on their own. You and I need prayer friends to help "dig us out" of the difficult and even dangerous places on our journey. Why not commit to being that prayer friend for someone today? Ask the Holy Spirit to show you someone who needs prayer support, and when you do, I believe He will provide the same for you.

Stay alert. Keep on praying. And your faith journey will be a beautiful adventure.

DeeAnn Bragaw

October 12

His Reluctant Prayer Warrior

*"I will answer them before they even call to me.
While they are still talking about their needs,
I will go ahead and answer their prayers!"*
—Isaiah 65:24, NLT

I had not planned on going to the Bible class with my husband at our community senior center. In fact, I did not even want to go. Yet I somehow made the decision that I would. Looking back, I now believe the Holy Spirit impressed me to go. I also believe He impressed me with what to take: a printed sheet with a prayer on it. I made a copy of my prayer sheet in black ink and laid it on my bed. Before leaving, however, I accidentally sat down on the prayer sheet, wrinkling it. I did not want to take a wrinkled copy. On my desk, I spotted a copy in color, so I grabbed that. Slipping my colorful prayer sheet into an envelope, I rushed out the door for Bible class.

The teacher was about to start class when we entered the center. I slipped over to her, handed her the envelope, and invited her to open it. She did and then took out the colorful sheet with the prayer quotation on it. To my surprise, she read it aloud to the class! Then she began to expound on the content! Upon finishing, she said, "I was not supposed to be your teacher today. The woman scheduled to present the lesson had an emergency and couldn't be there. Being notified last minute, I didn't know what I would present, but the Holy Spirit assured me I wouldn't have to worry about that. God would have it under control. He did. I started to read this aloud because the sheet was so pretty."

I was amazed. God had planned this all along. First, the Holy Spirit impressed me strongly to attend the class on that day. And what if I had not sat on the black-and-white copy and subsequently not exchanged it for the colored copy? It was the beautiful colors on the sheet that first caught the eye of the teacher and then engaged her enough so that she would share the content about prayer with the class! I am so humbled that God used me—a person who did not even want to go to class—to do His will. The first sentence on my prayer sheet read as follows: "Prayer is the answer to every problem in life. It puts us in tune with divine wisdom, which knows how to adjust everything perfectly."* May God help us follow the Spirit's lead!

Ruth Cantrell

---

* "Why Do I Worry About Anything When I Know That I Can Pray?," *Daily Word*, June 1952, devotional for Wednesday, June 18, 1952.

October 13

My Neighbor

Love thy neighbour as thyself.
—Mark 12:31, KJV

When you live in a small country town, you are privileged to get to know your neighbors. For twenty-six years, my husband and I lived in a small town in Alabama, United States of America. One day I happened to see some men working in a vacant lot as if preparing it for occupancy. I watched the progression each day. Eventually, they moved a trailer there. When they finally finished, I looked forward to meeting our new neighbors. I never saw anyone for days, not even a vehicle in the driveway. One day, as I was driving past, I saw a young lady going to her mailbox. I stopped and introduced myself and my hubby. She smiled and said, "My name is Elaine also—Deborah Elaine." I told her I had been waiting to see a vehicle in the drive, and she told me about her automobile accident and that she was no longer able to drive. I let her know that we go into town quite regularly, so she could ride with us whenever she needed to go. We exchanged numbers. She became a regular passenger, and I was happy to help.

I found out she suffered many challenges after her accident. We became close friends, and I helped her do many things around her home. I also invited her to church, and she went many times. As time went on, my husband, who is sightless, became ill. I explained to Deb but let her know I would help her when I could. Pete eventually had to go into the hospital. He stayed in for a month. When he finally came home, we drove past Deb's home and noticed the door was closed, which was unusual for her. We went by a few more times, and the door was still closed, so I stopped and knocked. No answer. We decided to visit her sister, and I asked if she was OK. Her sister gave me a look that told me Deb was not OK. She told me Deb had passed away over the Christmas holidays. We cried as she told me all the details.

My Bible says, "Love thy neighbour as thyself" (Mark 12:31, KJV). Who is our neighbor? Anyone with whom we come in contact. Though it could be very challenging to try to help Deborah while taking care of my husband, God was always beside me.

God, please help us to show compassion toward our neighbors. When it becomes overwhelming, remind us that You do not call the equipped; rather, You equip those You call.

Elaine J. Johnson

October 14

Divine Intervention

He shall call upon me, and I will answer him:
I will be with him in trouble; I will deliver him, and honour him.
—Psalm 91:15, KJV

The dress code for nurses has changed over the years. Formerly, a nurse's cap was considered part of the uniform. Once we nursing students successfully completed half the program, we became eligible for the capping ceremony. Along with my fellow students, I was ecstatic. My mother and my sister were excited as well. I would provide their transportation to the ceremony while my husband remained at home. Allowing enough time for the hour-long drive from Queens to Brooklyn (in New York City), I picked up my mother and sister around four thirty in the afternoon. Then I drove us to the school for the ceremony.

After the memorable program, I drove them back home. I did not arrive at my home until much later. I parked directly before the front door of our house. As I exited my vehicle in the dark, I was taken aback to hear what sounded like a stampede of horses coming in my direction. Quickly turning my head, my stomach tightened. No, not horses. Rather, I saw what appeared to be a gang of around five or six young teenage boys, and they were heading directly for me! Quickly surrounding me, they forced me into the back seat of my car.

"Where are your keys?" a tall boy gruffly demanded, pointing a gun at my temple.

Another had already wrenched my purse from my hands. "I'll see if they're in here," he said breathlessly, rifling through its contents.

Several others began interrogating me: "Is there anyone else in your house right now?" "How many are in there?" "Who are they?"

In my state of panic and shock, I just rattled off names at random. All of a sudden, the front door swung open, and my husband's form filled the frame. At this unexpected turn of events, the boys fled. My husband was simply looking out to see whether I was home so that our son, who was on the phone, could speak to me.

Talk about divine intervention—and foiled nefarious plans! My purse was gone, along with my driver's license and fifteen dollars in cash. But my keys were still in my fist, and I was alive!

In fact, I am still a witness to the truth of this promise: "God is our refuge and strength, a very present help in trouble" (Psalm 46:1, KJV). He never left nor forsook me!

Cora A. Walker (deceased)

October 15

Blessings

*"I will be your God throughout your lifetime—
until your hair is white with age."*
—Isaiah 46:4, NLT

Now that my hair is white with age, it is time for me to share some of the ways the Lord has cared for and blessed my family and me throughout the years.

My husband was a self-employed logger and usually went to work alone in the woods three miles from home. I would join him later. One day our two- and five-year-old daughters joined us, all going together. The girls and I waited nearby while my husband cut down a large pine tree. Suddenly, he called, "Honey, I broke my leg!" The tree had fallen amiss on the steep hillside. We quickly went to him, helped him into the car, and started the half-hour drive to the nearest hospital. What a blessing that I was there to help him when he needed it! Because we did not have medical insurance, the hospital did not want to admit him. When the admittance clerk learned he was a war veteran, however, the hospital arranged for an ambulance to transfer him to the nearest veterans' hospital. That development became a blessing that lasted the rest of his long life, for he always had funded health care after that.

After several years of his recuperating and working less, we found we could spend more time volunteering our services at a mission school in the mountains of southern Mexico. Our three children enjoyed going to school there, growing up bilingual, and helping with Sabbath School programs in nearby villages. We were also able to help, using a portable sawmill to cut lumber for building churches in small towns in the area. These years were a blessing to us and to the school. When the youngest of our children was ready for college, we needed to spend more time working in California. Our daughters became nurses; then one went on to become a doctor. Although our son did not think he would like to be a teacher, he did study education and ended up teaching at the same Mexican school he had attended as a youth.

Before long, it seemed, we had grandchildren who also loved going on summer mission trips! Two generations later, nurses, nurse practitioners, and physical therapists make up our group of grandchildren and spouses. *Thank You, Lord, for being our faithful God and the Giver of all blessings, even until our "hair is white with age."*

Betty J. Adams

October 16

You Will Not Fall

*Fear thou not; for I am with thee: be not dismayed; for I am thy God:
I will strengthen thee; yea, I will help thee;
yea, I will uphold thee with the right hand of my righteousness.*
—Isaiah 41:10, KJV

For years, I have wanted to paint a picture that I see in my mind, titled *Salvation Made Simple*. It would show Jesus walking along, holding the hand of a child, with the caption "Take My hand. You may stumble, but I will not let you fall." (I am still practicing my painting skills.)

We can all remember walking as a child with a parent holding our hand. It is easy for children to stumble over something. Yet how assuring it is to feel a stronger hand holding them up to keep them from falling. And when children grow to adulthood, they, in turn, hold the hands of their own children.

God is our loving Parent, and He has promised to uphold us with His "right hand." I have heard that "right hand" appears over one hundred times in the Bible. I have also heard that this term has several meanings. For example, it can simply indicate the hand on the right side of the body (Genesis 48:18), a location or position of honor (Hebrews 12:2), or giving help or strength (Psalm 18:35).

In Isaiah 41:10, God promises both to help us and to hold us up with the strength of His "right hand of . . . righteousness" (KJV). When we stumble, His strong grip supports us as we regain balance and become upright again. He keeps us from scraping our knees, so to speak.

Yet, in Isaiah 41:13, the writer states that God will hold *our* right hand. I have wondered about the significance of that. Though I do not have a specific answer, I do find comfort in the following comment that encompasses the assurance God gives us in verses 10–13 of Isaiah 41: "The heart of Infinite Love yearns after those who feel powerless to free themselves from the snares of Satan; and He graciously offers to strengthen them to live for Him."*

Praise God for His loving care and His strong right hand that keeps us from falling!

Elizabeth Versteegh Odiyar

---

* Ellen G. White, *Prophets and Kings* (Nampa, ID: Pacific Press®, 2005), 316.

October 17

Free to Choose

"Of every tree of the garden you may freely eat;
but of the tree of the knowledge of good and evil you shall not eat."
—Genesis 2:16, 17, NKJV

He came storming through the door, angrily muttering under his breath. I caught the words "Why did God let him do that?"

I do not remember what it was that upset my son so much, but I asked, "You want God to stop him? Would you like it if every time you wanted to say something hurtful to someone, God slapped His hand over your mouth and stopped you?"

My son had a mouth on him.

"And would you like it if every time you wanted to slug someone, God clamped your hands down to your sides and stopped you?"

My son got in fights.

"You want God to stop other people, but you don't want God to stop you—am I right?"

Free will for me but not for you. Do you like that? "I get to do what I want, but you don't get to do what you want." Or even better, "I get to do what I want, and you get to do what I want!" I know too many people like that!

The big question is, Do we really get to do what we want? Are we really free to choose? We find the topic of choice addressed right off the bat in the Bible. In the Garden of Eden, the serpent offered Eve the forbidden fruit. She could have said no and walked away. Hadn't God already told her, "Don't eat it"? But this snake hanging out in the tree said she should, and that it was good. "So . . . she took of its fruit and ate. She also gave to her husband with her, and he ate" (Genesis 3:6, NKJV).

Did God stop her from eating that fruit or from sharing it with Adam? No. And God lets you and me make our choices, too, even if they harm us or others.

God did not stop my son's friend from doing the wrong thing. Neither did He make my son do the right thing. But He did give my son a mother who could share the divine perspective, and He did give us His Word to offer divine guidance and the power to do all things well.

Pat Arrabito

October 18

The Immediate Answer

*It shall come to pass, that before they call, I will answer;
and while they are yet speaking, I will hear.*
—Isaiah 65:24, KJV

The thought of moving to Florida was so exciting. After living and working in New York City for more than twenty years, I felt it was time for a change of pace. My two brothers live and work in Florida, which was an incentive for me to do the same. Finally, the day of my departure from New York City had arrived. After a thorough check to make sure that I had all I needed to travel, I headed to John F. Kennedy International Airport. I had some mixed emotions over leaving behind loved ones, longtime friends, and my beloved church family.

The flight to Orlando was pleasant. Upon my arrival, a family friend met me and took me to my place of residence. However, it was not long before I began to question my decision to relocate. Did I make the right choice to spend the rest of my life here? Will I get a job soon? Will I find a church where I will feel at home?

The first few months of living in Florida were disappointing and stressful. I was not able to get a job as soon as I thought, and my finances were fast becoming nonexistent. One day I was at my wit's end: the rent was due, and I did not have enough money to pay it. Then I remembered the promise of my heavenly Father: "And my God shall supply all your need according to His riches in glory by Christ Jesus" (Philippians 4:19, NKJV). Beside my bed, I fell on my knees, pouring out my heart to my heavenly Father. While in prayer, my phone began to ring. Finally, I decided to answer it. On the line was a friend I knew from my days as a student in college. She had relocated to Florida years before I did. What she said astounded me. "I have been impressed to bring you some money." She had no prior knowledge of my current dilemma! The amount she gave me was exactly what I needed! I paid my rent that very day with much rejoicing. Before I even prayed, my heavenly Father had already set the wheels in motion to help me. While I was still on my knees, He had heard my plea for help and come to my rescue.

No matter how impossible things may appear for you right now, our heavenly Father is willing and able to hear His children's cries for help. Trust Him. He is just a prayer away.

Merita E. Joseph-Lewis

October 19

Rubbed Smooth

That our daughters may be as corner stones, polished after the similitude of a palace.
—Psalm 144:12, KJV

On a recent visit to the beach, I tried in vain to find an area not filled with rocks. I wanted to swim, not step around pebbles, no matter how beautiful they were. On examination, I noticed that the rocks were all smooth, and I thought of this text: "That our daughters may be as corner stones, polished after the similitude of a palace" (Psalm 144:12, KJV). Can you imagine that this is our Father's wish for us—to be polished stones, rubbed smooth and beautified?

How do we achieve this, our Father's goal? What is the process of rock polishing? How can a rough stone become beautifully perfect? Here is some insight into the process: A rock, God's daughter, must first be durable. No soft material can endure the polishing process. When God created us, He made us strong enough to withstand the storms that He knew we would undergo. For some, the storms occur as families struggle with health, financial, personal, or other challenges. Think of the woman who approached Jesus to touch the hem of His garment. Hemorrhaging for twelve years (Mark 5:25–34)! She had to be durable. For some, the storms come when we experience the realities of being the spouse of a man in a high position and being strong enough to hold his hand when he is facing his own storms. Never say, "I did not sign up for this." Instead, grab a pen and look for the place to sign your name.

Another observation: no matter how ideal the spouse or how beautiful the wedding is, your perfect family will be subjected to the storms that batter. Our rock cannot avoid these unexpected challenges. Think of the bruising from being literally tossed and turned! But consider how much more beautiful, how polished we become when the storm subsides. Any polished lady knows that beneath "that smile," there are often tears. Each storm polishes her more, making her fit for the palace. James advises: "Count it all joy when ye fall into divers temptations" (James 1:2, KJV). Count it all joy, friends; it is your Father's wish for you.

Let us embrace the ups and downs of the polishing. We may not realize it, but we are changing each day as we yield to the process. We are being rubbed smooth, but look how much more beautiful we are becoming!

Annette Walwyn Michael

October 20

Triple Trilliums

Go to the ant, thou sluggard; consider her ways, and be wise.
—Proverbs 6:6, KJV

My husband recently cleared dead trees from our rocky woodlot. As he drove the tractor over the shallow soil, he uncovered three white trillium plants. I knew they had no hope of life if they remained there among the roots and loose soil, so I carried the plants home. I looked for the perfect spot to plant them and found it in a partially shaded area. No other plants would interfere with these delicate trillium bulbs there. Then, with all the love and care I could muster, I gave these three treasures the best chance I could for a future life.

That was several years ago. Last spring two groups of trilliums were blooming in the front yard. This year I was surprised to see three groups. I knew I had planted only one little grouping. Now I was rewarded with nine beautiful blooms.

I remembered these multiplied trillium blooms recently when I heard a program on the radio where a naturalist explained how trilliums manage to spread through whole woodlots. I was amazed. As I listened to the naturalist, I thought of King Solomon's counsel to consider the ants (Proverbs 6:6) for their lessons of industry. You see, it seems that I owed my two new patches of trilliums to ants! When trilliums seed after blooming, ants collect the seeds, putting them in little soil storerooms. There, the ants munch on the seeds' gel coating but discard the seeds. So, when the spring sun warms the soil, the seeds sprout and grow new bulbs, though they will not bloom for a couple of years.

It is like that with our faith. A little gem of Scripture rests in the mind for hours or sometimes days before we can fully absorb its meaning. Then, suddenly, we understand what God is telling us through the "seeds" of Bible truth He has planted. As we share these treasures with others, our lives are enriched. These trilliums remind me that before Jesus came into my life, I, too, was lost on a rocky hillside. My pain and emptiness covered me just like the gel covered those little trillium seeds. Without someone to clear that away and plant me in just the right spot, I would never have sprouted and bloomed into the contented Christian I am today.

I can thank the "ants" of change for the future hope that I have today. I pray that my life will cause other little seeds of Christian growth around me to sprout and grow as well.

Patricia Cove

October 21

Making Wrongs Right

"You shall not steal."
—Exodus 20:15, NKJV

Each May I look forward to purchasing annuals to beautify the front and back of the house. But I have only recently discovered hanging baskets. My friend Maureen and her husband, Robert, have an abundance of flowers in the summer. In 2021, they got me hooked on hanging plants after Maureen volunteered Robert to make me some for the backyard fence. I purchased the flowers, which Maureen helped me pick out, and was pleasantly surprised when Robert made me eight hanging baskets and gave me some gladiolas and a bleeding heart as well.

Those who visited me marveled at what I did, but I had to give God and Robert the credit. I am a firm believer in teaching a person how to fish rather than giving them a fish. The following year I made my own hanging baskets by reusing the pots I had been gifted. This year was no different as I filled up my shopping cart with an array of assorted annuals. I was surprised when the cashier informed me that I qualified for a free item because of the amount I had spent.

There were so many hanging baskets outside the storefront that I went inside to confirm the free item. I understood the free item to be the jumbo flowers labeled "2 for $55.00." I picked up two plants but immediately wondered if I was to have taken just one plant instead of both. When I arrived home, I phoned the store. The person on the other end of the line confirmed my suspicions: I was to have taken just one of the plants, not both. I told him I would return the following day to settle things. Then I was impressed to check my receipt. That is when I noticed that I had been charged for *nine* trays of flowers instead of eight. I double-checked the receipt and recounted the flowers. I had a good laugh when I realized that I had been overcharged the same amount as the cost of the additional flowers I had taken.

The following day I went to customer service and informed the attendant that I had to make two wrongs right. I explained the situation, and she charged me $27.50 for the second plant. Then she gave me $2.50 that the store owed me. I felt free as I left the store. When we live our lives with integrity before the Lord, burdens truly are lifted at Calvary.

Sharon Long

October 22

The Unexpected Haircut

Study to shew thyself approved unto God, a workman that needeth not to be ashamed, rightly dividing the word of truth.
—2 Timothy 2:15, KJV

If there is one thing the pandemic has taught us, it is how to be self-sufficient—especially how to save money, because we can never tell how permanent our jobs really are. It was during this time that I learned to braid [put extensions into] my hair, with the help of what I call the "University of YouTube." I always knew how to comb and style my hair. But when I needed to have it braided, I visited styling professionals so that they could do what they do best. During the COVID-19 lockdown, most hair salons and barber shops were closed. The best I could do when having an opportunity to get out and about for a bit was to purchase hair extensions myself and experiment. Though I had no place to go, I still wanted my hair to look decent. Little by little, my practice made "improvement," and I got quite good at choosing the right texture of synthetic hair and doing my own installations.

One day I discovered some hair that was very affordable and closely resembled my hair. I thought, *This will work since I try to keep styles as natural looking as possible.* From time to time, I experimented with various textures. With each trial, I have always come back to the hair that most closely resembles mine. I never dreamed that very hair would get me into trouble!

Later, when it was time to take out my synthetic braids, I started cutting them out. Then, with astonishment, I realized that I had just cut out a length of my own hair, not the fake, synthetic hair! I had accidentally cut about two inches of my own hair! Because of the fake's resemblance to the real, I had not been able to tell the difference. All I could do was laugh it off. After all, it would grow back again—and no one would see it in the meantime.

However, it did make me think. When we allow ourselves to get so caught up and entangled in the lies of this world and what it has to offer, the time may come when we will no longer distinguish God's truth from the devil's lies. When that happens, we will risk "cutting out" God's truth from our lives. God gave us His holy Word so we can know the truth, and when the counterfeit comes along, we can clearly identify it and cut *that* out of our lives forever.

Candy Monique Springer-Blackman

October 23

Captive Thoughts

Bringing into captivity every thought to the obedience of Christ.
—2 Corinthians 10:5, KJV

I have very stubbornly curly hair that has a mind of its own! Any woman with my kind of hair knows what I am talking about. Just getting one's hair to go all in the same general direction can be a major undertaking. So I either go to a beauty salon and let my wonderful hairdresser deal with it, or I take one wet strand of hair after another and carefully wind it around a plastic roller and hold it down with a sturdy hairpin. Eventually, my hair dries either under the Southern California sun or under a dryer, and I am able to comb it out into a presentable format.

As I was going through this meticulous process this morning (my head is covered in multicolor rollers as I write), I thought of the apostle Paul's letter to the Corinthians. He shared what it means to be true followers of Christ. He used the expression "bringing into captivity."

My mind made a sudden connection: Just as my stubborn hair resists being "brought into captivity," I find that I, too, as a child of God, need to win victories in my life by submitting to Christ's discipline. I cannot do this by myself any more than my hair can place itself on my rollers. It is an intentional process of daily living out the purposes of Christ in my life rather than my own purposes.

When I was a teenager, I purposed never to wear makeup ever again. So I would grab my lipstick and rouge and powder and throw them as far as I could into the brush growing along an embankment in our backyard. Alas, I would wake up a couple of mornings afterward, looking haggard and wan and regretting my decision to discard the makeup. I would find myself furiously digging through the brush for the evidence of my erstwhile repentance and bring them sheepishly back into the house again. In my adolescent understanding of God, there was no hope for me in this merry-go-round kind of religion. Even so, I stuck with my religious faith, always in the hope of one day having the victories I so longed for.

In later years, I learned that I would need to leave to God the task of bringing every thought and character defect into captivity to the One who has already won the victory. My task is only to let Him do it.

Lourdes E. Morales-Gudmundsson

October 24

Singing the Lord's Song!

*By the rivers of Babylon we sat and wept
when we remembered Zion. . . .*

How can we sing the songs of the L*ord*
while in a foreign land?
—Psalm 137:1, 4, NIV

How can we sing the Lord's song in a strange land (with so many people dying or have died)? COVID-19 has affected our world on a global level. The pandemic of 2020 and 2021 impacted families all over the world with sickness and death. Lives, jobs, and homes were lost. Long lines formed at churches, community centers, and government charities as families sought food and clothing. So how can we sing the Lord's songs when there is so much pain?

Remember the story of Paul and Silas being thrown into jail for preaching the gospel? While in prison, awaiting a possible death sentence, they sang and praised God! They sang the Lord's songs from the depths of a dark, cold, and gloomy prison cell! Their songs ministered to other inmates and the jailer. They trusted their lives into the hands of God, who has the power to heal, deliver, or not deliver!

We, too, can sing the Lord's songs, even when our hearts are broken with grief. Our praises to God should not be dictated by circumstances. Our praise to Him is an expression of our complete trust and dependence on Him, regardless of our situation.

Ellen White writes, "We cannot but look forward to new perplexities in the coming conflict, but we may look on what is past as well as on what is to come, and say, 'Hitherto hath the Lord helped us.' 'As thy days, so shall thy strength be.' Deuteronomy 33:25. The trial will not exceed the strength that shall be given us to bear it. Then let us take up our work just where we find it, believing that whatever may come, strength proportionate to the trial will be given."*

So, despite the uncertainty of tomorrow, we will lift our hearts in praise to God. He holds the future in His hands. By faith, we will continue to trust in Jesus and sing the songs of Zion! "Let every thing that hath breath praise the Lord. Praise ye the Lord" (Psalm 150:6, KJV).

Jannett Maurine Myrie

---

* Ellen G. White, *Steps to Christ* (Washington, DC: Review and Herald®, 1977), 125.

October 25

The Utilities Account

*"It shall come to pass
That before they call, I will answer;
And while they are still speaking, I will hear."*
—Isaiah 65:24, NKJV

It was one of those beautiful sunny Sabbath mornings on the lovely island of Trinidad. I had just finished a wonderful worship session with my blood relatives all around the world (something we did every Sabbath morning). While I got dressed for the service at my local church, I sang the song "More Than Wonderful." As I sang, the words of the song seemed to come alive. Jesus *is* more than wonderful! I was wrapped up in the song. In fact, I was so happy that I fell in love with Jesus all over again. But this was certainly not pleasing to the enemy.

At that time, my church was in the midst of an evangelistic series for which we needed to move equipment back and forth. Just as my sons finished removing equipment from my SUV that day, I had an unfortunate encounter with the gate at the church. I could not believe it! I made this trip every Sabbath to the church, which was only one street away from our home. Why this unexpected damage to my vehicle? People know I cannot stand to get even a minor scratch on my car—and this was not minor! I turned around in the churchyard, checked the damage, and drove home to show it to my husband (for emotional support). Then I returned to the church to lead out in the song service. Only God helped me to make the return trip that morning and have the presence of mind to sing "More Than Wonderful"—with a new meaning.

On Monday morning, not knowing where I would get funds to repair the vehicle, I called the insurance company adjuster. He gave me a repair figure. As I checked through my accounts, I noticed some funds in one of them that I could not account for. When inquiring of the bank, I was told that the funds were from an account that had been opened twenty years prior when the home mortgage (utilities) account had been set up. Would you believe that this sum was double the amount I needed for the vehicle repairs?

Oh yes, Jesus is wonderful, amazing, and marvelous, just as the songwriter says. But, to this, I would add a further thought: We know that God, who sees the end from the beginning, knows what our future holds and just what we will need. When the future seems dark to us, we can trust His heart of love. He is God!

Jill Springer-Cato

October 26

God's Memory Room

And the spirit returns to God who gave it.
—Ecclesiastes 12:7, NIV

"I just cannot bear it," cried Melissa, who was curled in my lap, with tears streaming down her face. "Funerals are dreadful! Everyone sobbing. What does it mean that her spirit went back to God who gave it? Where does God keep it?" It was Melissa's first funeral experience. Unfortunately, it was for one of her playmates who had been killed in a hit-and-run accident.

"Once upon a time, when I was about twelve," I began, and Melissa's tear-stained face tilted up, eager for the story. "I was a pallbearer for a three-month-old baby who had died of scarlet fever. At the baby's memorial service, my father used the same verse from Ecclesiastes. Later, in response to my similar question, he replied: 'I don't know but I'm sure God has a state-of-the-art system for saving the spirit and DNA formula for every human being. It may help you to picture in your mind's eye the most beautiful room you can possibly imagine. The baby's [future] is safe with God—in His Memory Room.'"

"Is God's Memory Room more beautiful than the Amber Room? The one in Catherine's Palace in Saint Petersburg?" asked Melissa. "We saw pictures of it at school, and it was amazing!"

"My guess is that God's Memory Room is more wonderful than we could ever imagine, although the Amber Room could be a good start," I replied.

"If I'd known about God's Memory Room sooner, maybe the funeral wouldn't have been so dreadful. I could have told people about it." Melissa's little voice trailed off.

"The apostle Paul says we have hope, so we will not grieve like those who are without hope" (see 1 Thessalonians 4:13, NLT), I said, trying to encourage her own sad spirit.

"I'll miss her," said Melissa with a sigh. "But I like knowing her [future] is safe with God in His Memory Room."

"And think about how much fun you'll have when you next see her," I continued. "God will give her breath again someday. And this time, you'll be together forever."

"It'll be even *better* than before," said Melissa, smiling through her tears. "Much better."

You're right, Melissa, I thought to myself. *It will be even better than before.*

Arlene R. Taylor

October 27

From Panic to Peace

"This is my command—be strong and courageous! Do not be afraid or discouraged. For the Lord your God is with you wherever you go."
—Joshua 1:9, NLT

From the time we arrived at our campsite, the nearby forty or so young people drinking and toasting to "White Power" and racial slurs put me on edge. At four thirty in the morning, I yanked my husband out of bed, and we fled the area after overhearing plans to harm us. The trauma still makes me feel unsettled and unsafe, even in my own home.

"Of course," my confidant said, "your identity was attacked, and now you have to change your boundaries. You've always sought the furthest places, the most rugged experiences, and adventures. That is who you think you are."

I was operating on boldness, without wisdom about the world that we live in.

This week I had to adjust my self-imposed expectations and explore living in the moment, both wisely and bravely. My senses were still heightened, waiting for another assault on my personal space and identity. Yet those same senses guided me to better receive beauty too. I chose to enjoy the great support of patient friends, peaceful nature sounds, and low-key activities at a local park. Even though I had been to this place already, I saw it with fresh eyes. It is the same location, but this time I noticed the new season's foliage and even the changing boundaries of the place itself as ponds transitioned into meadows in order to serve new purposes in the ecological community.

With Jesus as my Guide, changes in the way I live my life will create a better world for someone else too. Not an environment of perpetual conflict, anxiety, anger, or hatred. But instead, a meadow of peace, boldness, and growth. Sometimes fences are broken down slowly, not with violence. Wisdom can be a terrifying process. Sometimes the more we know, the more there is to fear. Yet wisdom can also help us better appreciate the good times if we will let it.

Choosing peace, in spite of triggers and fear, can be an adventure in itself. And that, my friend, is a personal triumph, not an identity crisis!

Wendy Williams

October 28

Rejection

He is despised and rejected of men; a man of sorrows, and acquainted with grief: and we hid as it were our faces from him; he was despised, and we esteemed him not.
—Isaiah 53:3, KJV

People can be rejected because of their skin color, nationality, religion, economic status, age, or gender. Depending on one or more of these qualifiers, others may consider them to be inferior. Yet others may be despised for their "superiority": possessing a university degree, being a gifted musician, or having extraordinary abilities not shared by the general populace. Sometimes women's rejection of other women originates in feelings of envy or jealousy. Sadly, some cannot tolerate the success or superior abilities of others. Of course, men can also reject women who are able to do what they cannot, even driving a car in certain countries.

Whatever the so-called reasons may be, rejecting people is unfair. Rejection excludes, hurts, and isolates. And what is perhaps even a greater loss, rejection often makes impossible future interactions that could bring mutual benefits. Yet God has spread gifts among people for a purpose: He wants them to achieve their highest potential and use it for His purposes of love.

If and when we are rejected, let us take great comfort in knowing there is Someone who perfectly understands what rejection is. He understands everything about us. That Someone is Jesus. He was not rejected for being a foreigner because He lived among His own people. He was not rejected for following a different religion because He attended the same Jewish synagogues as did His fellow believers. Rather, He was rejected because the very ones who should have recognized, according to ancient prophecies, that He was the heaven-sent Messiah, turned on Him. Filled with envy that Jesus was the object of so much love and popular attention, they allowed their jealousy to consume them. In the end, their plans, along with His love, took Him to the cross. And He died for the very ones who were mocking and torturing Him.

Whenever you feel rejected, remember that you always have the love, understanding, acceptance, and support of Jesus. He knows everything about you. Wait prayerfully on Him as He transforms your pain from rejection into a blessing, not only for you but also for those around you. After all, He was rejected for you so that you can be accepted eternally by His Father.

Het Jane Silva Carvalho

October 29

Scars

But he was pierced for our rebellion,
crushed for our sins.
He was beaten so we could be whole.
He was whipped so we could be healed.
—Isaiah 53:5, NLT

As a little girl, I ran around with my brothers and did everything they did. Consequently, I have several scars to show for it. My first scar is in the middle of my forehead from when I was sitting in my brother's room, and one of my brothers was in the top bunk bed and pushed the bunk bed's steps down onto my head when I was three years old. I received three stitches for that one.

I have another scar in my left eyebrow. That one was caused by the same brother and resulted in twelve stitches. The scar on my forehead over my left eye was caused by the same brother and resulted in another twelve stitches. Another brother put me on the handlebars of my bicycle and rode recklessly down four or five steps and across the street until I eventually fell off, causing a scar under my chin.

All in all, I have had thirty stitches and four scars that resulted from something my brothers did. Even though my brothers are the reasons for my scars, I still love them very much. Every time I look at those scars, I remember exactly what happened and who caused them.

Jesus has scars that we caused. We are the reason for His scars. Every time He looks at His scars, He remembers exactly what happened. Even though we are the reason for His scars, He still loves us very much. "Jesus ascended on high from the field of conflict, bearing in His own person His bruises and scars as trophies of His victory, which was to result in annihilating the power of the first rebel, who [before he rebelled] was a chieftain in glory, an exalted angel in heaven. There was rejoicing in heaven, and the proclamation was carried to all worlds that the ruined race was redeemed. The gates of heaven were thrown open to the repentant race who would cease their rebellion and return to their allegiance to the law of God."*

Remember, whatever you are going through, Jesus has already paid the price of eternal life for each of us. Keeping our minds focused on His sacrifice will allay all fears and anxiety.

Pauline J. Maddox

---

* Ellen G. White, *Christ Triumphant* (Hagerstown, MD: Review and Herald®, 1999), 292.

October 30

A Perfect Gift

*Every good gift and every perfect gift is from above, and comes down
from the Father of lights, with whom there is no variation or shadow of turning.*
—James 1:17, NKJV

I looked up from preparing breakfast, only to see my husband in the hallway leading from our bedroom. He was wearing a happy smirk on his face as he danced to praise music playing on the radio. I joined him for a few seconds before we cut the dance short with a long hug. My heart was overflowing with praise and thanksgiving.

Less than a year earlier, the hospital had sent Earl home "to bed" after more than three weeks of mostly COVID-19 isolation. He was still testing positive for COVID when he was informed his hospital bed was needed for more urgent medical cases. Sadly, no rehab center in our county was admitting COVID patients. In the hospital bed at home, he looked worse than when he had been admitted to the hospital with a urinary tract infection (UTI).

Only one of twelve area home-help organizations was willing to send a caregiver into a COVID-stricken house—for a two-week quarantine period with the patient. And for $14,000! So I decided to undertake caregiving responsibilities with my daughter's help. But within a week, Earl needed professional care. A less harried hospital accepted Earl for a week, ending in two consecutive *negative* COVID tests. Earl was released to a rehab facility and returned home in much better shape than when he had first left.

Throughout the grief-causing pandemic, I wondered, *Why are some taken and others left?* After all, COVID claimed many people in decent health, often younger than Earl. So did each of the other conditions with which Earl was simultaneously afflicted in the hospital—dementia, pneumonia, and the UTI. All I know is that our all-knowing God chose to say yes to the petitions of this distraught wife, her family, her church, and her friends. In exchange for the "ashes" of disease, pain, grief, and fear, God has given Earl and me true "beauty" (Isaiah 61:3, NKJV). The painful shared hospital experiences have given us a contented sense of togetherness. We welcome each new day as a special gift graciously dispensed by a caring Father. "Oh, give thanks to the Lord, for He is good!" (Psalm 106:1, NKJV).

Lela Moore Gooding

October 31

Unexpected Noises

*Do not conform to the pattern of this world,
but be transformed by the renewing of your mind.*
—Romans 12:2, NIV

We were on a road headed to a beautiful overlook on the Oregon coast in the United States of America. This area has some of the prettiest coastline views, and I love to visit anytime I am in the region. This day, as we drove, we heard a noise that seemed to indicate something might have fallen off our pickup. I asked my husband if he had left his mug of tea on the bumper, which he denied. We did not see anything unusual in our rearview mirror.

After we had parked, I began to take pictures from a variety of vantage points overlooking the ocean. We walked up a trail and enjoyed the commanding views with waves crashing on the shore below. As we returned to the parking lot, my husband noted the hubcap was missing from the rear wheel. "Ah, that was likely what we heard making the noise!" Would we be able to find and reclaim the lost hubcap?

We drove back to our campsite, found a place to park, and continued the search on foot. There it was! I shouted to my husband farther up the road. It was resting against the tall grass, in the shadows, shiny side down.

Thankfully, we were traveling slowly enough that we heard the hubcap rolling away from us. Also, we had taken note of what happened and were able to go back over our tracks and retrieve the lost item. At any other time, we likely would have been unaware of the incident, traveling on a noisy freeway at high speeds, and never would have recovered it.

How aware are we of what is happening within us? To our bodies? Are they "making noises" that may indicate something is not right? Maybe there is a pain that was not there before, an unusual symptom, or something out of the ordinary? Perhaps we are traveling so fast through life that we have not taken notice of potential warning signs or have been too busy to stop?

I encourage you to push the pause button and give yourself a chance to be aware. Take stock of what is happening with your health, and take action before it is too late or your "hubcap" becomes impossible to retrieve.

Terri Lea Gibson

November 1

Mustard-Seed Faith

"You don't have enough faith," Jesus told them. "I tell you the truth, if you had faith even as small as a mustard seed, you could say to this mountain, 'Move from here to there,' and it would move. Nothing would be impossible."
—Matthew 17:20, NLT

Do you, like me, take little things for granted, things that we seldom think about? Recently, a friend sent me a birthday card, and along with it came a paper clip. It is not a regular metal paper clip but a prettily decorated lightweight cardboard paper clip. And guess what? It holds items together every bit as well as a metal paper clip. I have found it to be a helpful gift.

I got to thinking about so many other little things that help me stay orderly. A slim piece of ribbon, for instance, to keep stray wisps of hair out of my face. A safety pin to keep a hem from falling down until I can sew it. An eraser to help me correct written errors. A toothpick to dislodge a piece of spinach that might embarrass me if I am eating lunch with a friend.

Thinking on these small things caused me to consider a certain small thing, only one or two millimeters in size. Scripture tells us about the mustard seed. Jesus Himself spoke these words of Matthew 17:20, which is our verse for today. He certainly commended the ability of what a small amount of faith can do. He made it clear that even with mustard-seed faith, we can do wonders. If we are not doing so, it means that we do not even have a mustard-seed-size faith, for He prefaced His commendation of mustard-seed faith with, "You don't have enough faith" (verse 20, NLT). Why did He include that comment in His conversation in the first place?

The disciples had inquired, "Why couldn't we cast out that demon?" (verse 19, NLT). Jesus knew they had not yet acquired even mustard-seed faith. He wanted to encourage them to grow their faith like a plant, with tender loving care and daily nourishment.

We are modern disciples, and even with our morning and evening devotions, we have the opportunity to grow our faith. It is important to remember that if we tend our mustard-seed faith, it will grow into a strong, healthy, and vibrant faith. And what once seemed impossible will no longer be evident, for we will have found God's way to make the impossible possible.

Betty Kossick (deceased)

November 2

Rejoice, Pray Continually, Give Thanks

Rejoice always, pray continually, give thanks in all circumstances; for this is God's will for you in Christ Jesus.
—1 Thessalonians 5:16–18, NIV

The year 2007 will be forever etched in my memory. I remember it vividly. I was at work when my husband called to say that while he was filling a mug with water, the mug had just slipped out of his grip. "What?" I said, knowing something serious had happened. I rushed home to take him to the emergency room, where the doctor said he had experienced a stroke and that his right limbs had been affected. *Oh no, Lord! This is not how I imagined my life! My husband is paralyzed?* I was devastated. I was a young wife with small children. How would I manage taking care of him, raising the children, and dealing with our finances and home? I felt overwhelmed as I sat outside his room and wept bitterly. "Oh, Lord, please help me," I prayed.

The next day my husband's situation deteriorated as his blood levels took a turn for the worse. We were going to lose him. The doctors and nurses in the intensive care unit were trying their best to do whatever they could to save him. Those few hours were the most trying of times for our family. We fell to our knees, pleading with God to perform a miracle. As we prayed, our associate pastor visited the home where we were praying. He saw us on our knees, and when we told him what had happened, he knelt in prayer beside us. I asked him to anoint my husband. He agreed and took the elders and deacons with him for the anointing.

The news spread to our friends and family all over the world, and everyone prayed, asking God for a miracle.

God heard our prayers! Yes, my friends, God heard our prayers, and my husband opened his eyes on the third day and asked for me. What a joy to see him alive! God is amazing! Our prayers turned to praise and thanksgiving. We were so grateful for the marvelous miracle He performed right before our eyes.

We would do well to consider how the Lord uses the difficult times in our lives. With hindsight, we see the way He works things together for our good. This helps us gain strength for whatever the future brings. "Give thanks to the Lord, for he is good. His love endures forever" (Psalm 136:1, NIV).

Premila Pedapudi

November 3

Co-laborers With Christ

He that goeth forth and weepeth, bearing precious seed,
shall doubtless come again with rejoicing, bringing his sheaves with him.
—Psalm 126:6, KJV

The gospel commission given by Jesus to His disciples though all the ages, as recorded in Matthew 28:18–20, makes us all colaborers with our Master. As laborers in the Lord's vineyard, we are called to carry the seed of the gospel to everyone, beginning from our Jerusalem—our homes—to all parts of the world. The seed must be carefully planted in good soil, which represents the heart of people, then tended with care as it grows. God collaborates with us in soul winning and causes the seed to germinate, develop roots, and produce fruit.

It is a thing of joy for all farmers to see that the seed they have planted has grown into fully matured, fruitful plants, ready for the harvest. This analogy best describes the joy of witnessing how a sinner is saved, grows, and matures, and then goes on to win others for Christ.

Several years ago, I conducted an evangelistic crusade in another country. After the series, I met a young man in his early twenties who was vacillating between making a stand for God or not. I approached him and took a personal interest in him, encouraging him to give his life to Christ while he was still young. After a while, he decided to accept Jesus and was baptized. We kept in touch for a while, but I lost contact with him because I lived in a different country.

The years rolled by, and miraculously, my daughter came in contact with this young man, who told her the story of how he came to be baptized. He has grown in his faith and is now one of the leaders in the church where he was baptized. Moreover, he went on to get a master's degree in accounting and now works with the General Conference Auditing Service. He loves to work with young people in leading them to give their lives to Jesus. I reconnected with him, and great was my joy to hear his wonderful testimony. "Thank you, ma'am," he said, "for leading me to Jesus and for all the counsel you gave me. Today I am a child of God, and I am so blessed." His words filled my eyes with tears.

It is true: "He that goeth forth and weepeth, bearing precious seed, shall doubtless come again with rejoicing, bringing his sheaves with him" (Psalm 126:6, KJV)! Amen!

Omobonike Adeola Sessou

November 4

How to Grow Disciples

"You are My witnesses," says the LORD.
—Isaiah 43:10, NKJV

Inviting people to church is a good way to show you care about them. It is also a great way to introduce them to Jesus. But I am sometimes puzzled about how to keep the friendship going. The Bible, in Acts 3:1–12, offers some ideas.

1. *When you see a need, do what you can to fill it.* Peter and John met a lame man begging near the temple. They had no money, but they had a better gift. Peter said, "In the name of Jesus Christ of Nazareth, rise up and walk" (verse 6, NKJV). Before the lame man had a chance to think anything negative, Peter did something positive. He took him by the hand and lifted him up.

2. *Be available and encouraging.* The man, although no longer lame, still needed Peter and John's support. And they gave it. When we bring the good news of salvation to others, we do not want to drop it off like a package and drive away. We need to stay with them to carefully help unwrap the mysterious coverings that may obscure the gift of eternal life in Jesus Christ.

3. *Make use of God's promises.* When Peter lifted up the man, the Bible says that the man's "feet and ankle bones received strength" (verse 7, NKJV). When we encourage others with words and promises of Jesus, God is using us to help strengthen their faith.

4. *Be a friend like Jesus.* Have you ever had a friend invite you to a meeting or a gathering where you did not know anyone? What happens if she introduces you to someone you have never met and then she is called away? You are left standing there, trying to think of something nice to say. The situation can be awkward. You might begin to feel that you should have stayed home. When a friend is learning about Jesus, she needs us to stay nearby so she can be more comfortable being alone with Him.

5. *Be His witnesses.* Depending on how we respond to Christ's invitation to be His witnesses, we bring Him credit or shame. After Peter had healed the man, "all the people ran together to them in the porch which is called Solomon's, greatly amazed" (verse 11, NKJV). May we witness in such a way that people are drawn to the Savior, greatly amazed, and long to know more of His love. That is the goal.

Marcia Mollenkopf

November 5

More Than Morsels

*So they gathered them and filled twelve baskets with the pieces
of the five barley loaves left over by those who had eaten.*
—John 6:13, NIV

A look at the early history of the Seventh-day Adventist Church shows that many women devoted their gifts to God in carrying out His work. Women as well as men were placed in positions where they were needed. If we look at the social situation of women in the nineteenth century, that is exceptional. A church that owes its existence to a woman who is considered to be God's messenger—even a prophet—had to appreciate the fact that God imparts His gifts to all believers. The women of Adventist history are like a cloud of witnesses who encourage us to lay off all that hinders us from giving God our best and to run in the race, looking to Jesus (see Hebrews 12:1, 2, NIV). And today God still pours His Spirit on His sons and daughters.

Sometimes I feel women are overlooked in the story of the feeding of the five thousand. Only the men were counted, but women and children were there as well! All were served and fed. And they collected twelve baskets full of morsels. I am sure no woman left the baskets behind but brought them home to feed her village. The disciples did not take the baskets as they entered their boat. Jesus performed a miracle, blessing the five loaves a woman had prepared for her son. And today God takes the bread prepared by women and blesses it. Jesus is Himself the Bread of Life, and He gives bread in plenty, not just morsels. But sometimes women have to work with morsels, and God blesses their efforts.

In Jesus' encounter with the Canaanite woman, a mother pleads with Jesus to heal her daughter. Saying, "Even the dogs eat the crumbs that fall from their master's table" (Matthew 15:27, NIV), she shows she would be satisfied with a morsel of His attention. But with the words "Woman, you have great faith! Your request is granted" (verse 28, NIV), Jesus gave her more than a few crumbs. He gave His full attention and healed her daughter.

We can only reach the goal God has set for us if we *all* work together. Jesus did not wait for His culture to change before treating women with respect and appreciation. Let us treat each other with love and appreciation, especially, those who have done such a great service to this church and still do.

Hannele Ottschofski

November 6

A Calculated Plan

Do not be terrified by them, for the LORD your God, who is among you, is a great and awesome God. The LORD your God will drive out those nations before you, little by little. You will not be allowed to eliminate them all at once, or the wild animals will multiply around you.
—Deuteronomy 7:21, 22, NIV

One morning, while on spring break, I was reading Deuteronomy 7, where Moses explained how God would allow the children of Israel to conquer the Promised Land from the other nations. Moses specified that God would drive out the heathen nations little by little.

I wondered why God chose to do something of such great importance gradually when He could do it instantaneously. After moments of pondering, the revelation came. God might have been using this strategic method for a dual effect: destruction and reconstruction. In driving out the nations little by little (destruction), the Israelites would simultaneously have the opportunity to reconstruct their lives by progressively eradicating ungodly characteristics in themselves and deepening their faith in God.

I often struggle with the "need-it-now" syndrome, and so I almost always want my prayers to be answered immediately. Thus, I tend to get impatient when God uses the little-by-little approach when answering some of my prayers. Daily, I pray to God, asking Him to bless me with a godly spouse—a prayer I thought would have been answered instantly. I am still waiting for an answer, but after reading these two verses from Deuteronomy, I am reminded of something. God may not give me a husband instantly, as I think He should, because little by little, He is simultaneously preparing me to be a godly wife while growing my faith in Him.

Isn't it awesome to know that we serve the same God as the Israelites, and just as He was calculating then, He is calculating now because He changes not (see Malachi 3:6)? As we go through life, God may not answer all our prayers immediately, but some prayers He will answer strategically. God may be deliberately using some of our prayers to grow our faith in Him.

Growing faith in God takes time, and so God has to use different strategies to rebuild our faith in Him. Thus, God's little-by-little approach is the perfect remedy because it has a dual effect: it not only cures our need-it-now syndrome but also builds our faith in Him.

Sutania McBean

November 7

Beyond Our Wildest Imagination

"Before they call I will answer;
while they are still speaking I will hear."
—Isaiah 65:24, NIV

I mused in my mind about the change in my circumstances. Overnight I had lost all the sources of transportation to work that I had come to rely on over the past few years. Driving myself was now inevitable. This thought had been circling in my mind for a while but had now become an urgent need. If I wanted to make the daily commute to my job, I needed to get a car.

But how does one shop for a car when one has no idea what an appropriate car would be and what features to look for? A colleague consented to help me with my search. My budget was limited, and my mind was inundated with the opinions of others as to what I should be looking for. During our search, we found two vehicles that my colleague felt were good prospects. We agreed to return two days later to finalize the choice.

After my colleague failed to contact me as planned, we ended up having to set another day to go auto shopping. Later that evening, another colleague messaged to offer her car—a newer car with lower mileage—for me to purchase. I was able to purchase her car while she upgraded to a newer car. A deferred trip to the used car dealership resulted in an upgrade in the type and quality of car that I was able to purchase.

It is interesting how God orchestrates things in our lives. I had called her at the beginning of my car search, asking her for suggestions about where to find a good used car. She had remembered our conversation just that day and decided to make the offer to me. We were able to be a blessing to each other. God was so specific that He even told me the price to offer for the car.

God's ways are beyond our wildest imagination, and He is truly able to do more than we can even imagine. I do not know what challenges you are facing or what breakthrough you are waiting on the Lord for. Know that He has not forgotten you and has already answered your request. You will see the manifestation of this when the time is right, and you will clearly realize that God's timing is best. I pray you will find that what you thought was a disappointment is simply God's way of redirecting you to a greater blessing.

Andrea K. Francis

November 8

In His Perfect Time

You will arise and have compassion on Zion,
for it is time to show favor to her;
the appointed time has come.
—Psalm 102:13, NIV

My childhood school experience was difficult at times because I was a late bloomer. I was on par with my peers—except when it came to developing the physical aspects of becoming a woman. How I longed for those feminine markers, and I waited with great anticipation to be able to be like the other girls, all of whom wore brassieres and seemed to fill them voluptuously. I was bullied for something I had no control over. I remember one church lady saying, "You are a nice girl, but your chest is just too flat. If only it wasn't." This was done in the presence of others, and one of my male peers took the baton and ran around calling me "chicken chest" for the rest of that Sabbath afternoon. I was so conscious of my lack in that department that in the seventh and eighth grades, I began to stuff my bra with socks and tissue.

When the appointed time dictated by my biology and genetics had come, I began to notice some beautiful changes in my body. It would be fair to say that I no longer needed to fill my bra with socks and tissues.

I have realized that it is still possible to make adolescent mistakes as an adult. I do this whenever I compare myself against the apparent success of others, not accepting the uniqueness of God's timing for my life. Sometimes I am tempted to succumb to the temptation to fake it to fit in. Internalizing hurt from the subtle comparisons of critics is another mistake.

As women of God, we know each of us is unique. We are not to compare our paths and purposes with others. Second Corinthians 10:12 tells us that people who do these things are not wise. We must avoid listening to any bullying banter and focus instead on God's promises to us. A wise woman of God trusts that her life and purpose are unique and waits for God's timing.

Have you been upset over God's timing in providing what you think you lack? Are your peers getting married, having children, going off to school, or achieving success? Remember, at the appointed time, God will bless you in His unique way. The once barren areas of your life will become fruitful and grow beautifully in His love. Trust His perfect time for you.

Judelia Medard-Santiesteban

November 9

My Waymaker

"God . . . answered me in the day of my distress and has been with me in the way which I have gone."
—Genesis 35:3, NKJV

I felt overwhelmed. Things were not going well at all, and to add insult to injury, as the older folks would say, the two vehicles we owned were giving us problems, the washing machine was not functioning the way it should, and the list went on. I decided that morning to put all the issues before the Lord, including the fact that, with the exception of our son, the other three family members were unemployed. I determined to pray every hour, on the hour, which I did, beginning at 9:00 A.M.

As it approached 3:00 P.M., I sensed the Holy Spirit urging me to "pray now." I obeyed, and after praying, I sat for a few minutes, meditating on the goodness of God. At 3:02 P.M., the phone rang. I hesitated for a moment before answering, and to my surprise, it was a friend I had been thinking about the week before. We chatted for a bit, and I told her I had been thinking of her and planned to visit her at her office the next time I was in the city.

She then asked me, "Would you be interested in going back to doing legal work? A friend of mine is looking for a senior clerk." I was stunned. She continued, "So, if you would email all your information to me, I will forward it, as I am the one who recommended you."

Without hesitation, I blurted out, "Yes!"

My friends, I had decided not to return to that field, but clearly God had other plans. I saw this as His leading. I had been at home for the past six years, my husband was also at home, and we had been living on the little savings we had.

I sent my friend my application and résumé, and the very next morning I received a call at 6:30 A.M. for an interview the same day. Today I am employed, and my salary is almost the same as when I left my former job, where I had worked for thirty-three years—almost six years before. God heard the cry of His child that Sunday morning. He had been working behind the scenes, putting things in place, before I called. With my whole heart, I say, "Thank You, Lord!"

My prayer is that my testimony helps someone who is waiting in line for their blessing. Trust our on-time, faithful God. He is our Waymaker.

Brenda Browne-Ashe

November 10

God Did Answer!

"Before they call, I will answer;
And while they are still speaking, I will hear."
—Isaiah 65:24, NKJV

Glancing surreptitiously at my watch, my heart sank. Colleagues were waiting in the airport to whisk me away to my first speaking appointment—wherever that was. Over twenty hours in the air; only one in the customs office. (It felt like twenty!) Once in the airport, I had been pulled aside. The encounter went like this:

Officer 1: "Where are you staying in our country?"
Me: "The hosts have made hotel reservations for me."
He asked me where.
Me: "I don't know, sir. The hosts made all the arrangements."
Officer 1: "Do you have an invitation with you?"
I showed him an email.
Officer 1: "That's not a formal invitation. Where are you speaking?"
I told him at an annual medical convention, for one.
Officer 1: "Where is it going to be held?"
Me: "At the annual medical convention. I think at a resort about three hours from here."
Officer 1: "You think? Aren't you staying there? What's the name of the resort?"
Me: "I don't know." (It was not on the email.)

A second officer and then a third went through identical questions. Sadly, the same answers. In the fourth office, a woman shook her head and said, "We allow no one to enter our country without a local address."

Dear God, I breathed. *I have no address. I'm out of ideas. I'm exhausted and about to take another flight—back home. If You want me to speak here, please help!*

"Is there anywhere else you are scheduled to speak?" she asked.

"Yes," I heard myself reply. "I'm presenting an all-day seminar at Fulton College."

"Fulton College!" she exclaimed. "We know that college. It has an excellent reputation. Several of our officers attended there. Why didn't you say so to begin with?" (If I had known . . .)

Stamp, stamp, stamp. Passport in hand, I was in the lobby.

"Where have you been?" the leader exclaimed. "We thought you'd missed the plane!"

"No worries," I said. "I was having a prayer answered."

Arlene R. Taylor

November 11

The Locksmith

*Come, let us tell of the Lord's greatness;
let us exalt his name together.*
—Psalm 34:3, NLT

My phone rang; it was my son calling. "Mom, can you come get me? I've locked myself out of my car. I'm at Atwoods." Atwoods was a store near my house, but I was in town. I called my husband, David, and asked him to go and help Benton. He left right away.

David drove Benton to his home, where he got a key he thought was the spare key. Unfortunately, they discovered it was the wrong key. Apparently, Benton did not have a second key for his car. We wanted Benton to have access to his car, and we prayed that God would somehow help us to open his car, even though we could not figure out how to make that happen.

While David was trying to open the car, a family drove up in a Hummer. A lady smiled and asked, "Are you having trouble with your car?"

David explained what had happened.

The gentleman said, "I think I can help you. We have a towing service, and we help people get into their cars all the time. My place is just around the corner. I'll go and get my tools."

"How much do you charge?" my husband asked.

"Well, I generally charge sixty dollars, but since we are so close, I will just charge forty dollars."

"That sounds great!" David responded.

Soon, the family was back. They walked over to Benton's car, opened up a package, took out their tools, and within four minutes, Benton's car was open. When the gentleman saw Benton's Navy uniform on the hanger in his car, he asked, "Is your son in the service? Are you a veteran?" he asked, looking at my husband.

"Yes, to both questions," David answered, smiling.

"Well, I thank you for your service. And I thank you for your son's service. I won't charge you anything because I'm grateful to you both."

With that, my husband said thank you and goodbye to someone sent by God to help us.

Once we were both home and he had told me the story, I said, "Remember, we prayed, and God answered our prayer." With that, we said another prayer of thanks. God is so good; He certainly loves His children and helps them when we do not expect it.

Charlotte A. Robinson

November 12

Before I Call Him . . .

*"I will answer them before they even call to me.
While they are still talking about their needs,
I will go ahead and answer their prayers!"*
—Isaiah 65:24, NLT

It was our forty-ninth anniversary, and we were in Savannah, Georgia, United States of America, for the weekend. Just before leaving our hotel room to go for a walk along the Savannah River, I picked up my wallet. It was a beautiful evening, and many other people were strolling up and down the riverwalk. As we walked, we saw a riverboat docked and decided to cross the street to get a closer look at it. Then we sat on a bench nearby.

We watched the water as the sun set and the evening grew dark. My husband began taking pictures of the riverboat, the sunset, and me. We moved from one bench to another, laughing and posing. Around eight o'clock, we decided to go to dinner at our hotel's restaurant. We crossed the street and put our names on the waiting list. Before long, our names were called, and the hostess led us to a table by the window. We had sat down and begun to look at the menu when I suddenly realized I did not have my wallet!

"Honey, I can't find my wallet. It has all our money in it for this weekend! I know I had it when we were taking pictures on the riverwalk," I said. I remembered putting my wallet on the bench next to me when I got up to pose for pictures. Quickly, I rushed out and was about to cross the street when I heard a persistent tapping on the restaurant window. I turned and came face-to-face with a woman, who asked, "Are you, Pauline Griffith?"

"Yes," I responded.

She told me she had found my wallet on the bench and took it to the check-in desk at the hotel.

"What?" I replied; I could not believe my ears. I hugged her tightly and then ran back into the restaurant where my husband was standing at the window. I told him what had happened and then left to go to the check-in desk. While I waited for the elevator to arrive, it occurred to me that I had barely had a chance to whisper a prayer for help before my prayer was answered. My wallet had been found before I even knew it was lost! We had a delicious dinner and bought dessert for the woman who had found my wallet.

Pauline A. Griffith

November 13

God Knows Best

Trust in the LORD with all thine heart; and lean not unto thine own understanding. In all thy ways acknowledge him, and he shall direct thy paths.
—Proverbs 3:5, 6, KJV

You know how you plan your life, and you think you know just how it will turn out? Well, I have learned that sometimes things do not work out exactly as we think they will. I got married, and we had our daughter, Aprille, and that was it. We had expected to have at least two children, but it was not to be. So let me tell you how I became reconciled to having only one child.

When Aprille was in cradle roll at Dallas First Church of Seventh-day Adventists, in Texas, United States of America, the leader asked whether anybody played the piano because their pianist was moving away. I timidly raised my hand, and I had a new job!

A couple of years later, we moved to Stillwater, Oklahoma. One of the first questions I heard after walking into the church was, "Do you play the piano?"

Soon, I was helping with Vacation Bible School, teaching the youth class, and, yes, playing the piano.

We moved to Choctaw, Oklahoma, only a couple of years later and joined Choctaw Seventh-day Adventist Church, where we are still members. And sure enough, I was asked to play the piano and help in the primary class. Soon, I was the primary leader, Children's Ministries leader, and Communication secretary. I also volunteered at Parkview Adventist Academy, where Aprille went to school for ten years. I still volunteer in their library, many years later.

I now realize God knew me much better than I knew myself. If I had had several children, I would not have had the time or the energy to volunteer. But now, I have kids all over the place! Last month at the Oklahoma camp meeting, I was in the auditorium bathroom and heard a little voice from behind one of the shower curtains, "Hi, Miss Robin!"

"Who's that?" I asked.

"Grace!"

Little Grace goes to my church, and of course, she is one of many of my kids whom I meet unexpectedly. This thrills my soul. What a blessing! God knew what I needed. Isn't He amazing?

Robin Widmayer Sagel

November 14

Sabbath Bells

*Start children off on the way they should go,
and even when they are old they will not turn from it.*
—Proverbs 22:6, NIV

Ben was just six weeks old when I proudly carried him into the cradle roll room and introduced him to what I hoped would become an important part of his life—Sabbath School. We "ring-a-ling-a-linged" our Sabbath bells and "tick-tocked" our wooden sticks along with the clock at "half-past nine o'clock." And how we enjoyed welcoming one another by singing, "Who has come to Sabbath School?" Admittedly, the mothers sang more than the little ones, but it was not long before their sweet voices could be heard lisping along.

Ben's favorite activity was story time, and by the time he was ready to leave cradle roll, my mother-in-law could not believe the extent of his Bible knowledge. It made me feel good to know Sabbath School had become one of the highlights of his week.

As I describe Ben's experience here, I know many of you may remember the busy Sabbath morning routine. Perhaps someone asked you to teach a class, brush up on your rusty piano skills, and maybe even accept the responsibility of leading the department. I remember throwing myself into the new role and working hard to give the little ones the best Sabbath School experience possible. I spent hours preparing programs and decorating the Sabbath School room. I enjoyed every moment I spent creating a space that would hold special memories for each child.

We grow with our children and find ourselves moving from cradle roll through kindergarten and primary. Suddenly, they are juniors, and after you have served faithfully in the children's departments, it is time to hand over the reins to a new, younger mother. Everyone should enjoy leading out in singing and ringing the bells.

As I make this transition, I wonder where I will fit in. It has been so long since I was last part of the adult Sabbath School. While I may take a while to find my place, I am certain there will always be something more to do and many others to serve. I know I will ultimately find my place because this is where I choose to be. I love being in God's house each Sabbath. It is who I am. He created us all to serve. And you see, I remember ringing the Sabbath bells.

Linda K. Wolfaardt

November 15

What Is Your Story?

Then those who feared the LORD spoke to one another,
And the LORD listened and heard them;
So a book of remembrance was written before Him
For those who fear the LORD
And who meditate on His name.
—Malachi 3:16, NKJV

Ladies, how do you satisfy the urge to be creative—to feel a sense of accomplishment that brings satisfaction? Some might turn to baking; others to walking with camera in hand or perhaps working in the garden or making a gift for a friend. Some find their fulfillment in writing.

As I write this, I think of the widely divergent backgrounds of those who contribute their time, thoughts, and talents to making these devotional books possible from year to year. If you are one of those, you have felt that excitement when the acceptance notification comes. If not, why not consider it? I confess I am a self-appointed recruiter for writers, including those of you who have not yet let us hear your stories or learn from your experience. Those life lessons are such a blessing to those of us who read them.

My sister, Mary Jane Graves, has often been published in these books. I would read her devotionals, never thinking that I might have something to share. Then one day I found myself in a situation that seemed it would be perfect for a devotional. It almost wrote itself! It was published ten years ago when I was eighty-five years old. Since then, I have skipped a couple of years for lack of inspiration, but my latest attempt was emailed just a few days ago.

Each time I see the names of those of you who write, I want to know more about you. I turn to the biographical sketches in the back and learn where you live and a few other interesting details. I also check to see whether you are on Facebook, and if you are, I feel I know you a little better.

It is said that everyone has a story. It need not be any kind of dramatic experience. It can be some everyday occurrence from which you can draw a spiritual lesson that will turn your readers' thoughts to things of eternal value. And that is really what these books are all about.

"Everyone will share the story of your wonderful goodness; they will sing with joy about your righteousness" (Psalm 145:7, NLT). I do hope you will share your story with us. I look forward to reading it!

Lila Farrell Morgan

November 16

What Is Your Jesus Story?

Jesus used many . . . stories . . . to teach the people.
—Mark 4:33, NLT

Everyone loves a good story—old and young alike. Jesus recognized the power of a story and always had one tucked up His sleeve, ready to use wherever He found an opportunity. His stories were filled with "the familiar events of everyday life. . . . In this way He associated natural things with spiritual, linking the things of nature and the life experience of His hearers with the sublime truths of the written word. And whenever afterward their eyes rested on the objects with which He has associated eternal truth, His lessons were repeated."*

Jesus is our example in all things, and if He was never without a story, then what about us? Do we have a Jesus story to share with others? I love the story of the two believers who were joined on the road to Emmaus by Jesus. Not that they realized it at that moment. But once they recognized their Savior, they hurried back to Jerusalem, where they "told their story of how the Lord had opened their eyes. . . . The company heard this report in breathless silence. Some were inspired with new faith; others were incredulous. Suddenly Jesus himself was in their midst. His hands were raised in blessing, and he said unto them, 'Peace be unto you.' "†

Whenever we share the story of what Jesus means to us and how He has changed our lives, others are inspired and amazed. He is with us, and our hearts burn within us (see Luke 24:32). Do we hesitate to share our story? Think of the early church, how passionate they were to let the whole world know of their Savior! Their stories poured forth from hearts on fire to make Christ known. But today, too often, "the atmosphere of the church is so frigid. . . . The first works of the [early] church were seen when the believers sought out friends, relatives, and acquaintances, and with hearts overflowing with love told the story of what Jesus was to them and what they were to Jesus."‡ Oh, that this would be our experience! What does Jesus mean to you? Tell *that* story!

Karen Pearson

---

* Ellen G. White, *Counsels to Parents, Teachers, and Students* (Mountain View, CA: Pacific Press®, 1943), 140.
† Ellen G. White, *The Spirit of Prophecy*, vol. 3 (Battle Creek, MI: Seventh-day Adventist Pub. Assn., 1878), 217.
‡ Ellen G. White, *Testimonies to Ministers and Gospel Workers* (Mountain View, CA: Pacific Press®, 1962), 167, 168.

November 17

No Worries—God Is Near

Be anxious for nothing, but in everything by prayer and supplication, with thanksgiving, let your requests be made known to God; and the peace of God, which surpasses all understanding, will guard your hearts and minds through Christ Jesus.
—Philippians 4:6, 7, NKJV

Just the mention of the word *dentist* and the escalated phrase *dental appointment* immediately increase my heart palpitations. I am flooded with thoughts of "what if?" A feeling of helplessness overcomes me whenever I find myself situated in the dentist's chair, surrounded by the dentist, the assistant, and a table of sharp, shiny metal tools. At my last appointment, I was anything but calm as I sat, waiting for it all to begin. However, this dental appointment, unbeknown to me at first, would be different—a difference that would forever change my perspective.

Close to where I was seated was a large window that looked outside. As my attention became more focused on this scene, a revelation of God's love and His longing for us not to worry began to emerge, like the opening of a movie. I did not realize how long I had been focusing on the blue sky and how quiet my spirit had become. God had been preparing me for His message of love that would cast out my fear of dental worries—and life's worries.

Suddenly, I saw a bird appear, flying with outspread wings in large, circular movements into and then out of my view. I mused, *This is so interesting. Usually, there is a companion.* But all I could see was just this one bird. Then, right in front of my eyes, there appeared a second bird flying a distance from the first bird. You see, the first bird had never been alone. These two birds, while flying in and out of view, beyond what I could see through the window, were always there for each other. As my mind became more intrigued, a third bird joined the group. They all flew equal distances from each other but always close to one another.

What a lesson of love! It completely cast from my mind not only my dental worries but also all of the many worries of life that I carried—cares and anxieties that often bring tears to my eyes and cloud my mind from God's goodness. Now I could hear His still, small voice speaking to my heart, "No worries, child. I am with you always, and I will see you through."

Let us choose to guard our hearts and minds through God's peace today.

Cynthia Best-Goring

November 18

God Has the Last Word

And we know that all things work together for good to them that love God, to them who are the called according to his purpose.
—Romans 8:28, KJV

When I realized that I had been excluded from attending my own project at a large conference in Europe, I complained and took it to God. "It is not fair, Lord. I had the idea, and now others will use it, and I am not even there. I'm out!" The Lord heard my prayer and answered me through a dream. It was a short dream, but it left a strong impression. I saw one specific page from the *Adventist Review* of a year ago. The next morning I looked for the magazine and found the page I had seen in my dream. It was an advertisement, and it meant I would need to prepare to travel. It became necessary to discern whom I could trust from among the people around me because I knew I would need help. At that time, we all depended on snail mail, not email. It was in the early days of the internet, and it was not available in the heavily wooded area in which I lived. Someone would need to go to the city, about fifty miles (eighty kilometers) away, and collect all the mail for the workers, including me. Fortunately, I had some real friends who helped me.

After some weeks, I took a flight to England. When the airplane was flying over the capital and preparing to land at Heathrow Airport, I prayed, "Oh, God, I'm in London! Thank You!" It took me a few attempts to reach Bracknell, but soon after arriving, I was able to attend Newbold College for a summer English course. Since I had arrived two days early, I was able to attend the conference of Seventh-day Adventist librarians. That was wonderful because, besides being an English teacher, I was also the librarian at the school where I worked.

While at Newbold, along with my classes, I enjoyed wonderful accommodation, food, and several trips throughout England. It was awesome! In addition to all that, when I arrived back home, I was invited to teach at the Federal University.

Yes, "we know that God causes everything to work together for the good of those who love God" (Romans 8:28, NLT). When others "intended to harm me, . . . God intended it all for good" (Genesis 50:20, NLT). My friends, God has the last word because He is all-powerful!

Het Jane Silva Carvalho

November 19

Can't Sleep? No Problem!

And the Lord God caused a deep sleep to fall on Adam, and he slept.
—Genesis 2:21, NKJV

Do you have trouble with going to sleep or with waking up in the middle of the night and being unable to get back to sleep? You are not alone. According to SleepFoundation.org, approximately 62 percent of people around the world have problems sleeping, with nearly 70 percent reporting sleep disturbances at least once every night.* Some have chronic issues and deal with medical conditions, such as sleep apnea, narcolepsy, and insomnia. Other factors may include eating too close to bedtime, caffeine consumption, late-night screen time, and lack of exercise. But one of the main causes of sleep deprivation is stress. Our daily problems are keeping us awake at night.

I admit that many times the cares of this world prevent me from falling asleep. When I continue to toss and turn, I have found I am able to relax if I picture the following in my mind: I close my eyes and envision Christ as my Good Shepherd and myself as His little lamb. I crawl up into His lap, and He holds me tenderly, whispering peaceful words into my ear. His tender touch is very calming, and I am able to bask in His love. As my Protector and Provider, I thank Him for supplying my every need from the time He placed me in my mother's womb. Ever since, He has fed and clothed me, instructed and guided me, and rescued me from the dark places in which I have wandered. And most of all, I thank Him for giving up His life for me on the cross of Calvary. Then I claim that He alone is the Giver of sleep and ask Him to grant me the ability to rest. The next thing I know, it is morning, and I have slept soundly through the night.

Jesus is the Creator of all things, including sleep. He placed Adam in a deep sleep when removing his rib to form his helpmate, Eve. He knows our need for rest and restoration. All we need to do is ask, and He is willing to give. King David wrote, "I lay down and slept; I awoke, for the Lord sustains me" (Psalm 3:5, NASB). Are the stresses of the world keeping you awake at night? Try resting in the arms of Jesus, our Good Shepherd and loving Savior, and He will help you lie down in peace, for He has promised, "I will give you rest" (Matthew 11:28, NASB).

Karen M. Phillips

---

* Eric Suni and Kimberly Truong, "100+ Sleep Statistics," Sleep Foundation, last updated September 26, 2023, https://www.sleepfoundation.org/how-sleep-works/sleep-facts-statistics#insomnia-and-sleep.

November 20

God Provides

And my God will meet all your needs according to the riches of his glory in Christ Jesus.
—Philippians 4:19, NIV

My husband and I were living in the city of Loveland, Colorado, United States of America, in a comfortable home in a quiet neighborhood. We had loved our previous home in the foothills with acreage but desired to become debt-free so had made this move.

While visiting my dear friend who lived in a rural setting with a large garden, I noticed a home across their field that had a large storage garage with seven bays. I thought of my husband's passion for restoring old cars and trucks and thought how he would love to have an outbuilding like that.

A couple of years later, on our way to my friend's home, I saw there was a garage sale at the home I had noticed. We decided to stop and check out what they had. As my husband talked to the elderly owner, I felt a whisper in my ear saying, "Just ask him!" I handed my quarter to the gentleman for my small purchase, and then, smiling broadly, I looked him in the eye and said, "Would you also sell me your home?" I do not know who looked more surprised, my husband or the old gentleman! We were not looking for a new home; in fact, we were so happy with our current location, we thought it would be our forever home! The gentleman surprised me by saying, "It has recently crossed my mind that we may need to start downsizing." Before we left, I gave him our name and number and did not think much more about it.

Over a year later, I was surprised to receive a message from him, asking if we were still interested in his home! We quickly set up a time to tour their place. As we walked the acreage, we talked about how perfectly the home and property met our needs. With some negotiation, we were able to agree to a purchase price.

The Lord knew what we needed way before we did. The very next year the 2013 Colorado floods totally wiped away my in-law's home, leaving them homeless. Our new place had a lovely extra suite where they could live while we arranged to build a private mother-in-law apartment attached to our home. We have been so thankful to have them close where we could enjoy them and care for them as they aged. God provided far beyond our expectations.

Judith Woodruff Williamson

November 21

Timely Travel Documents

"Therefore I say to you, whatever things you ask when you pray, believe that you receive them, and you will have them."
—Mark 11:24, NKJV

Many years ago, my husband, Michael, and I set to planning a family vacation to Germany. We were all so excited. Jesse, our eldest who was taking German at secondary school, was eager for the opportunity to practice. But all the excitement in the foreground was overshadowed in the background with the fact that all four children's passports had expired.

Summer vacations are usually a busy time for many families, resulting in hectic schedules at the passport office. We prioritized applying for new documents. Fortunately, our home was a short distance from the post office, where we found applications and information packs. Passport pictures can also be taken there.

We completed this process three months before our departure date. And then the waiting began. In my mind's eye, I thought we would wait for about eight weeks, so I felt sure we had applied in time. After a couple of weeks, one of the applications was returned. There was something wrong with my son Nicolas's photograph. We quickly rectified the problem and returned the application the following day. We prayed every day during family worship for speedy processing and waited for answered prayer.

Two weeks later, the new passports began arriving. One, two, then three. Prayers continued, and thanks ascended for each one. Time went by quickly, and soon we were into the final week. But the passport for Nicolas had not yet arrived. We were due to fly out on Thursday. Monday and Tuesday came and went, and still the missing passport had not arrived. I walked into my eldest son's room that Tuesday evening and saw the most beautiful sight. Four boys all knelt in a circle, holding hands, praying for Nicolas's passport to arrive on time.

Early the next morning it arrived by special delivery. Our boys had a life-changing experience with the Living God. They knew, beyond a doubt, that He hears and answers children's prayers too. I was reassured to see them turn to God in prayer. Friends, there is power in the prayer of faith. Put it to the test today. God is faithful.

Cheryl-Ann Hudson-Victory

November 22

Where Is It?

*But let patience have its perfect work,
that you may be perfect and complete, lacking nothing.*
—James 1:4, NKJV

When our newly purchased refrigerator stopped working, my husband and I knew we would need to contact the store for assistance. Before making the call, we prepared ourselves to answer any questions they might have concerning the fridge. We realized that many of the answers we needed would be found on the receipt.

We were on a quest to find the receipt. Surely, we had carefully put it away for safekeeping. We searched the kitchen drawers. The receipt was not there. Where could it be? We checked the counter, and to our dismay, the receipt was not there. We checked boxes in the garage. We pulled items out of the shed and checked file boxes, but still, it was nowhere to be found.

Where is it? I said to myself.

"Could it have been tossed?" I heard my husband yell from the shed. I helped him carefully put the items back in the shed while wondering where the receipt could have gone. We went inside and searched the office drawers with no success. We desperately needed the receipt, but we could not find it.

Frustration was starting to set in. We knew it had to be somewhere, but where? I convinced my husband to take a break. When we had been in similar situations, we had learned that stopping and asking God for His guidance always helped. So we stopped, said a small prayer asking God for His help, and then went on to complete another chore.

Ten minutes after we had prayed, I heard my husband yell, "I found it!" I was giddy with excitement. Where had it been? Sitting in plain sight, in the very place we had already searched. It was not hidden by other items but lay on the very top of the basket. We were so relieved! But when we examined the receipt, we realized it was for another appliance. Nevertheless, we were encouraged by the events that had unfolded. We paused and thought for a moment. Then I had a eureka moment: "It's in the car."

"In the car?" my husband asked.

I repeated, "In the car."

Sure enough, the receipt was nicely folded, sitting in the center console of the car. We were so excited it had been found!

Today's verse reminds us that with God's patience and help, all things are possible.

Diantha Hall-Smith

November 23

Lesson From the Birds

Even if the fig tree does not blossom,
And there is no fruit on the vines,
If the yield of the olive fails,
And the fields produce no food,
Even if the flock disappears from the fold,
And there are no cattle in the stalls,
Yet I will triumph in the LORD,
I will rejoice in the God of my salvation.
The Lord GOD is my strength,
And He has made my feet like deer's feet,
And has me walk on my high places.
—Habakkuk 3:17–19, NASB

I dragged myself out to walk in my neighborhood one morning; my head hung low and my shoulders were burdened by all my problems. When I heard a buzzing sound, I looked up and saw a flock of white egrets burrowing their beaks on my neighbor's lawn. I paused and watched them intently, wondering what they had found to eat. I remembered God's promise, "Look at the birds of the sky, that they do not sow, nor reap, nor gather crops into barns, and yet your heavenly Father feeds them. Are you not much more important than they?" (Matthew 6:26, NASB).

My heart filled with joy at being reminded again that I can trust God with all my problems. He has told me that I am worth more to Him than the birds, and look how He provides for them! I felt secure in Him once again.

Whenever I wonder about my situation in life, God, in His providence, sends something to remind me He has my best interests at heart. He is my Father. What concerns me concerns Him. I simply need to continue to pray, trust, and obey. When the answers do not come as quickly as we think they should, let us challenge ourselves not to become discouraged, angry, or anxious. Remember how long Joseph prayed for deliverance? How long he waited? But through it all, he trusted God. Sometimes our prayers are answered immediately. Other times, like Joseph, we must wait a long time for the answer to our prayers.

We live in changing times, but God has not changed. He is the same, always and forever. So, even when the fig tree does not blossom and there are no grapes on the vine, let us continue to trust God and praise Him in the good times and the bad.

Heavenly Father, our struggles are very real. Please teach us to trust You and to hold on to Your unchanging love, no matter what situation we face. Amen.

Cornelia Estrella Sewer

November 24

Family Reconciliation

Bearing with one another and, if one has a complaint against another, forgiving each other; as the Lord has forgiven you, so you also must also forgive.
—Colossians 3:13, ESV

My grandparents had three daughters. They had four, eight, and six children, respectively. They grew into a closely knit extended family. Though distance separates us, we have maintained a bond that many desire. Our family celebrates every achievement and milestone.

My family is generally well-read, very vocal, and opinionated. Though discussions and debates can become very lively and heated at times, they are always held in a spirit of camaraderie. However, there is no perfect family, so there are rare times of disagreement or tension. In those times, Colossians 3:13 and the lessons from Jacob and Esau's reconciliation become even more relevant.

The story of Jacob and Esau's reconciliation is a model for Christian families, demonstrating the need for repentance, forgiveness, and divine intervention for its success. Jacob fled as a fugitive from his brother, Esau, whom he had cheated of his birthright to the land of his father, Isaac. He stayed with his uncle Laban, who did not deal fairly with him. Jacob eventually became overwhelmed by this ill-treatment and decided to return to Canaan. He knew he needed to reconcile with Esau, whom he knew to be angry and intent on revenge.

Demonstrating humility, Jacob instructed his servants to refer to himself as "your servant" when approaching Esau and to address Esau as "my lord." Jacob continued to use those titles throughout his encounter with Esau. In addition, he bowed to the ground seven times while approaching Esau. The fact that Esau ran to meet Jacob, embraced him, fell on his neck, and kissed him while each wept indicates repentance and forgiveness. The evidence of God's intervention is in Esau's response to Jacob's offer, his acceptance of the gift of reconciliation, and Jacob's acknowledgment of God's favor. Jacob noted that seeing Esau's face was like seeing the face of God and a sign of forgiveness and acceptance (see Genesis 33:10).

Dear Father, please help us to live in unity and to forgive in humility, just as God in Christ forgives us.

Annette L. Vaughan

November 25

Time Well Spent Is Time Invested

*Now when Daniel knew that the writing was signed, he went home.
And in his upper room, with his windows open toward Jerusalem,
he knelt down on his knees three times that day,
and prayed and gave thanks before his God, as was his custom since early days.*
—Daniel 6:10, NKJV

My daughter Karin Elyse invited me to join her holiday cookie-decorating class two months before she and her husband planned to celebrate the first birthday, first Thanksgiving, and first Christmas of their daughter, Kalia Vivian. Karin is an expert baker and cake decorator, always refining her skills and adding new ones. Yet I wondered, *Why another class when her days are already filled to overflowing?* That is when I was reminded that things are not always as they appear.

This gift of mother-daughter togetherness caught us laughing hilariously when Rudolph's nose would not stay in place. Time stood still as my daughter helped me, her former teacher, to perfect my handwriting using a frosting pen. Daylight gave way to night as I watched my daughter's gentle hands decorate Thanksgiving treats with her daughter's name laced delicately in three-dimensional artistic frosting.

Now, two years later, as I reflect on those shared hours, my mind wanders to the time I spend with my heavenly Father. My day usually starts before I open my eyes. Amazement is my morning-joy moment—a time when I spend just a few minutes experiencing an awareness of awakening. These few moments are like precious drops of rain on parched ground. Just enough water to awaken the soil and nourish the seed within, not overwhelming but enlivening.

Like time spent with my daughter, those waking moments cause time to stand still as I marvel at God's gifts of breath, sight, movement, and sensation of heart and lungs in their synchronized tune of thanksgiving within their perfectly crafted cage of protective bones. *Good morning, Lord,* is my greeting. A simple greeting of gratitude for life. *Thanks for taking the time to visit with me and remind me that I am fearfully and wonderfully made in Your image. Sinful though I may be, our time together this morning will reveal Your perfect will, grace, mercy, and love!*

My friend, with Jesus as our example, let us invest time with God and be blessed today.

Prudence Pollard

November 26

The Giving-Jar Project

"Give, and you will receive. Your gift will return to you in full—pressed down, shaken together to make room for more, running over, and poured into your lap. The amount you give will determine the amount you get back."
—Luke 6:38, NLT

As each of my grandchildren arrived, I gave them a small Mason jar and, with it, a desire to help nurture their love of giving. This is how the Giving-Jar Project was born. It has been growing, along with each of them, through the years. Here is how it works. Each time we visit, I give each of them a small white envelope with their name on it. Inside, there are one-dollar bills that range according to their age. Right now, Warren gets twelve; Brynn, nine; Sienna, six; and Raylee, three.

When I arrive, they get their giving jars and sit around the table. I hand out the envelopes, and they count their money to be sure Grandma did not make a mistake (and, of course, when they are small, this helps them learn to count).

I tell them they get to choose how much they give and how much they keep. Through the years, it ebbs and flows on who gives and keeps the most. I have, however, seen a trend over the years that my little tribe tends to be high in the giving area, for which I am grateful!

At Thanksgiving, we count the money to see what our total is, and the children, along with their parents, Katie and Matt, choose what the money goes toward for that particular year. Last year, they adopted a family of five for Christmas, and because Katie is one of the world's best shoppers, the family they chose had an absolutely fabulous Christmas.

Often, when people find out about our project, they donate too. We have caught friends putting money in our jars, and it is wonderful to see how contagious giving can be! We hope you will take this idea and start your own Giving-Jar Project. It may seem like a small thing, but it has made a big difference over the past twelve years as we have seen how God takes our little and turns it into much. We found that giving changes us as well as those to whom we give.

Once you catch a glimpse of what your gift can do, as God leads, you will be hooked! We found this to be true, and it is exciting to see how *giving* really is contagious! It is never too late to start! In fact, there is no better time than now!

Tawny Sportsman

November 27

A Thanksgiving to Remember

"If you extend your soul to the hungry
And satisfy the afflicted soul,
Then your light shall dawn in the darkness,
And your darkness shall be as the noonday.
The LORD will guide you continually,
And satisfy your soul in drought,
And strengthen your bones;
You shall be like a watered garden,
And like a spring of water, whose waters do not fail."
—Isaiah 58:10, 11, NKJV

I never know where the Lord will lead me next because He always takes me on an adventure when I work for Him. Years ago, I worked in a joint evangelistic meeting between the Church of the Oranges and the Berean Seventh-day Adventist Church in Newark, New Jersey, United States of America. On one occasion, the Church of the Oranges hosted a job fair that drew over two thousand people! We distributed over a thousand copies of *The Great Hope* and *Steps to Christ* and were given a list of almost three hundred names to follow up on. One of them was a young lady who had attended the job fair. She shared an apartment with her sister and five nieces and nephews. This family had experienced much tragedy in their lives. Over the next few years, I ministered to them, and two are now taking Bible studies.

I remember one Thanksgiving eve when the Lord impressed me to go shopping for them. It was the most memorable Thanksgiving of my life. Then something happened that deeply touched my heart. As I waited for the elevator after my delivery, this young lady came out of her apartment with all five of her nieces and nephews, ranging in age from three to fifteen. Lining up, from the youngest to the eldest, they each came and hugged me and said, "Thank you."

I stepped into the elevator with tears streaming down my face. As I walked to my car, I thanked God for once again answering my prayer. Each day I ask Him to let me be a rainbow in someone else's cloud, and He never disappoints me.

Early one morning I received the following email from this young lady. It read, "One day, I may die without saying goodbye to you, but I will never forget to say thank you because you hold the loveliest part in my life." The treasures of this world are of little value, but to know that, by God's grace, you have helped to lighten someone else's burden is of endless worth.*

Jean P. Good

---

* Adapted from Jean P. Good, *See What God Can Do* (Calhoun, GA: TEACH Services, 2020).

November 28

TY

Always giving thanks for all things in the name of our Lord Jesus Christ.
—Ephesians 5:20, NASB

When I was growing up, my mother taught my five brothers and me to send thank-you cards for Christmas and birthday presents. We did not think twice about it; it was something we just did. Over the years, we have moved from handwritten notes to electronic means to express thanks. For instance, there is the *TY* (thank you) we text to people who have done something for us. Also, it is not uncommon when using email for prompts to pop up that say, "Thank you" for some information we received or some act of kindness.

When I tell the children's story at church, I like to encourage the children to say, "Thank you," as they collect the lambs' offering. People like to feel appreciated, even if they are just dropping a few coins into the basket. A nice smile and a friendly thank you can go a long way to encourage generosity.

Unfortunately, over the years, it seems that etiquette has fallen away. It is always sad to see ingratitude. This leads me to wonder: If we humans notice the lack of gratitude, how might God feel? The Bible addresses the importance of expressing gratitude, especially toward God, who is the Source of "every good and perfect gift" (James 1:17, NIV). Since we are told that "if we ask anything according to His [the Father's] will, He hears us" (1 John 5:14, NASB), maybe we should phrase our prayers slightly differently. What if instead of saying, "Father, please save my children," we say, "Father, thank You for doing whatever it takes to bring my child closer to You."

It may sound strange to us to say thank you in advance. But not so with God. God wants us to believe that He hears us and will do what He knows is best. While He may surprise us in how He answers, we can show our belief that He will answer in His way and His time.

Being thankful is good for us. When we express our thanks and gratitude to God, it can bring smiles to our hearts and our faces. "A cheerful heart is good medicine, but a crushed spirit dries up the bones" (Proverbs 17:22, NIV). It seems to me that being thankful not only gives joy to the receiver but brings joy to the giver. So let us be generous in saying "Thank you" as often as possible to those around us and especially to God.

Sharon (Clark) Mills

November 29

The Missing Package

"It will also come to pass that before they call, I will answer; while they are still speaking, I will listen."
—Isaiah 65:24, NASB

Last summer I was looking forward to traveling from the United States of America to the United States Virgin Islands, though I felt a little anxious because I would be gone for a few months.

I was taking two of my grandchildren with me on vacation, and I had ordered a few things for them from Amazon to help keep them occupied during the long hours of traveling. The package was scheduled to arrive by 10:00 P.M. on Wednesday. I checked outside the door several times in the afternoon to see whether the package was there, but it was nowhere to be seen.

At 9:15, I checked my email and found a notification that the package had been delivered to my doorstep at 7:46 P.M. The usual photo showing the package was included in the email. I quickly went to see if it was there. Sadly, it was not. My heart sank because we were due to leave in only six days. There would be no time to reorder.

I wondered whether the package had been delivered to the incorrect apartment by accident. I went and looked by the doors upstairs and did not see it there either. I decided to go online and check with Amazon. I was instructed to wait forty-eight hours before reporting the missing package. As someone who believes that God is concerned about every detail of our lives, I prayed about the matter and went to bed. The next morning I went to the door expectantly and was overjoyed to find my missing package!

This experience reminded me of two things. First, we must remember to pray about everything instead of worrying. Nothing that concerns us is too small or unimportant to bring to the Lord in prayer. He loves to have us turn to Him with our joys and sorrows.

Second, God always hears and answers our prayers. We sometimes stop praying too soon. Keep praying, and keep trusting. He is faithful.

Dear Lord, thank You for Your promise that before we call, You will answer. May we never forget that You always listen to us and love to work all things together for our good.

Janice Fleming-Williams

November 30

No One Left Behind

For the death that He died, He died to sin once for all;
but the life that He lives, He lives to God.
—Romans 6:10, NKJV

In the Bible are many stories of things that were lost. There is one story about a lady who lost her coin. She spent a long time searching for it. This woman swept the floor diligently and found her coin. She was so happy and relieved that she called her neighbors to rejoice with her over finding the lost coin.

Another parable Jesus told, described in the old hymn "There Were Ninety and Nine," tells about a lost sheep. When one little sheep wandered away, the shepherd went out to find the wayward one, leaving the ninety-nine sheep. He searched and searched in the mountains and the ravines, and finally, after getting his clothes torn and dirty, he found his sheep caught in a thicket. He picked it up and, carrying it close to his heart, returned the lamb to the fold, where it was safe once again.

When I was young, our cat Tessie had kittens. She had the first one outside, so I brought them both into the warm laundry room, where she had another kitten. But she kept trying to get up and go outside. I put her face by the kitten I had brought inside, but she still wanted to go outside. Finally, I realized what she wanted. I put the newborn kitten back outside, and sure enough, Tessie brought it back in, lay down in her bed, and had three more kittens. I learned my cat Tessie could "count" and needed to go through the motions of bringing her own kitten inside.

When my boys were young, they had some neighbor boys over to play. After a while, I overheard one of the neighbor boys whisper, "Let's not play with another boy."

My boys were not sure what to do. "Why not?" they asked.

I said everyone should play together, and if they could not do this, they should go home.

Immediately, they decided they wanted to play together.

Jesus was all about inclusion. He did not want anyone to feel left out. After the disciples decided the children were a bother, Jesus encouraged the mothers to bring them to Him so He could bless them (Matthew 19:13–15). How I would have loved to bring my children to Jesus. Every time we exhibit a Christlike character, we are bringing people to Him. Let us not forget we are Christ's ambassadors on this earth! What an awesome responsibility we have!

Gyl Moon Bateman

December 1

"Look Behind You!"

Through the Lord's mercies we are not consumed,
Because His compassions fail not.
They are new every morning;
Great is Your faithfulness.
—Lamentations 3:22, 23, NKJV

I was excited! I was six years old, and for the first time, my parents were allowing me to walk to Friday evening vespers by myself with my friend Jill. It was always dark by 6:30 p.m. at the Kamagambo Teachers Training College in Kenya, where we lived, so when I left to walk to Jill's house, I carried my flashlight and carefully shone it down the road ahead of me. I did not want to step on a snake! Jill was ready when I knocked on her door, and we set off hand in hand, chattering excitedly. But strangely, as we passed the building with the campus generator, we both fell silent. Then, ringing through the silence, I heard a powerful, resonating voice, "Diane, look behind you!"

Startled and fearful because nobody else was nearby, I looked around and then turned toward Jill, clutching her hand, and said, "Jill, look behind us."

We turned and looked behind us. There, maybe three feet behind us, was a huge hooded cobra, raised up and ready to strike. If it bit us, we would be dead in a matter of minutes.

"Run! Run!" we shouted in unison and ran for our lives!

When we arrived at the church, panting and terrified, we asked each other why we had looked back. "I heard a voice say, 'Jill, look behind you,' and then you told me to look too," Jill told me, wide-eyed.

In amazement, I told her I heard the voice say *my* name! Tingling with wonder, we recognized that we had heard the voices of our guardian angels, who saved at least one of us from certain death.

I have never forgotten that experience and will never doubt God's existence and tender, personal care. Sister, what memories haunt you from the past year? Regrets, bitterness, sadness, or resentment? Did you leave problems unresolved, misunderstandings unclarified, or wounds unhealed? Did you make mistakes? Are you ready to try again? Your heavenly Father speaks to you with tenderness and power: "My dear daughter, look behind you!" Remember, "we have nothing to fear for the future, except as we shall forget the way the Lord has led us, and His teaching in our past history."*

Diane Duncan de Aguirre

---

* Ellen G. White, *Last Day Events* (Nampa, ID: Pacific Press®, 1992), 72.

December 2

The Lure of Sin

If we confess our sins, he is faithful and just to forgive us our sins, and to cleanse us from all unrighteousness.
—1 John 1:9, KJV

When I was growing up, children went outside and played games with their friends. We would play in the streets until the streetlights came on. Then we went inside, sat down, and had dinner with our families. Things are different today.

One day I wanted to go outside and play, but I was told I could not go. So I stood on the inside porch, looked out the window, and watched my friends. Then I decided to open the door and stand on the stairs just outside the door. Technically, I still was not playing with my friends. I stood on the stairs and watched everyone for a while. Then I decided to walk down the stairs and stand on the sidewalk that was connected to the stairs. I still was not playing. In my mind, it was "playing" that was the real problem.

After standing on the sidewalk for a while, I decided to walk down to the fence at the edge of our yard. From there, I had a really good view of my friends playing in the street. At this point, I was just a few feet away from where they were. Next thing you know, I was playing kickball in the street with my friends! Looking back on that day makes me think. This is exactly what happens with sin. We know what we want to do is wrong, but we end up taking little steps toward sin until we are completely involved. Sometimes we have compromised so much that we forget what we are doing is wrong.

As you probably guessed, I got in trouble that night. What I did was wrong, and there are consequences for doing what is wrong. It is the same way with sin. There are consequences but not just earthly consequences: "For the wages of sin is death; but the gift of God is eternal life through Jesus Christ our Lord" (Romans 6:23, KJV). Fortunately, as today's text tells us, we can repent of our sins, and we will be forgiven.

We should do our best not to take those little steps into sin. But if we do, we need to remember that we serve a loving God who will forgive us! He will also help us not to sin if we just ask Him. Praise God!

Elaine "Lainey" Lyons

December 3

What God Collects

You keep track of all my sorrows.
You have collected all my tears in your bottle.
You have recorded each one in your book.
—Psalm 56:8, NLT

I do not know how the collection began, but now there are hundreds of them in my house—snowmen. All different sizes and shapes. They *must* be smiling, happy-looking snowmen; what is the point of frowning or sad snowmen? My husband tried to put a moratorium on snowmen, saying no more could enter our home. But it was not like I was buying them. People just kept giving them to me. Most of the year, they are stored in boxes in the basement. But come December, you will find them in every room of my house and decorating my office at work. Their smiling faces fill our home through the gray winter months, bringing hope and joy.

I also have a collection of teacups and teapots. They fill the antique curio cabinet and corner hutch in our dining room. Almost all are from friends—some even from around the world, such as the adorable teapot from Paris that a friend brought me or the fragile glass teacup from Turkey I brought home from a trip. Each one brings memories of friendship and love, and it reminds me to stop, take a moment, and enjoy a cup of tea and conversation with a friend.

What do you collect? Did you know God is a collector too? He collects two things: our tears and our prayers. Psalm 56:8 tells us that God collects our tears and stores them in His bottle. Not just any bottle—His bottle. He writes down what brought each tear and records it in His book. He sees, and He remembers. Our tears—what brought us pain and what brought us joy—are important to Him. They are precious enough to collect and to remember.

He also collects our prayers. Revelation 5:8 talks about our prayers being stored in "golden bowls" before His throne in heaven (NKJV). You do not put just anything into golden bowls. Only important things. Treasured things. And God stores our prayers right before Him in gold. Revelation 8:3–5 tells us there will come a day when God tips these golden bowls and pours them out on the earth with fire. Let this challenge us to fill those golden bowls with prayers for loved ones—prayers of salvation and transformation—for God to collect, treasure, and pour out with power as He moves on hearts and changes lives.

Tamyra Horst

December 4

A Ray of Hope

"He alone is your God, the only one who is worthy of your praise, the one who has done these mighty miracles that you have seen with your own eyes."
—Deuteronomy 10:21, NLT

As I have worked with children in India, I have struggled, wishing I could help each and every one. There are so many children who are in need. These needs can be anything from help with obtaining a Christian education to having health problems with no money to hygiene care packages. It really breaks my heart to see the great need and lack of basics over and over.

Years ago, I met a young man who was going blind. Krishna attended one of our schools where the Adventist Child India (ACI) program helps fund sponsored children. He came from a very poor family who were unable to afford any kind of care. When I saw him, one eye was already mostly blind and was oozing pus. I was afraid it would move into the other eye.

Four years later, I received a phone call from this boy. I would like to share his story and the miracle he experienced with you.

Krishna went in for surgery for his eyes on January 1, 2022, with the help of the ACI Medical Fund. It took four long years of waiting for the operation as ACI worked to help him receive the surgery. We worried he would become completely blind before we could arrange the surgery. There was every chance of that happening.

It was such a joy to hear from and speak to Krishna by phone and find out that the surgery had been successful. He is well and can now see without any problems. He has a great job and is in a position to take care of himself and help his parents. We are grateful and amazed by this awesome miracle from God.

When we seek God's presence and request Him to intervene in our situation, we can see miracles happen! God has power over all creation, and He has the ability to work a miracle for each of us.

I am thankful that Krishna was given a miracle. If you need a miracle, I pray that you will experience one of your own someday and that it will remind you that our God has promised He "will never leave you nor forsake you" (Hebrews 13:5, NKJV).

Nancy Mattison Mack

December 5

Everyday Miracles

*Praise the Lord, my soul,
and forget not all his benefits.*
—Psalm 103:2, NIV

The sound of birds chirping in the trees filtered through my bedroom window. Nature's personal alarm clock was so much better than the shrill blast of my phone alarm. My mind drifted back to moments when, in my naïveté, I wished for a mighty move of God on my behalf. Intent on looking for the big miracle, I missed the many smaller miracles God was sending me every day.

I wiggled my toes and stretched. Smiling, I praised God that I could feel my limbs. And as I lay there thinking, I realized that I was truly blessed to be in my right mind and have a God who makes provision for me. At that moment, a light went off in my head, and I resolved to no longer wait or search for miracles with a magnifying glass. Since then, God has helped me to catch a glimpse of the miracles He sends on a daily basis.

God is concerned about the minute details of our lives. There is nothing about us that escapes His notice. He numbers the hairs on our heads and is aware of each breath that we take. When He tells us that we should not worry about our lives, that is exactly what He means. Why is this so? Because God is more than able to provide the things that we need. So often, He answers the prayers that we did not pray or edits the prayer requests that we make so that we can receive what is better for us.

Have you been busy focusing on all the things that are going wrong in your life? Do the cares of this life drown out the blessings God continues to bestow upon you? Take a moment to count the blessings God has given you. When you start to count your blessings, you will realize that you have so much for which to thank God. Open doors, closed doors, health, strength, and the very air that you breathe—we can never exhaust the list of all He has done.

Be encouraged as you go through each day and stop, not just to smell the flowers but to see the everyday miracles God is sending your way. You do not need to wait for that *big* event. Miracles are happening all around you every day. Just pause for a moment and take notice. You will be surprised by how many surround you.

Andrea K. Francis

December 6

He's Able! He's Able!

"For I know the plans I have for you," declares the LORD,
"plans to prosper you and not to harm you, plans to give you hope and a future."
—Jeremiah 29:11, NIV

The first three rows were packed, and some on the front row sat with elbows on their knees, leaning forward as I spoke at a men's prison. Such a thirst for Jesus is exciting to see. If only we yearned like that in every religious setting! When my friend Bev invited me to share, she said, "Bring the right vehicle, for there will be snow on the pass on your way back."

Before my talk, three men shared a verse and the reason they liked it. One shared Jeremiah 29:11, which is a reassuring verse and a good one about our identity in God. Ephesians 5:2 says, "Christ loved us and gave himself up for us, a fragrant offering and sacrifice to God" (ESV). And His gift does not end there because He extends His love through us. Ephesians 2:10 reminds us we are included in what God does, "for we are God's masterpiece" (NLT). Never, never, *never* think that your talents are not useful or are not making a difference.

After my talk, we met for prayer at the back of the room. Bev began, "Does anyone have a prayer request?" After each man shared, another would pray for the need. Bev added that I was to drive back over the mountain in the snow the next day. Three men offered to pray for me.

After leaving the prison, I was really curious about the weather, and sure enough, my weather app revealed snow on the mountain. The next morning, during my devotions, I did not see any verses with reassurance about the weather. As I pondered and prayed, four words came to mind: "He's able, He's able." I recognized it as a song and asked out loud, "Do you want me to sing the song?" So, I did. "He's able, He's able, I know He's able; I know my Lord is able to carry me through."* Then it struck me, *Wow! God wants me to know He will carry me through the snow!*

Soon after, I spoke at a nearby church, and it was such a blessing to be there. After a wonderful lunch, I needed to leave and marveled how God had really provided the whole way through. At the summit of the mountain, it was 34°F (1°C) and sleeting but not sticking to the ground. The prayers of those men really made a difference in the weather and, most likely, other unseen blessings as well. God sure is able!

Diane Pestes

---

* Paul E. Paino, "He's Able," in *Adventist Youth Sing* (Washington, DC: Review and Herald®, 1977), no. 57.

December 7

Another Look at Basketball

*For as we have many members in one body,
but all the members do not have the same function, so we, being many,
are one body in Christ, and individually members of one another.*
—Romans 12:4, 5, NKJV

Exercise has been a part of my life since I was about twenty-five years old. I loved basketball, so I became a referee because it allowed me to run up and down the court. I refereed for seven years. I only refereed men's basketball, so it was quite challenging. When the men fouled and ran to me, challenging my call, I enjoyed telling them to play ball and that this was not the time for a basketball clinic. Those were the days. Being in charge of a basketball game was one of many highlights of my younger years. I am now sixty-nine. Looking back, I see that we can learn a lot from the game.

I have taken two things from the game that I want to share with you. One is the value of teamwork, and the other is patience. We have learned in our Christian walk that teamwork is necessary to instill character while on our journey to heaven. In basketball vernacular, we must understand that in teamwork and the building of Christ's church, one can be a guard, another a forward, and another a center. There are, of course, many more positions for life's lessons. The Bible states in 1 Corinthians 12:12, "For as the body is one and has many members, but all the members of that one body, being many, are one body, so also is Christ" (NKJV). Working together with consideration for each individual personality and the unique contributions they add to the team, we must build the body of Christ.

Basketball teaches us patience. Have you ever noticed how one team can gain a lot of points in the first half of the game, building a lead, yet by the end of the game, they have lost? The same goes for us as we move down the highway of life. It will never do for us to focus on what we have done at the beginning of our journey. What will be key is how we have persevered and dealt with all life's hardships one day at a time in patience and victorious living. A crown awaits us through the sacrifice of Christ. "Let us lay aside every weight, and the sin which doth so easily beset us, and let us run with patience the race that is set before us" (Hebrews 12:1, KJV). With teamwork, patience, and God's grace, we will all win the game and enjoy eternal life!

Zandra LaMar Griffin-Willingham

December 8

The Gift of Health

*Gray hair is a crown of splendor;
it is attained in the way of righteousness.*
—Proverbs 16:31, NIV

During the third year of my physical therapy degree, our coursework required us to undertake many visits to various hospitals and clinics as part of our internship. We were told that we would be required to complete four clinical blocks, and each one would last for a month. I felt a little apprehensive about the experience because our class had never worked in a clinic setting for as long as a full month.

Each four-week block involved a different specialty and included working in a hospital setting, where any condition could be presented, and we were expected to be able to treat it. One of the specialties we worked in was pediatrics. It was challenging to see how many chronically disabled children came in to be assessed and treated.

During the four months of working in these clinical settings, I encountered many situations I had not faced before, which involved interacting with people on many different levels. These ranged on any given day from joyous to heartbreaking.

Being exposed to people who were extremely sick, many of whom were experiencing severe pain, opened my eyes and helped me realize how fortunate I am to have full use of my limbs and vital organs. I had never thought about that before. A healthy, fully functioning body is a gift we all too easily take for granted. Every day, as I entered the clinical setting, I would send up a word of thanks to the Lord for blessing me with good health.

Since working in the hospital, I have chosen never to take my health for granted. Health is a precious gift from a loving God. Once it is lost, it is sorely missed. Let us enjoy the privilege of health and not abuse or take it for granted. Give God all the praise for this wonderful gift. Determine with me to pursue a healthy way of life daily so that the Holy Spirit will best be able to use us as witnesses to others.

Thank You, Lord, for the incredible gift of life and health. Keep us ever mindful that our bodies are the temple of the Holy Spirit. Thank You for being the breath of life and for regenerating our weary souls.

Donna de Grass

December 9

Your Purpose Matters

"Well done, good and faithful servant! You have been faithful with a few things; I will put you in charge of many things. Come and share your master's happiness!"
—Matthew 25:23, NIV

We had just enjoyed a beautiful day of fellowship. Women had traveled from across England to attend a day of empowerment. As usual, when presenting on the topic of purpose or anything relating to purpose, we first dealt with and debunked any misconceptions that would hinder women from recognizing they had each been created with a divine purpose in mind. After presenting the topic of purpose, we had a question-and-answer session.

One lady began, "Dr. Nadine, I hear you speaking about this purpose thing. I somewhat believe that God brought us into the world to accomplish something great. I have a hard time understanding; is that a hobby or a passion but not something I can do as a full-time career?"

I was excited because I had heard that question so many times from women around the world, whether in person or virtually. Women often struggle, sometimes unconsciously, with believing they were created to support the dreams of others when, in fact, God has brought them into the world to do something significant—something that matters.

Many who know that God has called them to something greater than what they are currently doing still have internal conflicts because His call does not align with their ideas or it falls completely outside their comfort zone.

The solution to many of the world's problems may be in your hands, but too many of us have been told that our place is in our home; our voice should be silenced; and our ideas, kept to ourselves. God, however, wants us to know that we are not here by chance! We are not an afterthought. We are not a mistake, and the thing we are meant to do is essential because our purpose matters.

And if you have already rid yourself of these false beliefs, ask yourself what it is that hinders you from advancing in the work God has called you to do. As daughters of the Most High God, we can all look forward to hearing the words "Well done, My daughter! You have been faithful. Enter into the joy of your Lord" (see Matthew 25:23).

Nadine A. Joseph-Collins

December 10

In His Holy Dwelling

A father to the fatherless, a defender of widows,
is God in his holy dwelling.
God sets the lonely in families,
he leads out the prisoners with singing;
but the rebellious live in a sun-scorched land.
—Psalm 68:5, 6, NIV

Sitting at our dining room table one afternoon, my mother shared a dream she had the previous night. In her dream, an angel had shown her twin baby girls and told her they were the children God would give me in two years. As a single woman in my late twenties, this was a welcomed promise from God, and I mentally calculated a time line for the next two years. As the days and months passed and no new romantic relationship materialized, I forgot about my mother's dream. Eventually, my mother registered and underwent training to become a foster mother. As we shared a home, the evaluation included interviews with all adults in the home, including me. During my interview, I casually mentioned to the social worker that I was interested in adoption.

Two years later, as my mother prepared for her first foster placement—newborn twins—she sat at the same dining room table, folding baby clothes. As we talked, she commented that the social worker, who coincidentally happened to be the same one who had done our home assessment, had asked her if I was still interested in adopting. And if so, would I consider these tiny baby girls. Instantly, I knew these were the children in my mother's dream, and I cried. This was not how I wanted to start my family, but tearfully, I prayed for faith to trust God's plans. Two days later, we brought two five-pound bundles of joy home from the hospital.

Over the next few months, friends warned me not to get too attached because there were no guarantees the girls would even be available for adoption. And even if they were, the chances of a single woman being approved to adopt them were slim. But in my heart, I held on to the promise of God, and I trusted Him to make a way. After three years and multiple coincidences, or what we call *Godincidences*, the judge signed the paperwork legally making us the family God had created years before. Each time I look at my girls, I am reminded that God is still in the business of caring for the fatherless. He still orchestrates marvelous ways of setting the lonely in families. He still leads us with joyful songs that reflect His unfailing love.

Melissa Martinez

December 11

The Winter Chariot

The angel of the Lord encampeth round about them that fear him,
and delivereth them.
—Psalm 34:7, KJV

After completing my studies at Caribbean Union College in Trinidad, West Indies, I made the decision to continue my education at Columbia Union College in Takoma Park, Maryland, United States of America. My goal was to pursue a degree in biochemistry.

Reflecting on this experience, memories of my mother's unconditional love emerge. With a desire to provide me with everything I needed, she made sure I was prepared for my arrival in winter. Stephens and Johnson's Department Store had a special floor dedicated to winter travelers, but my mother went beyond that. She enlisted a tailor to craft a winter coat sewn specifically for me. She also took care of acquiring the remaining winter clothing items she knew I would need.

Amid loving advice and a flurry of activity, the day of departure arrived. Our home buzzed with family and friends offering well wishes for a safe journey. As we packed our suitcases and loaded into the car, a somber silence permeated. But it was soon replaced by anticipation of the journey ahead.

Leaving home weighed heavily on my heart as I bid farewell to my beloved family. The announcement of my flight number and departure gate intensified the sadness. We embraced, shared kisses, and sought divine protection through our prayers. On the plane, I yearned for the presence of my family. Unfortunately, it was an unattainable wish. Upon arrival at the John F. Kennedy International Airport, I caught my connecting flight and soon arrived in Washington, DC.

I collected my luggage and found a taxi driver who claimed to know the location of Columbia Union College. However, he eventually admitted he was lost. Trying to remain calm, I silently prayed for guidance when the driver suddenly turned threatening, took all my cash, and left me stranded with my suitcases. I was in a foreign land, lost, and penniless. Hope came in the form of a kind stranger who noticed my distress. She had two daughters at the college and offered to take me there. Grateful for her kindness, she safely delivered me to Halcyon Hall before disappearing. Looking back over my life, I can testify to the faithfulness of God. What a wonderful God we serve!

C. Marion Hudson

December 12

A Life Filled With Love

Live a life filled with love, following the example of Christ.
He loved us and offered himself as a sacrifice for us, a pleasing aroma to God.
—Ephesians 5:2, NLT

One sermon I listened to shared glimpses into the faith-filled lives of Moses, Enoch, and Abraham while linking their personal stories to the speaker's life experiences. When he mentioned that Enoch's life "pleased God" (Hebrews 11:5, NKJV), I felt elated and affirmed by Jesus. Every day I willingly put my life on the altar of sacrifice to be used by God however He pleases, especially for Sonny's sake (my autistic son) and for others who require lifelong support. I consider myself an ambassador for the King of kings, and I live my life in the Spirit. This means that if I feel impressed by the Holy Spirit to reach out to others and tell them about Jesus and share the gospel message of hope, I do it. My job brings me much joy and peace of mind, knowing that God is in absolute control over my life and the lives of my family members.

This job has also caused me intense pain and many tears, for not all Christians think alike. Heaven knows that I would never intentionally do or say anything that would bring disgrace to Jesus; however, I am subject to making human mistakes just like everyone else. This does not keep me from sharing my faith; it keeps me humble with a teachable spirit. If a "please forgive me" is necessary, I will say it without hesitation. I am sure that Sonny is reaping many blessings through his mom's chosen career and state of well-being.

"The king upon his throne has no higher work than has the mother. The mother is queen of her household. She has in her power the molding of her children's characters, that they may be fitted for the higher, immortal life. An angel could not ask for a higher mission; for in doing this work she is doing service for God. . . . Her work is for time and for eternity."*

There is something uniquely beautiful about a woman who grows from her struggles and uses the lessons learned to spread love and wisdom. Be the example that shows others how to live a life filled with love—"a pleasing aroma to God" (Ephesians 5:2, NLT)!

Deborah Sanders

---

* Ellen G. White, *The Adventist Home* (Washington, DC: Review and Herald®, 1980), 231, 232.

December 13

Snow Days

"Though your sins are as scarlet, they shall become as white as snow."
—Isaiah 1:18, NASB

Snow days are a thing of the past. The school my mom worked for declared all inclement weather days to be virtual learning days. A little piece of my heart died with that news. As a child, I would eagerly wait, with bated breath, after hearing the phone ring in the early morning. The excitement I felt at the possibility of a day off was close to unreasonable.

My parents' house sits off the road in the woods. On days when the snow was especially magnificent, I would suit up, grab my camera, and head out the door. The quiet whispers of birds or snow lightly falling off branches gave the silence enough life that it was not ominous or oppressive. I crunched through the snow, heading into the forest. Snow hung beautifully on pine branches and outlined deciduous trees. A cardinal flitted about, stark against the frosty landscape. The feeling I had was unlike anything else—ultimate tranquility. All imperfections lay hidden under pillowy mounds. You would never know broken-down farm equipment was here, except for the long-unused chicken coop that was too big to be completely covered by Virginia snow.

Scripture does not say whether there will be snow on the new earth, but I am certain the peace, contentment, and amazement will be present and magnified. The excitement of a snow day does not even compare! Best of all, our sins will not be there.

> He [God] will again take pity on us;
> He will trample on our wrongdoings.
> Yes, You will cast all their sins
> Into the depths of the sea (Micah 7:19, NASB).

As much as we want to try to fix what we have done, we stand out red, like the cardinal, against the pure holiness of God. When we give our lives to Jesus and open our hearts to Him, He does not just hide our sins; He takes them away. Thanks to His love and sacrifice, we will be transformed as clean, fresh, and beautiful as freshly fallen snow.

Dear Lord Jesus, whenever we see snow, may we remember Your promise of forgiveness and eternal life for those who love and serve You with their whole heart. Amen. *

Deidre A. Jones

---

* Adapted from Deidre A. Jones, "Snow Days," *Sabbath Thoughts* (blog), Highland Seventh-day Adventist Church, accessed November 29, 2023, http://highlandcounty22.adventistchurchconnect.org/sabbath-thoughts-blog/snow-days.

December 14

God's Special Encouragement

Praise be to the God and Father of our Lord Jesus Christ, the Father of compassion and the God of all comfort, who comforts us in all our troubles, so that we can comfort those in any trouble with the comfort we ourselves receive from God.
—2 Corinthians 1:3, 4, NIV

Our world is a dichotomy. As much as we need to be kind, encouraging, compassionate, and loving, there may be times when things go awry, words are spoken in haste, and behaviors can hurt or harm another. Though it is a world filled with troubles, it is also a wonderful world because God made it for us, and He is with us. We experience the harshness of life, but we also experience the love that God gives us each moment of each day.

An example of this is found in the Gospel of Luke, where we learn of the relationship between Mary, the mother of Jesus, and her cousin Elizabeth. They both found themselves in a position that left them vulnerable to ridicule. Elizabeth had been barren for many years, and as an older barren woman, she would have felt disgraced in a society where a woman who was unable to bear children was thought to be punished by God. Mary was a young woman, a virgin, and was pregnant. Although she was betrothed to Joseph, in the societal view, she was an unwed mother. But God had a greater purpose for both women. Through the workings of the Holy Spirit, Elizabeth became the mother of John the Baptist, and Mary became the mother of Jesus. John prepared the way for Jesus, our Savior. Jesus gave His life for us, showing us how to love and care for one another.

When the angel Gabriel told Mary about Elizabeth's pregnancy, Mary quickly went to Elizabeth. These women needed to give and receive encouragement from each other during this wondrous time in their lives. We all need love and encouragement on our journey. God often speaks His words of comfort through the love of our friends. Is there someone God has placed on your heart? Someone may need the kindness you can show them today. And if you are in need of encouragement, turn to the God of all comfort. He is near, my friend.

Carolyn Venice Marcus

December 15

Connections

*"Call on me in the day of trouble;
I will deliver you, and you will honor me."*
—Psalm 50:15, NIV

If it is God's will, nothing can stop it. If it is not, I would not want it anyway. This thought connects me with God when things do not go smoothly.

A former Burmese student of mine in a university in Thailand emailed and invited me to his forthcoming marriage in Kalaymyo, Myanmar. Attending Gin Suan's wedding would enable me to see the country (formerly Burma), which I had heard of in mission stories. I prayed for the trip to be God's will. One night I dreamed I was riding in a bus that crossed a narrow bridge spanning a fast-flowing river. I took the dream as a green light and made the arrangements.

Gin Suan's aunt Flora met me at the Yangon International Airport. After the greetings, Flora whispered, "We need to talk." She spoke seriously, and I sensed a problem. "The planes and buses to Kalaymyo are all fully booked until Christmas—too late for you to get to the wedding." She studied my face and paused as I absorbed the news. "Would you like to tour around Yangon until your return flight to Bangkok?"

"Wait," I replied as I offered a quick prayer for guidance. "God, I did not come here to tour Yangon. I came for a wedding. Please help me get to Kalaymyo."

I returned to Flora. "I need to call someone," I told her.

I dialed Rodrigo, a student I knew who was also going to Kalaymyo. Some Burmese friends were helping him find transportation. I had thought of traveling with him but had left Bangkok a day ahead. I explained my problem. Rodrigo called his friends, who just happened to be at the same airport. He connected us, and we agreed to meet. These friends suggested I take the bus that left two hours later. One of them had family who owned the bus company, and their drivers always saved one place for emergency cases. I took that seat.

The nineteen-hour bus ride was filled with interesting experiences and the kindness of total strangers. Most moving of all was when the bus crossed a fast-flowing river over a narrow bridge, just as I had seen in my dream. The trip started and ended with the help and grace of God. He helped me make all the right connections and helped me reach my destination.

Bienvisa Ladion Nebres

December 16

Driven to Pray

For now we see only a reflection as in a mirror; then we shall see face to face. Now I know in part; then I shall know fully, even as I am fully known.
—1 Corinthians 13:12, NIV

One Wednesday night I did something I rarely do: I attended my church's prayer gathering. That night the senior pastor led a devotional about the times when life has thrown so much your way, and you are not sure how you will make it. You feel like you are in a hole, and you keep falling deeper, with no visible way to climb out. You are so deep that you cannot see the light.

With no human way to get out of the situation, you are driven to pray. You are not praying because it is the right time of day or because someone told you that is what you are supposed to do. You pray because there is nothing else you can do.

That is exactly where I am, I thought as I listened to the speaker. I was in such a messy situation at the time, and I knew I could not fix it on my own. I had tried. But I know Someone who can fix any problem. *I must pray. I must tell God that I need Him. I need Him to take over my current situation and, indeed, my whole life. I do not have any other options; I must pray. I already know I cannot fix this. God can. I must pray.*

It was the Christmas season; all around me, people were wishing for peace on Earth and goodwill to men. But I did not feel any peace, and I certainly did not feel goodwill to all humankind. I needed help. I was driven to pray. I did not understand why I was faced with this situation. I did not ask for it. I did not cause it. When you are tempted to despair, when the darkness of that deep, deep hole has shut out all the light, and when you do not know where to turn or what to do, remember this: God has a plan.

"It is your privilege to be glad in the Lord, and to rejoice in the knowledge of His sustaining grace. Let His love take possession of mind and heart. Guard against becoming overwearied, careworn, depressed. . . . Turn your eyes away from that which is dark and discouraging, and behold Jesus, our great Leader, under whose watchful supervision . . . [we are] destined to triumph gloriously."*

Jean Arthur

---

* Ellen G. White, *Selected Messages*, bk. 2 (Washington, DC: Review and Herald®, 1980), 399.

December 17

Jesus' Best Christmas Yet

"I tell you the truth, when you did it to one of the least of these my brothers and sisters, you were doing it to me!"
—Matthew 25:40, NLT

I was eight years old when my world shattered. Months before, my dad had been taken from my house. As "Daddy's girl," I was devastated. Snow was falling, Christmas lights twinkled, and festive music was playing, but I felt no Christmas joy. The most important person in my world was missing.

Presents will make almost any eight-year-old happy, but money was tight, and there were no gifts under the tree.

Knock, knock. My mom opened the door and stepped outside. When she came in a few minutes later, she carried a box of brightly wrapped gifts and had a smile on her face and tears in her eyes. The process was repeated three times that day and continued in the following days. I do not remember how many people stopped by, but there must have been at least ten. Each one explained that they wanted to bring us a little Christmas joy. They hoped we knew how many people cared for us. By Christmas morning, there were more presents than I had ever seen or imagined! They spilled out from under the tree and were piled high around it.

On Christmas morning, after we ate our apple fritters and drank our hot chocolate, we all sat around the tree and read the Christmas story. I remember the feeling that started growing inside of me—thankfulness! Friends, churches, my school, and even the police department went out of their way to help make Christmas a little brighter for us. My little eight-year-old heart swelled with joy as I realized how many people loved and cared for us. The Christmas we thought we would have nothing was the Christmas we had the most.

Over two thousand years ago, Jesus told His followers, "Truly I tell you, whatever you did for one of the least of these brothers and sisters of mine, you did for me" (Matthew 25:40, NIV). When we do something for one of His children, we are doing it for Him. So maybe Jesus did not have the best first Christmas, but we can give Him the best He has ever had this year by helping a family in need, taking cookies to shut-ins, and making sure that His children feel loved. Are you ready to help Jesus have a wonderful Christmas?

Debbi Duncan

December 18

Friendship Lessons

Dear friends, let us love one another, for love comes from God. Everyone who loves has been born of God and knows God. Whoever does not love does not know God, because God is love.
—1 John 4:7, 8, NIV

Several years ago, I moved to Houston, Texas, United States of America. Initially, I told my husband I was too old to start over with new friends. I had lived in Atlanta, Georgia, United States of America, for twenty years, and I had a core group of friends—many of whom I considered family. I was determined not to make any new friends because I told myself I was too old to make new friends.

I told my husband my rationale: "I love you, so I will move, but do not expect me to make friends." He gently laughed at me.

After our move, I began working out at a gym daily. I noticed a young lady, and we spoke briefly. One day we struck up a conversation. I discovered that we were both teachers. And we were both busy with planning and plotting our Christmas vacations. Guess what? We ended up becoming friends.

God sent her to me because He had a lot He wanted to teach me—namely, I still had the capacity to become friends with someone new even at my age. And my new friend is a Muslim. I have learned so much about her life and religion. We both share a love for children and a love for God. She calls him Allah; I call him God. But we both call on Him. God provided another lesson in our friendship. I learned that love can build a bridge between strangers, making them friends.

John counsels us in his first letter, "Dear friends, let us love one another, for love comes from God. Everyone who loves has been born of God and knows God. Whoever does not love does not know God, because God is love. . . . Since God so loved us, we also ought to love one another. No one has ever seen God; but if we love one another, God lives in us and his love is made complete in us" (1 John 4:7, 8, 11, 12, NIV).

God has given each of us the capacity to love. It does not matter that we are different from one another. We can still find common ground. If we would all learn to love and accept others despite our differences, what a wonderful world it would be!

Paula Sanders Blackwell

December 19

My First Marathon

Therefore, since we are surrounded by such a huge crowd of witnesses to the life of faith, let us strip off every weight that slows us down, especially the sin that so easily trips us up. And let us run with endurance the race God has set before us.
—Hebrews 12:1, NLT

The fiftieth Honolulu Marathon took place in 2022. Although I am not a runner, I decided to sign up to do it. After previously participating in a virtual format, which allowed you the entire month of December to complete the 26.2 miles if you chose the multiday format, I decided I was ready for the real thing. Especially since I was not doing it on my own.

The Honolulu Marathon Clinic meets weekly from March until the week before the marathon in December. The clinic has various groups based on experience and speed. They even have a group for people who are recovering from health issues like heart surgery. Each week there are health talks related to training. Group leaders share tips they have learned over their years of running marathons. They promise that barring illness or injury, if you follow their training plan, you will finish the marathon.

On the morning of the marathon, I got up ridiculously early to catch a shuttle bus to the race drop-off with some new friends from my group. What excitement! We watched the fireworks and all the best runners go by. Finally, it was our turn to cross the start line. We enjoyed all the Christmas lights as the route wound through downtown. We saw a beautiful sunrise, and we saw the fast runners coming in toward the finish line. After we made the halfway point, we made the turn back toward the finish line, which we eventually all crossed, just like we were promised—if we followed the plan. I never thought I would finish a marathon, but it was so much fun, in large part thanks to the many people who came to cheer us on.

I had always read Hebrews 12:1, but now I have experienced it. I trained and developed my endurance. I left extra "weight" behind with a friend who met me midway to cheer me on (verse 1, NLT). I know I only finished the race because of the help and encouragement of so many. The hard work was worth it. All this excitement over an earthly race. Think how joyous we will be when we get to heaven! Let us all be part of the "cloud of witnesses" encouraging one another on to the finish (verse 1, NIV)!

Julie Bocock-Bliss

December 20

Joy to the World

"Do not be afraid. I bring you good news that will cause great joy for all the people. Today in the town of David a Savior has been born to you."
—Luke 2:10, 11, NIV

At this time of the year, it is easy to get caught up in the excitement of shopping and gift wrapping and forget the meaning behind the message of Christmas. This period is often referred to as the "silly season" and is characterized by a feeding and spending frenzy. However, the real silliness is found in the neglect of the greatest Gift ever given to man. Yes, we know Christ was not born on December 25, but He was born! And because He was, salvation has come to humankind. In one earth-shattering moment, God emptied heaven and sent its sweetest treasure—His only begotten Son—down to redeem His children.

Christ's mission was to connect us with the Father's heart of love. Instead of being born in a palace, He was born in a stable. Rather than royalty for earthly parents, He was welcomed by a carpenter and a young peasant girl. Instead of His birth being heralded by pomp and ceremony, shepherds ran through the darkened streets, proclaiming that the Messiah had come. Then, panting and out of breath, they entered a dusty stable and fell down and worshiped Him.

A crude manger filled with straw became the resting place for the Son of God. The glory of the Lord shone from the stable and transformed what was commonplace into something wonderful.

Today He wants to take your life and fill it with His presence. He wants to transform your hopelessness into hope, your heartache into joy, and your weariness into abundant life. He came to Earth so that you would remember who your Father is. He wants to empower you to live your life in an extraordinary manner.

That is His gift to you today—transformation. Offer Him the manger of your heart, and let His glory shine forth from your life. Then go out and proclaim boldly that the Messiah is coming to Earth again! That is your gift to others.

Cordell Liebrandt

December 21

Evacuate! Evacuate!

And he cried mightily with a loud voice, saying, "Babylon the great is fallen, is fallen, and has become a dwelling place of demons, a prison for every foul spirit, and a cage for every unclean and hated bird! . . ."

And I heard another voice from heaven, saying, "Come out of her, my people, lest you share in her sins, and lest you receive of her plagues."
—Revelation 18:2, 4, NKJV

I bought my elderly parents a smoke alarm that talks. When it detects the presence of smoke, it yells, "Evacuate! Evacuate!" I put this feature to the test one Christmas season.

My dad and I were peacefully warming ourselves by the fireplace one evening when I accidentally let the fire get out of control. My dad had warned me that the box I was trying to burn was too big. I thought I had it under control, but unfortunately, the greenery on the mantel caught fire and started to burn. The smoke alarm went to work and cried, "Evacuate! Evacuate!" While my dad rushed to the kitchen for water, I ran outside and grabbed the garden hose. I quickly put out the fire before it reached the popcorn ceiling. I felt so relieved it was not any worse! No one was hurt, and I watered all the plants at the same time.

I learned a couple of things from this experience. First of all, you are never too old to listen to your father's advice. It is even more important to listen to our heavenly Father's advice. I thought I had things under control, but boy, was I wrong. I have found that whenever I think I have everything under control in my own strength, things never seem to work out.

Second, the smoke alarm warns us when there is a fire. The Bible is God's warning to us living in the world. Revelation 18:4 warns us to come out of Babylon—to escape a fire and plagues so terrible that we cannot even comprehend them. Like smoke alarms, many of us have a Bible in our homes. But do we pay attention to its commands? Do we heed the warnings found in God's Word?

When the Bible tells us to evacuate and leave the things of this world, do we listen to the warning and act quickly? Or do we keep trying to take matters into our own hands? Is there something God's Word is warning you about? Will you listen to the call to evacuate? May we all listen to the warning and be ready when Jesus comes to take us home.

Mary C. D. Johnson

December 22

Swaddling Clothes

"And this will be the sign to you: You will find a Babe wrapped in swaddling cloths."
—Luke 2:12, NKJV

The shepherds watching their flocks on the hills between Jerusalem and Bethlehem were most likely watching temple sheep. Suddenly, a brilliantly shining angel appeared to announce the Savior was born. The first sign they were given was finding a Baby wrapped in swaddling cloths.

Swaddling cloths. Would they find the Baby unusually swaddled? Today babies are swaddled (wrapped tightly) in a small square of cloth. The Greek word *sparganoō* means "to strap or wrap in strips of cloth." Did the strips of cloth swaddle the baby like a blanket? Or, as some suggest, did they wrap around each limb to encourage the growth of straight arms and legs? If so, Baby Jesus would be found lying with arms and legs outstretched, foreshadowing the way He was nailed to the cross.

It is said Jews were required, when traveling, to carry with them strips of cloth for burial in case of accidental death. Finding enough spare cloth for burial was an undue burden for others. It is possible Baby Jesus was wrapped in the grave clothes of His earthly father, Joseph, pointing to His heavenly Father's redemption story: Baby Jesus was born to die so that we might live.

If I had been a shepherd that night, I probably would have protested. "Excuse me, glorious angel, did you just say that I will find a Savior who has emptied Himself of every power He had in heaven to become a helpless newborn? Are you saying that He entrusted His creatures with the care and protection of their Creator, even binding up and restricting natural movement? This is good news? To me, this sounds extremely risky, ill advised, and even life threatening. This is not my idea of a conquering Messiah!"

These shepherds carefully wrapped the temple's newborn lambs in strips of cloth to protect them against blemish. They clearly understood the sign of swaddling cloths. Did they recognize Baby Jesus as the Savior, the unblemished Paschal Lamb, the symbol of deliverance?

When I accept Jesus' unblemished life, death, and resurrection as my way to salvation, His swaddling and grave clothes prefigure my "robe of righteousness" (Isaiah 61:10, KJV).

Rebecca Turner

December 23

Lying in a Manger

"And this will be a sign for you: you will find a baby . . . lying in a manger."
—Luke 2:12, ESV

When the angel told the shepherds their Savior was born in the city of David, how did they know where to go? Would you have gone to Jerusalem or Bethlehem? Both are called the city of David. Surely, the angels gestured in the right direction, but maybe the shepherds associated King David with a shepherd boy of Bethlehem watching his sheep on the same hills. We know they reached the right town when looking for the Savior of the world.

The second sign they were given was finding the Babe lying in a manger. A manger is a feeding trough for animals. Most often, indentions were carved into stones to hold animal feed. Baby Jesus was found lying on a stone slab (in a stable) at birth—a sign foreshadowing the way He would be laid on a stone slab (in a cave) at His death.

The shepherds did not wait for morning. Surely, they breathlessly ran house to house, pounding on doors, waking up the town, asking if a baby had been born that night and if the stable manger was being used for a cradle, thus spreading the news of the Savior's birth.

If I had been a shepherd that night, I probably would have protested. "Excuse me, glorious angel, did you just say that a Savior, the promised Messiah, has arrived without pomp and circumstance in what is considered the lowliest, humblest, perhaps dirtiest—certainly the smelliest—place possible and is lying where His creatures come to feed? You say they are invited to freely eat His body and drink His blood? This is good news? To me, this sounds as if He is lying as a lamb waiting for slaughter. This is not my idea of a conquering Messiah!"

The stone manger was a sign these shepherds understood; lambs were fed at mangers. Some of these lambs later became Passover meals. Did they recognize Baby Jesus as the Lamb of God who would later say at His last Passover supper, "Take, eat; this is My body" (Mark 14:22, NKJV)?

When I accept Jesus as my Passover Lamb, He becomes my Deliverer. He leads my exodus from the darkness and tyranny of sin. He provides wilderness bread for me to eat at His manger. That stone slab symbolizes the Rock of my salvation, my strength, my strong tower, my refuge, and my fortress. "Blessed be my Rock!" (Psalm 18:46, NKJV).

Rebecca Turner

December 24

The Lord Is My Shepherd

The LORD is my shepherd;
I shall not want.
—Psalm 23:1, NKJV

With our two small children, my husband and I went as missionaries to Kenya, East Africa. Soon after we arrived, Susie became part of our family. That year had been especially hard for her. Her father had died, and her mother had been bitten by a snake and lost her lower leg. Now it was almost Christmas. Tall poinsettia bushes dressed in bright scarlet and massive jacaranda trees arrayed in myriads of blue blossoms heralded the season.

The day before Christmas, we packed the car with food for Susie's family. Perched on the roof rack was a large sack of maize. We placed cooking oil, salt, sugar, matches, bananas, and bars of soap in the trunk of the car. We added dresses and a few toys for Susie's little sisters from my Stateside Christmas stash. On Christmas morning, my husband got up early and went to our garden to gather beets, tomatoes, carrots, avocados, tomatoes, and greens. Then we added pineapples, oranges, papayas, eggs, and freshly baked bread.

Mama Salome, Susie's mother, had planted her field with maize and beans, which she carefully guarded day and night to keep out the warthogs—a major task for a woman with only one leg! What we did not know until we arrived that Christmas day was that robbers had stolen all her maize and beans. The family had eaten very little for three weeks. When we stopped near their mud-and-thatch hut, three skinny little girls stumbled out. As we unloaded our car, Mama Salome emerged from the hut, with tears streaming down her face. She thanked us again and again.

Within moments, Susie kindled the cooking fire. When the *ugali* (thick maize porridge) was cooked, Mama Salome invited us to eat. We replied, "You must eat first! Your girls are hungry!" She insisted that, as guests, we must eat first. We instructed our children to eat only a little—and very fast! Not until we had eaten did the girls eat, and oh, how they ate.

When we went into the little hut, on the wall was the memory verse picture roll I had given them on an earlier visit. It was open to the picture of the Good Shepherd. The Bible verse displayed was, "The Lord is my shepherd, I shall not want." Mama Salome had been awake all night, praying for food. And it was Christmas!

Dorothy Duncan (deceased)

December 25

The Lights of Home

In Him was life, and the life was the light of men.
And the light shines in the darkness. . . .

. . . That was the true Light which gives light to every man coming into the world.
—John 1:4, 5, 9, NKJV

Christmas is a magical time of stories, music, colorful lights, decorations, and special goodies. Woven in and around everything else is the story of Jesus' birth, God's most precious gift to us—the Light of the world!

The year I was nine, my mother bundled all six of us children into our little old Willys sedan for a trip to town. That was a special treat because we seldom got to go. She had been praying for some way to make Christmas special for her brood, and just that morning she had received a letter from Grandma with a check enclosed.

Before we tumbled out of the car in front of the general store, Mother carefully instructed us to "look but not touch" when we got inside. We gazed in wonder at all the lights and Christmas toys, not realizing that Mother was watching and quietly making her purchases.

As we piled back into the car, Mother looked worried. It was snowing hard. As we traveled, the younger ones were soon lulled to sleep by the rhythmic beat of the tire chains on the pavement. But as Mother turned off the pavement for the last two-mile homeward stretch, my brother Fred and I began to pray. Finally, the car lurched and then stopped. Our home was still a mile away. Mother knew walking would keep us warm. The snow reached over our boot tops, but we had to keep walking. Mother, Fred, and I carried the smallest children. After what seemed hours, we clattered into the house, thankful to be home and warm.

Our father, coming home from work, came upon our stalled car. His first thought was, *Oh, Lord, take care of my family.* He carefully followed our footprints, his arms laden with Mother's purchases. Oh, the relief when he saw the lights of home! *Thank You, Lord, they are safe!*

On Christmas morning, what joy as we each received one of those wonderful toys we had longed for!

We are trudging through a cold, dark world, but Jesus is still the Light, and He is beckoning us home. What joy will be ours on the great resurrection morning? He has given us the Light; will we follow it home?

Dorothy Duncan (deceased)

December 26

King of Kings

"The kingdom of the world has become the kingdom of our Lord and of his Messiah, and he will reign for ever and ever."
—Revelation 11:15, NIV

The coronation of King Charles III of the United Kingdom in May 2023 attracted attention around the world. In London, cheering crowds lined the streets to celebrate and share in the pomp and pageantry associated with the event. The coronation service itself is steeped in history, based on rituals going back almost a thousand years. It is essentially a solemn religious occasion, with hymns, Scripture readings, and a sermon, as well as the anointing, consecration, and crowning of the monarch. One aspect that caught my attention as I watched the telecast was that on entering Westminster Abbey, King Charles was greeted by a young chorister with the words: "Your Majesty, as children of the kingdom of God we welcome you in the name of the King of kings."

King Charles replied: "In his name and after his example I come not to be served but to serve,"* echoing Jesus' words in Mark 10:45.

There is no doubt that King Charles has already given many years of service and will continue to serve the people over whom he reigns. And yet, once the rituals were over, the king and queen returned to their palace. Jesus' service, on the other hand, involved an act of astonishing love and condescension—He gave up His heavenly throne to become a lowly human being in order to serve and save humanity.

The apostle Paul highlights Jesus' humility in taking on the status of a servant and dying on the cross in obedience to His Father's will (Philippians 2:6–8). The wonderful news is that our Servant King rose again, and "God exalted him to the highest place and gave him the name that is above every name" (verse 9, NIV).

By His grace, I hope to be among the vast heavenly throng celebrating our Savior King and singing, "Worthy is the Lamb, who was slain, to receive power and wealth and wisdom and strength and honor and glory and praise!" (Revelation 5:12, NIV). Will you be there too?

Jennifer M. Baldwin

---

* "The Coronation Service—Order of Service," Royal Household, May 6, 2023, https://www.royal.uk/sites/default/files/documents/2023-05/The Coronation Order of Service.pdf.

December 27

Heavenly Family Reunion

"At the same time," says the LORD,
"I will be the God of all the families of Israel, and they shall be My people."
—Jeremiah 31:1, NKJV

Michigan camp meeting in the United States of America was one of my summer highlights while growing up. My mother owned an eleven-bed rest home, and camp meeting was the only time she would go on vacation. The whole family packed up and went for the week, and to this day, I still have friends whom I met there. The Michigan camp meeting was one of the largest held in the world. It was a foretaste of heaven! I loved to watch the people who attended in their colorful clothing and hear them speak in their mother languages. The last year the camp meeting was held at that campground in Grand Ledge was 1988, the year after my mother died of cancer.

Camp meetings have long been a good way to foster relationships, and building friendships is very important to me. I recently got to see one of my best friends from Illinois. I also spent the weekend with a couple who were in my wedding in 1979. Lastly, I saw a friend who is a retired doctor who I went to the junior-senior banquet with at Andrews Academy. It was such a wonderful trip, seeing friends I had not seen for many years.

Connections often take place when you least expect them. Once, when our three sons were young, we took them to Disney World in Orlando, Florida, United States of America. On Sabbath, we went to a nearby church and saw two women who were student missionaries when my husband and I taught at the Seventh-day Adventist Language School in Seoul, South Korea, from 1980 to 1981. What a wonderful reunion we had, catching up on news from twenty years earlier.

Another example occurred on the third Sunday in July, when we have a family reunion on my father's side. I attended it with my parents every year and got to know all my cousins. As we grew older, we decided to keep the reunion going and encourage the younger cousins to attend. Our reunion has been going on for more than seventy-five years, with only one exception, when we had to cancel due to COVID-19.

There is a family reunion that none of us want to miss! When Christ returns to take His children home, He will gather all who have died, along with those who are awaiting His return, and we will never see death again! Redeemed by His precious blood, we will be reunited with our loved ones. What a day that will be! Jesus is coming soon. Maranatha!

Gyl Moon Bateman

December 28

We Still Have This Hope

*Looking for the blessed hope and the glorious appearing
of our great God and Savior Jesus Christ.*
—Titus 2:13, NKJV

From New Testament times onward, Jesus' followers have had this hope of His return and have waited for it. The blessed hope of Jesus' second coming was a topic our church pioneers constantly spoke of as they traveled around the country preaching and teaching. This hope burned within their hearts.

On October 22, 1844, some local Advent believers gathered on Ascension Rock on the William Miller farm in upstate New York, United States of America, watching the skies, waiting, and hoping. They were bitterly disappointed when Jesus did not return that day. Yet a faithful few still believed.

In the late 1800s, traveling evangelists began pitching tents and preaching that Jesus was coming soon. My great-great-grandparents, after attending one of these tent meetings, became believers and joined those looking for His return. All their lives, they looked for Jesus to come and fell asleep in "the blessed hope." My great-grandparents, then my grandparents, and then my parents watched for Jesus to come in their lifetimes, but finally, they, too, fell asleep.

During my four years in academy, the principal often told us time was short, and Jesus would likely return to Earth before we graduated. Over fifty years have passed since then.

One hundred and fifty years after the disappointment of 1844, I stood with my husband and children on Ascension Rock, gazed up at the heavens, and tried to imagine how those early believers must have felt. I remember wishing that Jesus would come that day.

However, 2 Peter 3:8 says that the Lord's time is not our time. With Him, one day is as a thousand years. While He was on Earth, Jesus told several parables about delays—a bridegroom who delayed his coming, and a master who delayed his return. So we continue waiting and watching, even though the Lord seems to delay His coming. He is "not willing that any should perish but that all" should accept His gift of salvation (verse 9, NKJV).

Let us not become absorbed in the things of this world, for everything in this world will soon pass away. I pray that our burning desire will be to share Jesus and the hope of His coming.

Beth Davis Nelson

December 29

The Traffic Ticket

The Lord shall judge the people; judge me, O Lord, according to my righteousness, and according to mine integrity that is in me.
—Psalm 7:8, KJV

I peered at the envelope, alarmed at what I saw written on it. As I anxiously opened it, to my dismay, it stated that I had run a red light. I clearly remembered the date I went to the city; however, I could not remember running a red light. "Lord, I don't remember running a red light. I will call and contest the charges." When I called, I was advised of the steps I needed to take.

I was given extra time before my case appeared in court, and on the day I needed to appear, I prayed, and my cousin offered to pray also. I drove to the city, making certain to arrive early. I announced my arrival to the clerk and told him my story, and he assured me that the judge might pardon me. Four or five cases were called before my name was called. After the judge read the charges, he asked, "Miss Hines, do you have anything to say in your defense?"

"Yes, Your Honor, I honestly did not know I had run a red light. I had been to the doctor for a procedure on my lower leg, and I was in pain. I am sorry." I apologized again and added, "I am asking for mercy, Your Honor." The ticket was for a significant amount, so I asked for mercy again, but to my dismay, none was granted. In fact, an extra fee was added to the ticket.

I was horrified and visibly shaken. No pity was shown. No mercy granted. I said to God, "Lord, I prayed! My cousin prayed, and You did not answer my prayer!" Immediately, I sensed the Lord say, "Yes, I did." The realization finally struck me. *I was not prepared*, I thought. *I had more than a month to pray and fast, and I waited to pray until the night before and the morning of my trial.*

I remembered that some problems required fasting and much prayer. I also remembered the five foolish virgins who were unprepared for the coming of the bridegroom. They were shown no mercy. The door closed on them.

My friends, we must be prepared. We must be ready, for the Righteous Judge will be coming soon, unannounced, and only those who have made preparations will be ready to enter the marriage feast of the Lamb.

Patricia Hines

December 30

God's Powerful GPS

I will instruct you and teach you in the way you should go;
|I will guide you with My eye.
—Psalm 32:8, NKJV

I was invited to a banquet, along with several members of my family. I felt so excited as I prepared my best dress with coordinated shoes and purse for the event. We entered the address of the event into the GPS and then set off to the banquet. We gave ourselves plenty of time and planned to arrive early so we could get a seat close to the front; we did not wish to miss anything.

The global positioning system (GPS) is a modern-day marvel invented by the United States Department of Defense for military use. It was allowed for civilian use in the 1980s. What a day that was! Most people loved the system; it reduced the need for paper maps, and drivers no longer had to constantly turn their heads to read road signs and numbers on buildings, which were not always visible.

We followed the directions to the banqueet carefully, and soon, the GPS indicated we were close to our destination. I checked the time, and we were early, as planned. But something was definitely wrong. We kept driving for a while but did not hear that we had arrived at our destination. Did we miss the announcement? We made a U-turn and tried again, but no destination announcement. This happened several times. After a while, I suggested we turn off the GPS and do a visual search. We eventually located the address, but we were slightly late, and our ideal seats were taken. We were sorely disappointed with the GPS and were reminded that the system is man-made and prone to problems.

The Lord also has a GPS, as indicated in Psalm 32:8, our verse for today. He said, "I will instruct you and teach you in the way you should go; I will guide you with My eye" (NKJV). The sixty-six books of the Bible are our GPS from God. In this world, we will feel lost and confused on our journey, but we have no need to fear. By faith, this GPS will guide us to our heavenly destination, where God is preparing a magnificent mansion and banquet for us. There are never any errors, delays, or misinformation with God's GPS because He is the Cartographer (the Maker of maps), Instructor, and Navigator. All He asks of us is that we faithfully follow His GPS instructions, and we will arrive at the right place right on time!

Sonia Kennedy-Brown

December 31

One Week

"Therefore keep watch, because you do not know the day or the hour."
—Matthew 25:13, NIV

The Cleveland Zoo in Ohio, United States of America, has an Asian Lantern Festival each summer that I had desired to see for some time. A few years earlier, my godsister had driven through it during the day. She decided it was not too interesting to view lanterns in the light, so she suggested we go at night and walk through to enjoy the festival fully.

Once the tickets went on sale, we invited a couple of other family members and friends and picked a date. Everyone was excited to attend. Of course, we had no way of knowing whether the weather would be good on that day. No one wanted to walk around in the rain or blazing heat.

The day finally arrived, and our group had a grand time. The lanterns were spread out and displayed throughout the zoo, and they were all so beautiful. We must have walked a good six miles that evening! Since it was dark most of the time we were there, not many animals were out for us to see. The lanterns had our full attention.

However, there was one attraction that piqued our curiosity: the corpse flower. I had never heard of it and wondered what it was. We leisurely walked up to the display and read about this flower. It had bloomed only four times in the past twenty-eight years. We discovered how it got its name. When in bloom, it has a pungent smell. Some say it smells like rotting flesh, hence the name. We took a couple of pictures and then moved on.

A few days later, the news began to run stories that the corpse flower was showing signs it was going to bloom! And it did; it was in full bloom exactly one week after our visit to the Cleveland Zoo! I could not believe we missed this rare event by one week. It would have been incredible to see (maybe not smell) it in person. The display we had just walked up to view now had lines where people waited an hour or more to see the blooming flower.

There is a one-time-only event soon to take place, and that is the second coming of our Lord, Jesus Christ. I do not want to miss it, and I am planning now to attend. Just as the flower gave signs it would soon bloom, there are signs that Christ's return is very near; "therefore keep watch" (Matthew 25:13, NIV).

Angèle Peterson

2025 Author Biographies

Kristeena Daniella Abbey loves to write and read the many devotionals shared by women from all over the world. She wanted to share her testimonies as well, so she decided to write for the Women's Ministries devotional. It is her prayer that her words will bless others in the same way she has been blessed. **July 23**

Betty J. Adams was born and raised in California, where she lived mostly until her husband of sixty-six years passed away in 2020. She now lives in Maine with her youngest daughter and helps her with her home scrapbooking business. Betty has six children, seven grandchildren, seven great-grandchildren, and three great-great-grandchildren. She enjoys reading, writing, and bird-watching. **Oct. 15**

Diane Duncan de Aguirre was born to missionary parents and lived in the mission field for over thirty years. She now serves the Lord at Pacific Press® Publishing Association in the International Department. Her daughters are her greatest pride, and Jesus' second coming is her greatest hope. **July 28, Dec. 1**

Isabel Cristina de Almeida is the retired mother of three young people. She lives in Brazil, where she loves to read, make friends, and be in contact with nature. **May 3, Aug. 9**

Sue Anderson has been married to her husband, Chuck, for fifty-eight years. They have two married daughters, three grandchildren, and three great-grandchildren. She is retired from the United States Forest Service and is a member of the Coeur d'Alene Seventh-day Adventist Church in Idaho. **June 23**

Lydia D. Andrews, PhD, CNM, RN, is a retired university professor of nursing. She and her husband, Newton, worked as General Conference of Seventh-day Adventist missionaries in Kenya and Ghana, Africa. She is the mother of three adult children and has four delightful teenage grandsons. She lives in Huntsville, Alabama, where she serves on the Prayer and Health Ministries of Oakwood University Church. She enjoys cooking, reading, traveling, music, encouraging young people, and spending time with family. **Jan. 22**

Edna Andrews-Rose, PhD, MSW, RN-PMH-BC, is a native Georgian now residing in Michigan. She serves as a nurse clinician at the University of Michigan Alzheimer's Disease Research Center. Her mother's death from Alzheimer's disease created a passion for facilitating workshops to educate and provide caregiver support and to recruit participants for studies of cognitive and movement disorders. Dr. Andrews-Rose's philosophy in life is to love God and know the joy of laughter and the gift of goodbye. **Feb. 28**

Pat Arrabito produces documentaries, films, and social media programs that focus on two most misunderstood but precious doctrines—the Sabbath and the state of the dead. She is mother to two grown children and two stepchildren and grandma to eight delightful grandchildren. **June 5, Oct. 17**

Raquel Queiroz da Costa Arrais is a minister's wife who developed her ministry as an educator for twenty years. She serves in South Korea as director for the Women's, Children's, and Family Ministries departments for the Northern Asia-Pacific Division. Raquel has two adult sons, two daughters-in-law, and four adored grandchildren. Her greatest pleasures are being with people, singing, playing the piano, and traveling. **May 25**

Jean Arthur lives in Silver Spring, Maryland. She is an attorney by training but retired from thirty-three years of service with local government. She now works as a substitute teacher in the local public school system. She is active in her local church and volunteers at church and in the community. She spends her free time gardening, traveling, bicycling, running, baking, and reading. **Dec. 16**

Flore Aubry-Hamilton loves the Lord, and she wants her light to shine for Him. Flore and her husband, George, live in Huntsville, Alabama. They enjoy working with disabilities ministries. **Sept. 13**

Viorica Avrămiea earned a BA in pastoral theology at Cernica Theological Institute, Romania. She also holds a master's degree in public health. Currently, Viorica works as an assistant director for the Sabbath School and Personal Ministries, Women's Ministries, and Health Ministries departments at Moldova Conference, Romania. She is also a Single Women coordinator at the Romanian Union. Viorica enjoys traveling, reading, riding her bike, telling stories, translating, and working for single women. **May 9**

Yvita Antonette Villalona Bacchus is a graphic designer. She works in the music department at her local church and loves to share about faith, God, and life. Yvita is grateful for the opportunity to bless and to be blessed through this devotional. **Feb. 15**

Noella (Jumpp) Baird was born in Jamaica. She is a registered nurse and lives in Edmonton, Alberta, Canada, with her husband, Alan, and three children: Alyssa, Natalia, and Eric. Her greatest pleasures are reading, singing, diamond painting, adult coloring, and meeting new people. Noella looks forward to Jesus' second coming when all will be made new, and she will see her two babies, Micah and Avery, again. **June 4**

Estelle Baker has served as director of the Women's Ministries department of the Northern Conference, South Africa, since 2017. In addition, she now serves as director of the Children's Ministries department. An educator by profession, Estelle taught at the secondary school level for fourteen years before joining the nonprofit sector as a human resource management professional for eight years. She is a single parent to twin boys who are both married and a proud grandmother of two, Gianna and Shai. Estelle praises God for leading in her life and for bringing her to this point—a life dedicated to service to Him. She counts it an absolute privilege to serve in the Lord's vineyard. **Sept. 20**

Jennifer M. Baldwin writes from Australia, where she works in risk management at Sydney Adventist Hospital. She enjoys family time, church involvement, and relaxing with crossword or sudoku puzzles. Jennifer has been contributing to the devotional book series for more than twenty-five years. **Dec. 26**

Annette M. Barnes lives in upstate New York. She works for New York State as a capital program manager and is a registered architect. Traveling is one of her passions. Annette is the head elder at her local church—the Joy of Troy. She loves God and is committed to serving His church and reaching the local community. **May 26, June 26**

Gloria Barnes-Gregory, PhD, MA, BSc, CM, is inspired by everyday experiences, especially interactions with her granddaughters. She and her husband, Milton, continue to serve others in health, family life, and leadership ministries, enabling others to make positive lifelong changes for themselves and to honor God. **Mar. 3, Mar. 25**

Dottie Barnett is retired and lives in a beautiful country setting in southeast Tennessee. For more than fifty years, she has been involved in children and adult Sabbath School leadership. Dottie has written a devotional blog for the past several years called *Whispers of His Wisdom*. She loves working with plants and flowers, mowing her large lawn, photography, and camping with her family. **May 16, July 4**

Gyl Moon Bateman lives in Niles, Michigan, and has three grown sons. She retired from working as a behavioral medicine nurse at a local hospital. Gyl enjoys pursuing her hobbies, being active in the local community and her church, and helping her sons at their local store. **Nov. 30, Dec. 27**

Miriam Battles is the mother of two adult sons and has been blessed with one beautiful daughter-in-love. She resides in Huntsville, Alabama, and works at Oakwood University as the director of Major Gifts and Planned Giving. She loves to travel and read. **Mar. 16**

Dana M. Bean is an educator from a small, beautiful island in the middle of the Atlantic Ocean—Bermuda. She loves the art of writing, reading, and capturing moments through photography. **May 7**

Cynthia Best-Goring lives in Glenn Dale, Maryland. She is a wife, a mother of two adult children, and a first-time mother-in-law. Cynthia serves as a Sabbath School teacher and enjoys being a recently retired principal. **June 30, Nov. 17**

Jennifer Billings is a former primary school teacher who resides in the United Kingdom. At present, she works with traumatized children as a foster carer. Jennifer supports the work in the children's department at church. Singing and playing music have been lifelong passions, gifts from God, which she now uses to teach young children to play the piano, leaving a legacy of children who play hymns in church. **May 20**

Paula Sanders Blackwell is an educator and writer who resides in Georgia. She is the author of a devotional book titled *Lessons From My Hard Head* and a ninety-day prayer journal. **Mar. 28, Dec. 18**

Julie Bocock-Bliss lives in Honolulu, Hawai'i. She is a lifelong member of the Honolulu Japanese Seventh-day Adventist Church. Julie works in a library, which is perfect because she loves reading so much! Her other hobbies include traveling, crafting, and giving gifts. She thanks God for the time and ability to enjoy her hobbies. **Dec. 19**

Patricia Hook Rhyndress Bodi has three children, two grandchildren, and a host of cousins and friends. The fresh hibiscus on her patio and putting together picture puzzles give her joy. She sends cards and notes to people who need a smile and a prayer. Patricia lives in California, United States of America. **Mar. 18**

Althea Y. Boxx, MPH, is a registered nurse with a background in both critical care and emergency. She is an ordained elder, serving with a passion for equipping members to minister through their respective spiritual gifts. Althea is currently a student at the Seventh-day Adventist Theological Seminary at Andrews University in Michigan, United States of America. She has authored a motivational devotional, *Fuel for the Journey*. She enjoys gardening, reading, writing, photography, and traveling. **May 8**

DeeAnn Bragaw is the Women's Ministries director for the North America Division of Seventh-day Adventists. She holds a master's degree in pastoral ministries and a bachelor's degree in education. DeeAnn previously served the Rocky Mountain Conference as its Women's Ministries director and Prayer Ministries coordinator. **Jan. 18, Oct. 11**

Marleni Brant-Pomare was born on the island of San Andrés. She lives with her husband, Mariano, in Florida, United States of America. They have two grown children, Narch and Narleesha. Marleni has been the administrative and academic director of Miramar United Methodist Preschool for the past sixteen years. She enjoys reading, walking, and quiet time. **Feb. 24**

Caren Henry Broaster is a high school English teacher at Houston Math, Science, and Technology High School, and she also teaches Dual Credit English Composition I and II at Houston Community College in Texas, United States of America. Caren is a member of the West Houston Seventh-day Adventist Church and taught Adventurers while her son, Corbin, and daughter, Haadiya, were in the program. They are now in Pathfinders, and she and her husband, Hubert, enjoy volunteering for the club. Caren loves to interact with her sisters in Christ in women's ministries, compassion ministry, and the church book club. **May 23, July 17**

Mary Head Brooks is a retired psychiatric nurse who lives in Georgia, United States of America, with her husband, Marshall. She has a passion for providing food for those who may suffer from food insecurity. Mary enjoys gardening, traveling, and spending time with her grandson, Mason. **June 7**

Kim Denyse Brown was born in Paris, France, and lives in Rockledge, Florida, United States of America. Presently, she is the Women's Ministries leader at the Bethel Seventh-day Adventist Church, in Cocoa, Florida. Philippians 4:8 is her favorite verse, and creativity through Bearing Light Expression is her passion. Kim has two adult children, Kimberly and Lemuel, and one grandson, Jaelin. **Feb. 3**

Vivian Brown, a retired educator, writes from Huntsville, Alabama. She has been a member of Oakwood University Church since 2006. Vivian recently celebrated her eightieth birthday and thanks God for His constant care of her and her family. She has been married to the love of her life for more than sixty years. Vivian is passionate about witnessing and is involved in several Bible-study ministries. She has enjoyed her Zoom Sabbath School class for over two years, where she motivates members to memorize scriptures. **Oct. 1**

Brenda Browne-Ashe is from the island of Antigua in the Caribbean, where she serves as the Women's Ministries island coordinator. A wife and mother of three—two girls and one boy—Brenda loves to work with women. **Nov. 9**

Marine E. Bryan, PhD, has two teenage daughters who light up her life as a single parent. She holds a PhD in health care administration and currently serves as a health care administrator for a reputable health care service organization in New York. Dr. Bryan is a coauthor and a prayer facilitator in the 24/7 United Prayer ministry. She currently serves her church as a Sabbath School superintendent. **Mar. 21**

Elaine Buchanan lives in Rawlings, Maryland, with her pastor husband. She has worked side by side with him since they started ministry in 2002. Her passion is doing in-home Bible studies, teaching the books of Daniel and Revelation, and sharing how God has changed her life. Elaine looks forward to the soon return of Jesus. **Sept. 16**

Elinor Harvin Burks resides with her soul mate, Winfield, a lay pastor in Leeds, Alabama. They enjoy pointing out God's creative genius in nature by demonstrating "Science for Kids" experiments at libraries, churches, schools, and community fairs. Mrs. Burks, a church treasurer, loves giving Bible studies, researching history, and making soap. She is a journalism graduate of Wayne State University in Detroit, Michigan. Mrs. Burks retired from the City of Birmingham, Alabama, in 2010 after twenty-four years of service. **Feb. 9**

Helen O. Byoune, EdD, resides in Georgia. She is ninety-one years young. A retired educator, she taught grades two and three and junior high English and social studies. Dr. Byoune is a learning-disabled specialist. She lived and worked for six years in the United States/British Virgin Islands as a diagnostician and adjunct professor. Dr. Byoune served for three years in South Korea as a Bible and ESL instructor and teaching supervisor. She is a mother of three, grandmother of one, and has three great-grands. Her leisure time is spent reading, writing, crocheting, and spending time with her granddog, Chi. **Jan. 23, Apr. 16**

Elizabeth Ida Cain is an educator by profession who works in human resources and administration, where she finds fulfillment in caring for employees in the workplace as Jesus would do. Elizabeth is a professional florist who enjoys teaching the art and cheering others with beautiful floral arrangements. One of her spiritual blessings is writing devotionals for the women's devotional books. She lives in Jamaica, West Indies. **Feb. 4, Mar. 7**

Hyacinth V. Caleb, born and raised in Antigua, presently resides in Saint Croix, United States Virgin Islands. She is a mother of two and a grandmother of six. Hyacinth is a retired educator who loves to read, write, and work outside in her garden. **Jan. 16, Feb. 10**

Florence E. Callender is a brain-based learning specialist, the founder of Innovative Lifestyle Solutions, and the creator of Learning Made Easy: Success Secrets for Parenting Dyslexia. She helps parents work with their struggling children so that they learn faster and easier, have a better school experience, and succeed in life. Florence currently resides with her daughter in Tennessee. **Mar. 30**

Ruth Cantrell is a retired Detroit, Michigan, schoolteacher and counselor. She and her husband, Ronald, relocated to Harvest, Alabama. Mrs. Cantrell has two sons, a daughter-in-law, and three grandchildren. She enjoys women's ministry, prayer ministry, reading, flowers, music, and organizing programs. **Sept. 6, Oct. 12**

Het Jane Silva Carvalho graduated with a degree in literature from the Federal University of Rio de Janeiro, Brazil, and has a master's degree in human sciences from the Federal University of Amazonas, Brazil. She worked as a teacher at various levels, including university, as well as in the area of literature evangelism. Het likes music, traveling, and reading. She volunteers in her church in the areas of music, treasury, missionary work, and children. Her favorite activity is distributing literature. **Oct. 28, Nov. 18**

Judy Casper lives in Idaho with her husband, Martin. She loves hiking in the summer and skiing in the winter. Mrs. Casper has run several marathons and is passionate about physical fitness. With a degree from Loma Linda University, she works remotely in the health information management field. Mr. and Mrs. Casper are active in their local church and look forward to the soon coming of Christ. **Mar. 31**

Eleasia Charles, EdD, MEd, MSc, BSc, JP, is a reading specialist and literacy coach. She has taught at the early childhood and tertiary educational levels and has focused her time on writing children's books to provide educational resources for struggling readers. Dr. Charles enjoys family time with her husband, four children, and two dogs, Bella and Spunky, and being active within her church and community. **July 20**

Suhana Chikatla is originally from India. She has two master's degrees and a doctorate. She wears many hats as a volunteer in the Children's and Youth Ministries department at her church. Currently, Dr. Chikatla is the Adventurer area coordinator for the North Alabama region, Pathfinder Club director, Master Guide club director for her church, Sabbath School teacher, multimedia personnel, and social media personnel. She and her husband, Royce Sutton, have a beautiful daughter, Rehana. **Aug. 19**

Precious Chitwa lives in Zambia. She is an economist by training and currently freelances as a content writer and editor. She loves to serve as a literature evangelist and belongs to a missionary movement called IMPACT: Inspired Missionaries Proclaiming the Advent of Christ Today. She also likes to read, write, and bake. **June 17**

Rosemarie Clardy enjoys walking each day with her husband and their two dogs. Together, they keep their community clean by picking up trash along a mile and a half of road. She is a volunteer and helper at Mount Pisgah Academy Seventh-day Adventist Church. **Sept. 12**

Sacha Clarke resides in Baytown, Texas, with her husband, Kelvin, and two sons, Chalum and Chasiah. She is a social worker by profession and is currently working to obtain her clinical license. Mrs. Clarke serves as head Sabbath School superintendent at her local church. Some of her hobbies include making wreaths and floral arranging. **June 11, Aug. 22**

Sherma Webbe Clarke writes from Bermuda, where she serves in her church in Women's Ministries and a variety of administrative roles. Her interests include sewing, photography, and travel. Sherma has contributed to previous devotional books and enjoys writing plays, short stories, and poetry. **June 10, Oct. 8**

Valerie Knowles Combie, PhD, is a professor of English at the College of Liberal Arts and Social Sciences at the University of the Virgin Islands, Saint Croix. She loves the Lord and prays for Jesus' second return. Through the years, Dr. Combie has served as a Sabbath School superintendent, teacher, and pianist for the church. She enjoys reading, writing, and gardening. **May 13**

Aminata Coote is the author of several Bible studies and devotionals for women. She blogs at Hebrews12Endurance.com, where she encourages women to study the Bible and follow the path God has set out for them. **Apr. 21**

Patricia Cove is a semiretired teacher. She volunteers at the local hospital gift shop and knits lap robes for elders. She and her husband, George, celebrated sixty-five years of marriage in May 2023. Their five children are all living busy, active lives. It is a very precious event when grandchildren and great-grandchildren come to visit. Mrs. Cove enjoys outdoor pursuits, including gardening. **Sept. 11, Oct. 20**

Sabrina Crichlow resides in Clifton, New Jersey, with her husband and two children. They attend the First SDA Church of Montclair. She was last published in the 2017 women's devotional. Mrs. Crichlow has also self-published a thirty-day devotional. She is a certified health coach, a certified life mentor, a motivational speaker, and the founder of iNAY (it's Not About You) Homeless Ministry. Her goal is to serve God and see everyone through the eyes of Christ. **June 20**

Anne Crosby lives in Page, Arizona, where her family ministers to the Navajo people. She is studying elementary education and has a music studio where she teaches piano to children in her community. In her spare time, Anne enjoys writing and participating in Children's Ministries at her local church. **Mar. 8**

Shana Cyr-Philbert, MD, MSc, is a family practice physician with a special interest in diabetes. She lives in Saint Lucia, West Indies, with her husband and young son, Nate. Dr. Philbert loves music, has sung in choirs from childhood, and is actively involved in the music ministry of the church. She is passionate about using music and medicine to change lives. **Apr. 2, July 21**

Rita Das is the wife of Dr. Nirobindu Das and the mother of two sons. She works as Women's Ministries, Children's Ministries, Family Ministries, and Health Department director for the South Bengal Section of the Northern India Union Section, where her husband serves as president. **July 8**

Jean Dozier Davey lives in the beautiful mountains of North Carolina, where she and her beloved late husband, Steven, made their home in 2005. She enjoys spending time with family, friends, and her two cats. Mrs. Davey also enjoys reading and encouraging others, and she is grateful for all that God has done in her life. **Jan. 20**

Sasha De Dios spends most of the year chasing stories to read or write. And if it can't be said with words, she loves to paint it. During the summer, Sasha likes to help with crafts and decorations for Vacation Bible School at her local church. Whatever she does, art and God are her constant companions. **Jan. 4**

Edna Bacate Domingo, PhD, MSN, RN, lives with her husband in Grand Terrace, California. A retired nursing professor, she remains active in running her nursing school. Dr. Domingo serves as one of the Sabbath School superintendents at Loma Linda University Church. She has three grown children and two grandchildren. Dr. Domingo loves nature and being with her grandchildren. **Mar. 22, May 1**

Lenora Dorf loves the Lord and has been called and chosen to "go ye therefore" from city to city in the United States, giving Bible studies and sharing God's love. She has a burden for souls, and it is like a fire shut up in her bones. Lenora is the mother of three amazing adult children and four beautiful grandchildren who all love the Lord Jesus. **Feb. 2**

Gail Dotski was born and raised in northern Michigan and has lived there ever since. She has five beautiful children and three gorgeous grandchildren. In her spare time, Gail enjoys playing her trumpet, doing cross-stitch projects, and coloring in adult spiritual coloring books. Her current project is to crochet an afghan for her five-year-old granddaughter. **Aug. 23**

Joan Dougherty-Mornan enjoys discovering God between the pages of the Bible and through life's experiences. She has two daughters and a son. Joan's hobbies are reading, writing, crocheting, and keeping busy for Christ. **Mar. 23, May 10**

Louise Howlett Driver, a missionary's daughter, pastor's wife, mother of three grown sons, and grandmother of four grown grandkids, lives in Idaho, where she supports her husband, who is still preaching and involved in helping others. She enjoys reading, gardening, and putting puzzles together. Mrs. Driver has been writing for this devotional since 1998 and is blessed each year. **Sept. 14**

Clody Flores Dumaliang is a retired metal health therapist from Los Angeles, California. She spends her leisure time traveling, hiking, and writing. Clody has been volunteering since her retirement. She has been married to her grade-school classmate for over thirty-five years, and they have a daughter, Victoria. **Apr. 12**

Debbi Duncan was born to missionary parents in El Salvador and moved to the United States as a baby. She loves to write, crochet, and read. Her greatest hope is to see her grandparents again at the resurrection and go home with Jesus to heaven, where there will be no more suffering. **Dec. 17**

Dorothy Duncan and her husband (both deceased) were missionaries for over thirty years, serving in Kenya, Mexico, Guatemala, El Salvador, and on the Navajo Reservation in New Mexico. They had a host of children of every color. Dorothy went to sleep, waiting for Jesus on January 6, 2020. **Dec. 24, Dec. 25**

Pauline A. Dwyer-Kerr holds two doctorate degrees. She is an advanced practice nurse and a professor of nursing. Dr. Kerr is a life member of the Cambridge Honors Who's Who. She has received numerous awards, including one for Childhood Amblyopia Prevention Screening. Dr. Kerr is an ordained elder and resides in Florida. She loves her children and grandchildren and enjoys the outdoors. **July 13, Aug. 29**

Yvonne E. Ealey, MEd, is a busy woman of God who cares for many. She is a retired teacher, an assistant clerk at church, and a busy homemaker. Yvonne enjoys praising God and writing about His goodness. **July 19, Aug. 27**

Fartema Mae Fagin is retired. She lives in Georgia, where she is actively involved in children's ministry. Fartema enjoys reading inspirational books, singing, and writing poems. **Apr. 28, July 2**

Melinda Ferguson lives in Rapid City, South Dakota. She works as a registered nurse in the local hospital. Melinda enjoys helping out with various church programs—especially the music. In her spare time, she visits family, loves to read, and enjoys hiking in the Black Hills. **Jan. 31, Apr. 22**

Janice Fleming-Williams is a retired church school educator, mother of two sons, mother-in-law, and grandmother. She enjoys reading and spending time with her children, grandchildren, relatives, and friends. Janice served her church as a Family Ministries leader for many years. She has a passion for happy marriages and healthy families. Janice and her husband live on Saint Thomas, United States Virgin Islands. **Nov. 29**

Marialyce Fordham gave birth to two children and has a lovely daughter-in-love. She enjoys spending time with her five grandchildren, walking, reading, traveling, and making new acquaintances. Her gift for making creative gift baskets is part of her ministry. Marialyce lives in Laurel, Maryland. **Aug. 7**

Shirley Sain Fordham is a retired educator, wife, mother of three married adults, and grandmother of eight. She enjoys family, friends, meeting strangers, technology, crocheting, scrapbooking, and her West End Seventh-day Adventist Church in Atlanta, Georgia. Until Jesus comes again, Mrs. Fordham will continue to live, love, laugh, and learn. **Oct. 4**

Andrea K. Francis is an educator by profession but proudly declares herself the eternal student. Through her work, she seeks to empower young people to actualize their God-given potential and help them build characters for eternity. **Nov. 7, Dec. 5**

Sylvia A. Franklin lives with her husband, Joe, in Rocklin, California. She currently works as a senior human resources generalist for Cooperative Agricultural Support Services in Sacramento, California. Mrs. Franklin serves as administrative assistant to the Women's Ministries director of the Pacific Union Conference of Seventh-day Adventists. She enjoys singing, planning events, and all the blessings the Lord generously provides. **Jan. 30, July 9**

Edith C. Fraser, PhD, is a retired college professor and counselor residing in Alabama. She has worked with issues for women, couples, and grief and loss (especially traumatic losses) for more than thirty years. Dr. Fraser has been married to Dr. Trevor for over fifty-three years, and they have two adult children. She is the proud grandmother of two grandsons and two granddaughters. **July 12**

Claudette Garbutt-Harding lives in Orlando, Florida, with her husband, Keith. They have been married for almost forty-five years. Now retired, she has a vibrant prayer ministry and encourages others to explore creative ways to pray. Mrs. Harding loves to write for the women's devotional and encourages other women to write. She helps with their editing. Mrs. Harding has written an autobiography, *16 to 61 and Beyond: A Teacher's Personal Journey*, which is available on Amazon.com. **Jan. 7, Apr. 5**

Marybeth Gessele lives in Gaston, Oregon, with her husband, Glen. She is a retired hospice caregiver. Mrs. Gessele enjoys sewing baby and lap quilts for various organizations. **Mar. 4**

Terri Lea Gibson, DNP, RN, is a nursing professor at Southwestern Adventist University. Leadership, community health, lifestyle nursing, and inspirational photography are a few of her passions, though reflecting the love of Jesus is the top priority in her life. She is blessed with over thirty-five years of marriage to Don, a retired pastor, and with her adult children, their spouses, and grandchildren. Terri loves to travel, engage in relationship building, and inspire nursing students. **Oct. 31**

Rita Gill serves in the Northern India Union as a departmental director. She enjoys reading; writing devotionals, articles, and stories; and spending time reflecting on nature. Mrs. Gill is blessed with a caring pastor husband, a son, a daughter-in-law, and an adorable granddaughter. She considers being a child of God as her greatest asset. **Jan. 17**

Jean P. Good is a native of Newark, New Jersey, and has been a literature evangelist since 1982. She is presently serving as the Allegheny East Conference publishing associate for northern New Jersey. Jean is the mother of five adult sons, thirteen grandchildren, and two great-grandchildren. She resides in Piscataway, New Jersey, and enjoys writing, decorating, and being at the beach. Jean lives each day to share the gospel of Jesus Christ with others, ministering to their temporal as well as their spiritual needs. **Nov. 27**

Lela Moore Gooding, Oakwood University emeritus professor of English, was an educator for forty-five years. She thanks God every day for her new job as caregiver and companion to Earl Gooding (Alabama A&M University professor emeritus), the brilliant man she married in 1965. Earl and Lela have five children—a son, a daughter, their spouses, and a goddaughter—and six grandchildren and three great-grandchildren. **Oct. 30**

Alexis A. Goring is a passionate writer with a degree in print journalism and an MFA in creative writing. She is an author of inspirational romance fiction stories and devotionals. Alexis loves following Jesus Christ and spending time enjoying delicious food with her loved ones. She's the founder of the *God Is Love* blog, where she teaches people about the God who loves humankind with all His heart. She enjoys photography as a hobby. **May 4, Aug. 1**

Raquel Gosling-George is an elder at the Baltimore White Marsh Seventh-day Adventist Church. She lives in Maryland with her husband, Errol, and two cats, Eclipse and Ashes. Raquel enjoys all aspects of church ministry, especially the Pathfinders and working with the youth. She loves nature, photography, puzzles, and helping others, and she lives by the motto "one day at a time." **Aug. 21**

Cecelia Grant is a retired medical doctor living in Kingston, Jamaica, and she longs for Christ's second coming. Her hobbies are gardening and listening to good music. Cecelia has a passion for young people, to whom she is always giving advice. She has been a contributor since 2010. **Feb. 7, Apr. 27**

Jasmine E. Grant is a retiree, a mother, and a grandmother who resides in New York City. She enjoys sharing the Scriptures and testimonies with folks in general, but Jasmine has a special place in her heart for young people. She enjoys teaching them about the Savior and encouraging them to excel in whatever they do. **July 10, Sept. 9**

Winsome Joy Grant writes from Valley Stream, New York. She is a retired mother and grandmother and continues to pursue her passion for writing. Winsome has been a member of the Solid Rock Seventh-day Adventist Church in New York for more than twenty years. She loves reading, appreciates nature, and loves animals, especially dogs. **Feb. 22**

Dawn de Grass is a retired teacher who taught English and biology. In her early years of retirement, she started painting and is most comfortable with oil painting. Dawn and her husband, Henry, have two daughters, two sons-in-law, and three granddaughters. She loves walking with her friend to keep fit. **Apr. 7**

Donna de Grass is a qualified physical therapist and holds an MA in the field of tuberculosis. She currently works as a researcher for a nonprofit organization that specializes in tuberculosis and HIV/AIDS. Her hobbies include yoga and reading. At the top of her bucket list is a trip to Antarctica. **Dec. 8**

Mary Jane Graves is old enough to remember that the "good old days" were not always so good! She is a widow, mother, grandmother, and great-grandmother and lives in North Carolina. **Apr. 23**

Carmalita Green is a registered dietitian in the Dallas-Fort Worth area in Texas. She enjoys participating in her Sabbath School class as a co-teacher. **Jan. 9, Oct. 2**

Cloreth S. Greene, MEd, MA, ABC, is an education and communications consultant from Jamaica who currently resides in Canada. She appreciates the outdoors, enjoys music and cooking, and is passionate about prayer, youth, children's, and health ministries. **June 18**

Glenda-mae Greene, PhD, writes from her wheelchair in the Canadian prairies. A retired educational administrator, she enjoys working with anyone who needs her help. Crafting devotionals is her testimony to the Savior's loving-kindness. **Sept. 15**

Zandra LaMar Griffin-Willingham is a retired captain from the New York City Department of Corrections in New York. She resides in Atlanta, Georgia, with her husband, Stanley, and two dogs, Alpha and Atlas. Zandra ministers to the hungry and needy on the third Sabbath of each month. **Dec. 7**

Pauline A. Griffith is a retired speech pathologist who lives in Huntsville, Alabama, with her husband, Dr. Wilfred Griffith. They have been married for fifty years and have three sons and five grandchildren. She attends the Oakwood University Church in Huntsville. **Nov. 12**

Diantha Hall-Smith is a daughter of God. She is the wife of a devoted Christian husband who serves in the United States Air Force and the mother of two beautiful children. Diantha was born in New York City, and has had the honor and privilege of living in and visiting interesting places domestically and globally. She enjoys writing, traveling, and spending time with her family. **Nov. 22**

Marsha Hammond-Brummel is a title 1 math teacher who lives in Claremont, New Hampshire. On weekends from May through October, she often can be found with her husband, Ken, at the historic Washington, New Hampshire, Seventh-day Adventist Church, telling stories of the early Adventist pioneers. **Jan. 28, Aug. 25**

Mary K. Haslam is a joycentric mother, daughter, sister, wife, and friend who loves people and adores God. She resides on a ranch in Texas, where she does everything from driving tractors to writing and singing. Look for her first book coming soon to shelves near you. **Jan. 19, Apr. 14**

Bessie Russell Haynes is a retired Seventh-day Adventist teacher who worked as a missionary teacher in South Korea for more than twelve years. She relocated to the Pacific Northwest in the northern part of Washington to be near her precious grandchildren—two living in Vancouver, British Columbia, Canada, and the other two near Seattle, Washington. Traveling, reading, writing, and gardening are her hobbies. She awaits Jesus' soon return! **May 17**

Kimberly M. H. Henry is a thirty-six-year-old registered nurse, originally from Jamaica, who immigrated to the United Kingdom on a skilled worker visa in 2022. Previously, she lived in the United States, where she worshiped at the Calvary Seventh-day Adventist Church in Bridgeport, Connecticut. **June 19**

Kathy-Ann C. Hernandez, PhD, is a writer, professor, and leadership expert. She is the founder of Value What Matters, a lifestyle brand focused on intentional living through the relationships we cultivate with ourselves, others, and our God. Dr. Hernandez is the author of *Waiting by the Brook: Seven Steps to Deeper Intimacy With God*. She lives just outside Philadelphia, Pennsylvania, with her husband and daughters. **Apr. 13**

Patricia Hines is originally from Jamaica, in the Caribbean. She is now retired and lives in Sebring, Florida. Patricia likes to write, enjoys music, and spends much of her days gardening. **Dec. 29**

Tamyra Horst writes from Bernville, Pennsylvania, where she lives with her husband of more than thirty years, Tim. An author, a speaker, and the Communication director for the Pennsylvania Conference of Seventh-day Adventists, Mrs. Horst loves being a mom to her two young-adult sons, being a friend to an amazing group of women, enjoying quiet time with a great book and a cup of chai, and sharing adventures with those she loves. **Jan. 5, Dec. 3**

Charmaine Houston is a health care professional who lives in Pennsylvania with her two children. She enjoys reading and running and completing half-marathons. **Feb. 20**

C. Marion Hudson earned a BS in biology and later an MBA and MSIS. She is a teacher of the Word and looks forward to the time when our minds will be in harmony with God's mind. **Dec. 11**

Cheryl-Ann Hudson-Victory is a registered nurse and ward manager, and she volunteers as the Health Ministry secretary in her local church. Cheryl-Ann is married to Nolan Victory, an attorney who serves in their church as an elder and Religious Liberty leader. They are the proud parents of four boys. Their local church is Aylesbury Seventh-day Adventist Church in the South England Conference. She likes to cook, bake, sew, organize church programs, and tell children's stories. **Jan. 21, Nov. 21**

Kaven Ible is a native of Bermuda. She graduated from Oakwood University in Huntsville, Alabama, and from Alabama A&M University. Kaven enjoys life and the opportunity to be a blessing to others. **June 25**

Shirley C. Iheanacho is retired and lives in Huntsville, Alabama, with Morris, her husband of more than fifty-three years. She is a church elder, writer, speaker, prayer warrior, ministry leader, and philanthropist. Mrs. Iheanacho encourages women to share their stories. As a result, more than seventy devotional articles by thirty-nine women have been published. Funds from her book, *God's Incredible Plans for Me: A Memoir of an Amazing Journey*, provide scholarships for needy female students. **Feb. 8**

Nilde Itin, MEd, is the associate director of the General Conference Children's Ministries. She is the wife of German Lust, an associate treasurer at the General Conference, and the mother of two young-adult children. Nilde earned an MA in education and has served in various capacities in South America and Asia. She enjoys helping women grow in faith and become influences for salvation through their lives, words, and acts of love. Nilde's favorite word is *peace*, and her favorite text is Philippians 4:7. Nilde loves outdoor life, organizing, serving, and spending time with friends. **Feb. 18, July 3**

Sharon Hudson Iyayi is a proud mother of two young ladies, the wife of Kingsley, and above all, daughter of the King of kings. She holds an MBA with a specialization in leadership and strategy and a second degree in industrial relations. Mrs. Iyayi runs her own successful company. She is an avid sports enthusiast and self-proclaimed foodie and actively serves as a community school governor. With a love for gardening running in her DNA, Mrs. Iyayi dreams of cultivating a lush subtropical garden, thriving in a country that experiences a diverse range of adverse weather extremes. **Jan. 13**

Evelyne Izeogu lives in Harvest, Alabama, with her husband, Chukudi. She is a retired finance manager. Mrs. Izeogu enjoys getting involved in personal ministries, writing, and telling children's stories. **May 6, Aug. 3**

Jonsaba C. Jabbi is a writer, storyteller, and emerging archivist currently living in Toronto, Ontario, Canada. Her passions include reading, scrapbooking, black histories, and women's issues. Currently, Jonsaba works at a local community arts nonprofit as a communications specialist. She has been reading these women's devotionals since she was a child and is privileged to have the opportunity to write for them as an adult. **Jan. 15**

Sophia Jaquez is currently a theology major at Union College in Lincoln, Nebraska. Her favorite Bible verse is Isaiah 55:8, 9 because it lets her know what an incredible, unpredictable, and wonderfully amazing ride she will experience when Jesus takes the wheel! With God in her life, life is one big roller coaster, and Sophia is excited to see where He will take her next. **May 30**

Greta Michelle Joachim-Fox-Dyett is a potter, writer, blogger, and educator from Trinidad and Tobago. She is married to her love, Arnold, and is the proud mama of an adult daughter. **Apr. 29, June 12**

Dawn M. Johnson, BA, MS, MPH, is an educator, financial adviser, and current PhD candidate. She enjoys writing, meeting people, and sharing the gospel with others. Dawn is a member of the Shiloh Seventh-day Adventist Church and is awaiting the imminent return of Jesus. She is a Jamaican currently residing in suburban Chicago, Illinois. **June 24, June 27**

Elaine J. Johnson and her husband of almost sixty years have moved back to her hometown after living for twenty-six years in their country home in Alabama. She has also reunited with her home church, Bethel Seventh-day Adventist Church. Mrs. Johnson's hobbies are reading, writing, and enjoying her grands and great-grands. **Oct. 13**

Mary C. D. Johnson is an enthusiastic high school Spanish teacher in California. She travels the world on mission trips whenever she gets a school break. Mary also enjoys scrapbooking, writing, cooking, playing the piano, and being outdoors. **Apr. 9, Dec. 21**

Sheila Johnson (deceased) resided in Trinidad and Tobago, West Indies. She was an avid gardener who also enjoyed worshiping her God, intercessory prayers for friends and family, studying the Bible, and sharing her life's testimonies to encourage and inspire others. **June 2**

Simone E. Johnson is a member of the Seventh-day Adventist Church in Goshen, Jamaica, West Indies. One of her favorite Bible verses is Jeremiah 29:11. **Sept. 28**

Deidre A. Jones resides in Mineral, Virginia, along with her husband and their Yorkie, Tuff. As a graphic designer, she enjoys assisting her church family with their communication needs. Since 2017, Deidre has written a blog called *Sabbath Thoughts*. She enjoys cooking, reading, and creating craft projects for the students at the school library where she works. **Dec. 13**

Mirlande Jordan, MD, has been a practicing psychiatrist for over twenty years. She lives in upstate New York with her husband of thirty-five years, Pastor Dr. Vernon Jordan, who pastors a Seventh-day Adventist congregation in Mount Vernon, New York. They have three adult children. Dr. Jordan enjoys ministry to young adults as well as children. She plays the piano, enjoys music, and is an advocate of health ministry. **Sept. 29**

Nadine A. Joseph-Collins, PhD, is a women's leadership expert and empowerment coach. She has dedicated herself to full-time ministry, resides in Atlanta, Georgia, and travels globally, empowering the prayer lives of others. Dr. Nadine has authored ten books, including *The Pursuit of Purpose: A Guide for Faith-Based Women to Break Free from Indoctrinations, Shatter the Mentally Constructed Glass Ceiling*, and *Uniquely Impact the World*. Dr. Nadine appeared on 3ABN's Dare to Dream *Urban Report* episode "How to Pray," which led to a thirteen-part program on prayer called *The Missing Peace*. She has a series on blessings that is headlined on Hope Channel, Kenya, and serves on the instructional team of Mark Finley's HopeLives365 Online University. **Dec. 9**

Merita E. Joseph-Lewis is a retired teacher who worked as an educator in New York City for many years. She currently resides in Orlando, Florida. Merita has three adult children, and she loves to write, cook, sing, and work in the garden. Caring for the elderly is her passion, which allows her to share the love of Jesus with them through songs and Bible study. **July 6, Oct. 18**

Mukatimui Kalima-Munalula is a gynecologic oncologist who runs as a way of relaxing. She recently became a first-time grandmother, and she adores her granddaughter to bits. Mukatimui lives in Lusaka with Themba, her husband, and their three children. She is currently working with the Ambassadors Club of her church. Mukatimui has contributed to two previous editions of the devotional books. **Sept. 2**

Carolyn K. Karlstrom recently moved home to the town of her birth in the state of Washington. She lives with her husband, Rick, and sweet kitty, Dusty. Mrs. Karlstrom enjoys bicycling, hiking, reading, writing, family, friends, and sharing Jesus with others. Her blog, *Carolyn's Corner*, can be found at carolynkarlstrom.com. **Feb. 14, July 5**

Sonia Kennedy-Brown lives in Ontario, Canada. She is retired and fills her time with reading, writing, witnessing, and tending her potted plants. Since the publication of her autobiography, *Silent Tears: Growing up Albino*, Sonia has become a motivational speaker on behalf of others with other disabilities. To learn more about the book project, contact her at soniab47@msn.com. **Mar. 2, Dec. 30**

Eva Cleonice Kopitar lives in Brazil. She likes to sing, read, and tell stories to children. Eva has four wonderful grandkids: Kaíke, Kaíza, Kauê, and Kaleb. Her biggest desire is for Jesus' soon return. **Feb. 26, May 12**

Betty Kossick (deceased) contributed to the devotional for many years. She worked as a freelance writer of varied genres and as a journalist, author, and poet for both religious and secular publications. In 2006, Betty published her memoir *Beyond the Locked Door*. She developed and edited *Front Porch Visits*, the newsletter for the Florida Living Retirement Community. Much of her work can be found by googling her name. Betty passed to her rest in February 2022. **Sept. 19, Nov. 1**

Mabel Kwei, a retired university and college lecturer, did missionary work in Africa for many years with her pastor husband and their three children. She now lives in New Jersey. Mabel loves to read a lot, paint, write, and spend time with little children. **Feb. 19, Apr. 25**

Erin Lambillotte is a writer and a full-time college student who has a deep love for connecting with others and sharing her ideas. Her favorite things consist of writing poetry, sitting in coffee shops for prolonged periods of time, and watching Hallmark rom-coms. Born and raised in Oklahoma City, Oklahoma, Erin now resides in Texas, where she is pursuing her bachelor's degree in both communication and English writing. **May 22**

Juliet L. Lucas Languedoc has been teaching for more than seventeen years. She is married to Pastor Jerry Languedoc. Mrs. Languedoc holds a BSIT/VA from the University of Phoenix and an MA in educational psychology from the University of the Southern Caribbean. She is a certified and commissioned teacher, an author, and a Teacher of the Year honoree. Mrs. Languedoc enjoys praying for others, meeting people, singing, witnessing, decorating, crocheting, sharing, and planting and grooming flowers. Her best friend is Jesus. **Apr. 1**

Raquel Bendita Larico is from Peru. She completed her degree in chemical engineering in 2010 and studied theology at Peruvian Adventist University from 2014 to 2018. In 2023, she graduated with a master's in geology at Loma Linda University. Raquel likes church involvement, hiking, listening to classical music, cooking, and reading, and she loves to write. Raquel would like to do missionary work, preach about the message of God's creation, and spread the three angels' messages (Revelation 14:6–10). **July 15, Aug. 24**

Wilma Kirk Lee, MSW, LCSW, is married to the love of her life, W. S. Lee. They have shared their lives for fifty-seven years. She is mother to Anthony, deceased; Adrienne, married to Carl Jones; and Amber. Mrs. Lee's title is GoGo to her three grandsons. She enjoys reading, crocheting, and listening to music. Her favorite color is purple. **Sept. 26**

Loida Gulaja Lehmann spent ten years selling religious books in the Philippines before going to Germany and getting married. She and her husband are active members of the International Seventh-day Adventist Church in Darmstadt, Germany. Both are involved in radio, prison, and laypeople's ministries. Loida's hobbies are traveling, nature walks, writing, and photography. **Apr. 24**

Joan M. Leslie is a native of Kingston, Jamaica. She currently teaches first grade in New York, New York, United States of America. Joan takes pleasure in reading and traveling. She recently published her first book, *Hi, My Name Is Book*. It is available on Amazon. **Feb. 6**

Cordell Liebrandt is the Women's and Children's Ministries director for the Cape Conference in South Africa. She also served for many years as a chaplain and pastor in the Cape Conference. **Apr. 19, Dec. 20**

Sharon Long was born in Trinidad but has lived most of her life in Canada. In 2015, she retired from the government of Alberta, Canada, after thirty-four years in child welfare. Sharon does contract work for the Alberta College of Social Workers and is active at the West Edmonton Seventh-day Adventist Church. She is the mother of four, grandmother of six, and great-grandmother of two. Sharon is passionate about people and is happiest when serving others. Every day above ground is a good day and a new opportunity. **Apr. 11, Oct. 21**

Rhodi Alers de López writes from Massachusetts, United States of America. She is the founder of an international prayer ministry and a ministry of restoration. Rhodi loves to share God's Word. Through her speaking and writing, she aims to inspire many others in their daily walk with the Lord. Find her blog at RhodiAlersDeLopez.com. **Mar. 15, Sept. 5**

Elaine "Lainey" Lyons lives with her husband, Darren. They have two beautiful daughters, Arielle, who is married to Chantze, and Gabrielle. Their five grandchildren—Ethan, SaNaii, Emma, Ellis, and Elmira—mean the world to them. The Lyonses own Korrior, Inc., a training, coaching, speaking, and writing company with clients worldwide. Elaine's desire is to spend time with her family here on Earth and, eventually, in heaven after the second coming of Christ. **Sept. 10, Dec. 2**

Nancy Mattison Mack is an American born in India to a missionary family. She is married to Bill. The Macks raised their family in Maryland, United States of America. When they were sent as missionaries to India to direct Adventist Child India, a donor-funded program for educating needy children, Nancy became the third generation of Mattison missionaries who have served India for more than half a century. Sponsoring a child's education is effortless at adventistchildindia.org. **Aug. 4, Dec. 4**

Pauline J. Maddox is an adult gerontology nurse practitioner working in the area of population health in Calhoun, Georgia, United States of America. She has four adult children and has been married to Victor Maddox for thirty-six years. Mrs. Maddox enjoys gardening, going to the gym, and spending time with friends and family. Her capstone article, "Cinnamon in the Treatment of Type II Diabetes," can be viewed online. It has had more than twenty-eight hundred downloads. **Oct. 29**

Rhona Grace Magpayo enjoys going on mission trips with her husband, Jun. A photography enthusiast, she loves to travel the world, capturing sunsets with her camera. Rhona always returns home to Maryland, United States of America. **Sept. 8**

Fe C. Magpusao is married to a pastor. She is a church schoolteacher and mother of two. Fe loves to travel to new places, hike, read, listen to music, and experience adventure. She holds bachelor's and master's degrees in education. **Sept. 21**

Mayra Rivera Mann lives in Lawrenceville, Georgia, United States of America, with her husband and works as the registrar for Atlanta Adventist Academy. She has two grown sons and a stepson. She loves traveling, reading, and scrapbooking. **July 16**

Carolyn Venice Marcus lives in North Carolina, United States of America. She and her husband have two amazing adult children. Carolyn is retired and was blessed to work for several years as a physician assistant. She enjoys walking, reading the Bible and uplifting books, singing, listening to spiritual music, and spending time with family and friends. **Dec. 14**

Melissa Martinez lives on the beautiful island of Grand Cayman but needs frequent trips to see mountains—the one wonder of creation Cayman is not blessed with. She counts herself doubly blessed with an amazing twin sister and twin daughters. **Aug. 11, Dec. 10**

Premila Masih serves the Southern Asia Division of Seventh-day Adventists as Women's Ministries director. She and her husband, Pastor Hidayat Masih, the Sabbath School and Personal Ministries director, have two adult children and two grandsons. Premila worked as a teacher for twenty-six years and served as Shepherdess coordinator at the Northern India Union. She has a passion for house decorating, reading, making friends, and ministering to women. **June 9**

Romina Lata Masih grew up in Fiji, where she first started serving as a pastor after accepting Christ and exchanging her Hindu faith for Christianity. After completing her MA in leadership, Romina lectured at Fulton College, Fiji. She has been a church pastor in New Zealand. Romina's husband also serves as a pastor, and they are raising their young son. **Jan. 26**

Fabienne Maslet writes from Martinique, a French island in the Caribbean, where she was born. Fabienne teaches high school physics and chemistry and is an elder in her local church. **Feb. 16**

Melody Mason is a follower of Jesus, lover of God's creation, writer, hiker, traveler, and prayer missionary. She works for the General Conference of Seventh-day Adventists in resource development for Revival and Reformation and is the coordinator for the United in Prayer initiative. Melody has authored two books: *Daring to Ask for More* and *Daring to Live by Every Word*. **Jan. 12**

Deborah Matshaya writes from South Africa, where she is a teacher. Deborah enjoys gospel music and has contributed many times to this devotional book series. **May 14**

Nicole Mattson currently resides near the beautiful shores of Lake Michigan with her husband, Terry. Both are avid nature lovers, but Nicole particularly enjoys hiking and exploring national parks. They are smitten with their seven grandchildren and enjoy every minute spent with them. **May 2**

Mary H. Maxson, daughter of the King, is a retired associate pastor (Paradise, California, United States of America) who resides with her husband, Ben, in Calhoun, Georgia, United States of America. For forty-seven years, she served God as an administrative church assistant in Women's Ministries (Argentina and Uruguay), as Women's Ministries director in two conferences, as director of ministry spouses, and as an editorial and administrative assistant with *Adventist Review* and Adventist World Radio. Pastor Maxson served for more than seven years as the director of Women's Ministries for the North American Division of Seventh-day Adventists. Her passion is to daily follow Jesus and disciple people. **Apr. 17**

Sutania McBean is a native of Saint Catherine, Jamaica, who now resides in the United States of America. She has been inspiring young minds as an educator for the past fifteen years. Sutania praises God for blessing her with a godly mother, Maxine McBean. **Nov. 6**

Linda McClellan loves to write, explore the beauty of nature, learn new things, and help others learn and apply helpful information. She finds great joy in her roles as woman, wife, daughter, sister, aunt, godmother, friend, coordinator, small-group facilitator, mentor, coach, clerk, Health Ministries coleader, colleague, learner, and corny joke teller. **Feb. 13**

Raschelle McLean is a fifth-grade teacher at Oakwood Academy in Huntsville, Alabama, United States of America. She is a mother of three sons and one daughter: Aaron, Josiah, Malachi, and Sarah. Raschelle enjoys cooking, singing in the choir, and spending time with loved ones. **July 27, Aug. 15**

Judelia Medard-Santiesteban is from an island in the Caribbean called Saint Lucia. She is a high school teacher of health and family life education and is involved in women's ministries and youth ministries. Judelia has authored two children's books that empower children to speak out against sexual abuse. Most important, she is "learning to lean on Jesus." **Nov. 8**

Annette Walwyn Michael has published two well-received Caribbean books. She has also been published in the *Adventist Review* and other periodicals. Annette is a retired English teacher and former assistant professor of English at Oakwood College. Married to Reginald, a retired pastor, she is mom to three adult daughters and the grandmother of eleven. **Jan. 25, Oct. 19**

Sharon (Clark) Mills is a retired educator who still loves learning. She enjoys spending time in nature, hiking, camping, being with family, serving God, and writing. Sharon is homesick for heaven and prays for the soon return of Jesus. **May 31, Nov. 28**

Marcia Mollenkopf, a retired teacher, lives in Klamath Falls, Oregon, United States of America. She enjoys a postcard ministry and loves to share God's Word. **Nov. 4**

Maureen H. Moncrieffe, EdD, resides in the sunshine state of Florida, United States of America, with her husband, who retired from pastoral ministry in 2019. She is a retired reading specialist and kindergarten teacher who enjoys tending to her flower and vegetable gardens, which give her enormous pleasure and fulfillment. Dr. Moncrieffe and her husband of over fifty years are blessed with five adult children and seven grandchildren. **Jan. 24**

Thessamar Moncrieffe, born in Jamaica and raised in New Jersey, United States of America, holds an advanced practice registered nurse degree. She is married and is the mother of three children. Thessamar's personal ministry is sharing her testimonies with others to hasten the spread of the gospel of Jesus Christ. **Aug. 5**

Lourdes E. Morales-Gudmundsson is a retired professor of Spanish language and literature. She has traveled worldwide with her seminar I Forgive You, But . . . and has published a book by the same title. Dr. Morales-Gudmundsson currently teaches a course titled Forgiveness, Personality, and Culture at La Sierra University. She serves as an associate head elder at her home church—Campus Hill Seventh-day Adventist Church—in Loma Linda, California, United States of America, and leads out in a Wednesday prayer meeting and study. Dr. Morales-Gudmundsson lives in Riverside with her husband, Dr. Reynir Gudmundsson, and is the mother of one daughter, Carmen, and grandmother to Juliana and Soffia. **Sept. 22, Oct. 23**

Lila Farrell Morgan, a widow, writes from a small town in the foothills of Western North Carolina, United States of America. She loves her four adult children, five grandchildren, and a growing number of great-grandchildren. Reading, contemplating the Creator's handiwork in nature, researching different topics on the internet, baking, and table games are her favorite pastimes. Lila looks for the positive in life and enjoys a good laugh. **Jan. 27, Nov. 15**

Valerie Hamel Morikone writes from southern Illinois, United States of America, and lives on a lovely farm she and her husband, Daniel, now call home after moving from West Virginia, United States of America, where they worked for the Mountain View Conference. Delighted to be near her son and daughter-in-law, she especially relishes more time with Daniel since they are both retired from full-time work. **Sept. 25**

Lleuella Morris is a Guyanese-born development professional and entrepreneur. She finds her calling in Isaiah 50:4 because she was called to develop both people and things. Lleuella likes to encourage others at every opportunity she gets. **Aug. 2**

Bonnie Moyers lives with her husband, Carl, and Milo, a ragdoll kitty, in Staunton, Virginia, United States of America. This freelance writer is a mother of two, a grandmother of three, and a musician for several area churches. **Sept. 17**

Denise Murray-Goods lives in Sydney, Australia, where she works as a journalist. She was a registered nurse for twenty-one years before switching careers. Denise has always loved working with people and hearing their stories. She is a mentor in her local Toastmasters club and runs a creative writing group. Being outdoors in nature while exploring the beautiful Australian coastline is one of her great joys. **Feb. 1**

Jannett Maurine Myrie, MSN, RN, is a medical missionary who finds great joy and fulfillment in sharing the love of Jesus with everyone. She is the proud mother of Delroy Anthony Jr. Jannett enjoys traveling, especially cruises, and entertaining, and she is an avid reader. Jannett is ever so thankful to Jesus for loving her unconditionally and blessing her to trust the plans He has for her and Delroy Anthony. **May 11, Oct. 24**

Cecilia Nanni earned a postgraduate degree in coaching, NLP, and team leadership, a degree in psychology, a master's degree in mediation and conflict resolution, and a master's degree in education, management mode. She has received an international diploma in volunteer management from UNESCO. Currently, Cecilia works as a volunteer coordinator in Central Asia. **July 24, Aug. 28**

Luisamaria Navarro, BSN, RN, lives in Texas, United States of America, alongside her awesome family of nine. She graduated from Southwestern Adventist University in 2023 and currently works with AdventHealth as a PCU (progressive care unit) nurse. Luisamaria enjoys being active in church, singing, and working with the youth. She also loves to spend time outdoors and with her family and friends. **May 28**

Charity Hanene Nchimunya is a Zambian national currently living and working in neighboring Tanzania. She is a wife and the mother of five and currently serves as the Women's Ministries director at Arusha International Seventh-day Adventist Church. **Jan. 8**

Bogadi Koosaletse Ndzinge is a retired educator, a writer of books, a motivational speaker, and a lay evangelist. She is a family woman with four grown daughters. Mrs. Ndzinge remarried in 2021 after her first husband went to rest from his labors in 2019. She loves to preach and witness and has served the church in various positions. Mrs. Ndzinge is currently the leader of the Voice of Prophecy department in her local church. She was previously published in this devotional book in 2016 and 2020. **Feb. 25**

Bienvisa Ladion Nebres recently retired from fifty-four years of teaching in Thailand and as a missionary in Africa with her late husband, P. P. Nebres Jr., and also in her homeland—the Philippines. She now hopes to spend time with her three children and their spouses and her five grandchildren and do what she enjoys—reading, writing, composing poetry, gardening, and listening to music. **May 15, Dec. 15**

Barbara Burris Neequaye, PhD, is a semiretired community college professor living in Charlotte, North Carolina, United States of America. She is the mother of one adult son and enjoys reading, writing, and going on cruises with her sisters. Dr. Neequaye is active in various church ministries. **Feb. 17, July 30**

Beth Davis Nelson is a fifth-generation Seventh-day Adventist. She has served as a church schoolteacher in Wisconsin and Illinois, United States of America, and in local churches as clerk, adult and children's Sabbath School leader, Communication secretary, and children's storyteller. Beth's stories have been published in *Our Little Friend*®, *Primary Treasure*®, *Guide*®, *Insight* magazine, and the *Adventist Review*. She and her husband, Wesley, have been married for forty-eight years and have two children and eight grandchildren. **Dec. 28**

Christine B. Nelson and her husband, Len, (both retired) have lived in Florida, United States of America, for over thirty years after relocating from Syracuse, New York, United States of America, in 1991. Trading snow for sunshine wasn't too hard to get used to. Christine was privileged to have submissions included in the 2012 and 2023 devotional books. **Mar. 11, June 16**

Maureen Nembhard lives in New York, United States of America. She and her husband, Lasville, have been married for forty-eight years. They have two daughters, a son-in-law, and three precious grandchildren. Maureen has been spending her retirement years in various servant leadership roles. She enjoys volunteering and traveling with family and friends. Maureen's hobbies include reading, writing, gardening, and other outdoor activities. **Jan. 6**

Linda Nottingham lives in Florida, United States of America, and teaches an adult Bible study class for her church. She is semiretired but serves as a mentor to women business owners. **Aug. 10**

Elizabeth Versteegh Odiyar lives in Kelowna, British Columbia, Canada. She has served God in church, in Pathfinders, and on mission trips. Elizabeth retired from managing the family chimney sweep business after thirty-three years. She is married to Hector, and they have twin sons and a daughter, all of whom are married and serving God. They also have five delightful grandchildren. **Oct. 16**

Sharon Okimi is retired but prefers to think of it as being retreaded! She is a wife, a mother of two adult children, and a grandmother of three teenagers. Sharon's personal interests focus on quilting and traveling. Quilts of Hope is her ministry to those needing encouragement. All she has accomplished has been by the grace of God alone. **Apr. 4**

Mary Opoku-Gyamfi is an accountant by profession. She was raised in a Seventh-day Adventist home and is passionate about the Word of God. Mary currently lives in Australia, where her husband pastors two churches. Mary is also a proud mum of three children: Michael, Jadon, and Janelle. **Mar. 14**

Lynn Ortel has an MA in counseling and is a licensed professional clinical counselor. She feels privileged to have served the church as conference director for Communications, Family Ministries, Women's Ministries, and Children's Ministries. Lynn also served as the conference Ministerial Spouses Association leader and currently volunteers in the Arizona Conference as Women's Ministries coordinator. Her personal mission statement is "to live a life of love" (Ephesians 5:1, 2). Lynn has traveled across the United States of America and overseas, sharing about the God who makes a difference in our lives. She is married to the wonderful Mike Ortel, and their three children have given them six grandchildren. **Jan. 2**

Sharon Oster is a retired teacher assistant living in Evans, Colorado, United States of America, with her retired pastor husband. She enjoys automobile day trips in the nearby Rocky Mountains. Sharon and her husband have three children and nine grandchildren. **Aug. 20, Sept. 30**

Hannele Ottschofski lives in southern Germany, where she has been active in many facets of women's ministries. Hannele is passionate about helping women develop their God-given gifts and using them to be the best they can be. She has written several books about women in church and society. **Jan. 3, Nov. 5**

Carey Pearson lives in Lithia Springs, Georgia, United States of America. She writes, sings, and works as a registered behavior technician in the Metro Atlanta area. She loves good music, good books, and making a difference in the lives of children with autism spectrum disorder. **Aug. 12**

Karen Pearson is a speaker, writer, and editor. She served as Prayer Ministries coordinator in the Idaho Conference of Seventh-day Adventists and as an associate pastor with her husband, Michael. She worked at Pacific Press® Publishing Association for almost ten years as director of Publicity and Public Relations. Karen currently edits the *E. G. White Notes for the Sabbath*

School Lessons and is the current editor for this devotional. Her greatest joy is to share stories of Jesus with others. **Apr. 18, Apr. 20, Nov. 16**

Premila Pedapudi is the administrative assistant for the department of Women's Ministries at the General Conference of Seventh-day Adventists in Maryland, United States of America. She is married to Joseph Kelley and is mother to a son, Praveen, and twin daughters, Serena and Selena (who are married to Samuel and Ebenesar)—all are a great support to her in her ministry. Premila is passionate about women's ministries and loves to sing, read, teach, and preach. **Nov. 2**

Kathy Pepper is a teacher and pastor's wife in West Virginia (Mountain View Conference), United States of America. She and her husband, Stewart, have a son, two daughters, a daughter-in-law, a son-in-law, and two lively grandchildren. Kathy's days are filled with teaching her students, working with her husband, and spending time with her family as often as she can. **Aug. 6, Sept. 7**

Sueli da Silva Pereira lives in Brazil, in Patos de Minas, state of Minas Gerais, and works at city hall. She is a Sabbath School teacher and enjoys music and writing for her blog. Sueli is married to Clarindo and has three children: Arthur, Eric, and Samuel. She currently participates in the instrumental worship group of the Central Church of Patos de Minas. **Jan. 14, Feb. 12**

Diane Pestes has written two books, *Prayer That Moves Mountains* and *Prayer Still Moves Mountains*, published by Pacific Press® Publishing Association. She is an international speaker who resides in Oregon, United States of America. She is known for her commitment to Christ and loves to recite Scripture in nature and post it on YouTube. She finds exercise relaxing and enjoys the grandeur of nature and traveling with her husband and mother. **May 19, Dec. 6**

Eshwaramma Peter was born, raised, and educated in Bangalore, India. She has served her church as a pastor's wife and her community as a teacher and principal. Eshwaramma now serves as the director of the Women's Ministries department in the South-Central India Union, where her husband is president. They are blessed with a son and a daughter and have two lovely grandchildren. She has a passion for ministry. **Aug. 8**

Angèle Peterson lives in Ohio, United States of America, and as the Holy Spirit impresses, she has contributed to the women's devotional over the years. However, Angèle longs for the day when these books are a thing of the past and we are in heaven. Until then, she continues to serve her local church in Oberlin and helps her sister keep the giving legacy of her family alive as vice president for the Carter Peterson McMillan Foundation. **Dec. 31**

Karen M. Phillips writes from her new location in eastern Kentucky, United States of America. She is happily married to her husband, John, and has four children and three grandchildren. She does volunteer human resources work for a number of different ministries. Mrs. Phillips also partners with John in their worldwide ministry, HeReturns. Her passion is proclaiming the Lord's end-time message and being an instrument in saving souls. **Mar. 20, Nov. 19**

Shannon J. Pigsley resides with her husband, Brad, in Council Bluffs, Iowa, United States of America. She has a full-time job but enjoys spending her free time camping, traveling, and doing photography. She also enjoys writing devotions for the Council Bluffs Seventh-day Adventist Church website, where she uses some of her photographs of nature. She has been the Women's Ministries leader at her church for the past six years or so and enjoys sharing her love for God and the many ways He has touched her life. **Aug. 13**

Prudence Pollard, PhD, is the mother of two adult daughters. She specializes in leadership development and holds appointments in the business programs at Oakwood University, Loma Linda University, and La Sierra University. Dr. Pollard is the author of *Raise a Leader, God's Way*, which is available from adventistbookcenter.com or as an e-book from Amazon .com. It is her firm belief that parenting is the most important work of evangelism a Christian can undertake. **Nov. 25**

Carina Prestes was born and raised in Brazil, where she became an architect and married her other half, Flavio Prestes III. Together, they studied at the Seventh-day Adventist Theological Seminary at Andrews University in Berrien Springs, Michigan, United States of America, to prepare for ministry. While at Andrews University, they completed their master's and doctorate degrees in religion. Currently, they serve as professors of religion at UNASP-EC (Adventist University of São Paulo), Brazil. **June 28**

Damaris Prieto is blessed as a pastor's wife and has been happily married to Pastor Luis Prieto for thirty-eight years. She is also blessed by her daughter, Sandra Gordon. Mrs. Prieto loves to help in women's and children's ministries, gardening, decorating, and reading. She works at the Oklahoma Conference, United States of America. **June 29, Sept. 18**

Beatrice Tauber Prior, PsyD, is a clinical psychologist, author, speaker, and owner of Harborside Wellbeing in North Carolina, United States of America. She is a grateful mother to a delightful daughter and wonderful son. Any moment Dr. Prior can spend with family, friends, and loved ones is a good moment. **Jan. 10**

Jessy Quilindo, originally from Seychelles, is currently the honorary Women's Ministries director of the Singapore Conference of Seventh-day Adventists. A clinical nurse by profession, she is studying counseling psychology to serve the women of her conference better. Jessy is married to Steven, her husband of more than thirty years. They have two young-adult sons. She enjoys cooking, home decor, and gardening but finds her greatest reward in women's ministries. **Mar. 10, June 6**

Liliana Radu is a pastor's wife and the Women's Ministries director for the Romanian Union Conference of Seventh-day Adventists. She enjoys organizing events and loves God's Word. Liliana is a teacher and a mentor for her children and for those in the school where she works. She likes to read, travel, cook, swim, and encourage people—especially women. **Feb. 5**

Shaila Rao is currently an English teacher by profession with twenty-three years of experience in teaching. She has led out in the church as children's Sabbath School superintendent, children's choir leader, guide for Master Guides, Pathfinder leader, and a short-story writer. Shaila loves cooking and singing. **Sept. 3**

Ricki-Lee Riley is seventeen years old and lives in New York with her mom and younger sister. She attends the Marie Curie School for Medicine, Nursing, and Health Professions and, at the time of writing, was a senior student. Ricki-Lee was awarded the 2021 Pathfinder of the Year for the Bronx Area by the Greater New York Conference. She currently serves as a youth counselor for her church's Pathfinder group. Ricki-Lee loves to write and participate in clubs in school and church. **Mar. 29**

Jenny Rivera writes from Brisbane, Queensland, Australia, where she works as a wound management stomal therapy specialty registered nurse. She is involved in the Sabbath School department at her church and shares her musical flute talent by playing in two different church orchestras. She enjoys traveling, reading, and spending time with family and friends. **Jan. 11, July 7**

Taniesha K. Robertson-Brown partners with her husband, Courtney, to raise two energetic boys, Preston and Prescott. She spends her days teaching her children, caring for her family, and serving in various ministries in her local church. While Taniesha received her training in education, her true passion is writing. She is the author of *Godly Families in an Ungodly World*. Taniesha loves the Lord and is keen on doing all she can to fulfill God's mandate for her life. **June 1, Sept. 27**

Charlotte A. Robinson has spent most of her life working and helping her husband raise three children. She has been published in *Our Little Friend*®, *Primary Treasure*®, *Guide*®, and *Insight*. After living with her parents near Ozark Academy for seventeen years, she moved to nearby Decatur, Arkansas, United States of America, when she married. She now lives on her late mother's property, where she lived as a child. **Nov. 11**

Jesseñia Robinson, born and raised in the Seventh-day Adventist Church, is a community health nurse whose aim is to be a lighthouse to those around her. She loves to encourage others on their journey with Christ through activity in the local church, conducting personal Bible studies, and various social media posts. Jesseñia also uses her website, jesseniamelise.com, to share resources with those seeking to deepen their relationship with God. **June 8**

Avis Mae Rodney writes from Guelph, Ontario, Canada. She is a retired justice of the peace and also a retired leader of Women's Ministries for the Guelph Seventh-day Adventist Church. Avis is blessed to be a mother, grandmother, and wife of Leon, her dear friend and husband of more than fifty years. **May 5, July 31**

Robin Widmayer Sagel lives in Choctaw, Oklahoma, United States of America, with her husband of thirty-seven years, David. She has a daughter and three granddaughters and works part time at the Midwest City Library. She also volunteers at the Parkview Adventist Academy library. She loves books! Her hobbies include reading, writing, public speaking, and baking. She has been published in *Our Little Friend*®, *Primary Treasure*®, *Insight*, and the women's devotional. **Apr. 3, Nov. 13**

Kollis Salmon-Fairweather resides in beautiful Central Florida, United States of America. She enjoys Bible studies and witnessing. Kollis plans to spend her remaining days working for the Master through outreach ministry. **Mar. 12, May 21**

Deborah Sanders lives in Alberta, Canada, with her husband, Ron, and her son, Sonny. In 1990, God blessed her with a successful writing and prayer outreach ministry, Dimensions of Love. In 2013, she selected the best stories and compiled a book of sacred memories, titled *Saints-in-Training*. She hopes her Sonny will use it to continue his witness for Jesus. **Dec. 12**

Jodi Scarbrough is a wife, mother, world traveler, third culture kid, and a child of the King. She loves to teach from the Bible and spend time gardening and hiking. Jodi currently teaches grades 5–8 in her local church school. **June 15**

Danijela Schubert, DMin (Fuller Theological Seminary), lives in Melbourne, Australia. Originally from Croatia, she has lived, studied, and worked in France, the Philippines, Pakistan, Papua New Guinea, and Australia. Dr. Schubert is happily married to Branimir. Together, they have two grown-up sons. **Mar. 26, May 27**

Jennifer Jill Schwirzer, LPC, EdD, is a counselor, author, musician, and speaker residing in Orlando, Florida, United States of America, from where she directs Abide Counseling and runs a nonprofit ministry. Dr. Schwirzer hosts the show *A Multitude of Counselors* on Three Angels Broadcasting Network (3ABN) and maintains an online presence at jenniferjill.org. **June 14, Sept. 23**

Kochuthresia Selvamony serves as the director of Women's Ministries at the Southwest India Union. She is the wife of Pastor Yovan Selvamony, the former president of the Southwest India Union of Seventh-day Adventists. Kochuthresia is blessed with two boys. The elder son, Samson, is married to Ajitha, and they work in Kuwait. The younger son, Jackson, studies at Andrews University, Michigan, United States of America, while working on his master of divinity. **July 29**

Omobonike Adeola Sessou is the Women's Ministries and Children's Ministries director at the West-Central Africa Division of Seventh-day Adventists in Abidjan, Côte d'Ivoire. She is married to Pastor Sessou, and they are blessed with four children. Her hobbies include teaching, counseling, making new friends, and visiting people. **Oct. 7, Nov. 3**

Cornelia Estrella Sewer writes from Miami, Florida, United States of America, where she has resided for the past twenty-two years. She is the registrar at the local church school. Cornelia enjoys working with children and served as an Adventurers director for twelve years. A native of Saint Kitts and Nevis, West Indies, she enjoys traveling, collecting currencies and coins, reading, and dabbling in writing. **Nov. 23**

Novalee Sherman enjoys reading articles, talking with friends, and writing in her spare time. **Mar. 27**

Victoria M. Shewbrooks lives and works in Bucks County, Pennsylvania, United States of America. She is an artist, illustrator, and photographer, sharing God's love visually with others. Victoria enjoys keeping a journal of God's work in her life. **June 13, Oct. 5**

Jo Shuck is a member of the Mesa Palms Seventh-day Adventist Church in Mesa, Arizona, United States of America. She's been an Adventist since being baptized in Newcastle, Wyoming, United States of America, in 2015. Jo currently serves as the Prayer Ministry leader in Mesa and writes a weekly column for the newsletter. **Feb. 27, July 14**

Debi Slack serves several ministries of the Seventh-day Adventist Church and is a graduate of Oakwood University. She has adult children, grandchildren, and great-grandchildren. **Aug. 16**

Heather-Dawn Small (deceased) was the director of Women's Ministries at the General Conference of Seventh-day Adventists in Maryland, United States of America. Previously, she was the Children's Ministries and Women's Ministries director for the Caribbean Union Conference of Seventh-day Adventists, located in Trinidad and Tobago. She was the wife of Pastor Joseph Small and the mother of Dalonne and Jerard. She loved air travel, reading, and scrapbooking. **Apr. 6, July 26, Oct. 6**

Yvonne Curry Smallwood enjoys spending time with God, family, and friends, as well as reading, writing, and crocheting. When she is not writing, you can find her in a craft store, purchasing yarn for the many crocheted blankets and afghans she creates and donates to a local hospital and nursing home. Her articles and stories have appeared in several publications. **Mar. 13, Aug. 30**

Debra Snyder was born and raised in Massachusetts, United States of America, but God led her to Nebraska, United States of America, and her husband, Kevin, in 2012. She is the mother of three wonderful children: Jacob, Samantha, and Steven. Debra is active in her church and enjoys writing, especially writing spiritual poetry. She loves connecting with others and sharing what God places on her heart about her life experience and how He has led in her life. To learn more about her poetry, email her at dlsnyder70@gmail.com. **Feb. 21**

Tawny Sportsman travels nationally and internationally as a speaker. She is an associate chaplain and the director of Take Heart Ministry, which began when she lost her husband of thirty-five years. Tawny reaches out to those taking the unexpected journey called grief, letting them know they do not have to travel alone. She designs programs and events for hurting hearts, and Tawny and her team provide tools, resources, support, and encouragement as they walk alongside those who are grieving. Tawny has a perfect daughter, a perfect son-in-law, and four perfect, delightful grandchildren. She resides in Sweet Home, Oregon, United States of America, and in her spare time, Tawny loves to hunt deer with her camera. **Apr. 8, Nov. 26**

Candy Monique Springer-Blackman is from the twin island Republic of Trinidad and Tobago. She attended Caribbean Union College, where she met her husband of nineteen years. They live in the Republic of Barbados, her husband's home country, and attend the King Street Seventh-day Adventist Church. There, Candy serves as a Sabbath School superintendent. She has a passion for decor. **Aug. 14, Oct. 22**

Jill Springer-Cato lives on the lovely island of Trinidad with her husband and two young-adult sons. She is a music minister who loves listening to local gospel music and is a member of the South Caribbean Conference Music Advisory. Jill is a church leader who is involved in all aspects of church life. **Oct. 25**

Summer Stahl lives in northeastern Washington State, United States of America, with her husband, who planted more fruit trees than she can keep up with. There are many things that describe who Summer is, but her favorites are child of God, wife, and mother. She loves reading, bird-watching, and flowers and is working on a Bible study on abuse. **July 1, Sept. 1**

Eva M. Starner, PhD, LPC, is an educator and counselor and has worked with families for more than thirty years. She is divorced and has facilitated her church's Divorce Care program (divorcecare.org) since 2013. Her children are her greatest accomplishment. Dr. Starner has three adult daughters and grandchildren whom she loves and spoils as often as she can while she waits for the soon return of our Lord and Savior, Jesus Christ. **Mar. 9, May 24**

Galina Stele, DMin, is the associate director of Women's Ministries at the General Conference of Seventh-day Adventists in Maryland, United States of America. Previously, she worked as a professor at Zaoksky Theological Seminary, Shepherdess coordinator, and director of the Institute of Missiology in the Euro-Asia Division, and then as a research and evaluation manager at the General Conference Office of Archives, Statistics, and Research. Galina is the wife of Artur Stele, the mother of an adult son, and a happy grandmother of one grandson. She was born in Kamchatka but grew up mostly in Kazakhstan, in the former Union of Soviet Socialist Republics. Galina loves reading, writing, gardening, cooking, and completing puzzles. **Jan. 1**

Ardis Dick Stenbakken is retired after serving as director of the General Conference Women's Ministries department. She edited these devotional books for seventeen years. Mrs. Stenbakken lives in Colorado, United States of America, with her husband Dick (see BibleFaces.com) in a home with a view of one hundred miles of the Rocky Mountains. She keeps busy with church activities, Bible study, occasional oil painting, and family. Mrs. Stenbakken is especially proud of her daughter, Rikki, and son, Erik, their spouses, and the four awesome grandchildren. She is passionate about women's issues and what the Bible says about women. **Jan. 29, Mar. 17, Sept. 4**

Keisha D. Sterling-Richards is an elder at Bushy Park Seventh-day Adventist Church, Central Jamaica Conference, and anticipates Christ's return. God has grown her faith via youth, health, education, women's, Sabbath School, and eldership ministries. She serves her community as a pharmacist, entrepreneur, health services operator, and medical intern. Keisha loves nature! **Aug. 26**

Rita Kay Stevens, a retired medical technologist, lives in Lacey, Washington, United States of America. She enjoys being involved with Women's Ministries in her local church. She is blessed with over fifty years of marriage to Jim, a former church administrator and evangelist. They have two adult sons, a daughter-in-law, and two grandchildren. She likes to travel, read, walk, and encourage others. **Mar. 6**

Carolyn J. H. Strzyzykowski and her husband, Stan, live in Saint Joseph, Michigan, United States of America. They enjoy as much time as possible with their families, including the baby great-grandchildren. After being a special education and adult education teacher for eighteen years, she served as a health care chaplain for twenty-eight years. Carolyn is an elder and volunteers at Life Plan and the senior center. They enjoy camping with the kids, gardening, and walking. **Apr. 10**

Carolyn Rathbun Sutton, a former editor of these devotional books, lives close to her children in northeast Georgia, United States of America. Though she recently lost her husband, Carolyn continues to volunteer in her local church and as an ambassador for Adventist World Radio. Creative writing, music, and Jesus still bring her immense joy. **Feb. 11, June 21, June 22**

Evelyn Porteza Tabingo is a retired cardiac nurse living in Oceanside, California, United States of America. She and her husband, Henry, are from the Philippines and have served as missionaries in East Africa. Evelyn enjoys reading, writing, gardening, music, and traveling. Spending time with family and her grandchildren is a favorite pastime. **May 18**

Bridget S. Taffe, originally from Jamaica, is a retiree who now resides in Huntsville, Alabama, United States of America. A pastor's wife and a mother of two, she has spent more than forty years teaching high school students. Bridget is an avid reader and a nature lover, and more than all, she enjoys sharing God's goodness with others. **Feb. 23**

Arlene R. Taylor recently retired from health care after decades of working with Adventist Health facilities. Still living in the Napa Valley of Northern California, United States of America, she devotes her time and energy to brain-function research, writing, and speaking. **Sept. 24, Oct. 26, Nov. 10**

Edna Thomas Taylor is a conference Women's Ministries coordinator, former church Women's Ministry leader, church elder, and entrepreneur. She is the mother of Junia, Jamila, and Jamaal, grandmother of Ammi, Najja, and Tyra, and great-grandmother of Aya. Edna writes from Tampa, Florida, United States of America. A musician, mentor, and motivational speaker, she enjoys reading, writing, and working with our "legacies"—young women. **Apr. 30, Oct. 10**

Rose Joseph Thomas, PhD, is the associate director of Elementary Education for the Southern Union of Seventh-day Adventists. She lives in the United States of America and is married to her best friend, Walden. Rose has two adult children, Samuel Joseph and Crystal Rose. She has two happy and fun-loving grandchildren, Adrian and Gianna. Rose loves to read, cook, and spend time with family. **Mar. 19, Apr. 15**

Stella Thomas is a retired public school teacher who has enjoyed working various jobs in retirement. Other interests include quilting, card making, word games, biking, walking, and piano. She lives in Maryland, United States of America. Stella is always grateful for our omnipotent, omnipresent, and omniscient heavenly Father. **June 3, July 22**

Diane Thurber is the president of Christian Record Services in Lincoln, Nebraska, United States of America. Christian Record Services' mission is to "empower people who are blind to engage their communities and embrace the Blessed Hope." To learn more, visit ChristianRecord.org. Diane and her husband, Gary Thurber, have two adult sons. **Apr. 26**

Monica Torrealba is a recipient of the Women's Ministries Scholarship Fund, which was made possible, in part, through this devotional series. She is a double major student at Andrews University, studying nursing and Spanish with a translation and interpretation concentration. Monica and her husband, both from Venezuela, plan to enter the mission field. She loves to cook for her family. Monica wants to know God in the deepest way. She loves the way He works and looks forward to showing His love to her patients and making a difference in their lives. **May 29**

Ann Trout and her husband, Steve, enjoy spending time with their two adult children and their spouses, and especially with their grandchildren. She teaches at a local community college and has published two devotional books. **Mar. 1, Aug. 17**

Rebecca Turner belongs to several small groups and loves to study the Bible deeply. Her mission in life is to encourage her friends and family to fall in love with Jesus. Rebecca is an editorial assistant at the General Conference Women's Ministries department and lives with her husband, Charles, in Maryland, United States of America. She thanks God for the privilege of being part of the lives of her four grandchildren because she missed out on having living grandparents during her own childhood. **Dec. 22, Dec. 23**

Annette L. Vaughan is originally from Barbados but currently resides in the Cayman Islands. She spent thirty-eight years as an elementary school educator and recently retired to pursue a legal career. Annette has a passion for studying and reading the Bible. Her other interests include traveling, writing, reading, photography, cooking, and homemaking. Annette has been happily married for over forty years to the love of her life, Bentley Vaughan. She loves God and people and cherishes her family. **July 11, Nov. 24**

Barbara J. Walker is an ordained elder in her local church. She is the director of the South Central Conference Women's Ministries for Mississippi, United States of America. She has served as director of the South Central Conference Morning Manna Prayer Ministries since November 2012. **Mar. 5**

Cora A. Walker (deceased) lived in Atlanta, Georgia, United States of America. She was a nurse, editor, and freelance writer. She passed to her rest in April 2021. **Oct. 14**

SanDia Waller, PhD, RDN, LMT, received her doctorate in nutrition and food science with a minor in biopsychology in 2008 from Wayne State University in Detroit, Michigan, United States of America. She and her family live in Michigan, where Dr. Waller homeschools, makes moisturizing creams, and runs Courage Club—a fun community seeking better health through vegan food meetups, activities, and informative health programs. Learn more at courageclub3@gmail.com and moisturebysandia.com. **July 25**

Lyn Welk-Sandy lives in Adelaide, South Australia. She has worked as a grief counselor and spent many years as a pipe organist. She loves church music, choir work, and playing the hand chimes. She enjoys nature, photography, and caravaning around outback Australia with her husband, Keith, serving where needed. She is a mother of four, grandmother of nine, and great-grandmother of seven. She has contributed to this devotional book for more than nineteen years. **Oct. 9**

Avonda White-Krause is a wife, mother, grandmother, and great-grandmother who lives in southwest Michigan, United States of America. She loves her family and friends, going to church, reading, computers, crocheting, gardening, and traveling. Avonda taught special education for thirty-three years and is now retired. **July 18**

Kimasha P. Williams is currently working as a communication professional in London, England, within the environment and civil society sector. She loves sharing her personal testimonies with family and friends and really enjoys writing. **Mar. 24**

Wendy Williams lives in the United States of America. She is the author of *They Called Us Baby*, a preventative book for children that informs about the dangers and grooming process of child sex trafficking in America. The book is available through AdventSource.org or NAD EndItNow. **Oct. 27**

Judith Woodruff Williamson is a retired dental assistant who lives in Loveland, Colorado, United States of America, with her husband, Wes. She has a married son in Alaska and a married daughter and two grandchildren who live in Germany. Mrs. Williamson enjoys traveling to visit them. She is also a porcelain artist who teaches painting classes, volunteers at her church, and loves her garden. **Aug. 31, Nov. 20**

Linda K. Wolfaardt has lived in Somerset West, in the beautiful Western Cape of South Africa, for most of her adult life. She has been married to Francois for thirty-two years and has two adult children, Ben and Katelyn. Linda has been blessed to travel extensively through her work. With all of life's changing seasons, one of her favorite Bible passages is Ecclesiastes 3:1: "There is a time for everything, and a season for every activity under the heavens" (NIV). **Nov. 14**

Yan Siew Ghiang lives in Singapore. She's been helping to care for her mother for many years. **Oct. 3**

Joan (Jo) Yelorda retired after working for twenty-five years as a probation agent. She then earned a master's degree in special education and taught in various school settings. Joan has been married to Pete for fifty-two years, and they have four adult children, three married, with six grandchildren. She enjoys Pilates, swimming, walking, guitar, reading, traveling, and spending time with her family and friends. Joan loves Jesus. **Aug. 18**